Dear Graduating Columbia Student,

Congratulations on your graduation from Columbia University! You have reason to be very proud of all you have achieved as a student at Columbia. Whether through academics, service, student groups, or otherwise, each of you has left an indelible mark on our community. We are confident that what you have learned at Columbia—both inside and outside the classroom—will enable you to succeed in your future endeavors and make a difference in the world.

As you plan for the next stage in your life, the Division of Student Affairs recognizes the significance of this transition. And wherever your plans may lead you, we think you will find the information contained in *Gradspot.com's Guide to Life After College* useful. It contains practical advice for life after college, including tips for managing your finances, building your career, and living on your own. I would like to extend special appreciation to our partner, the Center for Career Education, for helping us make this important resource available to graduates.

But your Columbia experience does not end with University Commencement. As you embark on this new adventure, we encourage you to remain connected. The pages that follow also provide information to help you stay involved and continue to make use of Columbia's vast resources. Attend events sponsored by the alumni offices, the Center for Career Education, and Athletics. Stay in touch with friends, return to campus for reunions, and enjoy programs sponsored by the Arts Initiative. No matter how you choose to continue your relationship with Columbia University, we look forward to your involvement.

In the interim, take advantage of this special time to celebrate your individual and collective accomplishments, reflect on the past few years, and enjoy the company of friends and faculty who have shaped your Columbia experience.

We wish you the best in all your future endeavor

D1383742

Kevin G. Shollenberger
Dean of Student Affairs
Columbia College and The Fu Foundation School of Engineering and Applied Science
Associate Vice President for Undergraduate Student Life
Arts and Sciences

Benefits & Services for Columbia Alumni

Columbia College and SEAS alumni enjoy numerous lifelong benefits and services offered by the College, SEAS, and University. Stay connected to Columbia and take advantage of valuable networking events, discounted NYC arts and cultural opportunities, career support library services, e-mail for life, and much more!

To learn more about staying engaged with your Alma Mater, benefiting from the support of your Columbia Network, and participating in Columbia alumni activities, contact the Alumni Offices below:

Columbia College
Office of Alumni Affairs &
Development
622 West 113 Street
New York, NY 10025
866–CC–ALUMNI (Toll Free)
ccalumni@columbia.edu

Fu Foundation School of
Engineering and Applied Science
Office of Development and Alumni Relations
500 West 120th Street
510 Mudd, MC 4718
New York, NY 10027
212–854–4472
seasalumni@columbia.edu

Columbia Alumni Affairs
Office of Alumni and Development
Columbia Alumni Center
622 West 113th Street
Mail Code 4525
New York, NY 10025
(877) 854–ALUM (2586)
(212) 851–1957 (fax)
alumni-link@columbia.edu

E-Mail for Life

The Columbia Alumni Association offers alumni free, Web-based e-mail. It features robust Gmail features with a Columbia address, over 6 gigabytes of free, Web-based storage, easy file attachment for outgoing messages, customizable name@xa.columbia.edu and no forwarding required. For more information, please visit: http://alumni.columbia.edu/access/s2_2.html

Columbia Arts Alumni League

Columbia Alumni Arts League (aka CAAL, pronounced "cal" as in "pal") members enjoy special benefits and discounts at more than 60 leading New York City cultural institutions. Connect with fellow Columbians and artists through exclusive arts events and stay informed about the arts, while supporting the arts at Columbia. Nearly 5,000 alumni from schools across the university enjoy CAAL benefits.

306 Prentis Hall
632 West 125th Street, Mail Code 5011
New York, New York 10027
(212) 851–1879
alumniarts@columbia.edu

Center for Career Education (CCE)

CCE offers a variety of career assistance to support alumni as they navigate and plan careers throughout their lives. Through individual career counseling, career development programs and workshops, job postings (LionSHARE), and career fairs and networking events, CCE supports alumni with career transitions, self-assessment, job search skills and tools, and career planning.

In addition, CCE encourages alumni to support the development of educational programs and employment opportunities for students and other alumni. Alumni are encouraged to share their career stories, volunteer as panelists, participate in networking events, include a profile on the alumni networking database, Columbia Career Connections, post job and internship opportunities, provide shadowing and other experiential experiences, and serve as a Columbia champion at their organizations. (Contact information can be found on the next page.)

Center for Career Education
Columbia University
East Campus, Lower Level
70-74 Morningside Drive
New York, NY 10027
212–854–5609
212–854–5640 (fax)
www.careereducation.columbia.edu

Columbia Career Connections

Network with other alumni by joining this online career network for Columbia University alumni and students. Visit alumni.columbia.edu/access/s2_6.html to sign-up.

The Columbia Libraries

Columbia Alumni may apply for a University Alumni Identification Card that grants renewable reading privileges. Alumni who wish to borrow books may obtain borrowing privileges for a $30 monthly fee.

Columbia University Libraries
535 West 114th Street
New York, NY 10027
(212) 854–7309
http://www.columbia.edu/cu/lweb/services/contacts/

Dodge Physical Center

All alumni may purchase a membership to use the facilities at the Dodge Physical Center.

3030 Broadway-MC 1900
New York, NY 10027
(212) 854–3441
http://www.gocolumbialions.com

University Registrar

Registrar services are available to alumni of Columbia University in the areas of transcripts, academic certification, diploma replacement, name changes, and release or withhold information. (Contact information can be found on the next page.)

ffice of the Registrar
olumbia University
)5 Kent Hall, MC 9202
40 Amsterdam Avenue
ew York, NY 10027
tp://www.columbia.edu/cu/registrar/docs/alumni/index.html

e Columbia University Club of New York City

>cated at 15 West 43rd Street in the heart of Midtown Manhattan, the Columbia
niversity Club of New York offers membership to alumni from all divisions of
olumbia University (including Barnard and Teachers College) as well as to all
rrent Columbia faculty, administrators, graduate and undergraduate students, and
olumbia certificate holders. Parents and children of Columbia alumni and current
adents are also eligible to become members.

West 43rd Street
ew York, NY 10036
2–719–0380
fo@columbiaclub.org

Jest and Conference Accommodations

uest accommodations on campus are available to parents, alumni, and guest
filiates of Columbia. Please make your arrangements well in advance of your
ticipated arrival as the number of guest rooms available is limited.

olumbia University Guest & Conference Housing
)60 Broadway – MC 3003
ew York, NY 10027
12) 854–0365
nferencehousing@columbia.edu

umni Travel Study Program

e Alumni Travel Study Program allows Columbia alumni to combine learning and
easure through domestic and international travel. The travel-study experience is
ten enriched by the participation of Columbia faculty members.

66) 3ALUMNI
tp://alumni.columbia.edu/attend/s4_1b.html

Gradspot.com's
Guide to Life After College

Written and Edited by
Chris Schonberger with Stuart Schultz and Tory Hoen

Edited by David J. Klein

We would like to extend a very special thanks to our amazing team of writers, whose research and writing were invaluable in the process of making this book:

Julie Fishman, David Pekema, Rachel Solomon, Arielle Sachar, Karen Keller, Aryeh Cohen-Wade, Theodore Bressman, Christine Margiotta, Rebecca Shore, Jennifer Pollock, Mandy Erickson, Jenny Williams, Lauren Levinson, Josie Swindler, Julia Bonnheim, Erin Hartigan, Erin Kandel, Orli Van Mourik, Jennifer Cunningham, Jake Tuck, Sean McManus, Stephanie Berger, Molly Martin, Richard Koss, Christopher Stella, Nick Schonberger, Courtney McClellan and Tom Wiseman.

We would also like to thank the following people for their contributions and support:

Antony Clavel, Matthew Demmer, Randi Hazan, Rachel Kinrot, Chris Nakamura, Lisa Harrow, Renee Bissell, Millicent Brown, Matty Marcus, Naledge, Dr. Valerie Young, Neilesh Mutyala, Steve Rosengard, Charlie French, Alexander Arapoglou, Nate Houghteling, Kyle Berkman, Greg Konover, Seth Robinson, Ben Herzberger, Chris Catizone, Davina Pike, David Lerman, Laura Swift, Arielle Goren, Andrew Smeall, Jamie Spitzer, Charlie French, Lisa Shichijo, Elise Minter, Jay Boggis and everyone who gave us feedback or commented on our website.

And last but not least, we'd like to thank our new publisher, MG Prep Inc., and the MG Prep Inc. team (Andrew Yang, Danielle Rothman, Beretzi Garcia, Evyn Williams and Dan McNaney) for standing behind us.

ISBN-10: 0-9841780-3-1

ISBN-13/EAN-13: 978-0-9841780-3-2

To order additional copies of this book, please visit: www.gradspot.com/book

Published by MG Prep Inc.

Interior design by Dan McNaney and Cathy Huang

Cover design by Aaron G. Lewis

Cover photography ©iStockphoto.com/Viorika

Acknowledgements

Chris thanks

Grandma and Grandad Griggs—for cups of tea, pints of bitter, and lots of love.

Stuart thanks

Andrew Yang for giving us the chance to do this, Chris Schonberger for making this book awesome, and Tory Hoen for giving this book a welcome new voice.

Tory thanks

Mum and Dad—for your support of both my education and the existential crises that ensued.

Table of Contents

Start Here

Why We Wrote This Book

Start Here

A few months after launching our website, Gradspot.com, we received an email from one of our users who was looking for help improving her living situation. After we pointed her to content on our site and answered some questions, she said something we haven't forgotten since: "If only you had been around when I graduated last summer, I probably wouldn't have ended up in Newark!" Now, no offense to Newark, but we fully understand her sentiment. After all, it was just a short time ago that we were leaving school and feeling completely unprepared to deal with issues like 401(k)s, sheisty landlords, and office politics.

Time and again, our peers echoed our concerns about being sent out to sea without a life vest, as have the graduating classes that followed after them. Some didn't have any clue what to expect, while those who were actually proactive enough to seek out resources found that they were either out-of-date or out-of-touch. Thus, we figured there was no better time to create a resource that could fill that void—first Gradspot.com and now this book. Ultimately, **our goal in these pages is to expose you to the issues that are most likely to arise in your first year out of school and to share the methods we and others have used to successfully navigate them.**

On top of all of the insights we picked up from our own experiences and included in this book, we've also called upon other recent grads and college students to share tips; reached out to a wide range of topic experts for their input; and trolled every other pertinent resource out there. We even set up a "Life After College Lab" to test out high-pressure showerheads, budgeting tools, and anything else that might make the transition a little bit easier.

Being twentysomethings ourselves, we understand what it's like to be a graduate today rather than in 1965. Times have changed, and we wrote this book to reflect the experience of a recent grad *now*. We hope you'll find it helpful and that it will ease the exciting, yet intimidating transition to life after college.

How to Use This Book

Gradspot.com's Guide to Life After College has many uses. You can prop up a wobbly chair with it, burn it for warmth when your parents kick you out the house, or "donate" it to your alma mater instead of making an actual monetary contribution.

Before you do all those things, however, we hope that you'll read it. While there is no set chronology to life after college, we've laid out the chapters in a way that approximates the general order in which you're likely to encounter different issues, from moving back home to coping with the pressures of a "one-year rut." To help you browse the book, we've created a very thorough table of contents and an easy-to-use cross-referencing system that will allow you to navigate among topics quickly. Ultimately, we hope each chapter will provide a solid foundation for overcoming a range of obstacles along the post-college road.

We've also compiled a list of links to all of the resources we mention in the book that you can find at gradspot.com/book. Many of the URLs listed in this book are obvious, but in instances where links were too long to include in the text, we've made note of it so it's clear that the actual link is available on our online resource guide.

While we can help you understand the basics, share tips and tricks about how to take the next step, and give you the tools to make informed choices, many of the decisions that need to be made are based on your unique situation and may require extra research. So even with all the acumen you'll pick up in these pages, we encourage you to be careful when dealing with major issues. Whether you're filing a tax return, choosing a dental plan, consolidating student debt, or doing anything else that we discuss in this book, always consult a professional for help if you have doubts. Remember, many of your choices now will affect you for years to come.

Visit Us at Gradspot.com!

Needless to say, no matter how long we make this book, there will always be more to discuss. If anything else comes up that you can't find in these pages, never hesitate to visit us at the online destination for life after college: Gradspot.com. There, we have additional guides, a Q&A section where anyone can post a question about life after college to experts and community members, and a community blog where users can share their own unique life-after-college experiences.

Enjoy the read, and good luck!

Author's Foreword

No matter how hard I try, I can't remember who spoke at my graduation. It's weird, because it's not like the whole day is a blank: I remember that it was raining and that I wanted a coffee from Dunkin' Donuts. I remember getting my diploma, massacring an hors d'oeuvres spread, and taking some pictures with the family of this guy I didn't really know. And I vividly remember telling a friend's mother that I was now "an incomparable Lord of Academia," a declaration that was met with an uncomfortable move away from me and toward the canapés. But what about those sage words that were meant to usher me into the "real world" with a sense of direction and purpose? The speech that my school probably paid $100,000 for me to enjoy on the most momentous day of my young life? No recollection whatsoever.

I guess there are two possible lessons here: 1) I have an extremely accelerated form of Alzheimer's, or 2) Inspirational words are nice and all, but they fade into oblivion once you've been sleeping on your friend's trundle bed for two months because the best job you can get is as an assistant lacrosse coach at a middle school. Essentially, this book is about avoiding these sorts of situations, or at least navigating them more seamlessly than I did. But if you'll humor me, I've got a few philosophical nuggets of my own to share before we get going. I would say "write this down" so you don't forget, but we've already done that for you.

Let's start with a quotation, as is customary on these occasions. Here's one from spiritual guru Eric Butterworth: "Don't go through life, *grow* through life." Probably my favorite line from Mr. Butterworth, whose M.O. is flipping the script on conventional wisdom. (He even wrote a book called *How to Break the Ten Commandments*, for goodness' sake!) But as much as we all feel the urge to put stuff like that on our Facebook profiles once in a while, I don't want to defer to truisms. The ones I heard before college turned out to be pretty off the mark, so why would I rely on any now?

For example, I'm sure a lot of people told you the same thing they told me before I arrived on campus: "Get ready for the best four years of your life." Well, that probably seemed like an exciting prospect four years ago, but what now? Does life really peak with Pimps n' Hos parties, dining hall dinners, and feigned enthusiasm for community service? Is studying for pointless exams really as good as it gets? Maybe it's time to reassess this "wisdom."

Don't get me wrong—there were definitely some times when I yearned to crawl back into the womb of university life in the first year after I graduated. Not only because the notion that your "best years are behind you" is incredibly depressing, but also because the simplicity of college life was tough to leave behind. As time has gone on, however, I've realized that life only improves after graduation. Whenever I want, I can cycle through my Facebook photos and Microsoft Word documents and pretty much relive college in 45 minutes. Great, I drank hundreds of beers and wrote some incredibly sick papers. Next!

For you, "next" may be a scary word right now because everyone keeps badgering you about the "next step." Where are you gonna live *next*? What are you gonna do *next*? How many episodes of *Next* are you gonna watch on MTV while you're unemployed? After the clear-cut expectations of college, it's tough to encounter so many question marks and not know how to proceed. But before you know it, you'll be checking your *Acapulco-lypse Now* album and thinking, "Yeah, those were the days in a way, but these days are more fulfilling in a broader sense."

In school, the best you can do is be considered cool and get A's. Great grades are all well and good, but here are two more lessons from post-college life: 1) Being cool in the college sense soon loses its cachet, and 2) Except for when you're slyly fudging your GPA on your resume, grades are yesterday's news. After college, by contrast, you can accrue legitimate respect from others. More important, you can go out on a limb and achieve something truly remarkable—something with a value that transcends letter grades. Get rich, cure eczema, create something beautiful…whatever. The sky is not the limit. That part of the atmosphere above the sky is.

And it is in this realization that we encounter the true meat and potatoes of life after college: opportunity and fulfillment. When you make your own opportunities outside of the predictable structures of school life, you will experience a more intense sense of accomplishment than you ever knew existed. No matter how you slice it, a victory in the real world will always feel better than an academic victory—the odds are tougher, fewer people are genuinely pulling for you, and the formula for success is less obvious. Navigate that unholy trinity and you are going to feel pretty good about yourself. And you should.

But honestly, I see no reason to worry. I mean, look at you—you're a new breed carrying an extremely valuable asset in spades: potential. You are tech-savvy and completely "wireless." You were all born in the '80s, except for a few degenerates and some people who went to "German school." You have literally

Start Here

burned so much "midnight oil" that you have caused a massive war. And statistically, ten percent of you are gay. Combine those last two facts, and you've successfully historicized the "don't ask, don't tell" policy.

So, at this moment, I urge each and every one of you to expand your conception of life after college to include a little thing called "dreams." Because as Ryan Seacrest put it, "You are America's Idol." Was he talking about Kelly Clarkson at the time? Sure, but right now you are all American idols. And just like Kelly back in the day, all you really lack is a little experience. That's where we can help. As you set forth into the world, let this book be your crib sheet to the Book of Life. *The Merriam-Webster's Spanish-English Dictionary* to your *Cien Años de Soledad*. The strategy guide to your own *World of Warcraft*.

Whenever you are feeling confused, just remember that those same idiots who said, "College is the best four years of your life," are now saying, "Life starts at 50." As Eric Butterworth would probably say to these people, "Make up your own mind before you try to make up mine." It's time to flip the script—life after college is where the fun really begins.

—Chris Schonberger

Chapter I: Holy $*%#, I Just Graduated!

Holy $*%#, I Just Graduated!

The last couple months of school are jam-packed with finals, parties, farewells, and finally…graduation. With so many things going on, this period can fly by in a disorienting haze of sadness and joy. But when you grab your diploma, drink your champagne, and walk out of the gates, be prepared for the heavy hand of reality to slap you right in your grinning face. The following questions will undoubtedly consume your mind:

What just happened? You graduated! Well played.

Am I still alive? Yes, you made it. Well done! Staying alive is half the battle.

Did I have sex? Hmmm. Really only you can answer that question.

What now? Have an ice cream sandwich and relax. We're here to help.

Up until now, everything has been decided for you and served up on a platter—or at least force-fed. You went to high school. You did your homework (sometimes). You went to college, chose a major, and, if you were lucky, that basically accounted for all the big decisions you had to deal with for four years. But now, maybe for the first time ever, it feels like the "next step" is not completely obvious. And worst of all, you feel like you need to decide what you want to do for the rest of your life *right now!*

This is a pervasive fear that the vast majority of recent graduates faces. It is completely normal, but also completely irrational because now is the first time in your life when you actually have the freedom to set your own timeframes—what's the rush? Take a six-month internship to see if publishing is right for you. Find a temporary gig or freelance to hold you over financially until you decide what you want to do next. Or take that two (or six!) month trip around the world you've always dreamed about because once you've joined the rat race, you might not have the opportunity to do so. At that point, it will no longer be assumed that a quarter of the calendar year is completely open for you to do what you want *or* that you'll be able to take a vacation that lasts more than one week.

You also don't have to figure out where you want to live just yet nor jump straight into a rental obligation. As long as you can bear your parents for a few more months, why not crash at home to give yourself time to sort everything out?

In this chapter, we'll help you ease into life after college and celebrate your educational achievements. We'll also navigate the slippery slope of living at home, share some easy ways to start earning money without making a career commitment, and help you plan the perfect post-college trip, whether that means a two-week jaunt or an all-expenses-paid gap year abroad. This is the time when you can start anew and set the tone for your life as a college grad. And whenever things get you down, just think about these two words: no homework!

10 Things to Do After Graduating

1) **Join a kickball league.** Already miss the college spirit? Rekindle the camaraderie from your varsity/intramural glory days while laughing at the guy in skinny jeans waddling to first.

2) **Apply to a reality TV show.** What do you have to lose (except dignity and the support of your family)?

3) **Become a bar trivia pro.** Utilize that vast wealth of knowledge you just accumulated by winning free drinks and the respect of thirtysomethings desperately trying to stay young.

4) **Travel.** The post-graduation trip is a classic move for those who can afford it, and even grads on a tight budget have plenty of options close to home. Read more on page 46.

5) **Learn to cook.** Once you're living alone sans a meal plan, the ability to whip up a fricassee will save big bucks and impress potential mates like the plumage of a peacock (or a she-cock). Read more on page 437.

6) **Spend time with your family.** Take advantage of the time you can spend with your loved ones now, because tomorrow you may be busy. Or they may be dead.

7) **Be a kid again.** Go home and rekindle all those old feelings you had as a child. Dust off your old Nintendo console. Hit a tennis ball against a wall and pretend it's Monica Seles. Whatever it takes to get that spring back in your step.

8) **Get in shape.** We're not suggesting you become the girl who's hitting the elliptical so hard that her legs are about to fly off, nor that tangerine-colored dude who exclusively does upper body and can barely run a mile. But at the very least, get rid of the lingering traces of your "freshman 15" (funny how it never quite went away) and motivate yourself to take the next step.

9) **Volunteer.** Before you become too "busy" making money for yourself, demonstrate a little of the philanthropic spirit for which you may or may not be famous. Find something that appeals to you personally and get involved. Read more on page 432.

10) **Write a book.** Or if novels aren't your thing, pursue anything that you're passionate about. Record songs, paint pictures, or write the screenplay you've been talking about for three years. Now is the time.

 Get a tattoo: My brother claims this is an awesome idea.

Moving Home

One of the most immediate issues facing the recent graduate is where to seek shelter after getting kicked out of the dormitory. If you're like most of your contemporaries (about 60%, according to a Monster.com survey), the default solution is your parents' house. And why not? Home provides many creature comforts, the rent is usually pretty competitive (i.e., $0), and cable is free. What's not to like?

Apparently, not everyone thinks it's such a no-brainer. If you believe the Baby Boomer-biased media, you'd think America had an epidemic on its hands. Yes, it's true—more and more college grads are moving home after graduation than ever before. As the naysayers like to point out, young people are making financial sacrifices early on in their adult lives while forcing

their parents to postpone retirement to support them. In her book *Generation Me*, sociologist Jean Twenge even goes so far as to suggest the underlying motivation for this trend is selfishness: Apparently, we are a generation of narcissistic daydreamers who would rather lounge at mom and dad's house thinking about our passions than worry about a mortgage. Sounds like the end of the world!

Ms. Twenge is entitled to her opinion, but the rulebook has changed since our parents first left college. The old paradigm of "graduate college, move out, start a career, get married, have some kids" no longer holds. Career paths are more varied but also more complicated than they once were, and it takes the average graduate several months (if not longer) to find a job.

If you're 35 and still getting yelled at by your mom for leaving the toilet seat up, then you might have cause for concern. But for now, don't beat yourself up about settling back into the nest, whether it's for a summer or a year. As long as you treat it as a temporary solution and show a little initiative to do *something* other than sit around reading *Twilight*, things will eventually work out. Here are some tips for navigating a potentially thorny situation.

Don't Fall Back into Bad Habits. Presumably, at least four years have passed since you really lived with the 'rents. They got used to daily life without you, and they probably liked it. Even if you have younger siblings, your departure to college meant one less mouth to feed, one less load of laundry each week, and far fewer ornery teenagers displaying horrible posture throughout the house. You'll do yourself a favor by seeing their side of the story and easing your way back into the Matrix. It's amazing how quickly that feeling of youthful entitlement can creep back into your psyche when you enter the house, but you don't want your selfish demands to come crashing down on your parents like a ton of bricks. Clean your clothes, wash the dishes, offer to buy (or at least fetch) groceries, and do some cooking. You can annoy them all you want and make them worry day and night, but don't make your return to the house feel like more *work*.

Make the Most of the Time with Your Family. Tempers fray easily in the pressure cooker of post-college life. As if jobhunting wasn't aggravating enough, being forced to give Ma Dukes a nightly recap of your progress can become extremely irksome. And ironically, it can be even harder if you've got a job. The last thing you want to do when you come home tired at the end of the day is to tell your mom all about the papers you filed and the copies you made—it salts the wound liberally. That said, it's wise to fight past the feeling of being smothered by your parents. Whether it's two weeks, six months, or a year from now, eventually you'll be on your own. Careers will force you to move around, significant others will demand that you go to their house for Thanksgiving— all sorts of things will ensure that you see your parents less frequently. Have dinner together, hang out with younger siblings, and make some memories while you have the time. Trust us, you'll feel better for it in the long-run. And if peace of mind doesn't motivate you, then just think of your civil behavior as remuneration for your room and board.

> ### Tips & Tricks: The economics of living at home
>
> It's undeniable: The number one reason grads move in with their parents is money. So whether you're trying to break into a low-paying industry or you haven't quite figured out what you want to do after college, check out the potential monthly savings that are available: $500 to $1,500+ on rent, $300+ on food, $65+ on cable and Internet, $50 on electricity, $50 on coffee, $10 on renters insurance…and those are just the basics. Unless your parents are asking you to shell out some extra cash (even then it's still a great deal), you could end up saving somewhere between $1,000 and $2,500 per month. Maybe living with mom and dad won't be so bad after all.

Holy $%#, I Just Graduated!*

Dad-juation (and Mom-juation). Parents also go through a transition after you graduate, so it's important to keep their interests in mind when you re-infiltrate their home. If they helped finance your education, they are probably pretty pleased about not having to pay another semester's tuition. Don't rain on the parade by finding new and less justifiable ways to be a financial burden. Give them space when they want to have friends over instead of sitting in the living room playing Xbox Live with headphones on—that's embarrassing for everyone. Overall, try to avoid giving the impression that your college career was a complete waste of time and money.

Save As Much Money As Possible. Whether you're jobless, interning, or stuck at a starting salary that can't support you month to month, the luxury of not paying for rent, utilities, or food can make a huge difference. However, if you go and blow any loot that does come into your hands on unnecessary extravagances, you will be doing yourself a huge disservice for the day when you do actually need to pay for things. Adopting a frugal lifestyle should not be that difficult, because let's be honest, living "la vida loca" (whatever that means) and staying with your parents don't necessarily vibe. Do you really want to be hitting the bar and playing tonsil hockey with strangers in your childhood bed? Save the money for a time and place when you can live a little more loosely. Who knows—the good budgeting and saving habits you start now might even translate to life beyond the nest.

Set a Schedule. Being semi-productive every day—or at least constructing an elaborate façade of industriousness—will help to get your parents off your back and make you feel more motivated. If you are already working, this shouldn't be too difficult. If not, wake up at the same time every day, and try to make sure that it's before noon. After that, try to do something useful. In *The Quarterlifer's Companion*, Abby Wilner and Catherine Stocker suggest scheduling at least one activity each day to help you on your job search: "It can be an interview, a trip to the library to do research, a trip to Kinkos to copy resumes, anything." It doesn't really matter what activity you choose to schedule as long as loafing around and being cantankerous does not become your *modus operandi*.

Enjoy the Fairies. Sometimes you will leave your room covered in soiled clothing, only to return later in the day and find it neatly ironed and folded on your bed. That is the Laundry Fairy. Or maybe one day you will be watching reruns of *Who Wants to Be a Millionaire* and suddenly dinner will magically appear in front of you. Thank you, Dinner Fairy! Some of us are lucky enough to have parents who, in spite of their better judgment, can't help but spoil us when we are around. Maybe your moving home is not cause for celebration, but you've still been gone long enough for your parents to miss you a little bit, and you also just achieved a great milestone by graduating. In other words, you are in good standing! Milk this situation as much as your conscience will allow you to, because when you move into your own place, those fairies will be slaughtered and subsequently resurrected as ruthless demons that will make your life infinitely more difficult.

Making It Long Term. Some people end up working or going to graduate school in the city their parents live in, and financially it might make sense to create a long-term arrangement that could span several years. This is a trickier situation that depends a lot on your relationship with your parents. If they let you do the things that you need to do to feel sane and you don't step on their toes too much, it can work out nicely and allow you to save money that you would otherwise be pouring down the drain unnecessarily.

At the end of the day, you need to be honest with yourself and make sure you are not stifling your potential by staying shacked up in the house. If you realize you need to spread your wings a bit more, you'll find a way to make it out.

Will Work to Buy Time

Whether you're at home trying to keep the 'rents at bay, you've moved out on your own but aren't quite ready for the 9-to-5 world, or you're just saving up some money to travel, there are plenty of ways to start filling your piggy bank sooner rather than later, almost all of which can be done without learning any new skills (unless you need a primer on "hustle"). Some are quick fixes to keep you afloat such as auctioning off your old CDs or being paid to shop (see page 43). Others include joining corporations without having to make full-time commitments, as in temping (see page 38) or working retail (see page 34). And below are some tried-and-true post-grad routes like tutoring, dog walking, babysitting, and more. The best part is that in all cases, you'll be able to maintain enough autonomy and flexibility to make it through the summer—and in some cases well beyond—without sacrificing the opportunity to watch every *Martin* marathon that comes on. Ready to get this money? Let's go!

Five Ways to Start Making Money Today

Exasperated by the job market already? Always dreamed of setting your own work schedule and indirectly giving the middle finger to "the Man"? There are plenty of ways to make some money—or even a *living*—that require no new skills and little to no start-up costs. All that's needed is some get-up-and-go and a liberal application of elbow grease. Here are five ideas, as well as tips on how to get started. If none of them strikes your fancy, learn how to apply the approaches that work in the below examples to anything you want in the "Make Some Extra Cash" template on page 35.

Tutor

You went to college. Many parents would very much like for their kids to go to college. Ergo, if you act like you know the secrets of the SAT or admissions essays, you can convince those parents to cut you some serious checks (anywhere from $10 an hour to over $30k a year if you stick with it for a while and

Holy $*%#, I Just Graduated!

27

bag some rich kids in the right market). This gig is practically custom-made for recent grads, so take advantage of your credentials while they're still fresh.

Is it for me? If you have a geeky love of standardized tests or you like teaching but don't want to commit to it as a career, tutoring makes a lot of sense. But be warned: Being a good tutor takes a lot more than just showing up and answering a few questions. Tim Urban, the founder of Launched Education (and a former *Apprentice* contestant), says it all boils down to that moment when Little Timmy shows up and says, "I did all my homework except for this really hard one. Can you show me how?" In other words, you can't just waltz in and expect that being "smart" will suffice. Even if you did well in high school and college, you will almost certainly have to crack open a book and make sure you're able to respond to questions when you don't have an answer key. You also need to have Zen-like patience to work with some of these little rascals until they really get the concept their teachers don't have time to teach them. You've got to develop the ability to handle parental expectations that may not be realistic, and connect with students who aren't excited to be studying or spending time with you. And most important, you'll have to actually produce results—that's really the only way to get more clients. But if you think you've got what it takes, then tutoring is a great post-college cash cow, ripe for the milking.

How do I get started? Generally speaking, no certifications are necessary to join the tutoring circuit, but you need to have a strong grasp on the subjects you're likely to teach. Once you've narrowed those down, there are two general approaches to tutoring—find your own clients or join an existing company.

Option 1: Join a company. The advantages to joining a company like Kaplan or Princeton Review are that you can start cashing checks pretty quickly; the disadvantage is your earning potential is stifled since you only get a portion of what each student is paying. When you start out, the company provides materials and students, plus you may get some classroom experience. The pay ranges from about $12 to $20 per hour, depending upon the market and the subject. To get hired you have to take a diagnostic test (it differs depending upon what you teach) and score around the 90th percentile. There's also an interview and training process that typically runs for a few days (the big companies have pretty high turnover so they're often looking for new recruits). Ultimately, if you just have a short-term work gap to fill before you do something else, this route might be your best option in terms of convenience and ease. You can usually work part-time hours while pursuing other jobs or classes.

In addition to the big names, there are many boutique test prep companies in every market that might be able to offer better rates but are generally more selective. Some of the better-known boutiques include Revolution Test Prep and Advantage Testing, as well as our distinguished publisher, Manhattan GMAT/ Atlas LSAT. The best of these test prep companies pay up to $50 to $100 per hour, but they're also more competitive, often requiring a 99th percentile score on any given standardized test, as well as prior teaching (or tutoring) experience and demonstrated ability. To get a sense of the boutiques in your area, check out Craigslist and do some Googlin' to see who's advertising for tutoring services locally.

Option 2: Do it yourself. While it's certainly easier to teach classes for a big company (they provide you with materials, students, and a space), you don't have to split the money pot if you get paid directly. (The national test prep companies charge dramatic mark-ups on your time, so if you're getting paid $20 to tutor someone, the parents of your students are often paying $40 per hour or more!) Entering the tutoring market as a free agent is definitely a tougher and more long-term approach, but such is the nature of entrepreneurship—bigger risks, bigger rewards!

The first and most intimidating hurdle, of course, is finding your own clients. Before you approach anyone, develop your pitch. What subjects are you going to teach? Why are you qualified? What is your teaching philosophy? ("Every student has different needs so each lesson must be tailored to the individual" is an oldie but goodie.) Retake any standardized tests that you want to teach if you didn't originally get as good a score as you would have liked, or brush up on materials on a topic you want to offer. Pulling together some original teaching materials, like a nicely designed handout with all of the key math concepts for the SAT, will create a sense of professionalism. And business cards and a website will help even more. Last, are you computer savvy? If you can provide off-site help through a video chat via iChat or Skype, you might also give yourself a competitive edge over brick and mortar shops.

Once you're prepared, target local schools (remember: private school parents spend money like it's going out of fashion) and show up well-dressed, well-prepared, and…ready to be rejected! Pitching a counselor, teacher, or school psychologist is not easy because it is a big deal for school professionals to recommend you—college-hungry parents can be crazy, and no one from the school wants to piss them off. Be patient; maybe you'll shoot bricks for the first four months, but by month seven you might have ten clients and you'll wonder how you ever considered quitting. How do you get from one to ten?

Holy $*%#, I Just Graduated!

Mine your personal networks—maybe your parents have friends or colleagues with junior high/high school age kids who want to go to your alma mater. Tell your friends. And then, prepare like a maniac when you finally get a client, because the only way schools and parents will keep recommending you is if you do a knock-up job.

Total start-up costs? Potentially none, though you'll want to work through some test prep books before you start (ask your friends if they have any first). If you're rolling solo you should put a little bit of money into making your presentation materials look snazzy and professional.

How much can I make? As mentioned above, Kaplan and Princeton Review pay about $12 to $20 per hour, and boutiques may pay a lot more. As for the D.I.Y. approach, you can hopefully pull in higher rates over time if you build a track record. You may have to start out as a bargain, particularly if you're tutoring people in your network initially. Eventually you should strive to charge rates closer to $30 or $50 (these are the prices you'll see for independent tutors on Craigslist across the country). With just a ten hour work week (3–5 clients) and an hourly rate of $40, you'd be raking in $1,600 a month and still have time for other activities and projects. Your goal as an independent tutor should be to have counselors and parents saying, "He/she isn't cheap…but it's worth it."

Pet Sitter & Dog Walker

Though tales of dog walkers making over $100k a year usually involve words such as "celebrity" and "whisperer," taking pups out for a stroll can be a fun way to make a few extra bucks, or even build a small business. And if you don't live in an urban area where people need walkers, you can always take care of their furry friends when they go on vacation. The plus is that pet sitting is almost always easier than babysitting—unlike a six-year-old, a dog won't ask you a million questions in an evening, unless you are on mushrooms at the time.

Is it for me? Any genuine dog-lover who is in good shape and moderately personable is a prime candidate to start a walking and sitting biz. That said, it's worth taking a reality check: You may like your golden retriever back home, but are you ready to hit the streets for two or more hours a day, rain or shine, and have a dog that's not your own poop on your rug?

How do I get started? Finding customers is the toughest part of starting your own outfit, and many full-time walkers will tell you it took them six months to a year to get a full slate of customers (that being said, it's not impossible to get a pooch or two pretty quickly, especially if you have dog-owners in your building/neighborhood). Since people treat their pets like their children, nothing will ever beat a personal recommendation. Thus, your first step should always be to tell everyone you know about your business—family, friends, dodgeball league acquaintances, old bosses and colleagues, et al. It's likely that at least some of them have dogs or know people with dogs. When that pool is maxed out, do some local marketing (flyers!) at apartment buildings and condo blocks, dog parks, pet stores, vets' offices, and anywhere else dog owners might assemble.

In addition to pulling together some basic marketing materials like business cards and a simple website, you'll want to get insurance. Pet Sitters Associates (PetSitLLC.com) offers membership and dog-walking insurance for $164 a year. This will cover you if your dog hurts another dog or person or destroys someone's property. And, if nothing else, it will also give your potential clients peace of mind. (Let them know on your business card and website that you're insured.)

If you really enjoy working with dogs and think a career in pet care might be for you, expanding your skills and going through an official program for dog training might be the natural next step. Look up local dog-training companies to see if they'll take you on as an apprentice. Finally, don't forget the increasingly popular trade of "doggy massage"!

Total start-up costs? About $250 for insurance, a website, and other promotional materials.

> **Tips & Tricks: Cheap business cards and websites**
>
> Whether you're pitching yourself as a dog-walker or a personal style guru, a business card can provide that little boost of professionalism and a way for people to remember you. For budget-friendly business cards and websites, look no further than VistaPrint.com. The site offers 250 business card for free (though it's probably worth paying the extra $3.99 to get the ad off the back), as well as a bunch of other promotional materials for little more than the cost of shipping. The ready-made website templates aren't exactly going to win any design awards, but they'll do the trick when you're first getting started. Just create a one- to three-page site with information for your potential customers and set up a unique email address to put on those biz cards (e.g., sophie@ downtowndogs.com). Another option is to create a free Wordpress. com blog and turn it into a landing page for customers. For instructions on setting up a website, see page 37.

How much can I make? Google the local competition to make sure your rates are competitive. In general, hard-working sitters and walkers can rake in about $10 to $20 for each 30-minute walk (more for dog-running), and $40 to $75 for an overnight stay. Just think: $10–20 for a 30 minute walk × 9 dogs (3 groups of 3) × 5 days a week = pretty good pay for staying fit and hanging with pups! And while "cash-in-hand" may not be a phrase the IRS likes, there's certainly nothing stopping you from keeping all the pup money in a brown paper bag, far away from any stimulus packages (where was the money for dog parks, anyway?). Then again, starting your grad career off dodging the law probably isn't the best idea!

Babysitter & Nanny

If you grew up reading the *Baby-sitters Club*, you've already got your homework out of the way. Taking care of local youths when their mom and dad head off for some alone time is not only a good way to make some extra money, but in some cases it can also be your ticket to traveling abroad for free. Open up a notebook—it's time to start your very own *Nanny Diaries*.

Is it for me? The most important thing to understand is that taking care of someone's children is a *major* responsibility—CEOs lose millions of dollars all the time, but the anger of their stockholders is no match for the wrath of a parent if you lose her child. Patience, energy, and organization are as important as a genuine love for kids—even when they eat dirt and spray you with Super Soakers. A love of travel may also motivate you if you're able to snag an au pair gig abroad.

How do I get started? As with dog-walking and tutoring, you need to be deemed trustworthy, so build a pitch that emphasizes your dependability and any relevant experience, even if that's just taking care of your five younger siblings. It's also helpful if you have or can obtain CPR and First Aid training, which you can find via most health organizations, including the American Red Cross, for between $20 and $100. Word of mouth is golden for getting gigs, but there are some agencies that place sitters and au pairs. One good website to check out is GreatAuPair.com, where you can post a profile for free and search for families. You do have to pay in order to get contact info (it costs $60 for a 30-day membership), but since many families purchase a membership, it is not always needed (you can just post a profile and wait for families to contact you). If you're looking to travel abroad but don't have the money, you can try the au pair route—check out TransitionsAbroad.com for listings in different countries. Finally, Craigslist is always worth a shot—go to the "childcare" section, which is under the "community" heading.

If you find yourself having trouble finding your first client, be sure to reach out to friends and family for easier-to-find gigs. Your neighbor who has known you since you were eight might not pay the best, but any gig you can get will build references and bullets on your babysitting resume.

Total start-up costs? None, unless you pay to get certifications or sign up for employment websites.

How much can I make? That's a tough one, as there are often nonmonetary benefits to nannying or being an au pair, like room, board, and the opportunity to travel to another country. (Some nanny jobs we've seen advertised even offer health benefits and salaries above $40k!) For plain old babysitting, we've heard quotes ranging from about $12 to $20 an hour, depending on the number of children, their ages, and what tasks are expected of you.

Waiter, Waitress, Bartender and Barista

Working at a Starbucks or the local faux-French bistro may not be the same as working for yourself, but there's definitely an entrepreneurial spirit and a ton of camaraderie amongst table servers, baristas, and bar staff who battle it out for the biggest tips they can possibly muster.

Is it for me? If you are talkative, energetic, and outgoing, any of these jobs could be a perfect way to pay the bills (or maintain flexible hours while you pursue other passions). It's very gratifying at the end of a shift to go home with a wad of hard-earned cash in your pocket. On the other hand, the job can be exhausting, and you may have to deal with the occasional overstressed manager and/or obnoxious customer.

How do I get started? Many restaurants in huge food cities (e.g., NYC, LA, Chicago, Atlanta) will not even consider you if you lack serving experience, so your first move should be to get a gig anywhere you can. A café or small chain restaurant will usually be the easiest place to get your foot in the door. You can also be a "host" at a restaurant with little to no experience. And for bartending gigs, one way to break into the biz is by attending bartending school. Classes usually run for two hours each weekday, over the course of close to a month, at which point the school should help you find a job placement. However, many 'tenders say it's not necessary to do a course and that experience, no matter

Holy $%#, I Just Graduated!*

where you get it, will be a lot more useful. So if you've got the confidence to fake the funk a little bit, try going for a dive bar or laidback restaurant bar, pick up some on-the-job training, and then go for tougher cocktail lounge or swanky bar gigs.

For all types of restaurant and bar work, Craigslist is your best friend, though coffee chains and larger restaurants/restaurant groups will generally have an employment page on their websites. Plus, you can always walk around your neighborhood of choice and ask if anyone's hiring. If you do this, make sure to dress professionally and bring a resume because they may decide to interview you on the spot. For best results, go during off-peak hours (e.g., morning or late afternoon). When it comes time to interview, dress up and make managers feel comfortable that you can carry a conversation without getting too casual. It's also good to study up on the establishment, and depending on the type of place, be conversant in the wine, cocktails, and food they serve. If you do get hired, avoid the temptation to offer too many hours because it will become a slippery slope with your manager and could throw off your work-life balance.

How much can I make? Since tips are the name of the game, it all depends on how busy your shift is. Instead of getting too frustrated, realize that the big nights make up for the crappy ones. So if you make $300 in four hours on a Saturday night, don't be too upset when you make $40 the next morning. It's not unheard of for experienced full-time servers to make up to $50,000 a year. At a coffee shop, where tips are limited, the potential payout is going to be slimmer. Starbucks, for example, pays anywhere from around $6.75 to $10 an hour depending on where you are in the country.

Retail

Retail doesn't quite have the same cachet as some of the other examples we've discussed, but these jobs are widespread and relatively easy to land—and as an added bonus, you could get some helpful discounts on your "real world" wardrobe or a new flat-screen TV. If any fools try to give you a hard time for working alongside high-schoolers, just remind them you're following in the footsteps of greatness: Madeleine Albright started her career selling bras at a Jocelyn's Department Store in Denver.

Is it for me? Do you like interacting with people? Can you be patient with people who just can't decide on the red with sleeves or the blue with no sleeves? Are you comfortable being a salesperson and dealing with customers who are pissed that their microwave broke? Can you handle long hours on your feet?

If you said "yes" to all of the above and you're knowledgeable about cell phones or shoes or anything else people buy, then retail may very well be a good money-making option for you today.

How do I get started? While some of the larger retailers maintain employment pages on their websites and throw positions up on generic online job boards (e.g., Monster, HotJobs, etc.), people tend to have the most luck by just walking into establishments at the mall or local shopping area and asking if anyone is hiring. Start by schmoozing with salespeople or managers—drop a little banter and display your knowledge of the store, *then* ask if they're hiring. Even if you're really desperate, you should try to focus on a certain type of store instead of hopping from Best Buy to J. Crew to Foot Locker, because prep-

> **Tips & Tricks: Santa Claus is coming to town…and he's got jobs!**
>
> In the world of retail, there's no better time of year than the "holiday season" (roughly October through December) to snag a paying gig. According to the 2007 U.S. Census, department stores added over 174,000 staffers between those months and did 14% of their annual business in December alone. What does this mean for you? If you're looking for a job near the holidays, head to the mall and fill in an application at Wal-Mart, Macy's, Target, and anywhere else with a HELP WANTED sign (you can also check their websites to see if they have employment sections).

Holy $*%#, I Just Graduated!

aration will be your greatest asset. At the very least, make sure you're familiar with the clothing lines or products being sold there. Also, get a good idea of the dress code. (While we would suggest erring on the conservative side, there may be cases when you should dress differently.) Last, make sure to always carry crisp resumes when pulling an employment-seeking pop-in.

How much can I make? Most employers are hip to the game: They know you're not going to stay forever, so they generally start out paying at minimum wage (the federal minimum is $7.25 per hour, but it varies from state to state) and then raise the rate if you stick around. Some big box retailers may pay a little more than smaller shops.

The "Make Some Extra Cash" Template

If you look at the examples listed above, you'll notice some common themes running throughout that can be applied to any number of entrepreneurial endeavors. So if tutoring algebra or evading projectiles from insane children isn't your cup of tea, here is a rubric you can follow to turn any skill you've got (or can learn relatively quickly) into a source of income.

Choose Your Talent. What are you good at, or what would you like to be good at? Can you parlay this skill into a service people would pay for? Is there a precedent for people paying for it, or would you have to create the market?

Examples: Music instructor, personal trainer, copy editor, bespoke chocolate-maker, landscaper, dock-builder, Ikea furniture constructor, driveway installer, computer fixer, chauffeur, personal chef, party promoter.

Become an expert. Even if you have honed the skill already, become an expert (or at least a good BSer) so you can convince other people to pay you to either perform your skill or teach it to them. Troll the Web for articles; find out the best books on the subject and hit the library; take a class or online tutorial. In some cases, an investment in a workshop or certification will boost your credibility and allow you to gain clients much more quickly.

Examples: Taking a homeotherapy workshop; reading books on yoga practice; studying up on a store's merchandise to get a retail position.

Develop your pitch and sales materials. Aside from knowing your stuff, how are you going to convince real, sentient humans to knowingly part with their money? You need a pitch that establishes you as trustworthy, knowledgeable, and capable. You also need materials, such as handouts, business cards, flyers, a website, and a lesson plan. The point is, make it look like this is something you are passionate about and not just a way to make a quick buck.

Examples: Make a video showing you acing various yoga poses and upload it to YouTube; give out free samples of your mail-order sweets at a farmers market; create a flyer for your guitar lessons and bring it to a local college campus.

Find clients. Ah, the thorny issue of clientele. For gigs like waitressing and selling those weird Cutco knives door to door, this is not an issue. But for other endeavors, you'll probably have to put on your marketing cap and think to yourself, "Who is my potential client, where does my potential client go (online or off), and how can I attract his or her attention there?" If you're living at home, you can try mining your parent's network or your childhood network, especially if you're providing basic services like house painting, mowing lawns, or shoveling driveways (which can easily make you $10 to $18 an hour). For example, if you were a college-level basketball player and you think you can run a clinic or one-on-one lessons for middle school students, try going to your old school and networking with any faculty who remember you. Finally, once you snag your first client, the best way to get more is through your performance, because word-of-mouth referrals will speak louder than any marketing materials you create.

Examples: If you're selling something fitness-related, target the gym. Pet-related? The pet store and park. Sex-related? The darkest alley you can find.

Grow responsibly. Once you've got some clients, it's off to the races to see how big you can get. If you're really making money as opposed to just a little chump change for the bar tab, then you may consider (ahem) paying taxes on your business, as well as making it an official legal entity. These steps will be particularly important if you decide to hire anyone and don't want to be screwed if they get you sued somehow.

Examples: Establish a single proprietorship for your copy writing business by hiring a local attorney or using LegalZoom.com. Create an LLC for your tutoring outfit by using MyCorporation.com.

Holy $*%#, I Just Graduated!

How to Create Your Own Website in a Few Easy Steps

For any of the entrepreneurial pursuits described in this chapter, creating a website devoted to your business can significantly boost your chances of success. But what if you don't know anyone who makes websites? The good news is that even with no prior knowledge of website building or computer programming, you can have a simple site up and running in no time.

The first step is choosing a domain name (i.e., your web address). Examples of domain names include Gradspot.com, CNN.com, and Google.com. Lots of domains have already been registered, so don't be miffed if you have to register SamsTotalTutoring.com instead of TotalTutoring.com. Buying a domain is incredibly easy—you can either purchase it via a one-stop shop like VistaPrint.com (see below)

> **How to Create Your Own Website in a Few Easy Steps continued…**
>
> or a domain registrar such as GoDaddy.com. If you do take the registrar route, there are always 10–25% off coupons floating around the 'net, so be sure to Google the name of the registrar plus the word "coupon".
>
> For most people, we highly suggest taking the super simple approach to building a website. This is accomplished by using a company that will register a domain for you, provide you with a premade website, and host it (i.e., make it available on the Internet). Once you purchase a website package, all you really have to do is choose a template and fill in the blanks on the pages of your new site (i.e., title your webpages, upload photos, and write some copy about your business). Tons of companies offer this one-stop service, including VistaPrint.com, LunarPages.com, and GoDaddy.com. Prices typically range from between $4.95 and $9.95 per month, depending on how complex a website you need (or, more to the point, how many pages you need and whether you want a unique email address). The only downsides to this solution are that your site is only customizable to degree and it won't be unique…but does it really have to be for your local tutoring service?
>
> If you really want a more customized website and are willing to spend some time on it, you have two options. One is to build it yourself, which requires either learning computer programming (not an overnight project!) or installing a free content management system (CMS) such as WordPress. The other is to hire a professional to do it for you from a site such as Elance.com, RentACoder.com, or Guru.com—or better yet, get a recommendation from someone you trust. While the professional approach may be more appropriate for some businesses, it's out of the scope of this discussion. However, you can find countless walkthroughs on topics such as hiring freelance programmers and using WordPress with a simple Google search. Good luck! ■

Temp Work

Pop culture has painted temps as gum-smacking receptionists and no-hopers dressing up in giant burrito costumes. But pop culture has led us astray before (like when it told us to listen to Fergie). So let's take a wider view. Traditionally, temping simply refers to a job placement where you work for an employer over a short period of time—on the job continuum, think of it as somewhere between an internship (but you get paid better) and a full-time job.

The cons of temp work are pretty obvious: You have little to no job security, the tasks are not always the most exciting, and there's often more pressure to not completely screw everything up than to do something outstanding. Plus, temping probably isn't what you dreamed of the day you got your diploma. But for a recent grad, it can be a great stop-gap option, particularly if you're not sure where you want to settle or you're looking to make some extra money while working toward something else (i.e., grad school, the end of *War and Peace*, or a singing role on *Glee*). And especially if you are trying to get a full-time job, temp work could be your best in-road: 90% of companies use temps, and the staffing agency Manpower reports that 40% of its placements go on to get permanent positions (just look at Ryan from *The Office*).

At very least, temp work can help you add bullets to a blank resume and build a new skill set as you begin to create your job-hunting story (see Chapters 3 and 4). In fact, many employers say they view temping as a sign of a good attitude and a strong work ethic—two great aces up the sleeve in an age when everyone thinks of our generation as entitled and high-maintenance!

Types of Temp Work

There are a few main categories of temp work you'll encounter. The most common is "temporary help," where a staffing agency hires you and then deploys you for however long you're needed. "Temp to hire," on the other hand, is basically like a tryout for the job. A third type you might see is "long-term staffing"—in these cases, staffing agencies recruit, screen, and assign workers to specific positions.

Under these umbrella categories, the temp world is as varied as the industries that hire temps, but unless you have some specific credentials (e.g., technical IT knowledge, lab experience, research or health care experience), the most general opportunities are in professional occupations (i.e., office/clerical) and industrial labor (think assembly line workers, food handlers, cleaners, etc.). For quick money, there's nothing wrong with arranging traffic cones or watching over an endless river of M&Ms looking for the overly bulbous ones. But if you also want to use your temp experience to build skills and dip your feet into career-oriented industries, you might be better served seeking work of the office variety.

Many of the functional positions companies fill with temps are in billing, payroll, office support, and data entry/processing. When tax season comes around, accounting and bookkeeping gigs see a major spike. Customer support centers also use temps to provide phone or online support for their products—at least the ones that haven't been outsourced to Bangalore. The pay levels ($12 to $20+ per hour; see page 43 for more) depend on your experience, skill set, and position—you'll notice various levels for different roles, like "Admin I" (very basic reception work), "Admin 2" (involves multitasking and answering to between one and three managers), and "executive assistants" (these positions generally require experience—up to three to five years—assisting CEOs).

All of the above positions can be found via staffing agencies, which we'll get to in a second. Once you get placed, most assignments last anywhere from a few hours to three or four months, and then you can go back to your contact at the agency to find something else. On the plus side, you won't have too much time to get bored, and working in a bunch of different offices is like career speed-networking, only less superficial. By the time you're done temping, you could have potentially made friends and contacts at several good companies—in this world we call "the working world," that's nothing to scoff at! In some instances you may even stay with a single company, working on an as-needed basis, and be in a good position to get hired if a full-time position pops up.

To learn more about the range of occupations available through agencies, check out the American Staffing Association's (ASA) website, AmericanStaffing.net.

The 411 on Staffing Agencies

It should be clear by now that the first port of call for any temp candidate is a staffing agency. These go by many other names—temp agencies, employment agencies, and so on—but the general idea is simple: Companies use agencies to find candidates for temporary roles, and agency recruiters work with you to match your skills with the right gig. In addition to providing access to employers, most staffing agencies also provide training to help you get work—the ASA recently reported that 90% of agencies offer some kind of free training, ranging from free tutorials on the latest versions of software applications to interview workshops.

A good place to start your search is with the big national agencies like Manpower (surprisingly not a porn site) and OfficeTeam (surprisingly not an office supplies site), which likely have offices in your area. Net-Temps.com also posts nationwide positions. However, you should also narrow your focus. Many staffing agencies specialize in a particular profession or field of business, such as general industrial labor, accounting, or secretarial work. Also, local agencies may be better suited for opportunities in your particular town or city. To find these more specialized shops, Terri Abbe, Director of Service Quality with Pace Staffing Network in the Pacific Northwest, suggests hitting up Google and the Yellow Pages (remember to try not only "staffing agencies" in your search but also "temp agencies," "recruiting," "employment agency," etc.). When you find some places, she recommends checking out their websites or calling them up to answer the following questions:

- Are there any testimonials from clients and employees? Are they reviewed on Yelp.com?

- Do they work with reputable employers, or places that seem sketchy?

- How long have they been working in the area? (Longevity usually means good connections to local employers.)

- Do they appear to have relevant jobs listed?

In a booming economy, signing up with one firm would be totally fine. But in darker days, Abbe recommends signing up with around three firms. You could go to even more, but play it cool—agencies may ask you who else you're working with, and if you list ten places it won't make them feel that you'll be worth their time.

How to Maximize Your Prospects

On the surface, the staffing biz sounds like the most efficient and awesome system ever. You show up, tell a recruiter what you want to do, then he or she tells you where and when to show up for work. If only life were really that easy! In reality, all the things that matter for a full-time job hunt—resumes, cover letters, interview skills, proper attire—are just as important when you're fishing for temp work, so you should refer to Chapter 4 to make sure you know the score on that front. However, you can also take some specific steps to get the most out of a staffing agency.

Brush up on your skills. Most of the jobs staffed by agencies are very functional, so assuming you pass muster as a normal and professional human being, getting placed is all about the right skills. And no, you can't just say you're a "computer wunderkind" and then figure it out later—you'll actually be quizzed on this stuff. Different specialties will require different skills, but for administrative work, for example, they'll check your proficiency with basic office tools like PowerPoint, Word, and Excel. Brush up before going in, or if it's a take-home/online test, find a friend who's a whiz to give you pointers (just don't tell the agency we told you to do that).

Be specific about what you want. Yes, you can be "down for whatever," and maybe you'll get placed in a range of jobs so hilarious that you can write your first novel about it. But for most people it pays to choose those agencies that can place you in fields that interest you. That way you can rack up relevant experience and maybe even launch yourself into a full-time position.

Always be on the ball. When you call an agency to ask about opportunities, never assume it will be a casual inquiry—be prepared to interview on the spot. This can be the difference between getting a job and getting blanked, because timing is crucial in the staffing world. When you go in to the agency, you should dress professionally (p. 254), bring references that you've told to expect a call (p. 197), and be open to jobs that might be under your ideal pay rate. Any placement is an opportunity to network and gain professional experience, and you really ingratiate yourself to the agency if you show you are flexible.

Cultivate your recruiter relationship. The fact is, recruiters deal with hundreds of candidates a week, so you want to stand out as a favorite. Send your recruiter a hand-written thank you note. Ask proactive questions about how to make yourself more marketable for the staffing firm, which may open up a helpful conversation about where you can improve. And again, present yourself as an open, flexible candidate to make the recruiter feel comfortable about putting you into employment situations. Finally, ask your recruiter for the best way to stay in contact with him or her. Should you call or wait for a call? Email? How often? Being considerate goes a long way.

The D.I.Y. Route

While staffing agencies are undoubtedly the easiest place to start out as a temp, you shouldn't feel beholden to them. You can also approach a company directly and offer your services in a temporary capacity, just as you might reach out to an employer and ask for an internship. Think about it this way: A lot of smaller companies might not work with temping agencies, but that doesn't mean they couldn't use extra help at busy times of the year. If you can propose a specific project or useful function, you might just get lucky. Once you're in the door, just prove you're indispensable and bada bing bada boom, they might want to keep you around.

Another potential move is to help out administratively at your parents' office for a while in return for a little off-the-top moola. If your parents don't have offices that fit the bill, maybe their friends do. It's likely that your folks wouldn't mind calling in a favor or two to get you out of the house!

The Payoff

So how much can you make? Typical hourly rates in most locations start at $12 to $15 an hour, but higher-level positions (like executive assistant or clinical trial administrator) might pay $20 an hour or more. Check out suggested hourly rates on your state's Department of Labor website and at Payscale.com. You can also check Craigslist for temp listings to get a sense of what people are paying in your area. If you're working with a staffing agency, they'll often provide basic health benefits, as well as vacation/holiday pay and even retirement plans. Assuming you're using temping as a short-term solution, the biggie here is the health insurance, which could be a lifesaver if you need to find coverage before you have a full-time job (see Chapter 7 for more on health care).

For the Lazy and Crazy

If all this talk of "pitching yourself," "starting your own biz," and "going to a temping agency" sounds exhausting, there are other, less active ways of keeping yourself afloat in those lazy months after graduation. This is the realm of making a fast buck and then never talking about it again! When going this route, the best advice we can give is to swallow your pride (you're going to need a few punch-lines for your memoir, right?), but also to **be careful and don't take unnecessary risks.** Just because your photo once appeared in your university's admissions brochure doesn't mean you should answer that Craigslist ad for "open-minded models." It's advisable to pack an industrial-sized can of common sense before venturing out into the world of random employment and money-making schemes.

Sell Your Stuff. Between the remnants of your college dorm and that box full of old slap bracelets taking up closet space, you are sitting on a cash cow of used stuff. In the age of eBay and Craigslist, unloading it is as easy as ever—you don't even need a garage. Ask the rest of your family if they want to get rid of anything as well, because they'll probably be happy just to get it out of the way. If you've got a lot of clothing in decent condition, Buffalo Exchange has

Holy $%#, I Just Graduated!*

locations across the country and will pay cash for your garments. Second-hand CD stores will take all your Nickelback albums (after you've uploaded them onto your laptop!), as will SecondSpin.com and CashforCDs.com. Try Half. com or the Facebook Marketplace in your school's network for textbooks, or head to Amazon to sell niche titles. And you can even sell your digital photographs for royalties on stock photography websites like iStockPhoto.com and Fotolia.com.

Holy S*%#, I Just Graduated!

Anyway, you get the point. Whatever you've got, someone somewhere probably wants it. You just have to be willing to put in some effort to connect with whomever that weirdo is. For example, when selling, it's been proven that sharing at least one picture makes a huge difference—take the time to take quality photos to make your stuff look credible and worth buying. In addition, when taking pictures, you should also put the object in context if possible (i.e., a plate shouldn't just be against a white wall, but on a table with a placemat and silverware). There are tons of other tricks for getting the most out of your online auctions; if you have stuff you actually think has some value, it's worth taking the time to search for online selling guides so you know how to maximize your profits.

Whore Yourself Out (Not Literally). We don't encourage prostitution, but now we're getting into the realm of all-out, no-holds-barred, Matthew-Lesko-in-a-question-mark-suit insanity. You can become an extra in a movie that doesn't involve showing off your "best bits" by checking the local paper or visiting Mandy.com, Backstage.com, and EntertainmentCareers.net. Most large movie studios pay the SAG union rate of $115/day plus snacks and a meal every six hours. If "acting" is not your style, scan Craigslist for other wacky jobs, like foot modeling, flyering, or writing a 14-year-old's history paper on Rosa Parks. Got a car? Check out FreeCarMedia.com to see how you can give your whip the NASCAR treatment and make anywhere from $50 to $500 a month "renting out" space on your vehicle.

Get Paid to Shop. If that sounds like a dream come true, you might want to look into a job as a "mystery shopper" (a.k.a. spotters, secret shoppers, anonymous audits, experience evaluators, virtual customers, etc.). Companies pay mystery shoppers to go to stores and provide feedback on the service that they receive—sometimes they even provide a script to follow. Pretend you are dehydrated and faint next to the board shorts. Inquire about gift-wrapping a 60-inch flat-screen TV. Who needs drama school? Generally, shoppers are rewarded with some combination of money, store credit, or merchandise—being Big Brother's little helper has perks. However, beware of online scams (i.e., you should never pay to become a mystery shopper; they pay you). If it seems shady, check in with the Better Business Bureau before proceeding. A good starting place is the Mystery Shopping Providers Association at MysteryShop. org. There, you can sign up with 100+ agencies to become eligible.

From Grad to Guinea Pig. Usually you have to pay exorbitant fees to get medication. So why would anyone pay you to take it? Well, they can't sell it until they figure out if it really screws people up—that's where you come into play! Be careful and don't jeopardize your health or sanity for a few hundred bucks. However, if you feel comfortable with the risks, there are many ways to pawn your body for financial reward within the medical world. Labs, universities, and hospitals nationwide are always looking for volunteers for scientific studies. Try a new flu vaccine, get a psychiatric evaluation, or get paid to sleep (though beware that sleep studies can be insane). The best approach is to contact a college or university in the area to inquire about research and testing volunteers—psych departments and med schools are good places to start. Also, scan the local newspaper and check the volunteer and "ETC" sections on Craigslist.

Medical "Donations." Who would have thought you could get paid to simulate reproduction? For guys, a vial of semen (about .7 ml) in the U.S. ranges between $200 and $3,000, but be prepared to feel emasculated if your seed doesn't make the cut. For ladies, the payoff is even higher, with eggs bringing in anything from a few hundred to thousands of dollars. However, depositing the ovum isn't as simple as knocking one off the wrist into a plastic cup—no surprise that men have it easier again! The whole process involves extensive medical testing, injections of fertility drugs, and a surgical procedure. For those who are a bit squeamish about "sex things," there's a more standard approach—the Red Cross no longer pays for blood donations, but plasma still earns a pretty penny. If you meet the donor criteria (healthy, 17+, over 110 pounds—what are we talking about again?) then you can get $20–30 per visit. Visits are limited to two a week with at least 48 hours between each one; check online for donation centers or call 1-800-GIVE-LIFE.

Answer Some Questions. You're a young, college-educated twentysomething who's just starting out life as an independent, self-financing consumer. So why not cash in on the fact that most companies in the country would love to know what you're thinking by taking part in focus groups and online surveys? Check out FindFocusGroups.com for paid listings—when deciding what's legit and what's bogus, look for companies you've heard of (or at least ones that list practical info like name, contact details, and the date and time of the focus group);

Holy $*%#, I Just Graduated!

avoid companies that promise outlandish money (if it looks too good to be true, it probably is); and remember to never give out your social security number. Another place to hunt for a focus group payday is Greenbooks.org. It's a site where companies can find facilities to do market research, but if you're sneaky, you can punch in your city, find places nearby that host focus groups, then go directly to their websites to sign up as a research participant. Jackpot! For lazier folks who don't want to leave the house, your best bet is online surveys. Start by going to EarnOnTheSide.com, a helpful resource that ranks paid online survey sites (and lets you know whether they're worth the trouble).

The Traveling Grad

Traveling after graduation is a time-honored tradition for many reasons, the most prominent of which is the fact that it's literally the perfect time to travel. You've been married to the books (or the booze) for four years now, so it's time for a belated honeymoon. And practically speaking, the chances of taking a two-month backpacking trip grow slimmer by the day once you're a working cog. We don't want to suggest that the clock is ticking on fun and exploration, but if you can pull it off, all of the pieces are in place for a great trip—youth, health, and a celebratory subtext. So why not get cracking on that "places to visit before I die" list? Remember: If a jaunt around Europe doesn't quite satisfy your needs, you can always go whole hog and consider a gap year (p. 56). And even if you're near-broke, there are still plenty of ways to subsidize your travels through international jobs and volunteer opportunities (p. 59).

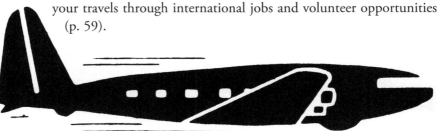

Choosing Your Travel Buddies

One common approach to post-college travels is to roll with friends with the intention of having "one last hurrah." As long as everyone's expectations are in sync, taking a graduation trip with your university cronies is an almost unconditionally good idea. But it's not always as smooth as expected. At the risk of sounding like curmudgeons, let us fly a quick cautionary flag.

Traveling is a lot different from casually hanging out, and even lovers can make bad travel buddies. Haggling over euros, getting jacked by Grecian purse-snatchers, and arguing about train schedules can drive a stake between you and your friend that could take months or years to decompose. So before you book a hostel, take a few moments to decide whether you and your "BFF" are travel-compatible. Here are a few red flags that could turn the post-grad honeymoon into *Turistas 2*:

- One of you is on a travel grant budget, and the other is on a trust fund budget.

- One of you likes foreign men, and the other thinks they are criminals.

- One of you is an adventurous eater, and the other is a McDonald's junkie.

- One of you likes to sight-see, and the other likes to beach-bum and party.

- Neither of you enjoys handling "logistics."

- Traveler's diarrhea...

If one or more of these situations gave you pause, it doesn't mean you have to throw the whole idea out the window. However, thinking about these issues before setting sail can help defuse some potentially frustrating arguments down the line. Ask your rich friend if he's willing to steer clear of the Four Seasons and see how the other half lives (or travels, as the case may be). Plan an itinerary that balances culture and clubbing if that will make all parties happy. A stitch in time will invariably save nine (of what we're not sure).

Brainstorming Trips

The main factors that go into planning the perfect summer trip are budget, duration, and companionship. But once those are settled, the fun part can begin—what do you really want to do? There are countless places to get your post-college groove on. Here are just a few ideas to get you started. Needless to say, you're going to have to do some further research to figure out the ins-and-outs of traveling to these places, but we hope this section will help spark a wanderlust. **Note: Before you set out for a foreign country, get your passport straight (see next page), and be sure to check if you need a visa or any vaccinations (p. 52).**

Holy $%#, I Just Graduated!*

The **"Generic European Backpackers" Trip.** Culture by day, booze by night, and an endless string of hostels packed with German ravers and cool but slightly arrogant Aussies. Yes, since back in the days of Peter the Great, there have been few travel routes more coveted than a jaunt around Europe. But who has the money? All those pints of lager, baguettes, and barrels of olive oil really add up. The good news is that while places like London, Paris, and Vienna aren't cheap, the summer is rife with cheap (or free) music and art festivals, and you can save money by purchasing food and drinks at grocery stores and traveling by train with a Eurail pass. For some fun in the sun, hit up Croatia's Dalmatian Coast or don some capri pants for a jaunt through southern Italy. If you're a smooth operator, you might be able to locate a nude beach or two. Who packed the binoculars!? **Book to Bring:** *Neither Here Nor There: Travels in Europe,* by Bill Bryson (and watch *Eurotrip,* one of the most underrated films of the past decade).

The **"Getting Plastered like an Irishman" Trip.** Ireland ain't cheap, but for rugged terrain, intriguing history, and unbeatable *craic*, a trip to the Emerald Isle delivers almost anything you could ask for (except good weather). Try to get beyond Dublin, which has plenty to see but may feel generically cosmopolitan to more seasoned travelers. (Go to a pub in the famous Temple Bar district and you're more likely to be served your Guinness by an Eastern European student than a true Irishman.) For the authentic experience, rent a car or hop on a bike and make your way from town to town. While the southern tourist trail is most popular, Northern Ireland mixes the fascinating political history of Belfast and Derry

Tips & Tricks: Passports

Before you can get enough stamps in your passport to compete with Bono, you need to actually have a passport. Be warned: Nothing sets a worse tone for a trip than arriving at check-in without the necessary identification documents. If your passport has expired, check the State Department website to find out where you need to send it for renewal. If you don't have your old passport, have never had a passport, or were under 16 when you received your most recent passport, you've got to trek down to the Post Office or your local City Hall and apply in person. You'll need a valid ID, two passport-sized photos, and proof of U.S. citizenship (e.g., a birth certificate). Generally, passports take about 4–6 weeks to arrive, but you can pay an extra $60 to get the expedited service (three weeks). If you're really in a bind (way to plan ahead!), nongovernmental agencies like PassportsAndVisas.com can handle business Mafia-style—it's around $59 for 8–20 business days and $169 for the 24-hour service.

with beautiful scenery along the Causeway Coast. And, believe it or not, some of the best surfing in Europe can be found on the west coast of Ireland around towns like Bundoran and Sligo. **Book to Bring:** *Round Ireland with a Fridge*, by Tony Hawks (not to be confused with Tony Hawk).

The "From Russia with Love" Trip. While visiting Russia in winter may lead you to drink vodka mixed with airplane fluid just to stay warm, the summer will allow you to see the sights in comfort and imbibe spirits for pleasure rather than survival. Moscow is architecturally stunning, combining the antique stylings of the Kremlin with the surreal domes of Saint Basil's Cathedral and the many imposing Stalin-era constructions. (When you visit Lenin's tomb, start singing "Imagine" and you'll surely win over a few tour groups in the process.) History buffs should also make a point of visiting Saint Petersburg, which has palaces galore and the majestic feel of an old European capital. Beyond the major cities, Siberia is apparently a pretty big place—grab your rucksack and start exploring. **Book to Bring:** *Notes from the Underground*, by Fyodor Dostoevsky.

The "Beach Rental with Friends" Trip. If you live on the coasts, you don't have to travel halfway around the world for a beach-bumming bender. Nantucket and Martha's Vineyard are popular destinations for East Coast grads, particularly those who favor ribbon belts and pants embroidered with pheasants. Out in Cali, those who can't afford Malibu still have hundreds of miles of beaches to explore. The key to making a beach week affordable is to share the rental with as many people as possible, cook your own food, and exclusively drink MGD (aka Mad Gangster Dancing). **Book to Bring:** Just wait until the end of the day and the beach will be littered with discarded bestsellers.

Holy $*%#, I Just Graduated!

Tips & Tricks: Hostelling

Let's call a spade a spade. When it comes to post-grad travel, you're not going to be staying in five-star resorts. You're more likely going to find the cheapest hostel around and shack up for the night. But hey, that's great. They're twenty-something meccas and can cost as little as $2 per night…including breakfast and dinner! Hostelling International is known for some of the best hostels around, and you can also search for traveler-friendly accommodations on Hostels.com and HostelWorld.com. In certain countries, hostels are referred to as dormitories and guest houses, so don't rule those out either. Since safety is always a concern when it comes to hostels (you shouldn't be concerned but just aware), referrals are always best. Recommendations from trusted guides like *Lonely Planet* and *Let's Go* are also useful.

Tips & Tricks: Cheap places, expensive flights

The one "gotcha" with super-cheap travel destinations like Southeast Asia and parts of Eastern Europe is they can cost an arm and a leg to get to in the first place. When planning your itinerary, remember to factor transportation into the budget rather than clinging to the fact that beers will cost five cents. Look into cheap connecting flights or around-the-world tickets (p. 53) to make the airfare affordable. Also look for deals on Kayak.com, Airfare Watchdog, Travel Zoo, and national carriers.

The "Superpowers of Tomorrow" Trip. Touted as rising superpowers (mostly by other, slightly condescending superpowers), China and India have dominated the press over the past few years. Pundits cast the growth of the two "Asian giants" as the ultimate articulation of globalization, spawning constant debate about which country will outpace the other as the next great industrial force. That means one thing for you: get there before they both look exactly like America! We're joking (sort of), but now is certainly a good time to explore these enormous, culturally diverse countries. From major cities like Beijing and Delhi to tourist destinations like the Great Wall and the Taj Mahal, the options are pretty much unlimited, and you can do it 5-star all the way or dirt cheap depending on your preferences. However, it's important to do some research beforehand, because both of these countries can be overwhelming without at least a vague plan of action. **Book to Bring:** *Siddhartha*, by Hermann Hesse; *River Town: Two Years on the Yangtze*, by Peter Hessler.

The "Soul-Searching in Southeast Asia" Trip. Have you seen *The Beach*? Dude, it's gonna be exactly like that! Let your inhibitions slip away as you eat a still-beating snake heart and feel its warm blood coat your esophagus. Live on a beach for a dollar a day and grow disgusting dreads. Shack up with a "ladyboy" and realize gender is just a state of mind. All jokes aside, Southeast Asia is a wonderful and extremely cheap place to visit, but from the food to the accommodations, its pleasures are not always ideal for the unadventurous. Thailand and Vietnam are the most popular destinations for backpackers, but the temples of Angkor Wat, located near the city of Siem Reap in Cambodia, are consistently touted as one of the alternative wonders of the world. **Book to Bring:** *The Beach*, by Alex Garland—obvi!

The "Ancient Wonders of the Middle East" Trip. Sure, some areas in the Middle East are not advisable travel destinations (e.g., Baghdad, Kabul, the Gaza Strip), but don't let that deter you from all the great places to visit there.

For those interested in ancient history, Jordan is steeped in Biblical lore, and Syria boasts the world's oldest continuously occupied city: Damascus. Israel, Lebanon, and Turkey offer rich culture and staggering landscapes—float in the Dead Sea, visit Bethlehem, and explore Istanbul's East-meets-West influences. Many travelers combine a trip to the Middle East with a stopover in Egypt; Cairo and the Great Pyramids of Giza are easily accessible from the Mediterranean and can serve as a launching point for a riverboat up the Nile. When heading to the Middle East, be aware that visiting heavily Muslim regions during major holidays like Ramadan can pose some logistical problems. Ladies, be sure to read up on appropriate clothing for visiting various locales and religious sites. You'll likely need a long skirt or pants, a long-sleeved shirt, and a scarf to cover your head (especially for visits to mosques). **Book to Bring:** *Exile*, by Richard North Patterson.

> ### Tips & Tricks: Understand seasonality
>
> You know what sucks? Spending three months planning your summer trip to Southern India only to find out after arriving that it's monsoon season and you can't leave the airport for the next five days. Always be aware of what season you're traveling in at your destination and how that will affect your travel plans.

Holy $*%#, I Just Graduated!

The "All-American Road Trip." Nothing says "I just graduated" like five dudes in a Jeep with the system blasting and the smell of B.O. wafting into the muggy summer air. Adventurous girls are known to take this journey as well, albeit in a slightly less pungent manner. The cross-country trip is a classic option—hit Vegas, Austin, and New Orleans, or take the high road through Chi-Town, Ann Arbor, and Yellowstone National Park. Cruising up and down the coasts is also an option, but whatever you do don't forget the golden rule of road trips: Whoever smelt it dealt it. If you have an early commencement, try to plan a route that allows you to crash all of your other friends' graduation parties. **Book to Bring:** *Fear and Loathing in Las Vegas,* by Hunter S. Thompson (the audio book).

The "Party 'Til You Die" Trip. It seems counter-intuitive to travel somewhere for the purpose of getting so lit up that you forget where you are, but it takes all sorts to make the world go around. If Mediterranean waters and all-night raves appeal to your animal instincts, the Balearic Islands are home to Ibiza, where mega-clubs like Space, Eden, and Amnesia (sounds like a science fair) have broken the backs of the world's hardiest party-goers. For a similar scene

Tips & Tricks: Vaccinations

We're guessing that you hope to come home from your post-grad trip with a memory card full of photographs and some cool souvenirs of your trip, not a case of Dengue Fever (we hear it feels like you have splinters in your bones). Prior to travel always be sure to check the Center for Disease Control for a list of suggested vaccinations. This way you can determine whether you want to spring for the vaccinations (they can be costly) or avoid the trip altogether. If you do decide to press forward, keep in mind that you'll need to get your vaccinations four to six months ahead of time. Speak with your doctor or check in with the American Society of Tropical Medicine and Hygiene or the International Society of Travel Medicine to locate travel vaccination clinics.

a bit closer to home, Mexico furnishes *muchas* tequila slammers in Cancun, Acapulco, and Tijuana. **Book to Bring:** Reading will make your head spin—bring a copy of *Pure Drum & Bass* and brace yourself.

The "Shredding in the Summer" Trip. Skiing during the summer is one of those mind-blowing experiences that will make you question everything you thought you knew about the world. Argentina and Chile are renowned for their great snow and beautiful scenery, and since it's winter there during our summer, the slopes are open for a post-commencement shredding session. (In Argentina, Cerro Catedral, located outside the city of Bariloche, is a popular destination for skiers, trekkers, and rock climbers.) If you want to stick to the Northern Hemisphere, Whistler in British Columbia is the capital of shorts-and-T-shirt skiing and snowboarding. **Book to Bring:** Just rent as many Warren Miller films as possible.

The "Camping with High School Friends" Trip. Cheap, cheerful, and potentially hilarious, this trip is a spiritual twofer, allowing you to reconnect with nature and the past at the same time. Pitching your tents within walking distance of a water park or mini-golf course is always a power move, but if you have the opportunity to go to a great national park like Acadia or Yosemite, you should definitely leap on it. **Book to Bring:** *SAS Survival Handbook: How to Survive in the Wild, in Any Climate, on Land or at Sea*, by John "Lofty" Wiseman.

The "Brazilian Hedonism" Tour. Few places on the planet get it cracking quite like Brazil (you know a place is crazy when the boys are born with mustaches). Ipanema Beach in Rio has great surfing, beautiful bodies, and amazing *caipirinhas*. Plus, you always have an enormous statue of Jesus looking over you—

a comforting thought, I'm sure. While chichi Buzios has been dubbed "the St. Tropez of Brazil," Salvador is one of the most laid-back party towns you're likely to find anywhere—the heavy Afro-Caribbean influence in the Bahia region finds its articulation in the nonstop smorgasbord of food and music. When you're all partied out, venture into the Amazon for some hardy trekking and wildlife-watching. The rapidly growing city of Manaus is the port of entry into the rainforest, and from there you can take guided camping excursions or make daytrips from the comforts of a jungle lodge. **Book to Bring:** *Brazil*, by John Updike.

The "Ché Guevara Wannabe" Trip. From the steakhouses of Buenos Aires all the way to the cigar shops in Havana's Old Town (note: Americans need a visa to get into Cuba—but maybe not for long), there's plenty of territory to cover in a trip based loosely on a dude whose face you saw in someone's dorm room. Grab a motorcycle and a diary, and don't forget to bring an Epi-Pen in case you go into anaphylactic shock. (If you don't know what that means, don't worry about it.) **Book to Bring:** *The Motorcycle Diaries*, by Ché Guevara.

The African Vacation. There are all sorts of reasons why people overlook Africa when planning trips. "It's too dangerous." "It costs too much to get

---

Tips & Tricks: Around the World ticket

The "Around the World" ticket is the stuff of legend amongst travelers. For better or for worse, there are a lot of myths circulated about ATW fares, but don't worry—you don't have to make it around in 80 days, and you don't have to sit in the cargo compartment. Let's nip those rumors right in the bud. The good news is they do exist, and for about $2,000 you can wend your way around the globe and see some truly amazing places. The bad news is that they come with restrictions galore, so you have to be flexible and red-eye ready. Check out world fares from airline alliances like Star Alliance, OneWorld Explorer, and SkyTeam, but make sure to pay close attention to the conditions, which usually include a mileage limit, a 12-month time limit, a minimum (generally 3) and maximum (5–10) number of stops, and an eventual return to the starting point (so if you end up trying to reenact *Seven Years in Tibet*, you can kiss your return fare goodbye). Most tickets also stipulate that you must travel in one direction, so you can't just get one to visit your lady friend in Paris for a year. All that said, the net result is monumentally more budget-friendly than buying a gang of one-way tickets, and you can pimp the system to get your penny-pinching self to some traditionally expensive locales. It pays to be flexible.

Holy $*%#, I Just Graduated!

there." "Hippos have killed more humans than any other semiaquatic animal." Though hippos are undoubtedly dangerous beasts, all of these excuses hold about as much water as the Sahara Desert. From the amazing markets of Marrakech to the world-class surf of Cape Town, there's literally an entire continent of amazing places to visit. Many companies offer safaris specially designed for the budget-conscious, and camping in the desert will always be free (if slightly unsafe). Explore the forests of Madagascar or track down lions in Tanzania. Just steer clear of current war zones (check the State Department website) and you're good to go. **Book to Bring:** *Things Fall Apart*, by Chinua Achebe.

The "Lord of the Rings" Trip. Peter Jackson's adaptation of the Tolkien trilogy didn't just teach us that the guy from *Rudy* has range—it also highlighted the stunning beauty of New Zealand. You can buy some novelty hobbit feet and recreate Frodo's journey, but that's just the tip of the iceberg. The famous Ninety Mile Beach may actually be only 55 miles long, but its dunes are still an incredible spot for some sand-sledding and ATV-riding. The secluded beaches around the Bay of Islands are not to be missed, and for eco-tourists/outdoorsy folks, there are more amazing national parks in New Zealand than you can shake a wizard's staff at. Best of all, the people are hella chilled out and friendly. **Book to Bring:** Start with *The Hobbit*, then see what else you can fit in your bag.

The "Trail of Chinggis Khan" Trip. For some, being in the middle of nowhere means that you made a wrong turn about 50 miles back and now your dad is yelling at you for breaking the GPS. But for others, the middle of nowhere is a place you go on purpose. Those who fall into the latter category of committed escapists need look no further than Mongolia, a country that ticks off all the requisite criteria for *remote*: 30% of the country is covered in dry steppe-land, about 30% of the population is nomadic, and the country is landlocked by two of the world's most intimidating neighbors, China and Russia. You'll almost certainly fly into the capital city of Ulaanbaatar, which combines Russian influences from its occupation (Cyrillic signs and distinctly Soviet architecture) with the energy of a changing nation—Mongolia became a democracy in 1990, and 60% of the population is under 30 years old. The city is a launching point for a range of outdoorsy trips, such as a trek to the Gobi desert or a trip to the über-remote Amarbayasgalant Monastery in far northern Mongolia, near the Russian border. If you're into horses, you can grab one for next to nothing and head out into the wild. You haven't lived until you've slept under the stars in a felt *ger* (the Mongolian word for yurt). **Book to Bring:** *Ghengis Khan and the Making of the Modern World*, by Jack Weatherford.

The "Temples and Tokyo Pop" Trip. When it comes to combining intriguing history with mind-blowing futurism, no destination can match the wonders of Japan. People-watching can keep you entertained for days in Tokyo's Harajuku neighborhood, the street fashion capital of the world, and the rest of the massive city offers constant stimulation—not to mention the best vending machines ever. To get to the heart of Japanese culture, though, you'll want to catch a lightning fast and immaculately clean train to Kyoto, where many of the awe-inspiring temples and shogun palaces are UNESCO World Heritage Sites. You can head to the stunning national parks on the northern island of Hokkaidō, or visit Hiroshima in the south to reflect on the devastation of WWII. Wherever you go, the fish on the sushi menu will be a whole lot better than you get back at home (though it should be noted that sushi is a delicacy in Japan, and they certainly don't throw back Philadelphia rolls like we do in the U.S.). **Book to Bring:** *Memoirs of a Geisha*, by Arthur Golden.

The "Sports Lovers" Trip. From major events like the World Cup and the Olympics to more offbeat affairs like the Highland Games and the Ashes cricket test, the summers are always chock full of international sporting extravaganzas. Depending on the profile of the event, you may need to get tickets well in advance, but sometimes just being around all the madness can be half the fun. Just don't become a sports hooligan—it's not a real job! **Book to Bring:** *Being Gazza: My Journey to Hell and Back*, by Paul Gasgoine.

Tips & Tricks: Getting around

Regardless of where you plan your post-graduation trip, once you've arrived at your destination, you'll most likely have four options for getting around: cars, buses, trains, and planes. While cars are straightforward (you rent one), the other three aren't always so obvious. Is a 24-hour bus ride for $15 worth losing a day of traveling when you can get a plane ticket for $50? While busses, trains, and planes are different across each destination, it's certainly worth doing some research prior to your trip. Can you book each at a travel agent, or will they rip you off? Are there local websites that provide bus and train routes? Can you show up at a train station or airport for a last minute deal, or will no one speak English? Even if you don't know where you'll be traveling once you get "there," knowing how to get around can be the difference between hitting an extra destination or not.

Holy $*%#, I Just Graduated!

The Post-College Gap Year

Maybe three months of traveling feels way too short. Maybe living at home doesn't appeal to you, but you also aren't too fired up about jumping straight into the rat race. Have you considered taking a year off?

We could devote a whole book to the subject of gap years—who knows, maybe we will! But let's not get ahead of ourselves. The point we want to make is there is a wide range of viable alternatives to finding a traditional job as soon as you leave school (for ideas, see the many volunteer and work opportunities starting on page 59).

After graduation, pressure to find employment and earn your keep doesn't just come from parents. Even if they are not particularly boastful, listening to your friends talk about their jobs and watching them charge extravagant dinners to their corporate cards can make you feel like you're stuck at the kids' table. But the thing about the kids' table is that it's mad fun (We still try to snag a spot there every Thanksgiving), and the thing about your friends' work stories is that they are full of smoke and mirrors. You have the rest of your life to work the proverbial 9-to-5, and a year delay is not going to sentence you to a permanent spot at the back of the pack. Doing what your friends are doing is not a good reason to discount a post-college gap year.

So what are good reasons to take a year off? Obviously, it's not the right choice for everyone. But if you decide to do it, make sure you have a goal and some semblance of a plan. Bumming around European cities to attend all-night raves on daddy's dime (if that's even possible) is not a great

> **Tips & Tricks: How to play time off on your resume**
>
> Unless you spent the year trying to beat *Mario Bros.* without getting small, time off is not something you need to hide from employers. The key is to not look like a directionless wanderer who will pick up at the drop of a hat and move onto something new. Employers like loyalty, but they also value a range of experience and a proven ability to be independent. Moreover, many companies report that employees who have taken gap years demonstrate greater maturity and stay on longer than their peers. So, in many ways, time off can make you an even more attractive candidate (especially if you went to Australia and got a nice tan). The important thing is to present your time off in a way that shows it had a purpose and wasn't just a ploy to put off the inevitable.

opportunity for growth and enrichment. Better reasons to take time off include learning a language, living abroad (in a more immersive way than a two-week villa rental in Cancun can provide), or volunteering, especially if you are burnt out from college or unsure of what you want to do. The point is that rushing into an unfulfilling job will only fuel the fires of a midlife crisis later in life, so at least give the possibility of a gap year some thought.

Confessions of an Undercover Adventurer: A Year "*Dans le Noir*"
by TORY HOEN

Working hard to achieve the American Dream is all well and good, but sometimes you need to say, "F you, American Dream," and get the heck out of Dodge. Sure, there are a lot of official and respectable ways to do this: Join the Peace Corps, get a Fulbright, or volunteer for any number of international NGOs. But all of those options require planning and foresight (neither of which is my strong suit), and sometimes you just need to hit the road…*now*.

After graduating and toiling for a year and a half in New York, I was starting to feel a bit conflicted. The combination of life in a matchbox-sized studio, 12-hour workdays, and a boss who regularly told me, "You can be replaced," was starting to get me down. I often found myself staring into a spreadsheet wondering, "This is my youth?"

Before long, visions of croissants began to cloud my thoughts, and the promise of pensive strolls along the Seine and cozy afternoons spent writing in cafes lured me to Kayak.com. A voice told me, "If you book it, they will come." *It* turned out to be a one-way ticket to Paris on Air India…and *they* turned out to be a year's worth of crazy French-flavored adventures.

As I researched my move to France, it became increasingly clear that French bureaucracy would become the bane of my existence if I allowed it to, so I came up with a simple solution: avoid it at all costs. Would Vasco da Gama have waited around for a visa? I think not. Bank accounts, cell phones, housing, jobs, professional and social contacts—these were all things that I hoped would naturally fall into place once I arrived (and unleashed my irresistible charm and rapier wit).

Holy $*%#, I Just Graduated!

Confessions of an Undercover Adventurer continued...

For the time being, I had a plane ticket, a short-term sublet, and enough savings to get me through the first few months. Beyond that, I would either A) Find a job that would sustain me, B) Find an aristocratic suitor who would sustain me, or C) Return home none the worse for having attempted an international escapade.

Feedback from others ranged from "You're so brave" to "You're such an idiot," but I took it all in stride. And once I got to Paris, things did fall into place. Of course, I had moments where I wondered what I was doing there as I committed one faux pas after another. But little by little, the faux pas grew less frequent, my French improved, my wardrobe became blacker, and I developed a culturally acceptable scowl.

I ended up finding a job that was a bit—how shall I say?—*dans le noir* (i.e., "in the dark," also known as "under the table" or, if you insist, totally sketchy). No, I was not a prostitute, but I worked in real estate, which might be worse. Regardless, it was enough to sustain me while I pursued my *real* dream of writing the next great American ex-pat novel (or something like that). I found a longer-term furnished sublet, bought a pre-paid cell phone, and managed to attract some pretty cool friends. Bank account? Who needs it when you've got a perfectly good underwear drawer? *Et voilà!* I was off and running.

A few months into my tenure in France, I was invited to a new friend's chateau, and as I sat in the *grand salon* sipping '83 Château Margaux with a giant taxidermy lion's head looming above me, I thought, "Paris was a good idea."

Yes, it was a gamble, and my existence was not really sustainable in the long-run. But I love France and I wanted to live there...is that so wrong? If the French can forgive Roman Polanski his crimes, I think they can forgive me mine.

I'm not advocating that you all run out and become illegal immigrants; this would not fly in many countries and could lead to some *Brokedown Palace*-style disasters. But a little fly-by-the-seat-of-your pants globetrotting never hurt anyone. You'll be surprised how rewarding it can be to throw all caution to the wind and become an international fugitive.

If you have a dream (or even a momentary impulse masquerading as a dream), I say: go with it. If you're wrong, you can always come crawling back. And if you're right, then you are in for many long wine-soaked nights of pontificating in *franglais* around a table of questionable French guys who self-identify as "philosophers."

Isn't this what your youth is for? ■

Ways to Travel Abroad for Free

If you're like most recent grads, you probably aren't working with much of a travel budget (let's just say that barring a lucky streak on the craps table, one Vegas weekend could be the closest you'll be getting to Paris and the pyramids for a long time). But international travel doesn't always have to be a self-financed endeavor. Nor does it have to be touristy. There are plenty of ways—some common, some a little strange—to support a globetrotting lifestyle or live in a different country for an extended period of time.

When approaching the job hunt, grads with a deep-seated wanderlust should consider careers that will allow for travel—options include the hospitality industry, being a travel-heavy salesperson (e.g., pharmaceuticals), working for an airline (even if you aren't in the air, you usually get ace flight discounts), joining the armed forces, and many others. However, there are also some slightly more spontaneous and grad-friendly opportunities that can be leveraged for a plane ticket, room and board, and Facebook albums that will be the envy of all your friends. From NGO volunteering to life as a hostel-hopping bartender, here are some ideas to set your travel fantasies in motion.

> ### Tips & Tricks: Travel resources
>
> There are as many approaches to travel as there are places to see in the world, and while some prefer a live-life-in-the-moment, fly-by-the-seat-of-your-pants approach, others globe-trot with such painstaking precision that you'd think they were searching for Carmen Sandiego. No matter what your steelo is, we suggest *at least* a little bit of forward-planning, if only to ensure you get the best deals, stay safe, and don't find yourself suddenly wishing you had taken some malaria pills after waking up in a sweaty fever with a sneaking suspicion that your spleen is enlarged. Before you hit the road, check out gradspot.com/book for a full list of useful (and grad-friendly) resources for travelers.

(*Note*: Traveling doesn't necessarily mean getting a passport. For someone from Maine, Mississippi might seem like it's on a different continent—and vice versa. If you want to get away from your hometown but don't necessarily feel like exchanging your USD for Vietnamese đong, you can pursue plenty of jobs that will allow you to relocate or travel around the country. See Chapter 2 for more on researching cities to live in the U.S.).

Teach English. You've probably heard stories of people who teach English in Korea for $3,000 a month and free housing. These gigs really do exist, and while not all English teaching positions are so lucrative (you may live on scraps—but at least you're in Venezuela!), they all offer a great opportunity to travel. Before you can teach English abroad, you've got to get certified. There are a number of certifications—most notably, Teaching English as a Foreign Language (TEFL), Teaching English as a Second Language (TESL), Teacher of English to Speakers of Other Languages (TOSEL), and Certificate in Language Teaching to Adults (CELTA). Courses will cost about $1,000 and usually take about a month to complete (many people travel to attend a course, though you can almost always find one close to home). Some schools will offer intensive one-weekend certifications, and there are also online courses you can take remotely. But while these quick-fire and at-home options might be okay for someone who just wants to dip his or her feet into the teach-abroad waters for six months or so, people who would like to seriously consider teaching as a career should invest in a full classroom-based course—you will come out feeling a lot more confident, and you get to bond with other future teachers who will become your best contacts for finding gigs around the world. In addition to word-of-mouth, there are a number of good websites for finding openings, including ESLCafe. com, TEFL.com, and ESLJobs. com. Remember that each school

---

Tips & Tricks: ¿Hablas español?

Do you speak a foreign language? If so, this skill could be a huge leg up on the international job market. You could work for an American company in their foreign office, using your knowledge of the local language to work with clients there. You could also use your bilingual skills to work for a foreign company, which will value the fact that you can communicate with both its native staff and English-speaking clients. Or, you can leverage your ability to speak one country's language to work in a completely different country—for example, you could help a German tour company in Berlin attract more Japanese customers. If you've got the motivation to learn a new tongue or you need a little review session, check out page 420 for a list of D.I.Y. language resources.

is different, and you'll need to make strategic decisions about which match your needs, based on location, teaching format, and pay scale.

Join the Peace Corps. Operating in countries as far-flung as Azerbaijan and Malawi, the Peace Corps is one of the most popular options for rough-and-ready grads to really see a developing country up close and personal. (You have to commit 27 months, so this one is not for the faint of heart.) In addition to having a positive impact on a community, the Peace Corps will help you accrue some benefits that will take you to the next step, like student debt forgiveness (p. 295), credit/financial aid at many grad schools (p. 176), and access to government jobs (p. 141).

Become an Au Pair. Childcare is apparently something that many families the world over feel comfortable farming out to a foreigner. Check out GreatAuPair.com to find gigs, and turn to page 32 for more information on becoming a babysitter/nanny.

Find other volunteer opportunities. There are countless organizations that need bright young volunteers, so don't feel bummed if the Peace Corps is not for you. Look for opportunities at WANGO.org, Idealist.org, VolunteerInternational.org, and TransitionsAbroad.com. Another site with a lot of international volunteer listings is GoAbroad.com. Note that certain organizations (e.g., some NGOs offering internships abroad) will charge you for the pleasure of building a well in a desert in the middle of nowhere. In some cases, this charge is realistic—these organizations are strapped for cash, so it's not like they can shell out to send a bunch of inexperienced workers abroad (think Habitat for Humanity). Other organizations might provide room and board but leave the rest (airfare, transportation, souvenirs) up to you—for example, Grassroots Soccer (grassrootsoccer.org) offers a 12-month internship but suggests fundraising a minimum of $10,000 to support yourself for the year. In any case, it's important to always perform your due diligence on an organization so you don't find yourself stranded with a crappy, money-grubbing "nonprofit" in the Ecuadorian rainforest. Check out CharityNavigator.com to see if the organization has been rated, or at least search around for message board discussions or testimonials about other people's experiences. And see page 146 to learn more about finding and exploring full-time nonprofit opportunities.

Join the WWOOFers. If you've ever longed to herd sheep in New Zealand, work on a vineyard in France, or help out on a family farm in Peru, now's your chance! WWOOF (World Wide Opportunities on Organic Farms) is an

Holy $*%#, I Just Graduated!

organization that helps people find short-term work opportunities (usually on farms) in exchange for free room and board. Since WWOOF operates around the globe, joining up is a great way to see a new corner of the world and to engage in a real way with the local community there. But be warned: WWOOF experiences differ drastically from country to country and farm to farm. Some require some pretty serious manual labor, so make sure you understand what's expected of you before you sign on to help harvest 50 tons of rice. Check out wwoof.org to see where you can go and how to get started.

Look for seasonal gigs at tourist hotspots. Here's a weird thing: If you go skiing in Utah in the winter, every worker you meet—from the lift attendant, to the sales clerk at the ski shop, to the girl pouring your après-ski beer—is from a different state or country. You think they're onto something? There's no reason you can't do the same thing in, say, Las Leñas, Argentina or Chamonix, France. For seasonal and tourism gigs, check out Net-Temps.com and CoolWorks. com.

Find a grant, fellowship, or prize. Before you graduate, see what travel grants and prizes your school has to offer. Foreign Languages, History, and other departments usually have programs you can apply for with a simple application or essay. In addition, Fulbright scholarships and other travel grants are always worth pursuing, though they can be very competitive. Try to find grant or fellowship programs specific to your interests. Mira's List (miraslist.blogspot.com) tracks opportunities for artists (e.g., writers' exchange programs, photography grants), and institutions related to your field of interest may have programs, as well. There are also awesomely random opportunities you can find, like the "Delaying the Real World Fellowship," which funds one twentysomething adventure a year. In fact, the "resources" section of DelayingtheRealWorld.com is a great place to find more info on travel opportunities.

Lead travel trips for students or adults. You'll likely need prior experience with a language or specific country (maybe you grew up somewhere else before going to school in the States), but leading others on an international adventure can be a great way to have an adventure of your own along the way. Check out Backroads.com, All About Visiting Earth (aave.com), or Putney Student Travel (www.goputney.com) to see if being a trip leader is right for you. If you can't get a job as a guide, you can also try joining the company in another capacity (maybe even as an intern) and working your way up to a position where you get to travel for marketing, research, or guiding purposes.

Get a job that'll take you places. Take a peek at the tip of the iceberg, just to get the wheels turning: diplomat, pilot, relief worker, consultant for an American company abroad (p. 138), paralegal for an American firm's foreign office (p. 140), travel writer, interpreter, and so on. Industries that often have international offices or work with foreign clients include advertising (p. 139) and PR, finance, oil, and the nonprofit sector (p. 146). In most cases it's easier to start out in the U.S. and then transfer to an office in another country. And while traveling for work is certainly exciting, just remember it's not the same as traveling for pleasure—in some of these lines of work, you have to prepare yourself for the possibility of being disappointed when you travel to Venice but never see much more than your hotel room and the inside of a client's office.

Wing it. You can always just buy a plane ticket and attempt to find work once you get to your destination. While this approach is not for everyone, you're sure to find others at the hostel with the same intentions as you, apparently locked in some sort of unspoken competition to see who can make it the longest without having to go home. Bar jobs and hostel gigs are two popular ways to sustain your travels—when you start relying on medical donations for the next train ticket, it may be time to rethink your plans. You could also be the manager for a traveling theater group, become a roadie for a band, or find a philanthropic foreign lover. Get creative! (Check out page 57 to read about how one Gradspot writer bought a one-way flight to Paris and survived to tell the tale.)

Holy $*%#, I Just Graduated!

Top Five Movies for Recent Grads
by Gritz

In one last-ditch attempt to help you delay the inevitable (see, we really are serious about "me" time), we've set up the ultimate post-graduation movie marathon. Invite over some friends, pop some Orville Redenbacher, and get ready to soak up some classic edu-tainment. Some of the films are inspirational, while others serve more as cautionary tales. All of them will fill in some of the gaps that your commencement speaker left out and prepare you for life after the summer after college.

The Graduate (1967). This is the ultimate graduation movie based on its name alone. And even though it came out ages ago, it tackles a timeless post-college conundrum: How do you find sex beyond the carnal conveniences of the dorm? Benjamin Braddock (Dustin Hoffman) discovers his

Top Five Movies for Recent Grads continued...

answer in the form of pop culture's most famous cougar (Anne Bancroft as Mrs. Robinson), but at what price? I guess the invaluable lesson of *The Graduate* is even if you're feeling a little lost and disillusioned after college, you shouldn't fornicate willy-nilly with older people. Because when you've got a generation gap staring you in the face, that's tantamount to sleeping with the enemy.

Into the Wild (2007). Whoa, depressing! Yeah, I feel you—this film is *mad* depressing. But watch it for two reasons: 1) Hal Holbrook is amazing and will make you cry. 2) It teaches the important lesson that there really is such a thing as "reading too many books." Post-grad life is all about balance—by obsessively reading Thoreau and hanging out by himself, Chris McCandless (Emile Hirsch) is extremely imbalanced (perhaps chemically so). While we can all agree that "selling out" and being materialistic are definitely two slippery slopes to avoid, hauling to the literally slippery slopes of Alaska might not be the best alternative.

The Motorcycle Diaries (2004). What better way to celebrate the end of college than by figuring out who that dude was that everyone had a poster of in their dorm room? As a medical student in 1950s Argentina, Ché Guevara (Gael García Bernal) gets on a motorcycle and embarks on an epic trip across South America with his college buddy. Along the way, they get into some typical 23-year-old shenanigans—chasing tail, drinking beers, and hitchhiking. But then Ché flips the script and becomes one of the most famous revolutionaries of all time. This flick is a must for any young grad with counter-cultural aspirations or a passing interest in the lives of people outside of the United States.

The Devil Wears Prada (2006). Bosses from hell, soul-crushing assistant-level jobs, and rocky transitions to a new city—*DWP* really covers the major challenges of the post-college transition in one fell swoop. Andy Sachs (Anne Hathaway) moves to New York City to pursue her dreams of being a fashion journalist. There, she becomes the assistant to Miranda Priestley (a.k.a. Anna Wintour; played by Meryl Streep), who runs the leading fashion rag *Runway* (a.k.a. *Vogue*). Like *The Nanny Diaries* (another good post-grad pick), this story comes from a *roman à clef* written by Wintour ex-assistant Lauren Weisberger. So, if you want to be a successful author, work for rich people in New York and then expose them. It's a foolproof formula.

***Kicking and Screaming* (1995).** No, not the one with Will Ferrell, which came out a decade later, but rather a cautionary tale that makes two very important points: 1) Sticking around campus post-graduation is invariably depressing, and 2) If you break up with someone who achieves even marginal success after school, it will quickly eat away at any façade of happiness that you attempt to foster. Point #2 is even more apropos in the Facebook era, when you can track your exes' every move while you sit crying in your squalid sublet.Cracking jokes about how you're unemployed and unmotivated is fun for a while, but it's not a sustainable existence in the long-run. (I guess that's point #3.) ∎

Holy $*%#, I Just Graduated!

Chapter II: Housing

Housing

Have you ever seen MTV *Cribs*? What about *Lifestyles of the Rich and Famous*? Well, unless you are really good at skateboarding or selling ringtones, your first pad definitely won't be featured on one of those shows. However, you will be able to *watch* them all you want, sans the irksome distraction of your mom yelling at you to "turn off that garbage." (You can also create the illusion of being on *Cribs* by owning *Scarface* and lining up all your Gatorades neatly in the fridge.)

Life beyond the dorm and your parents' house can be a bit intimidating if you've never had to take care of yourself before. But it's important to remember that even though some prisons are massive and have very good facilities, they still feel very claustrophobic and small for the simple fact that they are prisons. The golden goggles of freedom, on the other hand, can make the tiniest, coldest, most roach-infested room look like Buckingham Palace. Maybe that's a bit of an exaggeration. But like Paul Bunyan's height, it's an exaggeration with a point.

Let's be real about things: If you're like most recent grads, your first place is not necessarily going to be palatial. If it is, well played. But if not, don't fret. The important thing is that by moving to a new city and/or renting your first place, you are taking a huge step toward independence and personal responsibility. Having your own space will give you the breathing room you need to thrive socially and creatively. Furthermore, it will force you to become more self-reliant as you learn to deal with landlords, pay utility bills on time, buy your own groceries, and maybe even clean up after yourself once in a while.

In this chapter, we'll provide you with all the know-how you need to transition to life beyond the nest. After discussing the decision to move to a new city, we'll tackle the specifics of searching for a living space, signing a lease, living with roommates, and even buying a place. Ultimately, finding a nice spot can be one of the most annoying bees in a recent grad's bonnet, but where you sleep each night is so fundamental to your daily happiness that it's worth giving the process the respect and attention it deserves.

Choosing a Post-Grad City

So, you've made the decision to move out of the nest and make your way in the world. We salute you and sincerely hope that you didn't fall victim to a

Failure to Launch situation in which your parents secretly plotted to force you out of the house. Subject to a few restrictions, you now have the world at your fingertips. Close your eyes, spin the globe, and point. Gary, Indiana! Okay, forget that plan. A more logical approach may be in order.

Let's start with some real talk: The first city that you move to after college isn't necessarily the one you'll end up in for life. So go sow your nomadic oats. Always wanted to live in Austin before settling down in Philadelphia? Or how about Beijing before Kansas City? (Who said you have to settle "Stateside" right after college? Check out page 59 for ideas on how to take yourself international.) Now's the time to explore and experiment, when your responsibilities are at an all-time low and all you need to worry about, in most cases, is putting a roof over your head, eating food, and possibly repaying student debt (but no kids, mortgage, etc.). And if you end up somewhere you don't like, just move on to the next place. In the worst-case scenario, you move in less than a year. We promise, it's not a big deal.

When it comes down to the process of city selection, there are really two approaches: picking a city because you want to live there, or picking a city because you think it will maximize your job prospects. These aren't mutually exclusive, but it's worth considering the thought process behind each as you weigh your options.

Pick a City for Yourself

If you aren't the type that's rushing to make the "millionaires under 30" list (or you are that type but think you can do it without being in a business hub), you've got a ton of options for your first post-grad city. Is there a place where you've always seen yourself living, or a city that appeals to your gut for no particular reason? Some criteria to consider include the following:

- **Friends and Family:** Do you need to be around your friends and family, or do you want to blaze your own trail for a bit?

- **Cost of living:** This factor can be the difference between squatting and living (relatively) large. See next page.

- **Weather:** Are you a surfer, a skier, or someone who avoids going outside at all costs?

- **Demographic:** Do you want to be surrounded by other recent grads, stroller-pushing newlyweds, or incredibly old people?

- **Culture:** Do you want a city that has nonstop entertainment in the form of art and museum exhibitions, classical music, opera, Jonas Brothers shows, and other concerts?

- **Attitude:** Do you like a fast-paced or laid-back vibe?

- **Nightlife/Bar Scene:** Do you want to club hop, frequent the local speakeasies, or drink Trader Joe's wine at home while tearing through your Netflix queue?

Pick a City for a Job

If the "right job" is at the top of your priority list, we salute your self-starting 'tude and offer one piece of advice: Seriously consider what job you want before you pick your city. That's because once you choose the industry you want to break into, your city may be picked out for you (assuming you want to be in the hub). Richard Florida's *Who's Your City?: How the Creative Economy is Making Where to Live the Most Important Decision of Your Life* is a great resource for comparing post-college cities and getting a feel for which industries thrive in each. But to give you a sense of what we mean by hub cities, here is just a handful of examples:

- **Atlanta:** big business (e.g., Coca Cola, Home Depot, Delta), music

- **Boston:** engineering, consulting, venture capital

- **Chicago:** aerospace, finance, consulting

- **Dallas:** insurance

- **Denver:** telecommunications, environmental

- **Houston:** energy

- **Los Angeles:** entertainment, fashion, arts

- **Miami:** design, real estate, hospitality, anything having to do with Latin America

- **Nashville:** country music

- **New York City:** finance, fashion, advertising/marketing, publishing, law, new media

- **Philadelphia:** medicine, biology

- **San Diego:** biotech, health care

- **San Francisco:** technology (from computers to health), food and wine, start-ups

- **Seattle:** big-biz technology (e.g., Microsoft, Amazon), engineering, venture capital

- **Washington, D.C.:** politics, international relations, NGOs, and nonprofit

The Cost of Living Factor

The Economist uses an awesome system called "The Big Mac index" to assess purchasing-power parity in different countries across the world. The idea is that by looking at the comparative cost of a Big Mac, you can figure out if a currency is under- or over-valued. Within the U.S., we all use the same currency and the cost of McDonald's doesn't change all that much from place to place, but that doesn't mean the notion of purchasing power doesn't come into play. You can absolutely get "more" for your dollar in some cities compared to others. Rather than Big Macs, then, rental prices works as a pretty good proxy for the cost of living in various U.S. cities. And while it's not perfect, it's the biggest expense for most recent grads, so having an affordable rent generally translates into an affordable lifestyle.

Spending some time on Craigslist is probably the most accurate and comprehensive way to get a feel for rental prices for any given city. Going through the listings, you'll see clear price trends for one-bedrooms, two-bedrooms, room shares, house rentals, and any other housing options in different neighborhoods of a city. For a slightly less accurate shortcut, it's worth checking out RentBits.com, which provides frequently updated rental price averages across the country. (Just keep in mind that in some cities, you'd rent a one bedroom on your own, but in others you might split it into two rooms, so adjust rental figures accordingly.)

Another good way to get a snapshot of a city's affordability is using Sperling's Best Place cost of living calculator (BestPlaces.net/COL), which allows you to plug in two cities and compare the cost of key expenses like food, transportation, health services, and more. And for a really comprehensive statistical overview of the city you're researching, check out City-data.com.

You Don't Need to Move to Where Your Friends Are

There's nothing wrong with moving in with friends post-college (indeed, it can really ease the pain of transitioning), but don't move to a city just because your friends will be living there. Odds are, during the first few years after graduation, a diaspora of sorts will occur. Some friends might decide to chase their Hollywood dreams and move out to L.A. Others might move abroad for studies or "to find themselves." You don't want to be the one who moves to the city where everyone else lives, only to find out they don't plan on staying. Moreover, "keeping the dream alive" with high school or college buddies can turn out to be sort of depressing and stunt your personal growth. Move to where you really want to move, and in the end, you'll probably end up with some friends, anyway. (Note: This goes for significant others as well. You are not married, so there is no reason to act like you are. If you are married, mazel tov—just don't put your wedding photos on Facebook, please!)

Assessing Your Housing Needs: Cost, Neighborhood, and Space

Once you've chosen a post-college city to live in and gotten a sense of the most grad-friendly housing options (e.g., apartments versus condos versus houses), it's time to set some criteria to guide your hunt. The "sorting hats" of parentage and college housing offices are no longer responsible for assigning you rooms, so the onus is on you to figure out what you value in a living space, how

Housing

much you are willing to spend, and where exactly you want to live. To do so, it is necessary to balance the three main criteria for judging places: neighborhood/location, cost, and space (as well as any special needs or perks you can accommodate).

Neighborhood

In most cities worth living in, there exists a wide range of neighborhoods, each boasting its own inimitable flavor. Some are filled with hipsters who aspire to be starving artists even though their parents work for Fortune 500 companies. Some are filled with octogenarians, while others are havens for young families. If you are new to a city, get a sense of the landscape by reading guidebooks, grabbing local magazines and newspapers, and talking to people who have lived there. Walk around neighborhoods during the day and then go back at night so you can see what you can do and whether or not it feels safe—saving money is great, but if you are going to end up getting the shirt stolen off your back twice a month on the way home from work, maybe it's not worth living on "the wrong side of the tracks." Aside from safety for your body and belongings, think about whether or not you feel comfortable. Is the neighborhood diverse? Do you feel like you stand out in a way that doesn't feel right? Trust your gut, because as much as you think it might

---

Tips & Tricks: City versus the 'burbs

In some cities, downtown real estate is prohibitively expensive, whereas nearby suburbs are pretty affordable. In other places, you might find posh suburbs ringing a city that looks like Armageddon—go Detroit! The point is, every market in America has a vast range of prices, so you can't just do one quick scan of Craigslist to decide whether or not you can afford to live in a particular city. You need to dig deeper. Find out where the most popular places for people commuting to the city are—studies have actually shown that commute time is one of the most important factors towards day-to-day happiness. Maybe you can't afford a place in the best neighborhood in the city, but a place a half-hour train ride away might be half as much. You've got to weigh your priorities and think about why you want to live near that city. If you think it's the best place to build your career because it's an industry hub (p. 71), perhaps it's worth sucking up a tough commute at first. But if you are moving to a city because you think it would be fun to live there, be realistic—living an hour away is going to get pretty tiresome, and maybe you'd be better off in a cheaper city where your budget can get you closer to the action.

Housing

motivate you to work harder, it sucks to live in fear and dread of returning to your own pad at the end of the day. Here are some more pressing concerns to consider:

- **Proximity to Work.** Will an hour commute to and from work make you want to impale yourself on a rusty spike? If you drive, what will the morning traffic be like? Would you rather wake up half an hour later every weekday or be closer to your friends on the weekends? A good way to estimate your commute is to get transit directions from your potential neighborhood/pad using HopStop.com and Google Maps.

- **Proximity to Transportation.** Can you get everywhere you need to go without a car? Note that if there's an express bus, train, or highway to shoot you to work in the morning, it might be easier to live in a different area or town than it would be to live geographically closer but three trains and a ten-minute walk away.

- **Cost.** Basically, can you afford it? (See page 77.)

- **Safety.** We'll just mention it again so as not to get sued. (Just kidding—we really do care about you!) Use sites like NeighborhoodScout.com, City-Data.com, and Homefacts.com to get safety info on the neighborhood.

- **Convenience.** Grocery stores, banks, and pharmacies should be easily accessible, or else you might get aggravated and/or hungry.

- **Other.** How much do you value being close to friends, restaurants, bars, parks, and anything else that will make your life more convenient and enjoyable?

Top Five Tips for Moving With and Without a Mover

Whether you're moving out of your college dorm or into your new place (or both!), you are going to have to deal with the arduous task of transporting all of your stuff from point A to point B. Here are some tips for moving solo, or with the help of a professional mover:

Housing

Top Five Tips for Moving With and Without a Mover continued…

1) Prepare. Figure out what you'll need (e.g., boxes, tape, truck) and secure it before moving day so you won't have to scramble. If you wait until the last minute like every other kid in College Town, USA, you may be stuck riding the Greyhound. This eventuality, in turn, will give new meaning to the word *depressing*.

2) Get help. Ever tried to load a mattress into a car/truck on your own? Now imagine trying to repeat this process with all of your furniture. Ask friends and family for help. If that backfires, then scour Craigslist for freelance strongmen. You don't need to be a hero.

3) Pack smart. Save some cash by getting your packing materials online or from a hardware store. Also, put some thought into what goes in each box and how to avoid wasting space. Storage/packing is an art form that should be treated with due respect.

4) Wheels. Check U-Haul, Budget, and Penske to see what kind of ride you will need and compare prices. On pickup day, arrive early to get first dibs. When loading up, remember to distribute weight evenly. If you are renting a trailer, make sure the truck and/or your car has a hitch to attach it to.

5) Assume it will be annoying. I don't care what people tell you; moving yourself is a big pain in the butt. If you have the cash, do yourself a favor and spend it to hire movers.

Moving with a Mover

1) Make a reservation. This is not your Intro to Philosophy term paper—just because you are paying someone else to do it for you doesn't mean you don't have to give it any thought before the date of pickup. Most moving companies recommend making a reservation two to four weeks ahead of time.

2) Comparison shop. In comparing movers, you will naturally want to consider pricing, but you also want to learn a bit about the company that will be sending someone to pack all of your worldly goods into a truck that could double as a getaway vehicle. Make sure your mover has insurance and uses fulltime staffers that will be mindful of their own job security when moving your stuff.

3) Check the fine print. Once you are given an initial estimate, it is helpful to rattle off any potential obstacles you envision to ensure the movers don't hit you with any hidden fees. Do they charge an additional fee for large items like an armoire? Will the company transfer your goods mid-move to a different truck (thus increasing chances of breakage)?

4) Get directions. If you are at a point of indecision about where you want to live, hiring a mover in the hopes that they will make the decision for you is probably not the way to go. Printing out specific directions ahead of time will save time and money. It will also force you to pick a place to live and thus prevent the possibility of homelessness.

5) Pack yourself. Not only do movers generally charge by the hour, but they also won't care if all of your belongings are supposed to be sorted by "awesomeness factor." Moreover, they will charge a premium for packing supplies, and use way more boxes than is necessary. Handle this part of the process on your own and then use the pros for what they do best— heavy lifting. ∎

Housing

Cost

How much you are willing to pay is pretty much up to you, though we encourage you to think about saving your money rather than blowing it on an unnecessarily extravagant pad. In economic terms, rent is a *sunk cost*, meaning it cannot be recovered once you've paid it. It is not an investment that will accrue value over time (unlike buying a place, which you can learn more about on page 115). On the flip side, the place where you sleep and spend most of your free time has a huge impact on your happiness quotient. Just keep things in perspective when you are hunting. If two apartments are essentially identical, but one comes with a gym in the building and costs $100 more, don't think, "Wow, this apartment building is so much better because it has a gym!" Rather, you should think, "Would I pay $100/month for a gym membership?" Rent is money you never get back, so make sure you put it toward the things that are actually important to you on a day-to-day basis. Also, remember that

> ### Tips & Tricks: Flex/convertible apartments
>
> Before you start wheeling and dealing on the real estate scene, make sure you are familiar with the industry lingo—not understanding the terminology on a listing can lead to a lot of wasted time and maybe even a grave mistake. One concept that is particularly relevant to recent grads living with roommates is that of a flex apartment, also known as a convertible. These terms refer to apartments that have the space (generally in a large bedroom or off the living room) to add an extra bedroom by putting up pressurized walls. So a "flex three" or "convertible three" is a two-bedroom apartment with room for a third. It does not mean that it is a three-bedroom that can be flexed or converted to four, so if you have more than three people look elsewhere. Like a convertible car, these apartments are usually pretty cramped, and unfortunately you can't pop the roof to get more sunlight. However, this type of arrangement can make the rent much more manageable for recent grads on tight budgets. (For more real estate speak, see page 88.)

roommates can significantly cut the cost of living (see page 105 for more on "Roommate Living").

Another thing that can defray costs is a bad economy. For recent grads, one of the unforeseen benefits of an economic downturn is that rents take a dip. Places that would previously have been prohibitively expensive may actually fall within your range. In addition, many brokers are willing to waive their fees (or management companies will offer to pay them on behalf of tenants in order to fill apartments and even offer months for free). Rents become more negotiable than ever, so check out our tips for negotiating (p. 94) and be bold! While a financial meltdown like the credit crunch will likely make your job hunt that much tougher, it may make your house hunt a bit easier.

Recession or not, the key question is how much is reasonable when it comes to rent. Property prices vary so drastically from place to place that geography plays a huge role in this decision, but a wise recent grad budget (p. 316) would have you spending around 35% of your monthly income on rent. That might not be possible in the most expensive cities, but you should never spend more than half of your salary on rent and utilities (so if you make $35,000 a year and bring home $2,000 a month after taxes, Social Security, and health care, your rent should be a maximum of $1,000 per month).

It's important to settle on a range before you start hunting to avoid wasting time looking at places you can't afford. To set that range, you need to get a sense for the average rents in the place you're hunting so you don't get swindled or go in with an unrealistically low budget. Just scour Craigslist listings, review RentBits.com averages, talk to friends and coworkers, and call up a few brokers for an overview of the market (you don't have to commit to work with them). When you actually start seeing places, be very explicit in asking about the average cost of utilities and the services each provides (generally trash removal, water, and maintenance).

Space

As the fictional British broadcaster Alan Partridge once pointed out, "People always go on about space. But people forget, you can get lost in space!" Though your getting lost in your first pad is about as likely as Baghdad winning the next Olympic bid, the fact remains that space is not always all it's cracked up to be, particularly when it comes at a high premium.

We should note that you could probably rent an old farmhouse in Mississippi for the same price that it costs to live in a cramped Manhattan studio, and in many ways that's an awesome idea. But for now let's assess the realities of city living. When looking at an apartment or house, think about how much natural light it gets and how important that is to you. If you end up renting a convertible, will the added room block out most of the light? Next, assess the floor plan, which is generally much more important than the square footage number quoted on the listing. Do you have to walk through another bedroom to get to the bathroom? Are the hallways awkwardly narrow? Finally, think about your unique lifestyle and needs. If you live with a social group of friends and you plan to spend most of your free time at home together, then maybe it's worth sacrificing large bedrooms for a bigger living room and kitchen. But if you want to spend your evenings watching (and then re-watching) *Bridget Jones's Diary* in peace, hold out for a suitably comfortable bedroom. Finally, if you have worked out a rental scheme in which you and your roommates will pay different amounts, make sure you look for places where the rooms match their respective price tags.

Perks and Special Needs

If you require wheelchair-accessibility or you own a pet, you'd better make sure that any building you look at can accommodate these needs. Beyond the essentials, you need to determine how much you value the various "bells and whistles" of the living facility.

Housing

- **Laundry.** A laundry room (or better yet a washer and dryer in the apartment or house) should be a major point of investigation. However, bear in mind that laundry rooms cost money, so look around the neighborhood before ruling out a laundry-free building—there may be a Laundromat next door that will wash, iron, and fold your clothes for little more than it would take to use the machines.

- **Kitchen.** A refrigerator, stovetop, and oven are basic, but a dishwasher can be a godsend to a busy and lazy grad. That said, if you never cook at home (let alone eat outside the office), maybe it's irrelevant. Determine your cooking needs and aspirations, then proceed accordingly. You can also roll with paper dishes and plastic silverware to make things easier. Just don't expect Al Gore to show up at your dinner parties. If you're subletting or joining an existing house share, ask about whether the kitchen is already equipped with shared items or whether you would be expected to contribute your own dishes, pots, pans, and so on

- **Gym.** Having a gym in your building, community, or house is pretty fresh, but again, assess your actual schedule and habits. Does your job provide a gym membership somewhere better? Would you prefer to work out at home or closer to work? Have you even worked out since '99? Maybe it's not so crucial after all…

- **Doorman and/or Security.** What kind of security is in place for residents? Is it a gated community? Are there night patrols? (And if so, is it because the surrounding neighborhood is a warzone?) In cities, a doorman apartment is not only safer, but also more convenient when it comes to dealing with packages, guests, and other building-related issues. However, if packages are your main concern, remember that you may also be able to get them shipped to your office. If it's not a typical "doorman building," is there security on hand or a number you can call in case of emergency? Needless to say, having this type of staff on the premises almost always means higher prices, so decide how much these services are worth to you.

- **Patio, Balcony, Outdoor Space, or Roof Access.** If you like "grilling and chilling" as much as Bobby Flay does, a little deck space can be very agreeable, but that doesn't mean you have to splurge on the penthouse. Many apartment buildings offer shared roof or garden space,

Housing

and some apartment and condo complexes have interior parks and/or lawns where you can commune with nature to your heart's content.

- **Parking.** Do you need it, and are there cheaper alternatives?

Types of Housing

The housing options available to you will vary from city to city, and even neighborhood to neighborhood. Maybe you're ready to move downtown into that "super cute" two-bedroom that you and your best friend have been dreaming about since you were in the sandbox together. Or, maybe you've decided the time has come to find a shared house full of vegan communists and cause a ruckus (by slipping cubes of steak into their bulgur). Either way, there is a place for you, but it's up to you to find it (or create it). For most recent graduates, the options are split into the following categories:

Apartments. Ever watch *Frasier*, *Friends*, or *Two Guys a Girl and a Pizza Place*? Well, these shows provide a somewhat skewed portrayal of what apartment living is like, but you get the idea. When you rent an apartment, you are usually renting a unit in a larger building, apartment community, or townhouse that is owned by a landlord. The landlord sometimes manages the building directly or hires a management company to oversee everything from rent collection to building upkeep. The other tenants in the building are renters as well (or a mix of renters and owners), and depending on the building, the length of tenancy can be short- or long-term, though most leases are a minimum of one year.

Condominiums. Condos can be in large buildings with the same look and feel of an apartment, or they can be independent/attached units in a more spread-out development. The key distinction from apartments is that they are owned by individual owners who, collectively, form a Homeowner Association (HOA). In addition to caring for their own units

---

Tips & Tricks: Sublets

The term *sublet* refers to an arrangement (usually short term) in which an existing lease is passed on to a third party by the original lessee. In layman's terms, someone who is already renting an apartment rents it out to you. This can be a great option for people who want to "try out" a city or neighborhood before formally renting a place there, or who just want to avoid a more formal renting procedure. Another plus: Sometimes a sublet will be furnished! For more information on sublets, go to the "Sublets" section on page 100.

---

individually, they pay association fees that help to maintain the common areas of the building/development, as well as any shared facilities and amenities on the premises. These facilities and amenities can be pretty swank—look for sweet perks like fitness centers, sundecks/gardens, garages, or even pools and tennis courts. Because the units are privately owned, condo owners are willing to invest money in the maintenance of the facilities in a way that many standard management companies will not. That extra TLC can be a double-edged sword. On one hand, owners are likely to be accountable and responsive if you have any issues or need maintenance to be performed (assuming they didn't rent you the condo and then go on a year-long meditation retreat in Tibet). On the other, they may be (overly) protective of the property and make strict stipulations about what you can and cannot do while living there. For more information on condo rentals, see "Specifics of Renting a Condo" on page 96.

Houses. In some cities, it's more common to rent houses (or "apartments" within individual houses) than it is to rent an apartment or condo in a managed building or complex. The process of searching for a rental house is much the same as searching for other types of housing, but once you find one, there are a few new variables that go into the mix (got your snow shovel?). If you're considering this option, check out "Specifics of Renting a House" on page 98.

"The Housing Hunt" section starting on page 85 is applicable to all rental options.

Confessions of a Nomad: The Modern-Day Odysseus
by GRITZ

Nomad, n.

1. *A member of a group of people who have no fixed home and move according to the seasons from place to place in search of food, water, and grazing land.*

2. *A person with no fixed residence who roams about; a wanderer.*

After living with my mom in Washington, D.C., for the first fall after I graduated, I decided to seek fame and fortune at an Internet start-up in New York, where I shacked up with my best friend from college and his parents. Everything was going great until I was fired three weeks later, less than 24 hours after I had signed a sub-lease on a place with my buddy. Suddenly, I found myself at the most daunting crossroads of my post-college life: Should I bail out and go back home to D.C. with my tail between my legs, or should I soldier on with no job and zero prospects? Needless to say, my hubris got the better of me, and thus my life as a nomad began.

Over the next eight months, I would live at six more locations, including two couches, one hotel, a solo sublet that everyone I know refused to visit, and a room that leaked dirt from the ceiling—when I woke up in the morning, I often felt like someone had tried to bury me alive. Sometimes, I wished they had finished the job.

Though it's rarely easy, the nomadic lifestyle is a reality for many recent grads that move to a new city before securing employment. But while job hunting, apartment hunting, and sleeping on a different futon every couple of weeks can be an exhausting endeavor, there are many hidden benefits to the life of a wanderer.

First, a good nomad will have to develop admirable social graces if he plans to make it for very long. Be it an aunt or a friend of a friend from college, your host is doing you a huge favor by providing you with room and maybe some board, so you have to be on extra good behavior. Clean up after yourself, keep your things neatly packed away, leave the house as often as possible, and always bring your own towel (and bedding if possible)—no one wants your grime on their linens. On a similar note, don't bring a "tenderoni" back from the bar unless you are staying with your best friend. When you're a nomad, the whole idea is to snag a spot in someone else's bed! The need for a roof over your head actually adds a bizarrely Darwinistic subtext to the act of flirting, because getting it cracking means free shelter and another night of survival in the concrete jungle. (Needless to say, I never actually achieved this level of nomadic prowess. Boo-hoo! I guess that is the price one pays for having uneven facial hair and eczema—conditions which are only exacerbated by the nomadic lifestyle.)

Housing

Housing

Confessions of a Nomad: The Modern-Day Odysseus continued…

Next lesson: A nomad shall become extremely resourceful and knowledgeable about the city where he or she subsists. On the one hand, you may become familiar with many different neighborhoods, which will come in handy if you ever decide to get your own place. However, you will also need to develop the ability to kill time on the streets, ideally for free. Sometimes you will have to wait for your host to get home, or you'll wake up on a Saturday morning and literally not know where you are going to sleep that night. Lurking around a city is an art form that requires a little outside-of-the-box thinking. Street performers become your TV; Barnes & Noble is not just a bookstore, but also an opportunity to catch up on world affairs and use a semiclean toilet. Best Buy is the rec center, where kids play Xbox and lounge in gaming chairs all day. Help yourself out by using some of the money you're saving on rent to join a nice gym—it will serve as an unofficial clubhouse where you can shower, utilize various hygiene products, and hang out if you have nowhere else to go.

Finally, the consummate nomad shall develop an intimate appreciation of life's necessities. If you are going to be nomadic for any extended period of time, you will need to scale down your belongings to a bare minimum. A few changes of clothes, toiletries, a pillow, and a towel are really all you need—wait until you find a place before calling in the PS3s, humidifiers, and other household luxuries. When it comes to food, channel your Neanderthal lineage and learn to be a hunter-gatherer. This involves pulling moves like eating all of the free samples at Whole Foods and taking home food from buffets for dinner. (You can also become a "freegan" and literally eat out of the dumpster.)

At the end of the day, being nomadic can be an invigorating experience, because you haven't really lived until you've sat on a park bench wondering whether or not you might have to sleep there. Also, if things go well, the experience can reaffirm your faith in humanity. The modern-day nomad is a sympathetic character that people love to help, so foster good etiquette and enjoy the fruits of others' hospitality! ■

The Housing Hunt

Back in the days when the West was still wild and the Oregon Trail had yet to become an incredible video game, the U.S. government used to sponsor "land runs" in which homesteaders would line up with their wagons, wait for a gun blast, and race to claim a subsidized plot of land. It was pretty insane, but in the end, the most motivated and aggressive settlers got the land.

These days, the process has changed drastically with the advent of real-estate brokers, Craigslist, and actual laws. Nonetheless, in cities like New York and San Francisco, the general vibe is not so different from those days of yore. Crazy competition for the best apartments is driven by the fact that 1) Many twentysomethings want to live in the same areas and in similar types of apartments, and 2) The majority of recent grads move in and out of apartments at the same time of year.

If you're lucky, you have a couple of weeks set aside solely for hunting. For those who will be working during the search, be prepared to wake up early and spend some lunch hours racing around to different places. It's not uncommon to see between ten and 30 places, so it can be a grueling process. In some cities, using a broker can help facilitate the process, but if you're a lone hunter with time on your hands, you can certainly get it done on your own. In the meantime, you'd better familiarize yourself with the secrets of subletting (p. 100) and maybe even being a nomad (p. 82).

But enough small talk—it's time to make moves. Survey the land (on the Internet), load up your wagon (with the proper docu-

> ### Tips & Tricks: How to be a super hunter
>
> When it comes time to seal the deal, you're going to have to gather a whole bunch of money and documentation for the landlord. Preparing these items in advance—and even bringing filled-in forms and documents with you when you visit places—can be the difference between getting the lease and seeing it slip through your fingers. Indeed, the competition for housing can be so fierce that anything you can do to improve your candidacy helps. Consider getting a guarantor even if you don't think you'll need one. Ultimately, landlords have no obligation to be fair when it comes to deciding who will get the place (no "first come, first served" policy applies here), so you want to make an effort to look like the richest, most responsible candidate of them all. (Go to page 92 to find out exactly what landlords require from prospective tenants.)

Housing

mentation), and get ready to throw some 'bows in the pursuit of the perfect pad. Go West, young man! Or, as the case may be, Go East, young woman!

Attacking the Market: D.I.Y. vs. Working with a Broker

There are essentially two ways to find housing: get a broker or search on your own (or do both simultaneously). Depending on where you live and what type of living situation you seek, working with a broker may or may not be an option. Brokers are more prevalent in certain cities (e.g., Boston, New York, Chicago), and they tend to work directly with management companies that oversee specific apartment buildings or sometimes with the Homeowners Associations of condo complexes. Whether you decide to work with a broker or not, brace yourself for a healthy dose of stress and annoyance. Hunting down your own dwelling can be an all-consuming process, but once it's settled, you can throw a housewarming rager and you'll soon forget what a pain in the ass it was. Here are some of the pros and cons of using a broker versus hunting on your own.

Option #1: Do It Yourself

Conducting an independent search is a good idea if: 1) You have the time; 2) You want to save money by avoiding brokers' fees; 3) You're planning to move into an established house share or a sublet; or 4) You're looking to rent a condo or apartment directly from the owner or a management company. (Management companies usually run big buildings or apartment complexes, and they'll almost always have a central office you can visit or call to inquire about open units.) While looking for "no fee" housing requires a bit of creativity and a lot of perseverance, it is an entirely viable option and a good way to save cash at this fiscally precarious moment in your life. To ensure that the hunt goes as smoothly as possible, check out these savvy hunting tips.

- **Sound the Alarm.** Let family, friends, and coworkers know you're in the market for a new place. Ask friends about their search to get a list of good websites and management companies. Also, if you like a friend's building, have him or her ask the super if there are any apartments up for rent. Some buildings and management companies offer "Refer-a-Friend" rewards to tenants who bring others in, so you may help your friends cash in. (If you end up renting a place with this policy, don't forget to take advantage in the future when you hear of someone who is looking—or at least demand that your friend who referred you buys you a burrito). Word of mouth is especially useful when it comes to subletting (p. 100), as people often seek to sublet to friends or friends-of-friends before making a public announcement. Use your social networks (e.g., Facebook, Twitter) to let people know you're looking and to see if they have ideas.

- **Go to the Source.** This is often the best strategy. If you've narrowed down your search to a neighborhood, visit each building in the surrounding area and ask people going in or out whether there are apartments available, or try to find the number of the management company (sometimes found on a plaque in the entranceway) and call directly. Even if they don't have an apartment in the building you're calling about, they might have one nearby. If you're looking for a house, cruise around the neighborhood looking for FOR RENT signs.

- **Craigslist.** In most cities in the United States, Craigslist reigns supreme as the go-to resource for housing. Everyone should start here, if only to get a sense for the market. If given an option, begin by searching under the "No Fee" section, where you will find apartments being rented directly by management companies or condos being rented directly by owners. Occasionally, brokers may list apartments in this section with the caveat that they will absorb any fees, therefore making them "No Fee" from the standpoint of the tenant. As always, beware of Craigslist fraud—if it seems too good to be true, it probably is.

- **Other Resources.** Beyond Craigslist, different cities have their own local resources, such as Rentvine.com in Denver and RentersResource.com in Houston (a list is available via gradspot.com/book). Ask friends and coworkers what they used. In addition, scour classified ads in local publications (or on their websites). If your city has a college or university, check with their housing office to see if you can tap into any listing services or resources they provide for grad students and/or faculty members. Some schools even lease rooms to interns on a short-term basis, especially during the summer (see page 158).

- **Photos.** When checking out photos online, look for any fine print that indicates, "Photo is similar to actual apartment." This is a trick that some brokers or companies use to lure people in before showing them the actual apartment—which is often a total dump. In real estate, if it seems too good to be true (state of the art appliances and a private terrace at a dirt cheap price), it almost always is.

Housing

- **Making Contact.** When responding to different listings via email or phone, try to get as much info as possible (e.g., exact street location, price, size, and layout). Then be ready to run over to see the place at the first available time slot or during an open house. "No Fee" housing moves particularly quickly. Slow and steady may win some kind of race, but it isn't this one.

Decoding Ad Speak in Real Estate Listings

When you start hunting for an abode, you will quickly learn that real estate listings are a veritable study in the art of the euphemism. The more fluent you are, the more efficient you will be in your search. As a rule of thumb, avoid any online ads that feature flashing lights, size 98 font, or exclamation mark abuse. Beyond that, here are a few translations to help you on your way. Note that use of these words does not always mean you can yell "You lie!" at your computer. But if you have a bad feeling about a listing (or, most important, there are no photos accompanying the listing), they should be viewed with healthy suspicion.

"Cute"/ "Cozy"/ "Adorable"/ "Intimate"—It's tiny and may lack basic features like closets and storage-space. Your bed (if you can fit one) may very well take up the entire bedroom and/or apartment. On the upside, it will be cheap to heat (just add more fiber to your diet).

"Full of Character"/ "Charming"—Dirty, rundown, decrepit, and potentially located in a poorly maintained building.

"Bohemian"/ "Funky"—Indicates there is something "different" about this place. Could be anything from lingering marijuana fumes coming from the neighbors' apartment to pornographic murals on the living room wall. Be sure to ask for details.

"Never Lived In"/ "State of the Art"—It will be freshly painted, and the appliances will be new, but don't confuse newness with high quality. You may encounter even more maintenance issues in a brand new place than you would in a more weathered spot.

"Quiet Neighborhood"—Sometimes known as a "boring" and/or "secluded" neighborhood. Might make you feel like you're living in a slasher flick.

"Lively"/ "Animated Neighborhood"—Prepare to be kept awake at night by traffic/revelers/the sports bar on the first floor of the building.

"Up-and-Coming Neighborhood"—Everyone loves an underdog, but you don't necessarily want to live in one. If it's really "up-and-coming," find out what's setting it back from arrival at the "nice neighborhood" promised land. Most importantly, make sure it's safe.

"Great Location"/ "Convenient To [Some Place Cool]…"— Perhaps the most subjective of all real estate descriptors. Do they mean it's literally walking distance to a place you'd want to go, or walking distance to the 45-minute train that takes you to that place? Ask for a precise address and Google map that sucker. ■

Housing

Option #2: Real Estate Brokers

If you're moving to a city where brokers are accessible, they can be very helpful, especially if you're hunting for the first time or are completely unfamiliar with the city. The main advantage to using a broker is that they go through all of the listings for you to separate the wheat from the chaff, and they can show you a lot of apartments at once, thus saving a lot of time. They may also have exclusive access to rentals you would not find on your own, and they can sometimes get better deals from management companies than you could negotiate yourself. Traditionally, broker fees run between 10–15% of the yearly rent (though this can vary by city), but

in a tough market, many brokers are willing to negotiate or waive their fees entirely—or management companies may agree to cover the fee for you. For this reason, a bad economy is a good time to use a broker, even if you wouldn't have done so otherwise.

Some brokers are great: resourceful, empathetic, and not criminal. But many are none of the three. So if you do seek their services, you have to learn how to cut straight to the real talk—it's helpful to always keep in mind that they are working for you (make them earn it!). You shouldn't have to pay anyone until you actually find a place, so feel free to work with a number of brokers simultaneously. Word of warning: They may drop you if they find out, but *c'est la vie*. There are plenty of brokers in the real estate sea. Here are some rules of engagement to keep in mind:

- **Fix a price.** First figure out the highest rent your budget will allow. Then shave off a couple hundred dollars to account for the broker fee (if applicable).

- **Finding a broker.** Try to find good brokers by asking friends what companies and specific brokers they used. Or do a Google search to locate brokerages in your city. Finally, peruse Craigslist, as it will often connect you to individual brokers or brokerages.

- **Play the field.** Work with several brokers, but be (or at least pretend to be) serious with each. If a broker senses you will come through as a potential renter, he or she will go above and beyond to seal the deal. If you think you're getting brushed aside, remind the broker (in a tactful way) that there are many others who are just a phone call away.

- **Get a schedule.** The first dirty broker trick is to try to up-sell you by showing places way out of your price range, and then bringing you to a dilapidated hut within your actual budget. Ask for an itinerary before seeing any apartments, then nix anything that doesn't fit your range. If that doesn't leave anything left to see, tell the broker to get back to work or take a hike.

- **Under pressure.** The second dirty broker trick is to pressure you into settling on a place by mentioning the six other people waiting to put in an application. Whether those six people actually exist or are merely figments of the broker's screwed-up imagination, you may never know. Don't let the broker pressure you into a hasty decision. That being said, if you know you like it, mount up and take it—those six people may be out there after all.

- **Do some recon.** The Better Business Bureau is a good place to check up on the credentials of specific brokerages.

- **Negotiate.** Go for the gold. The recent economic crisis puts you in a great position to negotiate. For tips on how to go about it, see page 94.

- **Beware of contracts.** If a broker wants you to sign anything, read it very carefully, and remember that the window for negotiation closes once you lay down a signature.

Final Steps: Applying and Signing the Lease

If you thought *finding* a place was a struggle, you are in for a treat, *mon frère*. Actually sealing the deal is half the battle (more so in some cities than others), and in most cases it involves an infuriating mix of timing, luck, and favoritism. No matter where you are, some prep work and a light sprinkling of gamesmanship can give you the head start you need to score that sweet pad. While it's not always necessary, it never hurts to pull together the necessary documentation beforehand and bring it with you when you visit places to give yourself an advantage over others who are less prepared. You might come off looking like an over-eager spazz, but sometimes the biggest spazz gets the worm. Keep in mind that your docu-

> ### Tips & Tricks: Read the lease (and take pictures of the apartment)
>
> Don't be lazy—this is a healthy portion of your salary we're talking about, so make sure you are not committing to anything that will bite you in the booty. For example, did you plan to leave for three months in the summer and sublet your place? Some buildings and landlords do not allow subletting, so check the fine print. If you can't decipher the legalese, try to find a lawyer to go over it with you, or let a wiser person take a look. If you can't find anyone with a good sense of the red flags to look out for, Nolo.com is a great resource for reading about renters' and tenants' rights—it's full of helpful tips and explanations of various legal components of rental agreements. Once you've actually signed the lease, take pictures (with date and time display) of the space when you first move in so that you have evidence of that giant crack on the ceiling that the landlord will likely try to deduct from your security deposit when you move out.

Housing

ments may need to be notarized (the same goes for guarantor's forms, which are discussed below), and if you have any roommates they will probably need the same documentation as well.

What You'll Need

Not every landlord requires exactly the same items, but you will almost always need to provide some combination of the ones listed below. Once the process is done, make sure anything you handed over is returned to you.

- **Copy of Photo ID.** Driver's license or passport should suffice, no matter how unfortunate the photos.

- **Letter of Employment.** Must verify duration of employment, position, and salary. Ask your boss or your company's HR department to provide it for you and don't be intimidated to make this request as it's expected. If you don't have a job yet, you'll probably need a guarantor (see next page).

- **Two Most Recent Pay Stubs.** Get 'em from work.

- **The First Two Pages of Your Tax Return.** Some places require just the past year, while others require the past two years. Bring both just to be extra safe.

- **Most Recent Bank Statement.** Get it from the bank or online. The idea here is to look as rich (i.e., secure) as possible. If you have a savings or investment account, bring statements from those as well.

- **Copy of Previous Lease (If Applicable).** Make sure the lease has the previous landlord's info and let's hope there are no skeletons in the closet. If things ended poorly at your last place (often the case for people who rent during college), pretend you spent the last few years living with your parents or in dorms.

- **Letters of Recommendation.** In the absence of written notes, names and phone numbers of personal or professional references should suffice.

- **Rental Application and Fee.** The application will be provided by either the landlord or broker. Most often it is filled out on the spot, but occasionally it can be done in advance if there is a particular

Housing

building or management company to which you are confining your search. The fee (about $50) is used to process the application and run a credit check.

Guarantors

Most management companies require that a tenant's yearly income be above a minimum level, up to about 40-45× the monthly rent (income of roommates can be combined). For a $2,000/month apartment that means you have to make between $80 and $90K. If you don't stack this type of money (you're not alone), you may need a guarantor to co-sign the lease. The guarantor agreement is provided by the landlord or management company and requires some basic personal and financial information. Signing it legally obligates the guarantor (usually a family member or close friend) to pay rent if you default. He or she must earn a greater percentage of the rent—up to 80–90× the monthly rate—but combining the incomes of two guarantors is often allowed. Even if you can hack it alone, having a guarantor is never a bad idea, since it makes your candidacy that much more attractive. Take note, fair homesteaders: Some landlords won't accept guarantors from "Homestead states" (Texas, Louisiana, and Florida) because residents in those states are protected if the tenant defaults on payments (and landlords don't want to deal with that).

If you don't know anyone who is willing to act as your guarantor, there are options. Websites like Insurent.com can help by acting as your guarantor (for a fee that varies depending on your credit score). If you go this route, make sure to factor the guarantor fee into your overall housing budget.

Get Your Money Right

On top of the application fee, there will likely be other lump sums of money to pay either upon application or at the lease signing. Unfortunately, you will usually have to pay a bit more than just the first month's rent—that arrangement usually only works at a halfway house. Below is a list of what you'll need (note: landlords often require the security deposit and first month's rent to be on separate certified checks or money orders—no personal checks or credit cards).

- **Broker Fee.** If you go through a real estate agency that charges a broker fee, the norm is 10–15% of the yearly rent. If the management company is covering this fee for you, they will pay the broker directly.

Housing

- **Hold Deposit.** Used to reserve a place prior to lease signing, this fee is generally just deducted from the security deposit. If you have a change of heart, it will be deducted from your bank account instead.

- **Security Deposit.** Paid at lease signing or move-in, this charge ensures that damages are covered. It is usually equal to one to two month's rent and refundable as long as the space is left in the same condition as when you moved in. Note: If you're renting from an independent landlord or individual owner, he or she may waive the deposit or be more lenient about the amount.

- **First Month's Rent.** Essentially another security deposit to lock it down once and for all.

The Negotiator's Toolkit

You may be a recent grad on a budget, but you're no sucker. As such, you have every right to negotiate and try to get the best possible deal for yourself (even if you're talking $1,000 off the rent instead of $100,000 off a house purchase). When going into battle, be strategic—it's all about striking that balance between being too pushy and being a pushover. These real estate people are slick, but you're slicker. And particularly when the economy's struggling, you're in a great position to get a better-than-average deal. Here is some helpful info to help you negotiate your way to real estate bliss (or at least contentment).

Working with Brokers. If you're using a broker, you may have better luck negotiating their fee instead of (or in addition to) the actual rent. Many brokers will waive fees when they're low on clients. If your broker won't budge, have him or her talk to the management company to see if they will pick up the broker fee on your behalf. An empty apartment or house is a landlord's worst nightmare; he or she may be willing to cover the fee if it means locking in a good tenant (hopefully that's you). When there's a larger management company in the mix, it is sometimes difficult to know where the buck stops with regards to decision making. Ask your broker or landlord who the head honcho is, and then be assertive about setting up a face-to-face meeting if possible.

Timing. From a landlord's point of view, a lower-paying tenant is better than no tenant at all. If you time it right, you can end up getting a great deal on a property that would otherwise have been vacant. Keep in mind that landlords are more willing to give deals at the end of the month (assuming the lease would start on the first day of the next month) than they are to give them at the beginning of the month when they still have a few weeks to find a tenant. In terms of seasonal strategy, late summer/early fall and late spring/early summer tend to be very busy times for turnover, so try avoiding the rush by hunting during the "off season." You'll have less competition, and will have a better chance of differentiating yourself in the eyes of your landlord.

Building Type/Size. In larger apartment buildings that are managed by one or more rental companies, negotiating can be tough, as the management companies often adhere to strict policies and can be unwilling to work with you the way an independent landlord might. Consider renting from the landlord of a smaller building or from a private owner; you may have a better chance of establishing a personal rapport and negotiating effectively.

Doing Your Homework. Before trying to negotiate your rent, talk to friends and do online research to try to find out how much people are currently paying for properties like the one you have your eye on. The more you know about the market, the savvier you will seem. If you find that a similar property is being rented somewhere for less than what your landlord is asking, use that price as a starting point for negotiations. Some brokerage websites list their rents for each property, and these rents can fluctuate. If you notice that the rent for your apartment is now listed as $200 more than it was a few weeks ago, call your broker and/or landlord out and ask him or her to respect the rent that was previously listed.

A Discount for Paying Upfront. If you can swing it, ask the landlord for an overall discount in exchange for your paying the first few months' rent upfront. She will have more money in her pocket, and you will save overall. This option requires that you have enough liquidity to pay the first few months in one lump sum; if you can, everyone wins.

Turning on the Charm. No one wants to give a deal to an a-hole. Most landlords (especially those who oversee smaller buildings or rent out their

Housing

The Negotiator's Toolkit continued...

own properties) are looking to find nice, reliable tenants. If you make a great first impression, they may be more lenient about rent in order to keep you on their team. Consider bringing letters of reference or a copy of your (good) credit report to negotiations in order to prove what a desirable tenant you are. And don't forget to smile. (See page 284 for more on credit and credit reports.)

Offering Your Services. Keep it above board, but don't hesitate to get creative and offer to help your landlord out in various ways (e.g., painting, shoveling snow, garbage removal) in exchange for a rent reduction. If the landlord feels that having you as a tenant will be advantageous to him, he will be more likely to give you a break.

Re-negotiating. After you've been in the place for a year (or, if you're renting month-to-month, for a substantial amount of time), you are in a good position to renegotiate your rent—or at least to request that your rent not be increased. If applicable, point out how you've paid on time each month, how you've made improvements/repairs to the property, and how you've been a stellar tenant overall. If they play hardball, send that sass right back at them and let them know you can take your money (and your good behavior) elsewhere.

First Month Free. Particularly in large apartment buildings and communities, it's common to get the first month free as an incentive to sign a lease. If it's not offered, ask for it. If you can find a similar apartment that's offering this deal, use it as a bargaining chip at the place where you really want to live. ■

Specifics of Renting a Condo

The process of searching for a condo is not so different from standard apartment hunting, but when it's time to sign a tenancy agreement, there are some distinctions you need to know. The big wildcard is the Homeowner Association (HOA) that governs the building. The HOA has no legal authority over you as a tenant, but that doesn't mean it won't have a significant presence in your life. For starters, the HOA often reserves the right to approve or reject potential tenants (which is why it may take longer for your rental application to be approved than if you were renting a house or apartment). Before you commit to a condo, make sure to read through the HOA's covenants, conditions, and restrictions (CC&Rs), which cover everything from noise disturbances to parking space allocation to tennis court use (if you're lucky enough to have scored a tennis court).

Ultimately, your landlord is the direct member of the HOA renting to you, and that person is responsible for meeting all requirements for membership. But in reality, whether it's you or your landlord who screws up, you will end up paying the price in the form of an eviction. From your standpoint, the trick is to make sure the contract clearly outlines the tenant's versus the owner's responsibilities in relation to the HOA. Keeping in mind that everything is negotiable, here are a few things to watch out for when going over your rental contract.

- Who is responsible for paying HOA fees? (Usually it's the owner.)

- Who is responsible for performing (and paying for) maintenance within the unit? (Usually a combination of the tenant and owner.)

- What about common areas? (Usually the HOA or a superintendent.)

- Who should initiate repairs/maintenance, and what is the procedure for doing so?

- Which of the complex's facilities and amenities do you have access to? What are the terms of use?

- As a tenant, are you eligible to use any external gyms, spas, or golf facilities that have contracts with the HOA?

- Are you allowed to attend events put on by the HOA (BBQs, etc.)?

What is provided for in the condo in the way of furniture and/or appliances?

- As a tenant, are you allowed to attend the HOA's monthly board of directors meetings?

- What is provided for in the condo in the way of furniture and/or appliances? Are you allowed to attend events put on by the HOA (BBQs, etc.)?

Housing

- Can you paint and/or alter the appearance of the condo? What is provided for in the condo in the way of furniture and/or appliances? Are you allowed to attend events put on by the HOA (BBQs, etc.)?

Rent-to-Own

In some cases, renting a condo can be the first step towards buying a condo. When you're asking the questions above, inquire about potential Rent-to-Own options, which will allow the rent you pay now to go toward an eventual down payment on the unit should you choose to buy it. Consider it a test drive—rent it first, and if you think it's nice and you start to feel more financially stable, look into a purchase. If you're really serious about entering into this type of agreement, consider hiring a lawyer to help you sift through the fine print. There are huge financial benefits to this type of agreement, but you may end up paying unanticipated taxes and fees along the way. For more information on buying property, read the "Buying a Place" section on page 115.

Specifics of Renting a House

If you're in a market where it's the norm for recent grads to rent houses, there are some compelling reasons to feel like you're trumping your apartment- and condo-dwelling cronies. Bigger rooms, more privacy, a yard, a parking spot, space for awesome pets—these are all typical benefits to living in a house. But the problem with houses are twofold: More space means more stuff to deal with (lawn, driveway, a roof, etc.), and the nature of house rental agreements is that you have to accept a little more responsibility than your friend who's wedged inside a shoebox in a building with hundreds of other people. Heavy is the head that lives in a castle. So before taking on the responsibility of renting a house, make sure you weigh the pros and cons carefully. That picket-fenced pad with the basketball hoop in the driveway seems great now, but you might be singing a different tune when you're expected to deal with the giant hornets' nest that you failed to notice behind the backboard.

To break it down clearly, here are the specific issues you'll have to deal with as a house renter:

- **Management Issues.** The status of your landlord may not be as "official" as it would be in a managed apartment building; make sure you're clear on the rental terms, and discuss your tenancy rights with whoever's renting you the house.

- **Maintenance.** What is your landlord responsible for, and what are you expected to take care of on your own? Consider housecleaning, lawn mowing, snow removal, garbage disposal, and routine maintenance like plumbing and electrical issues.

- **Higher Bills.** Houses are big and therefore more expensive to heat and clean. That creaky farmhouse might be charming, but unless you can heat it using the residual energy from your dance parties, prepare to cough up some cash during the colder months. Same goes for air conditioning in the summer.

- **Roommates.** Given the obvious size considerations, you'll almost always have a roommate—or eight—in a rented house. Whose name will be on the lease? What happens if someone doesn't cough up the rent? Check out page 105 for tips on roommate living.

Let's run through the management and maintenance a little more so you don't stumble blindly into the house from hell.

Who's the Boss?

When you rent a house—or a room in a house—you will most likely be renting from an individual owner or a landlord who owns and manages a few houses in the area. As a result, these arrangements are often less formal than those you might negotiate with a large management company that oversees apartment buildings. If you're renting a room or rooms within a house, your "landlord" might be the family who owns and occupies the rest of the house. They probably don't think of themselves as real-estate biz folks per se, just people looking for a little extra income. The benefit is you might be able to bypass all the "official" stuff like credit checks and guarantors, and if the owner is nice, you might get looked after a lot better than you would in a big building. Casualness can be tricky though, so it's good to be clear about rules and protocols before you move in so the owner isn't suddenly all up in your grill telling you to babysit her kids.

If you're renting an entire house, it's likely that your landlord might work full-time in real estate or be a local business owner who does a little real estate on the side. When you're looking at each place, inquire about whether the landlord lives in the neighborhood—often it will be someone who owns three houses on a block and lives in one of them. And while you might want a little privacy on the day you host your Naked Slip'n'Slide Festival, it's generally nice to know the owner's close at hand if a problem arises.

Indeed, it's also very important to figure out how problems get dealt with in and around the house. Many concerns are similar to the ones that come up in apartments and condos, but make sure your lease clearly outlines who is responsible for the following issues that are specific to houses:

- Weekly garbage / recycling removal (a.k.a., do I have to do anything except toss my garbage bags and Mountain Dew cans out on the driveway?).

- Snow removal (a.k.a, I better not have to shovel).

- Exterior and lawn care (a.k.a., who trims my hedges and gets rid of the family of possums in the tree outside my bedroom?).

- Paying for minor repairs and major maintenance issues (a.k.a., what happens if the roof leaks or the staircase collapses?).

- Parking (a.k.a., do I get a spot or do I need a sticker to park on the street?).

Negotiating Rent

Handy with a leaf blower? Passionate about re-grouting bathroom tiles? Up for babysitting your landlord's kid? If so, you may be in a position to negotiate your rent in exchange for helping out around the property. For advice on how to do this, see our "Negotiator's Toolkit" on page 94.

Subletting

If you need something shorter-term than a standard year-long lease, or all the aforementioned renting shenanigans just seem like way too much work, subletting might be a good move for you. In a sublease agreement, you rent directly from another renter, so the whole thing's a lot less formal. There are risks to not holding the lease (keep reading), but assuming all goes well the benefits of this practice are three-fold.

First, subleases provide greater flexibility for short-term stays. A regular lease will usually last at least one year, but you can always find people subletting their apartments for almost any amount of time, from a week to many months.

This arrangement is ideal if you want to "try out" a city before signing a longer-term lease, or if you are unsure of how long you will be staying. Second, many sublets come furnished and, if it's very last minute (i.e., the sublessor is getting a on a plane in two days and needs to rent the apartment ASAP), you can get lucky and score a great deal. Finally, subletting usually allows you to avoid all the "red tape" associated with actually renting your own place (like getting a guarantor). The formality of the arrangement varies depending on the parties involved, but it's unlikely you'll have to produce all of the paperwork that is required of lease-holding tenants.

Sublets come in all shapes and sizes. You can sublet a studio or one-bedroom and have the place all to yourself, or you can sublet individual rooms within larger apartments, condos, or houses. The latter move can be a great way to meet people in a new city, but make sure you ask the right questions and get a clear sense of the house vibe before moving in (see page 107).

Looking for a Sublet. Many of the strategies listed in the "Do It Yourself" section on page 86 apply to sublet hunting as well. Because sublets are flexible arrangements, they can be found in any number of ways, but here are a few places to start.

- **Word of Mouth**. A great place to start, especially if you're not psyched about the idea of living with complete strangers. It's very possible you already know someone (or someone who knows someone) who is looking to rent out his or her room for a certain amount of time. Leverage your networks to let the world know you need a roof over your head, and think outside the box. Sure, you'd prefer to move into a room in a furnished penthouse, but if your friend's grandmother has an unused guest room you could inhabit for a few months, don't turn your nose up at it. You could probably negotiate milk and cookies into the deal.

- **Craigslist.** The Holy Grail for all things housing-related, sublets included. Check the "Sublets & Temporary" section for the city of your choice, and then start sifting! Make sure to take note of whether the sublet is furnished or unfurnished, whether utilities are included in the listed rate, and whether there are any other "special" conditions involved in the rental (e.g., will you be expected to walk your new roommate's Shih Tzu?).

Housing

- **Sublet.com.** This site allows you to search many sublets—furnished and unfurnished, long-term and short-term. The only hitch is that you must pay for membership to find the contact information (the price for two month's access ranges from $10 to $85.) The owners of Sublet.com also own Cityleases.com and Metroroommates.com, so it's really like having a tri-membership. It's worth a shot if the first two approaches fail you.

Visiting Sublets. Always visit the sublet (and meet any roommates you might have) before making a decision. If you are moving across the country and can't visit, ask for detailed photos, speak to the tenant(s) on the phone, and make sure you're clear on the layout of the apartment. You don't want to find out after the fact that your roommate has to walk across your mattress to get to the fridge.

Due Diligence. In order to avoid unpleasant surprises once you've moved in, make sure you clarify the following issues.:

- *Circumstances.* Why is the sublessor subleasing the room? If you will be moving in with roommates, how do they know each other? Have they had previous subletters?

- *Building and management.* What's the building like? Has the tenant had any problems with the landlord, management company, or board of owners?

- *Rent.* How much is it? Will you pay the sublessor or the landlord directly? If you are going through the person who sublet the apartment to you, what will happen if they then fail to pay the rent to the landlord on time? Does rent include utilities? How and when are utilities paid for?

- *Security deposit.* Will you be required to cover a portion of the security deposit? What happens if you accidentally punch a hole in the wall while watching a Jane Fonda aerobics workout on VHS? Note that if you pay a security deposit directly to the tenant, they may not be able to pay you back until they get their original security deposit back from the landlord at the end of the lease. Will this delayed repayment work for you?

- *Maintenance.* If there is a problem, are you expected to deal with it (or, worse still, pay for it)? Will the sublessor be easy to contact if you can't figure out how to fix the problem?

- *Communication (also known as, "Is he or she going to be in the Ecuadorian rainforest the whole time?").* Will you have the green light to make game-time decisions on repairs if the sublessor isn't available? Do you know who provides the utilities, cable, and Internet, and can you contact the providers if need be? Is the super responsive and helpful when something needs to be attended to?

- *Furniture.* Will the sublet be furnished (partially or completely)? Will you have to bring thing like sheets, towels, or kitchen supplies? (You probably want your own linens regardless—we won't go there.)

- *Roommates.* Will you have roommates? If so, consult the "Finding Compatible Roommates" section on page 105.

- *Kosher-ness.* Has the sublessor cleared the arrangement with the landlord or board of owners? Some buildings forbid subleasing, so you don't want to end up getting tossed out through no fault of your own. (Of course, you can always try to fly under the radar and hope for the best.)

- *Think about the future.* If your sublease takes you to the end of the original lease, you may be in a position to take over the lease and stay in the apartment. Play it right and this move could be a good way to "test-drive" an apartment before making a commitment.

Meeting the Roommates. When you meet your potential "landlord" (the sublessor) and/or potential roommates, use your instincts about whether the situation feels right. It can seem like an audition, but play it cool. Remember: You are being interviewed, but you're interviewing them as well. Don't let your desire to pass the "personality test" and be liked overshadow the importance of finding a place that makes sense for your lifestyle and individual needs.

Signing an Agreement. We'll be honest—this may not happen. Whether they are negotiated with friends or strangers, sublets are often fly-by-the-seat-of-your-pants arrangements, and, as a result, they can be disconcertingly casual. But unless you can trust the person completely or the sublease is extremely short, it's best to sign a legal document that outlines the conditions of the sublease. (If you don't have a buddy/colleague/dad who's a lawyer at your disposal, go to TenantResourceCenter.org to download a standard sublet contract.) Make sure the contract clearly outlines how rent will be paid, how maintenance will be performed (and by whom), the length of the sublease, the procedure for paying/returning the security deposit, and any other special circumstances (see "Questions to Ask and Things to Watch Out For" in previous section).

Housing

Renters Insurance

Many recent grads never even consider purchasing renters insurance because they either A) falsely assume that the landlord's insurance covers the tenant's belongings, B) don't think they own much that's worth protecting, or C) are too lazy and/or busy to think about it. However, the reality is that owners insurance (paid by the landlord) only covers structural damages to the building, and if you ended up buying that plasma TV, Tempur-Pedic bed, and shiny new MacBook Pro, you might have more to protect than you think. Renters insurance generally covers stuff like fire, smoke, theft, vandalism, and lightning. And while it protects all of your personal belongings, it also has other unexpected benefits—for example, it provides temporary housing should you need to relocate or wait for repairs to be made, and it covers medical and legal expenses if someone gets hurt in your crib and sues you. With typical plans starting at $150 per year (with a max around $300, depending upon how much coverage you request), it's not such a ridiculous thought after all. Insurance giants Allstate, Geico, Liberty Mutual, and State Farm all offer coverage, and you can contact them directly. But as with any insurance policy, be sure to comparison shop like there's no tomorrow (or perhaps like there is a tomorrow in which your toilet turns into Old Faithful and floods the whole apartment). Be sure to check out Esurance.com and NetQuote.com, and no matter where you find the individual policies, dig in to make sure you're not paying for any unnecessary bells and whistles.

GradGuard, an insurance agency geared towards recent graduates, also points out two important pieces of renters insurance fine print: First, you can usually choose either "cash value" coverage or "replacement value" coverage—cash value factors in depreciation of items at the time of damage or

> ### Tips & Tricks: Trouble paying rent? Throw a party!
>
> In Harlem in the 1920s, tenants who didn't have enough money to cover their monthly rent would call up some musicians, invite a bunch of friends over, and then pass around a hat and ask for donations. And it worked (in fact, these rent parties are considered by some to be a driving force in the birth of jazz). Today, this harebrained scheme sounds more like the setup for a terrible movie. But if it helps you avoid eviction and people have some fun in the process, you may just end up looking like a genius. And if nothing else, maybe the art form of tomorrow will emerge in the apartments of today's unemployed grads. Or maybe everyone can just play *DJ Hero*. Whatevs.

Housing

loss, while replacement value pays the cost of buying an item of similar kind or quality today. Second, renters' policies generally have a $2,000 total limit on stolen jewelry, but you can easily get additional coverage if your jewelry exceeds that amount and you want that coverage. (Random factoid: If you're thinking of getting a dog, be wary that many insurance companies are reluctant to give policies to people with more aggressive breeds such as Dobermans, Rottweilers, Pitbulls, and German Shepherds.)

If you do decide to get a policy, make sure to write down model numbers, purchase dates, and the places where you bought each item, and also take date-marked photos or video footage of all your stuff so that you can share it with your insurers as proof of ownership if you ever need to make a claim. Keep a copy of this list in your email or somewhere *outside* of your apartment. After all, a list that only becomes relevant if your apartment burns down probably shouldn't be stored in your apartment.

Roommate Living

Ah, roommates—can't live with them, can't live without them.

Actually, you can live without them, but it's more expensive and sometimes sort of lonely. If you were the type of person in college who preferred the privacy of a single room, don't overlook the fact that you still lived in a dorm full of students that you could fraternize with on a whim. Living alone in post-college life can be a bit more solitary, and sometimes it's nice to have someone to come home to at the end of the working day (or the end of the job-hunting day, as the case may be).

Sometimes, however, it is not nice at all—particularly if you come home to find your roommate smearing chocolate mousse over his naked body while listening to the *Ducktales* theme song. The sword cuts both ways, as they say (the good news: sometimes that sword cuts the rent in half). If the above image doesn't put you off and you do decide to shack up with a roomie (or eight), consider what you are getting yourself into and how to make it work.

Finding (Compatible) Roommates

In this menagerie, there are three distinct beasts: friends, strangers, and lovers. (Sometimes the first two can morph into the third, but only if you are a complete masochist.) Alternatively, try to link up with other apartment seekers via friends, family, and alumni networks. Finally, Craigslist and other housing-

Housing

focused websites are useful resources if you're looking to sublet or find an apartment/house share arrangement. Always be cautious when it comes to living with strangers. Craigslist can help connect you to great people who share your interests and lifestyle, but it is also a hotbed of maniacs. Let common sense be your guide, and consider taking a friend with you when you go to see potential properties.

Friends. As long as you don't allow things to get too "college," living with friends can be a nice way to ease the transition into the "real world." However, it's not necessarily going to be all gravy, all the time. Getting kept up by a noisy roommate might have been passable the night before your noon lecture, but waking up at 7 am every day will make you a bit more conservative in terms of what you deem to be appropriate nighttime behavior. New responsibilities like getting your own food, paying rent, and trying to be moderately clean can draw unspoken tensions to the surface. However, if you are good enough friends with your roommate, you will hopefully be able to work past any problems and still find that there is a modicum of love left in your hearts at the end of the day.

Strangers. Depending on where and when you're moving, you may not necessarily be moving in with friends. Living with strangers might make you a little uneasy, but for some, it can be a smart option and a good way to expand your horizons. For instance, if you are looking to create a specific type of living environment for yourself, you might want to consider looking for others who share your vision of what makes a happy home. Whether you want to maintain a "locavore" kitchen, set up an artistic collaborative, or live by a nudity-only policy, seeking out others who are on the same page can be a great way to establish the "house vibe" you're looking for.

For some, the decision to live with strangers is dictated by your fiscal situation. In these cases, you will still want to establish a set of house rules in order to keep the peace. It's one thing when it's your friend who is meticulously picking the marshmallows from the Lucky Charms, but it's quite another when it's that random dude that you've decided to shack up with. Make sure you're all on the same page about house rules and things should run smoothly. If you become friends then you've got a "cash back" situation on your hands, but the more realistic goal should be to get along moderately well. Stack the odds in your favor by always meeting each and every roommate before making a decision.

General compatibility issues include the following:

- *Smoking.* Will your roommate be smoking tobacco, weed, or crack on a regular basis? Probably something to broach before move-in day.

- *Pets.* Don't try to hide your ferret: They'll smell it from a mile away!

- *Lifestyle.* Is your prospective roommate more of a homebody or a 24-hour party person?

- *Work schedule.* Depending on the bathroom situation, the morning shower rush can be a real source of frayed nerves (and split ends).

- *Significant others.* Do any of the roommates have boyfriends or girl-friends who are always around? Two roommates can quickly become four when you factor in significant others.

- *Gender.* Are you cool living with someone of the opposite sex?

- *Race and sexual orientation.* Beware of racists and bigots!

- *Religious and/or dietary needs.* Kosher? Deathly allergic to nuts? Be clear about your needs, and make sure you can respectfully comply with theirs.

- *Pro-dance party or anti-dance party?* 'Nuff said.

- *Other.* Cleanliness, weird habits, etc.

Lovers. Shacking up with your boyfriend or girlfriend is definitely an aggressive post-college move. The most important thing to consider is your motivation. The only real reason to move in with your significant other is if you both think it is the right time to up the ante. Doing it to save money or because it seems convenient will probably lead to tears, so don't take it too casually. For better or for worse, living together will push your relationship to its limits and give you a better sense of whether you're compatible enough to build a long-term future together. Remember all those nights when you said, "Let's not sleep over," because you wanted to play *Tony Hawk's Pro Skater* or watch *Sex in the City* reruns with a carton of Chunky Monkey? Well, now you *have* to sleep over, so you'd better hope that your mate is understanding of your idiosyncrasies (like the fact that you have a nonnegotiable "underwear drawer policy").

Housing

Laying Down the Ground Rules

No matter whom you end up living with, you have to sort out paying the rent and buying the cleaning supplies. Otherwise, you'll either be evicted or carried out on your couch by an army of rats while the Pied Piper upper-decks your toilet. Here's how to keep it all in check:

- **Lease.** The lease question is a tricky one. If you want ultimate control over the apartment you may want to keep the lease in your name, but not having your roommate's name on the lease also means you become the landlord by proxy. You'll be responsible for getting the rent together on time, or covering the whole rent yourself if your roomie decides to jump ship.

- **Rent.** Will one person pay more due to certain privileges like a bigger room or parking spot? Rooms can be pro-rated based on square footage, but you may also want to take other things into account like closet space, number of windows, or proximity to the bathroom.

- **Utility bills.** Divide the duties—if one person covers cable, the other should make sure the lights stay on. And if you only watch Hulu and your roommate keeps the cable box in her room, maybe she should pay more of the cable bill. Consider signing up for automatic bill pay (p. 303) to reduce hassle and avoid late payments.

- **Groceries.** Decide up front whether food will be separate or shared so that tension doesn't arise when someone lays a finger on your Butterfinger. There are some things the apartment will regularly need, like toilet paper, napkins, and trash bags. Will these items be bought as needed by whomever, or should there be a monthly Costco outing to stock up Y2K-style?

- **Furniture.** You may have some stuff left over from college, but chances are it's been thoroughly "compromised." Figure out what's usable and then discuss who will bring what. If items need to be bought, decide whether the cost will be split or if one person will foot the bill and maintain sole ownership. (See our tip on splitting furniture on page 319.)

- **Visitors.** How late is too late and how long is too long? Does your roommate's extended family plan on flying in and forming an Aero Bed flotilla on the living room floor every weekend?

- **Chores.** Keep in mind that people have different cleaning habits—some tidy up every day, while some do a big *Trading Spaces*-style overhaul once a month. If your roommate cleans less often than you do, don't try to force him or her onto your schedule. Instead, try to make a compromise with other chores or get him or her to pitch in for a maid service.

Moving In and Setting Up Your Pad

You sealed the deal on a place and probably found a roommate. Do it big! It's almost time to pitch a reality show to Fox called *How to Be the Consummate Recent Grad*. First, you'll need to take some steps to make your pad livable—some irksome logistics (fitting your king mattress through the front door), some necessary preparations (making sure there's running water), and some fun stuff (deciding whether to put the mirror on the wall or on the ceiling above your bed). Be prepared to dip into the bank account again, because couches and cable don't usually come free. To help you out, here are some tips and tricks for setting up your first post-college pad.

Nail down move-in days. If you're moving into a house, then this won't be an issue. But if you're moving into an apartment or condo, there may be specific move-in days and times (e.g., weekdays only from 9am to 5pm). Even during these allotted hours, you should think strategically about parking and how you're going to get your van o' stuff as close to the door as possible. (For more moving tips, see page 75.)

Order utilities early. Moving into an apartment or home without cable and/or Internet is annoying, but moving in without electricity may actually be illegal in some states. Plan ahead and find out what the building provides and what you need to set up yourself. Electricity can be handled in a matter of days (or even the day of the move-in), but cable and Internet can take several weeks so it might be worth making an appointment in advance. If you're moving into a house, you may also be responsible for sewage and water. You can find sewage and water utility providers from either your landlord or a quick Google search.

Housing

Furnishings. In college, a mattress, a chair, and a few hangers may have sufficed, but you're an "adult" now, so you probably want some stuff, like a couch for guests to sit on and plates off of which one can eat food. This is where the spending comes into play, and you've got to be careful to not let it spiral out of control. To defray costs, look to buy second-hand goods (check local colleges for people moving out of dorms and their college houses/apartments for great deals); see what you can scrounge from parents and grandparents; check out budget-friendly retailers like Ikea, CB2 and Target; and always comparison shop. Make a checklist and, if you have roommates, figure out how to split costs on various shared items. Do you have pots and silverware? (See page 441 for a breakdown of basic kitchen items.) A bed and desk? A television and computer? A window AC unit? What about toilet paper and paper towels? Cleaning supplies? A floor lamp or two? If you're starting with nothing, it's not unheard of to pay in excess of $1,000 to $2,000 for all of the goods you'll need for your first place. Before buying big items, measure the doorways, rooms, and elevator to make sure that anything you purchase can actually make it into your place and then fit where you want it to go. And remember: This stuff is all pretty discretionary so if you want to stick with an airbed and a candle, go for it. Just don't burn the place down or expect any potential hookups to be thrilled about the prospect of sleeping over.

Fix up the place. Often the landlord will make sure your place gets spiffed up before you move in—fresh paint job, new bathroom fixtures, removal of the mountain of Burger King bags left by the prior tenant. If you haven't already negotiated this service into your lease, it can't hurt to request some improvements. Or, if need be, you can do it yourself—something as simple as painting some walls with a fresh coat of paint (or those cool stars that light up in the dark) can really make a place feel like your own. Other seemingly small things make a difference as well. If the light bulbs make the bedroom look like a cell for mental patients, swap them out for some eco-friendly compact fluorescents (or less shaded, higher-watt bulbs that are less eco-friendly but look nice). Other quick-and-easy upgrades include installing high-pressure showerheads and putting some nice shades or curtains on the windows. Prior to any upgrades, just confirm with your landlord that you can make them and that you won't have to, for example, repaint when you leave (unless you're comfortable doing that).

VOIP is the new landline. While most grads are comfortable just using a cell phone for all of their communication needs, some people still like the old-time comfort and convenience of a landline. The good news is, a much cheaper alternative is available called VoIP (Voice over Internet Protocol). For approximately $15 a month (comparison shop among VOIP providers like Vonage and others), you can sign up for a phone line that runs through your Internet but works with any phone you currently have (you plug the phone or base station directly into your router). For those of you worried about Internet outages, most VOIP providers will forward all calls to your cell in the event of your Internet temporarily going down. Skype is another option that you just download for free online. Calling other Skype users is free, but you have to pay to call actual phones.

Prepare for problems. Rodents, bugs, and floods are just a normal part of being a renter, so it's better to be safe than sorry. Run through a safety check and get to know your new 'hood. Do you know where the closest hospital and police station are? Upon moving into your new place, collect some emergency contacts: the local police department, hospital, pest control, a plumber, and an electrician. Also, make sure that your smoke and carbon monoxide sensors are working. If you aren't comfortable fixing a particular problem and can't find an easy fix on websites such as DoItYourself.com, then call your super (if you have one), landlord (if it's a repeat problem), or a professional (if it just won't go away). See page 113 for more tips on super and landlord relationships.

Meet the neighbors. From the bag lady in the next apartment to the family of 15 in the house across the street, the best way to deal with neighbor issues is to preempt them. Upon moving in, stop by and introduce yourself. This way if any problems do arise, you're already on a cordial basis and it's easier to politely say something like, "Would you mind not playing Megadeth on full blast at 4am?" If a problem persists even after you've confronted the offending party, either speak to your landlord/super or the police (if you're really ready to escalate it to that level).

Set up automatic lease pay. Instead of having to remember to pay your rent each month (even the best of us have been late), consider setting up automatic bill pay through your bank (p. 303). It can save you from late fees and you can always cancel your payment prior to payday if necessary. Usually a landlord will let a late payment or two slide, but the more dependable you can be over time, the better position you put yourself in to get good treatment, renegotiate your rent, and receive positive references in the future.

Housing

Top Ten Ways to Go Green in Your Apartment

These days, it's not so much "go green or go home" as "go green in your home." Making some environmentally friendly tweaks in the crib is not only easy, but it will also cut down on your gas, water, and electricity bills. Everyone wins!

1) **Change your bulbs.** Compact fluorescents last up to ten times as long as incandescent bulbs and use a quarter of the energy. You do the math!

2) **Look for certified Energy Star products.** An Energy Star TV set can use 30 percent less energy than an uncertified one, and an Energy Star washing machine can save more water than one person drinks in a lifetime.

3) **Temper your climate control impulses.** Experts suggest setting the AC to 78°F (an insistence on 72°F will cost you 39 percent more energy).

4) **Kill the "energy vampires."** Unplug appliances like cell phone chargers when you're not using them—they keep sucking down energy even when nothing's connected.

5) **Buy organic and recycled products.** Organic mattresses, sheets, and towels are increasingly mainstream and affordable. Opt for recycled glassware, clean up with eco-friendly household products, and get a reusable shopping bag for trips to the grocery store.

6) **Downsize your fridge.** Most recent grads don't keep much more than beer, milk, and a few condiments in their refrigerator, so why go for a massive energy-guzzler?

7) **Build good habits.** There are so many easy ways to save water and energy that people overlook. Turn off lights when you leave the room, don't run the water while you're brushing your teeth, and take shorter showers (consider installing a low-flow showerhead). After a while, these habits will become second nature.

8) **Use your dishwasher wisely.** Only run your dishwasher when there's a full load and always use the energy-saving setting. Savings earned: 100 pounds of carbon dioxide per year. If you're doing dishes by hand, use cold water.

9) **Buy some plants.** Houseplants not only add a little color to the room, but they also suck down pollutants and purify the air in your apartment. Just remember you'll have to water them once in a while.

10) **Get a home energy audit.** Many utilities providers offer free home energy audits to find where your home is poorly insulated or energy inefficient. You can save up to 30% off your energy bill and 1,000 pounds of carbon dioxide a year, according to the Inconvenient Truth peeps.

Dealing with Housing Issues

As a renter, you don't have as many rights as an owner. For example, you're probably not allowed to put a sauna in the bedroom closet. Oh well! But one nice thing about renting is that, assuming you have a fair lease, whoever rents to you is theoretically supposed to make sure you are a happy tenant and deal with problems when they arise. As with anything in life, the service you receive has a lot to do with personal relationships. Thus, the most important step first-time renters can take to ensure a good living situation is to hobnob with the head honchos—in most cases, this means the **landlord** and the **superintendent.** In some condo and house rental situations you just have a landlord, but the point is still the same: These people can single-handedly make you a happy camper or a miserable squatter, so it's worth figuring out their role and making nice from the get-go.

The Super

If your place has a super, he or she will probably be the person who gets you settled in your new digs, informing you of all emergency numbers and contacts, showing you the circuit breaker, and walking you through the ins-and-outs of your apartment. Going forward, the super is also your maintenance safety net. He or she is not there to help you replace a light bulb or kill a cockroach in your tub—you can handle that yourself with a little liquid courage. Rather, supers are the last line of defense—call them only after you tried to fix the problem yourself or when a situation arises that you clearly can't deal with alone (e.g., there was a flood and now there's a hole in your wall). Granted, you can call them for every little issue, but then you'll end up being known as the recent grad who cried "rat." Your super will probably set some ground rules

Housing

Tips & Tricks: Tipping

The only thing worse than an overflowing toilet is an overflowing toilet that won't be fixed for a week. Tip the super $50 to $200 around Christmas time and make sure he knows his hard work is appreciated (even if the work really isn't that hard). If the building has doorpeople, be sure to tip them too, since they are in charge of your packages, dry cleaning, and take-out. Depending on how many visitors you have, how often you receive deliveries, and how well you are treated, tips for doormen should range from $10–$80. If you're in a building with a ton of people, make sure you know who's relevant to your life; you don't need to tip all forty people on staff. You are the recent grad, after all. No need to go all Daddy Warbucks.

with you before you move in, but unless there's an emergency, you should only contact him between 9AM and 9PM. After you've dealt with your super a few times you'll get a handle on how helpful he's willing to be.

Some condos have supers (though they're not always called that) who oversee the common areas of the building. When there's a problem in your individual condo, however, you should go directly to your landlord (the owner). If it's an issue in a common area, you should still go through your landlord and ask her to take it up with the super and/or HOA. In some circumstances, your landlord may put you directly in touch with the super of the building, but that is decided on a case-by-case basis. Hopefully, you develop a direct relationship with the super at the beginning so there's no need for an intermediary. (Just don't be telling the super to help you install a Murphy bed when you haven't cleared it with the owner.) If you're renting a house, your landlord should help you with any issues, or else hire and pay for someone to fix a problem.

The Landlord

The landlord is not just a person who takes your money each month and laughs all the way to the bank (though he is that too). He or she is also supposed to be responsible for any problems with the building. Has the super still not fixed that leak in your ceiling you've complained about five times? Enough is enough: Call the landlord directly. Your lease will include some legalese about the "habitability" of your apartment, and that basically means that the landlord must resolve anything that makes your home unlivable (e.g., lack of clean water/heat/sane neighbors). If the situation is not rectified, threaten to stop paying rent or bring in the real authorities: an attorney, the police, or the Department of Housing and Communities.

Sometimes, you might be in hot water with the landlord. Perhaps you were too busy with your new job and forgot to pay the rent. Usually, landlords will charge you a late fee, but if you've been a good tenant, they tend to waive it. But what if you can't make the rent one month? Instead of just ignoring the problem, you should speak with your landlord and see if you can work something out—most of the time it's not a huge deal. However, if the worst-case scenario occurs and your landlord tries to evict you, be sure to know your state's tenant rights and contact the Department of Housing and Communities. A landlord can't just kick you out without the law behind him, and that process usually takes about six months.

Buying a Place

You might be thinking that we've officially lost the plot. You're an intern with piles of student debt and zero credit history—how the hell are you going to buy a house or an apartment!?

Admittedly, buying a place is not feasible for everyone in the first few years out of college, but it's not as insane an idea as it might seem at first glance. While property markets are well beyond most recent grad budgets in places like Boston and San Francisco, many cities are *relatively* affordable. We understand that you might not want the headache of mortgages, insurance, and other home-owning responsibilities, but under the right circumstances there are two compelling reasons to take the plunge: economics and peace of mind.

Rent, as we discussed before, is a completely sunk cost—it does not appreciate in value and you will never get it back. In many cities popular among recent graduates, rents are inordinately high because landlords know that we need housing and are willing to pay a lot for it. Property that you own, on the other hand, can be an investment that can appreciate over time, sometimes quite significantly if you buy wisely. Also, since homeowners get a sizeable tax break on their mortgage interest payments, the total costs of owning a home can be similar to or even less than what you would otherwise be paying in rent (see exhibit below). Thus, in many cases the real challenge of buying isn't making monthly payments but rather gathering enough loot for the 20% down payment.

If you do decide to go for it, however, you should look for a place that you actually want to live in for at least a few years and that you think holds good value, rather than treating it solely as an investment. Otherwise, you will drive

Housing

yourself crazy worrying about how every little problem that comes up (in your house or the market as a whole) will affect the value of your "investment." Instead, consider it a "consumable investment," and recognize that this is the place that you're going to be living in for the next five to ten years, which can be a reassuring and exciting sentiment.

Needless to say, there is a huge amount of research and preparation that goes into buying property, but we just wanted to put the thought out there for people who hate seeing $1,000 go down the drain each month. If you expect to be in one place for at least 5–10 years and you're making a healthy salary that you can reasonably expect to maintain, at least consider it. And remember, even if you have to leave before you think it's time to sell, you can always sucker the most recent crop of recent grads into renting it while you bide your time.

(Note: If condo ownership appeals to you, go to page 98 to learn about the "Rent-to-Own" option on some condo rentals.)

Buying Versus Renting

When you discuss buying an apartment, people might ask you where your decision comes out in the "rent versus buy" equation. In other words, is the monthly cost of owning less than the monthly cost of rent, or vice versa? You might be surprised to learn that, on a month to month basis, it is sometimes cheaper to own. Check out this chart to see how the financing breaks down:

Price of House/Apt.	Cash Down @ 10%	Total Monthly Payment[1]	Year-end Tax Savings[2]
$100,000	$10,000	$640	$1,890
$150,000	$15,000	$959	$2,835
$200,000	$20,000	$1,279	$3,780
$250,000	$25,000	$1,599	$4,725
$300,000	$30,000	$1,919	$5,670
$350,000	$35,000	$2,239	$6,615
$400,000	$40,000	$2,558	$7,560
$450,000	$45,000	$2,878	$8,505
$500,000	$50,000	$3,198	$9,450
$750,000	$75,000	$4,797	$14,175
$1,000,000	$100,000	$6,396	$18,900

(1) Total Monthly Payment includes mortgage repayments and apartment/house maintenance. However, it does not include the tax benefit of owning a mortgage. We did not include the benefit in this number because we wanted to look at the monthly cost of owning a house/apartment, and the tax benefit only accrues at year-end when you file your taxes.

(2) Since we don't think you should ignore the tax benefit all together, we wanted to present the annual tax savings you would receive at year-end.

Notes

- *Assumes interest rate of 6.0%, a tax rate of 35%, a 30-year mortgage, and that monthly maintenance is proportional to purchase price.*

- *Some simplifying assumptions were made. For example, we assumed average maintenance fees, but it can change depending upon real estate taxes, amenities, and the general level of home upkeep.*

While the "rent versus buy" question is one way to assess the short-terms economics of home ownership, you also have to keep in mind that the appreciation or depreciation in the value of your the home (i.e., the price today versus when you sell) is an equally important factor in the long-term decision. Since the long-term part is a lot harder to predict, it's important to buy a place because you really like it, not solely because you think it's a good investment. That way, if the market lets you down, at least you aren't left with something you never even wanted in the first place.

Housing

Chapter III: Career Options

Career Options

Here we stand at the true crossroads of the post-grad experience. While commencement day serves as a communal ceremony to mark the transition into the "real world," there comes a more important moment of reflection when you stop reminiscing about the time you streaked the quad and instead look yonder toward the future. Whether it's a day, a week, or a year after leaving campus, the real transition begins when you face your destiny and boldly declare, "Yes, I am ready to begin my career, and maybe I'll even consider moving out of my parents' house!"

The young grad's declaration of independence is usually followed by a spazz attack of varying degrees of intensity. As it turns out, the freedom to determine your own course is not only exciting, but also pretty terrifying. The trick is to avoid thinking of every job-related decision as a make-or-break moment in your life; instead, think about your career as a constantly evolving story. While the good old hand of fate will work its tricks like it always does, you are the hero and you have the power to change the course of your tale whenever you want. As long as you keep the forward momentum going and don't kill anyone (never a good career move), employers will be interested in hearing it.

As you set out, remember that even great stories can have pretty crappy openings ("They call me Ishmael"…snooze!), so don't get caught up waiting for the perfect beginning. People will be more than happy to give you all sorts of half-cooked advice about choosing your first job, ranging from the New Agey ("do what you love, dude") to the depressingly practical ("whatever pays the bills, young 'un"). Somewhere between the existentialist and realist approaches, you may find something that resonates with you and sets off a light bulb. But our take is that finding "the right job" is more of an active process than a philosophical one.

The first step, as cheesy as it sounds, is simply to expand your frame of reference and realize that there are a *lot* of options out there (see page 133 to start brainstorming). But at a certain point, you've got to bite the bullet and go for something. If you like it, then you've chosen well; if not, then you've at least narrowed down the field and picked up some valuable perspective. Finding the job you love often comes down to a process of elimination. That's totally fine—who wants their story to be completely predictable, anyway?

In this chapter, we'll help you size up the job market, figure out what you might want to do, and then find the openings that interest you most. In addition, we'll highlight a few popular options like government and nonprofit work, as well as some of the ways you can avoid the rat race and take control of your career destiny. Then, once you've got your targets in the crosshairs, move on to Chapter 4 for all the tips you'll need to follow through and get the job.

Top Five Things to Do Before You Get a Job

It's often said that "searching for a job is a job in itself." Like most maxims, there's some truth to that, but it would be insane not to do anything else with your time. In fact, the worst thing that you can do while job hunting is to do nothing but look for employment. There are a bunch of things that you can do to improve your prospects before you even have a "job"-job, and many of them have the added benefit of keeping you sane. In fact, any of these five options is a fantastic way to begin your career story.

1. Get an internship or volunteer (paid or unpaid) position. This common exchange of your time for experience and a few resume bullets not only makes you a better job candidate, but it also allows you to get your foot in the door of an organization and to build your network. (For more on internships, see page 156; for information on volunteering, see page 432).

2. Build a new skill set. When you have nothing else to do, learn something! This can be anything from mastering a language that will help you secure a niche job, to developing a skill like computer programming that will allow you to freelance for money. And today, with the plethora of free tutorial websites and local meetup groups, you can easily do all this for free (see page 418). One thing is for sure: Employers dig skills.

3. Consider graduate school. If you didn't land a job right out of college but you know you're interested in a career path that requires an advanced degree, now may be the time to get the testing and essay writing out of the way. When the time comes to actually apply and you're bogged down with work, you'll be thankful you already have this stuff done. (For more on grad school, see page 161.)

4. Freelance or temp. Sometimes you just can't afford to take that unpaid internship or double-up on student debt and go to grad school. When that's the case, consider freelance (p. 151) or temp work (p. 38).

Essentially, you'll be earning cash and getting your foot in the door of various companies. There are countless tales of freelance and temp gigs turning into full-time paying jobs.

5. Travel abroad. While we all have dreams of jetting around the world à la Brangelina, traveling after school doesn't always have to be expensive, nor does it need to involve the adoption of foreign orphans. You can hostel-hop or even find a money-generating gig out of the country, like teaching English as a second language. Maybe you can even find a grant from your school or a national organization. (For more on traveling on the cheap, see page 46.)

No matter which option you choose to pursue, make sure that you can leverage it to help you secure career opportunities down the road. ■

Understanding Your Ideal Job Profile: Function, Organization, and Industry

Whether you're ready to pursue a job today or are just planning ahead, it's a good idea to start looking at jobs in terms of *function*, *organization*, and *industry*. To do so, think about how your friends tend to talk about jobs. "I'm good with numbers—I think I'd make a fine accountant," one person might say. "Ever since I threw up on Mickey Mouse after riding the teacups at the Magic Kingdom, I've loved Disney; it's my dream to work there," says another. "Ladies," exclaims the third, "Just look at me: I mean, how could I *not* work in fashion?"

These declarations of intent may all sound similar, but there's a subtle difference between them. Check it: Accounting is a specific job *function*, and you can do it at many different companies across almost any industry (every business needs to keep its books in order). Disney is an *organization*, and its size dictates a lot about it (including the fact that it's large enough to employ that

Tips & Tricks: Let your newspaper guide the way

One simple litmus test for figuring out what job you should get is suggested by Lindsey Pollak in her book *Getting from College to Career*: Start picking up the paper every morning and see what section you gravitate toward. Do you hone in on the front page or flip straight to the arts section? Are you more interested in the stock prices or the box scores? It seems kind of silly, but it makes sense. As a whole, a good newspaper provides a representative swath of what's going on in the world. Whatever you find most interesting is probably where you should focus your efforts.

creepy person in the Mickey Mouse suit). Finally, fashion describes an *industry*, but it leaves a lot of questions unanswered. Does your friend want to be a model? Would she like to do public relations for an up-and-coming designer? Or how about working as a buyer at a national department store?

Understanding these distinctions is crucial to a smart job hunt. One trap a lot of recent grads fall into is immediately obsessing over a specific position (e.g., "I want to be the editorial assistant for the music reviews section at *Rolling Stone*"). While it's great to have a particular goal, you severely limit your chances of success in the job market if you maintain such a narrow view of what your first job should look like. As headhunting pro Maxine Martens says, "Instead of looking at one job, you should be saying, 'Who needs me?' and, 'What [function] do I want to do?' When people are very focused on the specific job, it has less resonance."

By all means, apply to your dream job, but don't forget to apply to other similar jobs, as well. By looking at how job functions, organizations, and industries play into one another, you can begin to make sense of the job market and where you will eventually fit into it. To help you get started, we've provided an overview of your options as they relate to these three areas.

Industry

From the advertising-obsessed *Mad Men* fanatic to the travel nut who selects hotels based on the thread count of their sheets, some people find themselves intrinsically drawn toward a specific industry. That's cool, and we say follow your instincts. But sometimes, it's worth seasoning those instincts with some reality sauce. For example, if you want to get into the newspaper industry, it's likely going to be difficult to find a good opportunity in the current climate, so maybe you can figure out how to pursue the same function—writing—in a new media environment. Alternatively, it might pay to focus on the industries with the brightest or the safest prospects (see "Which Industries Are the Safest in a Recession?" on the next page).

Here's a smattering of industries to whet your appetite.

1. Hospitality (e.g., hotels, restaurants, clubs, bars, resorts)

2. Retail (e.g., boutiques, chain stores, department stores)

3. Commercial Finance (e.g., banks, investment firms)

4. Real Estate (e.g., construction, investment, management)

5. Consumer Goods (e.g., household products, toy manufacturers)

6. Fashion/Beauty (e.g., cosmetics companies)

7. Publishing (e.g., book publishers, magazines)

8. Journalism/Media (e.g., newspapers, blogs, TV, radio, online video hubs)

9. Energy (e.g., oil companies, solar panel producers)

10. Entertainment (e.g., film, music labels, talent agencies)

11. Software (e.g., Oracle and Microsoft)

12. Aerospace (e.g., plane manufacturers, NASA)

13. Insurance (e.g., automobile insurance, home insurance)

14. Telecommunications (e.g., cell phone network providers)

> **Tips & Tricks: The wide world of health**
>
> While many people associate a career in health with becoming a doctor, being an MD is just one option amongst many that contribute to the wellbeing of humans. There are a ton of different jobs in health care—you could do sales for a pharmaceutical company, work in PR at a health care firm, become a social worker, deliver care in developing countries with a nonprofit, and more. If you have a particular skill or interest, chances are there's a way to explore or leverage it within the health care sector.

Career Options

15. Health (e.g., hospitals, device manufacturers, pharmaceuticals)

16. Government (e.g., political offices, various state and federal departments)

17. Education (e.g., schools, administration)

18. Food and Beverage (e.g., beer and wine companies, snack food companies)

19. Agriculture (e.g., farms, government organizations)

Which Industries Are the Safest in a Recession?
by Alexandra Levit

Alexandra Levit is a nationally syndicated Wall Street Journal columnist and author of such books as New Job, New You: A Guide to Reinventing Yourself in a Bright New Career *and* They Don't Teach Corporate in College. *We asked her to weigh in on a question we've been asked repeatedly by the Gradspot community.*

A lot of people ask about the best types of jobs to pursue during an economic recession. It's not surprising that when people see constant news about ailing industries like finance and print media, they wonder if *all* jobs are likely to disappear in the next five years. What I tell them is this: While no job in the world will ever have complete security, there are many industries that are considered more "recession-proof" than others. Here are a few of my favorites:

Health Care: While the debate about health care is divisive, you can bet there will be a lot more government spending making its way to the industry. There is already a major labor shortage in nursing, and this is only bound to increase as the boomers continue to age and need more services, more often. Others will continue to get sick and be treated whether they can afford care or not. In fact, according to the site WheretheJobsAre.org, there are more than 54,000 projected hires in medical and public health positions by 2012.

Education: Children in the United States are still guaranteed schooling until the 12th grade, and many states are perennially experiencing teacher shortages, especially as a large number of current teachers reach retirement age. Also, laid-off or unsatisfied adults are returning to school in record numbers, creating opportunities in adult education. (See page 169 for more on teaching degrees and careers in education.)

Accounting: Don't lump this one in with "finance." It has been hot since federal regulations forced companies to get serious about their books a few years ago, and when times are tough, more people look for accountants to help them pinch every penny they can. To become a Certified Public Accountant (CPA), you'll need to pass the Uniform CPA Exam, which requires serious studying and potential prep courses beforehand. Google "State Boards of Accountancy" to find the eligibility requirements to sit for the exam in your state.

Agriculture and Utilities: The economy may be sickly, but the first things people pay for are food to eat and gas to heat their homes. These jobs are not affected by the loss of discretionary income and will remain intact.

Local Service Sector: Every town needs at least one plumber, electrician, and hairstylist. During a recession, just make sure you live somewhere where the demand outweighs the supply.

Local, State, and Federal Government: The government keeps on chugging, even when the country's in a hole. Generally speaking, budget cuts don't tend to affect the jobs of public safety officers, court clerks, administrative service managers, and other such positions. (For more information on government jobs, see page 141.) ■

Career Options

Organization

Many people will zero in on a particular organization where they want to work. But what is it about that organization that they like? Is it the actual company (e.g., they've wanted to work for F.A.O. Schwartz ever since seeing *Big*)? Or is it the "type" of organization (e.g., small, large)? These are two very important factors when considering which organization you want to work for.

If you are dead set on a specific company and want to get your foot in the door today, focus on the long-term and don't let the quality of the jobs offered today derail your pursuit. Few people would willingly choose "intern" or "administrative assistant" from a lineup of job titles at a company. But if you ask them if they want to be an "account manager" or a "vice president" at that same company, they'd probably sing a different tune. Sometimes you just have to start in the proverbial mailroom.

While we're all about your applying to your dream employer, just consider that it might not be wise to put all of your job-hunting eggs in only the basket of a single company. After all, what happens if there's a hiring freeze? According to Jason Hill, a managing partner at a staffing firm in New York, you should always pursue your dream company while also casting a wider net: "If you want to work at Goldman Sachs, for example, you should be thinking, 'Who are Goldman's competitors?' And then you should network with people at those firms, schedule informational interviews, and research what the companies are all about." You should also be looking at companies that act as feeders into the company that is your first choice.

Whether you've chosen to pursue a specific company or not, it's important to recognize that each organization fits into a general 'type' related to its size, culture, and way of doing business. Clearly, there are organizations that buck the trend (in the same way there are Swiss people who are actually quite bellicose). But it's worth considering the most common pros and cons associated with each so that you can figure out which types fit your personality, skills, and career goals best.

Large Corporation (e.g., Target, JPMorgan, Johnson & Johnson)

Pretty much any company whose ads you've seen or products you've used would fall within this category.

Pros: Formalized training, extensive benefits, job security (sort of), room for advancement, resume-building, geographically diverse assignments (including international locations), vast resources.

Cons: Bureaucratic, potential to be pigeonholed into functional role, lack of autonomy, slow advancement, "corporate" culture off-putting to some people.

Career Options

Professional Service Firm (e.g., Skadden Arps, Deloitte, Ogilvy & Mather)

These are firms that provide financial, legal, accounting, advertising, consulting, or other services to large corporations.

Pros: Hands-on training, high-level work, very good benefits, strong network-building potential, large class of young colleagues, resume-building, great pay.

Cons: Intense work schedule, tough to maintain work/life balance (i.e., you may travel frequently or be constantly on-call for clients), lower job security (if a client leaves, firm loses staff), high turnover typical, managers inconsistently interested in junior staff, very hierarchical.

Start-Up Company (e.g., Twitter, Bonobos)

This is a growth-oriented new company that is in its early stages of development. If it's a real start-up, you probably haven't heard of it yet, unless someone you know is working there or you surf the start-up blogs. (For more on start-ups, see page 139.)

Pros: Exciting pace, quick advancement, skill-building, ability to influence decisions, relationship-building with colleagues, low bureaucracy, chance to gain equity, less "corporate" environment.

Tips & Tricks: Look at mid-sized and small companies

Particularly in a competitive job market, it's key to expand your search beyond big companies. Smaller companies can have specific hiring needs at any given time, and their scale allows them to be a bit stealthier than their unwieldy competitors. To capitalize as a hunter, you too must be stealthy, because opportunities at these companies don't always show up on job boards. A great first place to start is *Inc.* magazine's "Inc. 5000" (available at inc500.com). It's an annual report of the fastest-growing private companies in America, many of which have 50 employees or less. In addition, be vigilant about tracking industry news to see who the new movers and shakers are. If a company just received venture capital funding, launched a breakout product or service, or got acquired by a larger entity, be the first one at the gates to vie for openings that arise from an expansion or reshuffling. In this case, showing up at the gates might mean cold calling. The good news is, you're a lot more likely to get through to someone in a hiring position at a smaller company than when you attempt to navigate the labyrinth of a large corporation.

Career Options

129

Cons: Limited resources, low job security, low success rate, potential low pay, lack of good benefits (sometimes), high commitment (expectation to "live and breathe" the company), less structured.

Small Business/Office (e.g., doctor's office, independent store/service)

These are businesses with staffs of 100 people or less. Most businesses fall within this category.

Pros: Low bureaucracy, flexibility, skill-building/practical know-how, high client interaction (good if you're a people person).

Cons: Fewer resources, lower job security, less generous benefits, often personality-driven, less well-known/reduced resume cachet, ceiling on advancement, functionally oriented roles.

Nonprofit and Government (e.g., Clinton Foundation, Department of Labor)

In very simple terms, these are organizations or entities that work towards the achievement of a specific goal or that tackle/manage a set of issues (rather than seek to make a fiscal profit). Examples include all branches of federal, state, and local government, as well as NGOs, museums, universities, hospitals, and local charitable organizations. For more on government jobs, see page 141; for nonprofits, go to page 146.

Pros: Pro-social mission, job security, good work-life balance, potentially interesting work.

Cons: Bureaucratic, slow advancement, potentially low pay, frustration arising from lack of funding and/or resources.

Function

Every grad should have a dream. But once you've finished indulging abstract fantasies like

---

Tips & Tricks: Top entry-level employers

If you're not sure which organizations to target, why not start with the ones most likely to hire someone of your experience level? Seems like a smart move to us. Luckily for you, every year CollegeGrad.com compiles a list of companies that hire the greatest number of entry-level employees, which includes familiar names like Verizon Wireless, Progressive Insurance, and Boeing. But have you ever heard of BearingPoint, Epic Systems, and Schlumberger? It's definitely worth taking a browse through the list over at collegegrad.com/topemployers, which also includes a link to their top internships list as well.

having "a career in film" or "working with animals," it's time to think about what you actually want to do on a day-to-day basis. This doesn't mean you should give up on film and/or animals (after all, the *Air Bud* director did pretty well for himself). It simply means that you should be honest with yourself about whether going on coffee runs for a director or grooming show cats will really fulfill you on a daily basis and help you meet your career goals. While a prestigious company or the allure of a certain industry may seem cool for a second, the things you actually *do* at work are what will determine whether you are happy or not and move your career forward.

If you think you know exactly what you want to do professionally, then speak to people who are doing it and figure out if you can jump in right after college or if you're going to have to take a more circuitous route from a job-function perspective (i.e., it's a great idea to work for an accountant before you decide to become one). In order to truly succeed you also need to enjoy what you're doing. So if the thought of sitting at a desk behind a computer all day (note: playing video games and surfing Perez Hilton doesn't count) scares you, you should consider a job that involves more extensive and regular face-to-face interaction, like a sales position or a job in a hospitality organization. If you like to play with spreadsheets and numbers, then maybe finance or accounting would be a good fit. And if you're not sure what you'd like to do at all, talk to people who perform different functions and ask them what their typical day looks like. They may give you the old "my job is so exciting, there is no typical day" line. Don't let them off the hook that easily; ask them what their most boring day looks like—and find out how often these days occur. Better yet, try to follow them around for a day or two.

In addition, when exploring job functions, recognize that in the working world you can often leverage your natural talents more fully than you did at school. In academia, there are few classes where being hilarious or being able to sweet-talk clients really helps you that much. But out there beyond the ivory tower, there are jobs that match all sorts of talents. Do you have a nice way with children? Do you have an extraordinarily refined palate? Can you stay up extremely late? All of these are marketable skills in the working world. The key is to determine where your talents will be valued and then figure out how to sell them effectively.

If you're still not sure what the hell we mean by "function" and are slightly scared we're talking about something to do with math, here are some examples of high-level functions to give you an idea:

1. Management

2. Sales

3. Advertising

4. Finance

5. Operations

6. Accounting

7. Human Resources

8. Research/Product Development

9. Design/Production

10. Technology

11. Legal

12. Copywriting

13. IT

14. Sales

15. Public Relations

A company of significant size will have staff in every high-level function described above. For example, at General Mills there are Managers, Marketers, Finance Staff, Operations Staff, Accounting, Human Resources, R&D, etc. They'll also have more specialized functions. And there are even more functions that don't even require the confines of a big corporate structure. To explore these, step into The Wide World of Jobs!

The Wide World of Jobs

Sometimes the pre-graduation job rush can make the working world feel remarkably small and generic. As so many of your classmates vie for similar jobs, it's easy to forget that in addition to traditional career paths, there are thousands of niche jobs (and just plain bizarre jobs) that might appeal to you if you keep an open mind. Take the time to consider jobs that you may have never heard of—they are often the most interesting. We don't necessarily expect you to find your calling by looking at the list below, but here are 51 not-so-average jobs to get the wheels turning…

Environmental Engineer	Internet Entrepreneur	Franchise Owner
Archaeologist	Graphic Designer	PR Executive
Nonprofit Fundraiser	Sommelier	Dog Walker
Astronaut	Advertising Salesperson	Chef
Civil Servant	Photographer	Fashion Buyer
Car Reviewer	Website Programmer	Video Game Tester
Travel Writer	College Student Advisor	Interior Designer
Tutor	Musician	Personal Assistant
Pharmacist	Social Worker	Radiologist
Alaskan Crab Fisherman	Ski/Surf Instructor	Tour Guide
Teacher/Professor	A&R Rep	Flight Attendant
Wedding Planner	Head Hunter	Blogger
Construction Manager	HR Manager	Actor
Real Estate Agent	Farmer	Financial Advisor
Paralegal	Talent Agent	Art Gallery Manager
Management Consultant	Truck Driver	Actuary
Stock Agent	Airline Pilot	Computer Systems Analyst

Career Options

Changing Industries, Functions, and/or Organizations

As your career story evolves, it's likely that you will want to switch it up in terms of the function you play at work, the type of organization you work at, or the industry in which you work (or all three). There's no reason why you can't try out a number of different combinations over the course of your life, but be strategic about how you do so.

"You can change your functional area or the industry you're in, but it's tough to change both at the same time," says Michelle Kedem, a cofounder of recruitment firm On-Ramps. For example, if you do HR for a pharmaceutical company and you really want to do marketing for a book publisher, you might consider using your HR background to snag a publishing job and then change functions once you've established yourself in the company.

Another approach to making a big switcheroo is to be willing to start at the bottom, possibly even as an intern. In some cases, grad school (p. 161) can also provide a natural way to shift toward a new career, though you need to go into it with a clear goal. Beyond that, there's always good old-fashioned elbow grease (and luck).

Researching Career Options, Companies, and Industries

Whether you've decided to pursue a specific career or are just exploring your options, there are a ton of online resources that provide background information on companies and industries as a whole. These sites also provide cover letter and resume writing advice, job search tips, and useful tools. For our advice on resumes and cover letters, check out Chapter 4.

Gradspot.com (listed first due to contractual obligations!). If you don't find what you're looking for in this book, check out our website for over 100 survival guides and tons of other content to help you with your job hunt (and anything else life after college throws your way).

Vault.com. If you haven't come across it yet, Vault is a key piece of weaponry in your job-hunting arsenal. The website offers free company rankings in many different industries that can provide a useful overview of who the players are in any given field. The most invaluable tools, however, are its industry guides ($15–$20), which provide a pretty good rundown on what employers are looking for in that industry, along with sample interview questions and other goodies. And while the job board section is kind of a dud, the comprehensive company guides ($16.65 per month) have relevant information on specific companies (though you can most likely find a lot of the same stuff with some Googling). Just make sure to check with your college career office before shelling out any cash; many colleges offer their students free access to Vault.

WetFeet.com and Glassdoor.com. WetFeet is an extensive online "magazine" for job seekers, providing articles about the job search, as well as industry and company overviews. It's a good complement to the job-hunting tips you'll find on Gradspot. Glassdoor is like a cheat sheet for interviews: Previous candidates who interviewed at particular companies give the lowdown on the questions they were asked. It also provides company reviews and salary information.

Occupational Outlook Handbook (www.bls.gov/oco). Produced by the Bureau of Labor Statistics, this handbook provides you with important information for a ton of different jobs—including education and training required, earnings, working conditions, and what the role entails on a day-to-day basis. If you have some idea of what job or field you might like (i.e., "I want to be an engineer but am not sure what kinds of engineering work is out there"), this is a resource that will allow you to dig deeper.

Salary.com. It's basically what it says it is: information on how much you will make in certain jobs in a given geographic location. If you're thinking of moving to a new city to pursue a job, match up your expected salary with average rents to see if you'll be living large or living on the streets (p. 72).

Your college's career office. Your school's career center is the last bit of college handholding you will receive on your way out the door, so take advantage of it. Your career center may provide information on getting a job (where to look, how to write

> ### Tips & Tricks: The X-factor: job location
>
> In addition to industry, organization, and function, there's a fourth factor to consider when weighing job options: location. For example, if you grew up in a certain area and want to stay there, your search should reflect that. Or, if you're just dying to live in Seattle, you should look for a job with one of the big employers in the vicinity (e.g., Amazon) and adjust your industry goals accordingly. And if you're dead set on a certain industry and willing to take a risk, you may be better off moving to the hub of that industry. For a sample list of big industries in popular recent grad cities, see page 71.

Career Options

your resume, how to dress, etc.), have industry and company reconnaissance, and even offer resume review, mock interviews and other job hunt preparation services.

We've just highlighted the key resources you need to research a variety of careers. However, they are by no means the final word. Some other helpful websites include QuintCareers.com, OneDayOneJob.com, and JobWeb.com. And don't forget about actual people—chatting with people you know can also help to crystallize your goals and help you figure out how to make the next step.

Interview: Doing What You Love

After meeting at the University of Pennsylvania, emcee Naledge and producer Double-O formed the rap duo Kidz in the Hall. In 2006, they released their critically acclaimed debut School Was My Hustle *on Rawkus Records. We talked to Naledge about translating an Ivy League degree into a rap career.*

What other careers did you consider when you left college? I was interested in music journalism, public relations, and possibly advertising. Whatever I ended up doing was going to involve the world of media and entertainment.

How did you make the decision to pursue music full-time? I did what most of us artists call "jumping off the ledge." I just quit my job cold turkey and told myself I was going to either sink or swim. I lived for a year as a starving artist in Los Angeles. Eventually I made enough contacts and got enough people interested in my music that I knew a deal was going to come. I wouldn't have been able to survive if it wasn't for the money I saved while I worked at a public relations firm.

Did you receive any discouragement from parents, friends, or teachers? My parents supported me 100%. To most of my teachers, hip-hop music was a foreign world, so they would often stress to me that I needed to use my education as a backup plan. Most of my friends thought I was crazy to not go the conventional route and get a corporate job. Most of them didn't think that I could really get a record deal. Oddly, they are the same ones that say they believed in me all along.

Do you have any advice for recent graduates who feel pressure to get a traditional job instead of pursuing their passions? Chasing your true passion is always going to be more rewarding, but it is key to be realistic about your situation. Sometimes you will need to supplement your passion with a "9-to-5."

Are there good and bad reasons for getting involved in a creative industry? The monetary return is not always great, but you will be much more emotionally rich. ■

Where to Actually Find a Full-Time Job

A job search is a rite of passage, and no rite of passage would be complete without a ritual. Don't worry, you don't have to shave a Labradoodle and burn its hair in a terra cotta oven—this ritual is all about making a commitment to scan job listings on a regular basis. It can become a bit of an obsession, but that's okay—you don't want to miss out on an awesome job just because you don't have your head in the game.

After browsing the major sites like Monster.com, CareerBuilder.com, Indeed.com and, yes, Craigslist, it's time to get down to the nitty-gritty. Each industry has its go-to destination for job postings, so it's important to know where to look. While you're at it, always take advantage of any job leads your school can send your way.

Your Alma Mater. Recent college grads have three unique and effective resources at their fingertips, and many grads get their jobs through one of these avenues:

1. *College Office of Career Services.* Not only will the office hook you up with other alums on similar career paths, but it may also furnish you with openings from companies that are specifically targeting your

Career Options

school, on-campus interviews, and networking sessions with companies interested in hiring.

2. *Alumni networks.* For some reason, Hoyas like helping other Hoyas, Tarheels follow Tarheels, and so on and so forth. Contacting fellow alumni can put you on the receiving end of some odd reminiscences (you might not want to know about the Class of '66's penchant for streaking), but it is a must for anybody on the job hunt.

3. *Professors.* Often, the people with the coolest jobs are the ones who were set up by professors that took an interest in their futures. Think about professors with whom you've developed a special rapport and talk to them. They might have some great ideas.

Investment Banking & Consulting. The best time to apply for an entry-level finance or consulting position is in the late summer to early fall, a year before you'd start working. Since most major banks and consulting firms have structured programs for their entry-level employees, they hire the majority of their recent grads during this time. Your first step should be to try applying through your career office, which may have preexisting recruiting relationships with companies. However, if you've been otherwise instructed, or a specific firm that you're interested in doesn't recruit on your campus, you can apply to any of the major banks and consulting firms directly through their websites. Investment banks like Citigroup and Goldman Sachs accept online applications, as do consulting firms such as Boston Consulting Group, Bain & Company, McKinsey, Monitor, and Mercer. Note that this list doesn't even scratch the surface for potential employers in these fields. You should also check out a financial headhunter organization (e.g., glocap.com) that can find you placements at a

---

Tips & Tricks: Networking now and later

The job hunt is an involved—not to mention competitive—process. Making a commitment to start networking early and often will be invaluable as your hunt heats up. If you're not sure about what you want to do, exploratory networking is a good first step. Talk to as many people as possible to get a sense of what fires you up (or makes you want to ralph). Once you're ready to start applying for jobs, then you can start doing some opportunistic networking that will help give you an edge over other candidates. Go to page 198 to learn the networking essentials you'll need to pull off a *coup d'*employment once you're on the hunt.

Career Options

variety of companies, though these companies will generally only work with more experienced candidates.

New Media & Marketing/Advertising. In light of the shifting forms of consumption from traditional media to innovative online formats, marketing/advertising is an incredibly interesting field to get into right now. New media gigs are listed on PaidContent.org and MediaBistro.com, and start-ups are always on the lookout for marketing directors, researchers, and content producers (keep reading for a list of job boards for start-ups). Joining one of the major marketing/advertising companies (e.g., Grey, Ogilvy, BBDO, Digitas, Razorfish) might be a smart first step. Check with your career services office for firms that recruit at your school, and browse the career sections on the websites of any companies that pique your interest.

Publishing & Journalism. If it's a career in publishing or journalism you seek, check out Mediabistro.com, Ed2010.com, Mandy.com, journalism school listings, IWantMedia.com, and even *Variety*. For listings in the book world, BookJobs.com and PublishersMarketplace.com are good options. After surveying those resources, it often helps to go straight to the source in this industry. Track down your favorite websites and publications online, then check to see if they have a "Careers" section. Don't be dismayed if you only see internship programs—while we know you see yourself as editor-in-chief, sometimes internships are the only way to develop the contacts and clips you'll need to get there. (For more on interning, see page 156.) You should also find out who owns the magazine/newspaper/website where you want to work. For example, the Condé Nast media empire includes *Vogue*, *GQ*, *Wired*, and *The New Yorker*. Maybe you know someone at a publication that falls under the same umbrella as the one you want to work at, or maybe you can get a gig at *Teen Vogue* but not *Vanity Fair*—at least you'll gain access to the Condé Nast HR department (and what we hear is a ridiculously delicious cafeteria). That connection alone will give you a leg up on the competition when the next *Vanity Fair* position opens up.

Start-Ups. Becoming CEO of a start-up company is easy—just make some business cards and announce your new position on your Facebook profile! However, another (usually better) option for getting involved with a start-up company is to join an existing one. There are thousands of new companies started each year, and there are two distinct approaches to finding the opportunities they create. The first approach is to check out niche sites that list start-up jobs. These include VentureLoop.com, Startuply.com, PartnerUp.com, HotStartupJobs.com, and StartupZone.com, as well as the job listing boards

Career Options

Tips & Tricks: Don't spend money to get a job

Regardless of which career resources you end up using, check with your school's career office prior to shelling out cash for any subscription fees that might pop up. More often than not, career offices will offer free subscriptions to their students and alumni. That said, be prepared to shell out a few dollars here and there for resume photocopies at Kinko's, stamps for mailing applications, etc.

---

of entrepreneur-focused blogs like TechCrunch.com (which is tech-focused), PaidContent.com (publishing and media), and more. The other way to look for an opportunity is to work in reverse: First find the start-ups and then see if they're hiring (keep in mind that a successful start-up— i.e., the type you want to work for—is continuously growing and most likely looking for people). To do this, you just need to stay on top of the industries you're interested in, because people will always be talking about up-and-coming companies. Check out industry rags, read more general magazines like *Entrepreneur* and *Inc.*, and follow relevant blogs and Twitter feeds (p. 212) to stay up on the latest news.

Paralegal & Lab Work. For paralegal positions, check out ParalegalJobs.com, EmploymentSpot.com, or the paralegal jobs forum at Indeed.com. Besides searching for paralegal positions, also look for "legal assistant" gigs. These terms are often used interchangeably, although there is actually a paralegal certification, which requires a bachelor's degree, some coursework, and passing an exam (many firms don't need you to be certified). Along with looking at job boards, identify large firms in your city by going to Vault.com and ILRG.com. Once you've found them, go straight to the companies' websites, which should have an employment section and information about the nature of the position and the experience requirements. If you're considering law school, being a paralegal is a great way to see up close if the lawyer life is right for you. For lab jobs, check out eLabRat.com, lab positions at Indeed.com, or postings at university medical schools.

Entertainment. Want to be a big-time shot caller in Hollywood? Working at an agency is the traditional route for getting a foot in the door in Hollywood, and everyone has to start in the mailroom before moving up to a "desk" (basically acting as an agent's assistant). You can look for these entry-level gigs at Variety.com or go directly to the websites of agencies like United Talent Agency (UTA) and William Morris Endeavor. What about working on a TV show? Or how about theater and music? Again turn to Variety.com but also check out Mandy.com. Mediabistro.com, EntertainmentCareers.net, HollywoodReporter.com, and EntertainmentJobs.com.

Government & Nonprofit. Finding government jobs is unlike searching for any other for-profit opportunity. As a result, we've devoted an entire next section to them. We also discuss the nonprofit industry in detail starting on page 146.

"Other." If you don't see the industry you hope to enter here, don't despair. In fact, the best way to find a job remains your alma mater's career office, because if a company lists a position there, you know it has a vested interest in your school (and, by extension, you). Unfortunately, not even your career office will have every job you want. If it doesn't, head over to your dream employer's website and apply directly. If you

> ### Tips & Tricks: Get ahead of the job market
>
> In a depressed market, the top jobs go fast. Savvy hunters know to cast their nets wide. This isn't to suggest you shouldn't aim high, but while hunting for your dream job, don't overlook second-tier opportunities. It's likely that you are well-qualified (or even over-qualified) for many of these gigs, which increases your chance of landing one. While less-savvy hunters spend their time and energy vying only for the top jobs (often in vain), they miss out on less "glamorous" openings by the time they figure out they should have been looking at them. While the idea of taking a job that might be "below you" is a little depressing, it ensures that you'll stay in the game and puts you in a position to move up as the market improves. Sometimes getting ahead means starting from the bottom up. It might feel like a step in the wrong direction, but you'll meet new people, expand your network, and pick up skills that you can leverage to get a great job when the market softens.

know the industry that interests you but not the companies that might have openings, check out one of the job information resources we listed on page 130 to find lists of the top employers by industry. Finally, you can always cold call a company to find out what positions they have available. You've got nothing to lose, and you could end up being tipped off about a job that has not yet been publicly announced.

Government Jobs

Though Walmart is forever doing its damndest to catch up, the largest employer in the United States remains the government, so we thought it made sense to dig a little deeper into various opportunities offered by Uncle Sam.

Career Options

A lot of grads think about government jobs in extremes, conjuring up visions of low-paid, bored public servants who wile away their days as a cog in the bureaucracy, or slick, trench coat-wearing FBI agents who graduated at the top of their Ivy League class. But when you consider the thousands of agencies at the federal, state, and local levels, there's no way to stereotype government gigs. And as the Baby Boomers head towards retirement and money from the government stimulus package starts getting kicked around, there are expected to be over one million government jobs created over the next ten years.

In addition to offering an unlimited variety of positions, the government is an ideal employer for recent grads because it offers excellent job security (workers joke that only an act of Congress could threaten their job); a reasonably good salary (salaries start at $27,000, and long-term salaries can exceed $100k); and great benefits, retirement plans, and student debt forgiveness ($10,000 per year, up to $60,000 total).

If we've piqued your interest, let's consider some of the options you can pursue at the three main levels of government: federal, state, and local. Before you dive into this job pool, be sure to clean up your Facebook profile (see page 182); we hear the CIA is a stake-holder.

Federal Jobs

The federal government alone has over 1.9 million employees. That's not hard to imagine when you consider that it's composed of over 100 different agencies, from the Department of Education to the CIA. And the best part? They're all understaffed! Enter you.

Pick an Agency, Any Agency

The first step in looking for a federal job is to figure out what's important to you. Do you have a finance background and want to apply it to monetary policy at the Fed? Did September 11th change your entire *raison d'etre* and inspire you to help protect America in Homeland Security? Regardless of your goals, a great place to start exploring opportunities is the exhibit published by the U.S. Office of Personnel Management's (OPM) that matches undergrad majors to agencies, located at http://www.usajobs.opm.gov/ei23.asp. Or, you can begin by just browsing a list of federal agencies at USA.gov. Finally, take some time to check out "The Best Places to Work in the Federal Government" (data.bestplacestowork.org)—the result of an annual employee satisfaction report—as well as "Where the Jobs Are" (data.wherethejobsare.org), a continually updated report of projected job openings at agencies. Just keep in mind that as you peruse the smorgasbord of federal agencies, some might be located in D.C., while others (85%) are scattered across the U.S., and 44,000 position are housed abroad.

Classifications of Jobs

There are two different ways that federal jobs are classified: according to preferred applicant criteria and according to pay scale. When it comes to applicant criteria, Competitive Service positions are open to anyone, but Excepted Service positions favor candidates with specific credentials (e.g., veterans).

Pay is measured according to the General Schedule (GS) pay scale, which ranges from GS-1 to GS-15. As a recent college graduate, you should be looking at jobs classified between GS-5 and GS-7, which have average starting salaries of between $27,000 and $33,000, respectively. If you go to grad school first, you'll be able to enter most agencies at GS-9, with a starting salary of $44,000. (See page 161 for more information on grad school.)

Where to Find Federal Openings

Once you've determined which agency might make sense for you, the best place to look for an opening is www.usajobs.gov. While a majority of federal government opportunities are listed there, some will be listed exclusively on the specific agency's website, and thus it's always worth looking at both. You can also give govcentral.monster.com a glance—it's more of a free for all, but you never know when you might find something perfect that you would have otherwise missed.

Applying to Federal Positions

When applying, attention to detail is key. Many agencies will enable you to fill out an entire application online (usually through www.usajobs.gov or their own website), but be mindful that your resume for a government job will have to be more comprehensive than one for a private sector application (see page 185 for more on resumes). Many agencies will request a resume that lists all of your work experience, the number of hours you worked per week at each, and what you were paid. So don't be surprised if your resume goes beyond one page; this is the one time that's okay. For certain jobs, you'll also have to complete a Knowledge, Skills and Abilities (KSA) assessment. Throughout the application process, resist the temptation to lie, even about drugs. The truth will

Career Options

come out, whether through a polygraph (administered if you require security clearance) or extensive background checks.

When interview time rolls around, treat it just like you would any other job (see page 218 for interview tips). Be prepared to explain why you want a government job, why your past experiences position you as a strong candidate, and why you'll add value to the team, agency, government, and ultimately, country.

Selected agencies: Agriculture Research Service, AmeriCorps, Census Bureau, Central Intelligence Agency, Consumer Product Safety Commission, Corporation for National Service, Department of Labor, Department of Education, Department of Health and Human Services, Department of Homeland Security, Department of Transportation, Federal Bureau of Investigation, Federal Reserve Bank of Chicago, Federal Trade Commission, Library of Congress, National Park Service, Patent and Trademark Office, Peace Corps, Smithsonian Institute, US Air Force, and many more. (For a more comprehensive list, visit www.govtjobs.com/jobsourc.html.)

Capitol Hill

Remember that annoying kid in middle school whose sole aspiration was to be elected as the student body president? Fast forward ten years and he or she is probably working in D.C., proudly proclaiming, "I work on the Hill!" While many people use the terms "Capitol Hill" and "D.C." interchangeably, Capitol Hill actually refers to a specific subset of the federal government—most notably, positions with congressmen, senators, and lobbyists. Not surprisingly, it's a breeding ground for politicians and people who want to network with decision-makers. While the pay is not great and the hours can be more grueling than other government jobs, many people think Capitol Hill is an unparalleled place to start a successful career in anything.

Finding Capitol Hill Jobs

There are two approaches to looking for opportunities. The first is traditional networking. Try to snag a position with a representative from your state and comb your personal network to see if you have any connections. If that route doesn't have legs, you can default to job boards. RCJobs.com and OPAJobs.com offer a smattering of full-time opportunities, and HillZoo.com offers a mixture of full-time and intern work.

While working around any congressperson can be a big career boost, we recommend zeroing in on issues you really care about and then searching for the representatives that focus on those issues. Are you interested in legislation regarding refugees? Did you write a thesis on health care? Are you passionate about environmental policy?

Again, attending graduate school will open more doors in which to place your foot, but you'll have to decide for yourself whether the time and money spent on grad school are necessary for what you want to do professionally.

Working on Capitol Hill

The most common entry-level positions are Staff Assistant gigs. Essentially, you're the representative's slave: You'll have to answer the phones, sort through mail, receive appointments, do research, manage interns, and generally be the office factotum. Ultimately, however, your lifestyle will depend upon the representative that you work for; if he or she is a "family person" that goes home by 7pm most nights, so will you. But it could easily go the other way. In addition to Staff Assistant, you should also consider interning (interns are called "pages" on the Hill), which is a great way to test the waters and get a foot in the door.

State & Local Agencies

State and local governments employ approximately eight million Americans and are planning to hire another 1.4 million within the next ten years. When job prospects are looking rough, this is the employer to turn to.

The Difference between Federal and Local and State

Local and state governments are literally the local versions of the federal government, with some extra offices. For example, there's a Federal Department of Transportation, and there's a local and state one, as well. There's Congress, and then there's the State Assembly. Conveniently enough, local and state positions are easier to snag, and you have more geographic security because you know you'll always be working in your state. According to the Bureau of Labor Statistics, work schedules are also more lenient. On the flip side, the pay scale for local and state positions is slightly lower than federal, but it's still competitive.

Tips & Tricks: Campaign

Whether you volunteer for a political campaign or work as a full-time staffer, the experience you'll get in this high-stakes environment can be huge when you're applying for a government job. Look out for local election posters, browse local papers for major legislation, and stop by your city or town hall to see if there's any way you can lend a hand. Candidates and groups pushing legislation will have websites providing clear instructions on how to join the cause. And don't think this is only appropriate if you want a job on Capitol Hill. It can also help if you want to pursue opportunities in state and local government, as well. The best part is that if the campaign goes well, there might be a job waiting for you when your boss becomes mayor (or whatever he or she was running for).

Finding a Local or State Position

Locating job opportunities on the local and state level is a bit trickier than it is on the federal level. Most state agencies won't post jobs on major boards, instead keeping them on their own websites. Tracking them down requires some handy-dandy Googling and use of the admittedly shady-looking directory of local and state government job websites found on 50statejobs.com/gov.html. Govcentral.monster.com is worth a shot—when you search it, make sure to include "State of…" and "City of…" as keywords. If you're more interested in the local politician route (e.g., working for a state assemblyman or mayor), you should take a similar approach as you would for finding a Capitol Hill job (see page 144). Look for connections, browse the boards, or find issues that matter to you and then match them with politicians' causes.

Selected state and local agencies: State Assembly, Tax and Finance Department, Thruway Department, Job Bank, Power Authority, Department of Education, Department of Health, Office of the Advocate for Persons with Disabilities, Department of Civil Service, Department of the Lottery, Liquor Authority, Office of Children and Family Services, Department of Labor, and more (especially depending upon which city or state you're looking at).

Nonprofit Jobs

Although the government is a nonprofit entity, most people associate nonprofit work with "doing something good for the world," not working for the Department of Transportation. But even this distinction is thin—there are over ten million U.S. citizens working for nongovernmental nonprofits, and you can be sure that not all of them spend their days saving Africans or dispensing aid to hurricane survivors. So before you dive into the nonprofit world head (or heart) first, let's take a moment to consider what types of jobs are available, as well as the challenges and rewards you can expect if you take the plunge.

The (Very) Wide World of Nonprofit Jobs

If you can think of a cause you care about, there's most likely a nonprofit that focuses on it. But in addition to things like "rehabilitating dogs with no legs" and "teaching inner-city kids to play badminton," you should think about the institutions and services that serve the greater good—such as public television and museums—since many of these are operated on a not-for-profit basis too. To give you a sense of how varied the nonprofit sector is, here is just a handful of organizations that fall under this umbrella: *American Cancer Society, American Red Cross, Bill & Melinda Gates Society, Carnegie Hall, Council of Better Business Bureaus, Inc., Ford Foundation, Habitat for Humanity, The Metropolitan Museum of Art, National Geographic Society, Planned Parenthood, Ronald McDonald House Charities, National Public Radio, United Nations, The Natural History Museum, and The World Wide Fund For Nature.*

Tips & Tricks: How to get past the resume robots

Because some companies and hiring centers get such an enormous volume of applications, they actually use automated computer programs to serve as a preliminary screening mechanism for resumes. One such resume-scanning system is Resumix, which is used by government agencies. It may sound like something out of *Minority Report*, but it's the way things are, so you need to know how to sweet talk the robots (hint: they have no feelings!). The trick is to "optimize" your resume for the process of being trolled by keyword crawlers. Software like Resumix creates "skill buckets" for every job, based on keywords—if your resume does not contain the skills searched by the robot, then it's *adios, amigo.* Your best bet is to study the language used in the job posting and parrot it back in your resume. ResumeEdge.com suggests that if the posting doesn't actually mention specific skills, you should search for similar jobs and use them to create a list of the top 25 skills required for that job. (You may also be able to find relevant skills by reading profiles of professions on Vault.com.) In addition to skills, the robots will look for required years of experience (if appropriate) or any other basic qualifications, so make sure you meet these and include them in your resume.

Career Options

The Importance of Funding

Unlike for-profit organizations that are capitalized by their shareholders or government organizations that are funded by taxes, nonprofits live and die by funding, which comes primarily in the form of donations from individuals and other organizations (including the government, in some cases). The result is one hell of a double-edged sword for an employee of a nonprofit. On the one hand, it's incredibly exciting to be able to focus all of your effort on a specific cause instead of worrying about financial returns or the public at large. On the other hand, depending upon the economic and political environment, funding can tough to come by, and when the well runs dry, your hands are tied.

The funding issue also trickles down to the everyday realities of nonprofit work in two key ways. First, since resources are so limited, nonprofits can only afford to hire individuals who are able to add value starting day one, which makes it more difficult for a recent grad to snag a nonprofit gig. Second, most nonprofit organizations' employees are generally paid less than an individual fulfilling the same functional role in a for-profit job. (Presumably you're not considering nonprofit work as a get-rich quick scheme, though.)

Ultimately, funding issues may be a hard pill to swallow, but if you're the type to say, "Let's do the best we can with the resources we have," you may flourish in this line of work.

Browsing and Evaluating Nonprofits

Just because a nonprofit supports a cause you believe in doesn't necessarily make it a good organization. You need to research it as you would any other company. The first place to turn is CharityNavigator.org, which provides reviews of nonprofit organizations based on their effectiveness and funding. If you don't know which nonprofits you want to investigate in the first place, a great resource is the "Causes" application on Facebook; just browse through the hundreds of thousands of causes to find associated nonprofits. Once you're sure you believe in an organization's mission, its funding should be the second-most-important characteristic you focus on. A great place to turn to in order to gauge an organization's financial health is GuideStar.org.

If you can't find your target nonprofit in any of these places, that doesn't necessarily mean it's a money-laundering operation. Call them directly to make sure they're a registered 501(c) organization (i.e., a licensed U.S. charity); if you're interested in working there, they should be willing to answer all your questions about funding and milestones.

Nonprofit Considerations

Nonprofits are certainly their own beast. If you choose to go into this line of work, there are a few challenges you're likely to encounter that may be less pronounced (or completely nonexistent) in the private sector jobs.

- **Stretched Workforce.** Because nonprofits are often forced to operate with limited resources, many of them are small in size or stretched for manpower. As a result, employees are often asked to wear many hats and accept a lot of responsibility. For example, you might be hired as an administrative assistant but find yourself working on marketing and accounting as well. Employees are often expected to be motivated by the mission and to put up with low compensation as a result.

- **Slow Progress.** Let's be honest, clothing the homeless and feeding the hungry isn't something that can happen overnight. But because of the stakes, it can be draining to feel like the end goal is never in sight. The trick is to focus on incremental progress and small-scale change. Burnout is common in this type of work if you don't figure out a way to manage your expectations.

- **Bureaucracy.** Given the funding structure of nonprofits, there can be a lot of red tape involved when it comes to revising their missions or shaking things up internally. Even making small changes to how things are done can require seemingly endless paperwork. It's not that big of a deal, but it's also frustrating to know that you have to spend hours filling out forms when you'd rather be working toward the organization's goal.

Applying to Nonprofit Jobs

Nonprofits in general don't plaster job postings all over newspapers, websites, and colleges like for-profit organizations might. Instead, they tend to list openings primarily on their websites or major nonprofit job boards. If you are down to wade through hundreds of openings, then the folks at Idealist. org will quickly become your best friends. (Idealist.org also publishes a free e-book about nonprofits, which you can download from its resources section.)

Career Options

In addition to Idealist, The Foundation Center (http://fconline.foundation-center.org/) offers a great jobs newsletter.

Once you apply for a nonprofit job, steel yourself for a competitive process. While your passion for the cause is practically a prerequisite, it's your relevant skills and prior experience that will set you apart. Remember that nonprofits need people who can fulfill specific functional roles just like for-profit companies. Do you want to be a researcher? Do you want to be in admin (e.g., accounting, HR, fundraising)? Do you want to deliver relief services and be "on the ground?" Thinking about where you fit into an organization is crucial when you're on the job hunt.

Alternative Routes to Finding a Nonprofit Opportunity

If your heart is dead-set on a specific organization and you don't have the skills to snag a position today, look for volunteer positions (p. 432) or internships (p. 156) that will help you build your story, skill set, and resume prior to applying. Another approach is building skills in the for-profit sector and then using those skills to transition to a nonprofit down the line. Indeed, nonprofits often value candidates with private sector experience because many of the job functions are transferable, and they may have important connections to fundraising sources. If you do decide to take this roundabout route into the nonprofit world, just be sure to stay involved with the causes you care about through volunteering or pro bono work. Those private sector paychecks can be addictive though, so watch out!

Another way to dive right into nonprofit work that's custom-made for recent grads is through term of service opportunities. These include positions with organizations like AmeriCorps, the Peace Corps, and Teach for America, and they usually require an initial training period before you're sent off into the field. While they might not pay you a salary, they sometimes provide stipends, benefits, places to live, debt forgiveness, tuition help, and more. (Note: AmeriCorps and Peace Corps are both government agencies, but they provide work opportunities that people would associate more with "nonprofits" than traditional government work, and as a result, provide a great introduction to both the government and nonprofit sectors.)

Freelancing

Are you someone who literally can't stand the idea of working a 9–5? Do you want to set your own hours, name your own price, and rarely get fully dressed? If so, freelancing might be for you. It may take a while to establish yourself, but once you hit your stride as a freelancer, you can work from anywhere, determine your own schedule, accept or refuse projects as you wish, and drink on the job!

Beyond flexibility, freelancing is a great way for recent grads to explore various interests and skills without committing to a full-time position. Plus, in the age of outsourcing, it's becoming increasingly common for companies to seek outside consultants and freelancers who can work on a project-to-project basis. Freelancing is something you can do at the beginning of your career, in between jobs down the road, or even on the side if you have a full-time gig that allows you enough time to work on other projects.

But before you tear up your resume and change into sweatpants, hear this: Getting started as a freelancer is not easy. Instead of job hunting once and then settling into a company, you must be constantly on the prowl for new projects and clients. Once you actually have those clients, it can feel like you have ten bosses instead of just one (even though none of them give you benefits—another drawback of the freelance game). And in addition to doing the actual work, you have to act as your own marketing team, building your brand and getting the word out that you're available for hire. One satisfied client should ideally lead to the next, but in the meantime, prepare to pound the pavement (or the 'net) and live on pasta and PBR. (For tips for marketing yourself, check out the "Make Some Extra Cash" template on page 35.)

What Skills Can I Sell?

Freelancing makes most sense for people who have an existing talent or skill that can be converted into freelance work (e.g., graphic design experience), but anyone can take classes and workshops to gain bankable skills (e.g., massage therapy). Below is a brief list of possible paths to consider.

- Teach a foreign language/translate
- Copyedit for businesses or publications
- Tutor students or adults who want to brush up on a specific subject (p. 127)

Career Options

- Give lessons (music, karate, meditation, whatever you can credibly teach)
- Be a personal chef/cater private events
- Teach yoga/private fitness training
- Astrology (learn to read peoples' charts)
- Dog-walking/pet-sitting (p. 30)
- Be a wedding or event photographer/videographer

Don't overlook the fact that what begins as a freelance experiment could morph into a start-up and ultimately a real company. Be on the lookout for growth opportunities, if that's what you're after. Below, we'll dig into four common examples of freelance pursuits to give you a sense of what to expect and how to get started.

Writing and Editing. If you're a writer or editor, you may be able to find assignments via Craigslist, Indeed.com, MyJambi.com, Sologig.com, Mandy. com, Ed2010.com, or Mediabistro.com. If you're really serious, you'll purchase a copy of the most up-to-date *Writer's Market* (or become a member of the website for $29.99), a resource for writers that has contact information for hundreds of magazines, journals, and agents you can pitch. It also provides pay ranges and guidelines for query letters (i.e., written pitches). Those pay ranges vary drastically, but you can expect anything from $5 per review on a random start-up music website to upwards of $0.50 per word at a legit publication. It's also very common to see gigs that don't pay but will offer "great exposure and resume credentials." Don't take their word for it! If you've never heard of the publication or website, do some research into circulation and web traffic (you can use Compete.com to see how many visitors a site gets), and decide whether you think an article published there will give you credibility when you pitch bigger fish. Writing stuff you don't want to write for other people is not worth it (after all, you've got your own coming-of-age novel to work on), so make sure each assignment fulfills one of three criteria: 1) It will be a great "clip" for your portfolio; 2) It will help you develop a relationship with an editor at a place you want to write more for; or 3) It pays well (or is just cool enough that you're willing to do it for free). Even after you start getting regular gigs, brace yourself for the inevitable ups and downs of the writing world.

Programming. If you have a knack for problem solving, logic games, and cracking awesomely dorky jokes, programming might just be your calling—and a lucrative one it can be. Freelancer programmers can usually bill at $50 to $150 per hour once they've proven their mettle. You can look for gigs on Craigslist, Elance.com, Guru.com, and RentACoder.com or contact programming shops to see if they're looking for any freelance help. However, in an age where everyone and their grandma has a start-up idea, it's definitely worth mining your personal contacts and your parents' network for potential work. Perhaps most important, you should leverage the robust communities that exist in the world of programming—each programming language and platform has its own community—not surprisingly, all of the members live online and share information about gigs.

Graphic Design. You may consider yourself an artist, but you still have to eat. Graphic design is a great way to exercise your creativity while still making a living (not to mention that graphic designers are just plain cool). Large companies regularly farm out design gigs to freelancers, so if you have a degree in this field (or have amassed enough knowledge to know what you're doing), you should be able to break in as a freelancer without too much trouble. Knowledge of the Adobe Suite (PhotoShop, InDesign, Illustrator) is a must, and depending on what type of design work you are doing, you should research other software options as well. But you can figure all that out on-the-fly. According to Benny Gold, a San Francisco–based designer who has worked with companies like Burton and Nike, "The strongest skill you need for design is being able to develop concepts. Almost anyone can learn the programs, but your concept abilities will set you apart." Pay is either hourly ($25 to $200 depending on experience) or project-based ($350 is an average fee for a custom logo design). In graphic design, it is essential to have a website where potential clients can browse your portfolio and familiarize themselves with your capabilities. Your site will become synonymous with your identity as a designer, so it's important to make sure it's well-organized and aesthetically impressive. While it's smart to remain

> **Tips & Tricks: Resources for freelancers**
>
> No matter what your skill or service, there are many resources online where freelancers can connect with each other and potential clients. If you're tired of working alone, visit MeetUp.com or Google for coworking organizations to find freelancer groups where you can get to know others who share your lifestyle. Post an ad on Craigslist and scan the "gigs" section. There's some weird stuff in there, but you may find legit work as well. Ifreelance.com and freelanceauction.com are other sites you can browse according to skill set. Solvate is a company that contracts with freelancers and matches them up with companies who have specific project-based needs. Finally, there are tons of freelance job boards like elance.com, Amazon's Mechanical Turk, oDesk, and many more so it's worth taking a look around.

Career Options

Tips & Tricks: Freelancers are citizens, too

In other words, just because you're a free-lancer doesn't mean you don't have to pay taxes or go to the doctor. If you're fully self-employed you'll have to keep track of your own income and file taxes quarterly (search around online for information on how it works—freelancers love to procrastinate by sharing tips on message boards and in blog posts). If a given employer pays you $600 or more for your services in a given year, it is responsible for providing a 1099 Misc form (see page 341). If you don't receive it by January, follow up and see what's happening. In terms of health care, there are many options for getting insurance without the aid of an employer, such as individual plans, short-term plans, and the Freelancer's Union. For more information on insurance options, go to page 357.

versatile as a designer, you might want to consider finding a "niche" (album covers, T-shirts, blog design, etc.) that you can market in order to distinguish yourself.

Social Media Guruing. With all new technologies come new jobs—rumor has it Larry King was just a pauper on the streets before the television came along. For our generation, "social media" is the newcomer on the scene, and as such it's considered something we inherently understand better than the wrinklies up in the boardroom. As organizations begin to realize the power of viral videos, Facebook fan pages, blogs, and all that other good "Web 2.0" stuff, they're increasingly looking for new blood to shake up their old-school marketing departments. You can actually get full-time jobs with major companies (e.g., Dominos, JetBlue) as a "social media manager" these days, but a knack for these tools can also be leveraged into freelance consulting gigs. (Word to the wise: There's a lot to know—don't assume you're an expert just because you spend four hours a day on the 'Book). To find opportunities, check out SocialMediaJobs.com (look at the "Consultants" category) and Mashable.com's job board. You can also try techie sites like Elance.com and Odesk.com to find people looking for social media experts. But if you're low on experience, start small by pitching yourself to smaller organizations that aren't necessarily looking for a social media pro until you tell them they need one (e.g., charge $500 to teach the nice silver-haired ladies at the library what Facebook is). Try approaching a local museum, a pizza parlor, or one of your parents' friends who has a small business—you might even do it for free the first time. If your strategies work, there's nothing stopping you from finding new clients and charging a lot more to build out a company's online presence, create a viral Twitter campaign for a tutoring company, or shoot promotional YouTube videos for a nearby Yoga studio.

Still Undecided? Make a Venn Diagram!

When our writer Gritz graduated from college, he decided to put his fate in the hands of the most powerful mathematical concept in the world: the Venn diagram! The Venn diagram is used throughout the modern world to solve problems large and small, and it was single-handedly responsible for bringing together Jay-Z and R. Kelly on *The Best of Both Worlds*. So why wouldn't it work for a recent grad looking for a job? Let's see how the experiment panned out.

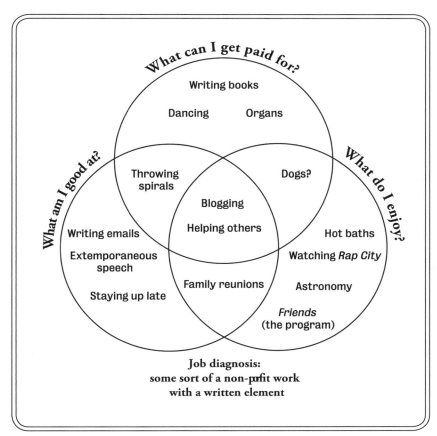

Internships

Don't underestimate the power of a great internship as an important piece of your career story. While there are plenty of examples of people who land great jobs right out of college, more often than not, getting to the gig you really want requires a long-distance run, not a sprint. One of the best stepping-stones to full-time employment is an internship—or several. In fact, the **intern pool is by far the most common source of new hires at many companies.** While you may not yet have the skill set to be a strong candidate for your dream job, as far as competition for internships goes, you're a great white shark in a pool of guppies. Your college degree makes you a superstar candidate, so leverage it to get your foot in the door of a company where you might ultimately like to work.

Once you've landed an internship, your job duties may involve a trip or two to the local latté purveyor, but don't get caught up in the details. Internships are a great place to start out—they provide a setting to learn new skills, network, bolster your resume, and dip your toe into an industry to see if you actually enjoy it. And just as important, taking an internship can help you maintain momentum in your job hunt instead of getting frustrated because nothing's opening up or a particular company is beginning to look like an impenetrable fortress. (Yes, you should absolutely continue to look for jobs *while* you're interning, and many companies will encourage you in this process.)

Hopefully we've sold you on the fact that internships are a great catapult for an enterprising young grad. Once you snag one, treat it as an audition for a role in the main cast. Here are some tips for getting a foot in the door and making the most of your experience as an intern. Haters, step off!

How to Find Great Internships

Finding an internship is not entirely different from finding a full-time job, so be sure to check out the job listing resources section on page 137. In addition, here are some more great resources geared specifically toward internships:

- **Your alma mater.** Check with career services and the alumni office to research various internship options. Make sure to ask whether your school has strong relationships with any programs in particular.

- **The website of the company where you want to intern.** If it has an employment section on its site (usually listed in the "Careers" or

"About Us" sections), you can usually find details about the internship program there.

- **Books.** There are plenty of books with profiles of different internship programs. You don't need to buy them—just spend an afternoon at a bookstore or the library and see what you can find. *Vault Guide to Top Internships* and *The Best 109 Internships*, both by Mark Oldman, are good places to start.

- **Lists of top-rated internships.** *BusinessWeek*, Vault, and CollegeGrad. com all publish rankings of the best internships, so track these down. The *BusinessWeek* one even includes information on pay and the percentage of interns that get full-time offers.

- **Quarterlife.com.** Through its affiliation with "The Intern Queen," this social network provides a decent smattering of internship opportunities easily accessible from one of the top navigation tabs, though it should be noted that the listings skew toward media-related fields.

- **Cold calls.** It's easier to cold call a company and offer free labor than it is to ask for a job (however, there are fuzzy laws about unpaid internships so they may say "no" even if they want you). Find a company that interests you but doesn't have a formal internship program, and see if they'll take you on. This approach can be particularly effective at small to mid-sized companies (see "Tips & Tricks" page 129).

Do Your Homework

Not all internships are created equal. Some places take on interns without thinking too much about what they're going to do with them, whereas others have excellent programs designed for maximum immersion. To separate the wheat from the chaff, you'll have to do some research. Once you've identified a few programs that interest you, visit InternshipRatings.com to see how different companies' programs are rated. More important, track down some people who have previously interned at the companies you're interested in (try Facebook, LinkedIn, and school networks) to ask what they thought of the experience. Don't forget to see if they have any particular advice for the interview process.

For tips on how to go about preparing your application and interviewing, check out Chapter 4.

Career Options

How to Thrive at an Internship

Once you've landed an internship, hit the ground running and make the most of the opportunity from day one. Even if you're only planning on being there for a few months, treat it as if it were a "real" job—you never know, it might become one. Here are a few tips on what you can do to stand out from the other 'terns.

- **Don't act like you're too good to get coffee.** There are three reasons people make you get coffee in an internship: 1) They want to break you down and make you aware of your inferiority (see *The Devil Wears Prada*); 2) They are too lazy (or hung over) to get it themselves; or 3) Everyone in the office goes on coffee runs and sometimes it just happens to be your turn. The second two scenarios are far more common than the first. Still, even if there is a little bit of hazing going on, having an ego won't help anything. Someday, you'll be the one in a position to tell people what to do, and then you can either exact your revenge on the world or make it a better place by being nice to your interns. (Most likely you will start out saying you'll never make them do menial tasks, but then you'll make them do them anyway, because the cycle is more powerful than any of us realize. It's the same mentality that keeps fraternity brothers organizing elephant walks and sorority girls dousing each other with ketchup. Don't fight it or the whole system will crumble!)

- **Avoid the "nervous intern" syndrome.** Every office has an overly nervous intern. This intern is very sweet and

---

Tips & Tricks: Intern housing

To avoid being the intern who gets caught squatting in the conference room, plan ahead and think outside the box in terms of where you might live. If your internship is in a place where you have friends or relatives (or, better yet, parents), there's no shame in shacking up with them for a little while to save on rent. Buy an air mattress for $50 and make yourself scarce; if you have several potential sponsors, you can move around to avoid overstaying your welcome. (For more tips on living off others, see "Confessions of a Nomad" on page 82.) You can also ask the company you're interning for if it has any subsidized housing options or suggestions for affordable housing. If it's a summer internship and you're located near a university, you may be able to rent a room in a dorm. Finally, check out sublets (p. 100), and bear in mind that going in on housing with one or more roommates can significantly defray the cost of living.

well-intentioned, but ultimately a pain in the butt that no one wants to deal with. He or she walks around on eggshells, afraid that any false step will literally set the building on fire and ruin the entire company…forever. Remember: When you're an intern, no supervisor is going to put you in the room with the red button. Nothing you do is going to be do-or-die, so if you're given an assignment, don't ask a million and one questions about how to do it—at that point, the person who assigned it to you might as well have done it himself. Instead, try to get as far as you can on each project, and if problems arise, then pose a few thoughtful questions at one time.

- **Become indispensable (and be proactive).** Is there a task that you can do better than anyone else in the office? Then work it to the max, and the company may have no choice but to hire you. If you're not getting enough work, don't sit around IMing your friends and bemoaning the fact that you're not being given the opportunity to prove yourself. Get up and walk around the office. Introduce yourself to people who may not be in your immediate work area and see if you can help them. Anticipate ways to make your supervisor's life easier and then execute. Unfortunately, the chance to shine is not guaranteed, so do anything you can to show your supervisor what you've got before your internship is up.

- **Make connections.** The "only speak when spoken to" approach won't get you too far at an internship, and here's why: Interns come and go, but full-time employees are set in routines that they may have fostered over the course of many years. If they're friendly human beings, they'll interact with you, but some people will just go about their business as if you don't exist. It's not necessarily that they're rude, they're just busy, and taking you under their wing is not part of their job description. For this reason, it's on you to put yourself on colleagues' radars and make them want to teach you, give you work, or mentor you in other ways. For the most part, you can easily accomplish this by introducing yourself and asking some questions. This simple act will puncture that weird workplace aloofness and put you in a position to make an impression. Sometimes the memorable intern gets the job (just make sure you're remembered for your hard work and not for always leaving your fly down).

- **Remember why you're there.** The hardest part about internships is staying motivated. Your stipend might be laughable (or even nonexistent), but don't get hung up on the details. Instead, you've got to think like a benchwarmer trying to be a starter. If you're dazed and out-of-shape when you finally get put in the game, people aren't likely to be impressed with what you can do. So stay on point, and be ready to pounce. Otherwise, why are you there? Slaving away for peanuts is a waste of your time (and the company's) if you're just going to slack your way to the finish line.

Before You Leave an Internship

Any respectable "things to do before leaving the office" checklist should include stealing a few paperclips, getting digits from any other cute interns, and coyly dropping hints that you like cupcakes as the final week approaches. More to the point, though, it's important to be strategic about your exit for the same reason we've already discussed: You're a blip on the radar for many people whose entire professional lives take place in the office, so it's up to you to ensure that you're not forgotten the moment your log-in privileges are revoked.

There are three simple steps to leaving with your head held high and your Rolodex brimming with new contacts. First, initiate a real conversation with your supervisor about prospects for the future. If there's no official evaluation process, ask for feedback—a major goal of an internship is to learn what employers see in you and how you can improve. If that supervisor seems to like you, get a reference

> ### Tips & Tricks: Can I look for jobs while I'm interning?
>
> Of course! In fact, that's precisely what you should be doing. In the broad sense, "job loyalty" is not a big deal at internships because everyone's on the same page about your ultimate goal (i.e., to get a job, there or elsewhere). If people like you at your internship, they should either be looking to hire you as a full-time employee or help you move on to your next opportunity. Be respectful of your position and your duties (browsing job-hunting sites while you're at work is not a good move), but don't be shy about taking time off for interviews or networking engagements you can't reschedule. If you get a job elsewhere and have to leave your internship early, so be it. That's the whole point!

letter, or at least ask if it would be okay to list him or her as a reference in the future (see page 197). Second, say thank you and goodbye to anyone and everyone you interacted with in the office. If you haven't started one already, now is the time to get a networking spreadsheet going (page 204), because you never know who might be in a position to help you in the future. Finally, take away anything from the office that could be of use as you take the next step. Did you get a great handout about financing or sales techniques? Did you have a good rapport with a client whose contact information is going to be trapped in your work email if you don't get it ASAP? Think about what you've learned and whom you've met, and make sure you're not leaving anything behind that you can't get back.

Grad School

Going going, back back, to college college…This urge strikes many recent grads after their first forays into the real world, and it's definitely an impulse worth investigating. Whether you decide a business degree is the best way to advance your career, you realize you need a master's to pursue your dreams, or you just have a yearning to be back in academia, there are graduate degrees to match almost any intellectual or professional goal. There are also good and bad reasons for getting them. While you are allowed to remain in semi-aimless mode as an undergraduate, a worthwhile graduate experience requires a certain degree of focus and purpose. Moreover, it often requires a hefty investment of money, both in terms of tuition (though there are ways to reduce the burden; see page 174) and sacrificed income while you're in school. It would be impossible to cover all of the pros and cons of each unique type of graduate degree in the space of this book, but we hope to provide some useful guidelines for thinking about this big decision.

Career Options

Five Good and Bad Reasons to Go to Grad School

Good reasons:

- An advanced degree is required for the job you want to do.

- You are switching fields (or want the opportunity to do so).

- You have the opportunity to study abroad and can afford it.

Five Good and Bad Reasons to Go to Grad School continued…

- Your employer is willing to pay for or subsidize it.

- You want to be an academic or professor in a given field.

Bad reasons:

- You're bored.

- You want to avoid the job hunt. (Newsflash: Graduate students have to job hunt too.)

- Your boyfriend/girlfriend/bestie is going.

- To "see if I like [fill in the blank with some obscure field]."

- You miss "Thirsty Thursdays." ∎

Deciding What You Want to Study

We're tempted to say: "Well, well, my friend. If you don't know what degree you want already, you're probably in the wrong building. Now scurry along, rapscallion." But no! It's not always immediately obvious how advanced degrees are valued in different fields, or even which degrees make sense for which fields. In his book *No Sucker Left Behind: Avoiding the Great College Ripoff*, Marc Scheer makes the following recommendation for choosing a degree that will help you meet your long-term professional goals. Instead of thinking, "What degree would I get if this were a perfect world and education did not have to serve a purpose beyond a noble pursuit of the Truth?" try this approach on for size: "I like that person's job—I wonder if I need a degree to get there." In other words, think about the job (or at least the field) you ultimately see yourself in, then do some research into the educational backgrounds of people whose careers you hope to emulate. In addition, reach out to department heads at different schools (keep reading to find out how to find them) and ask pointed questions about who enrolls in their program and what careers they tend to pursue upon graduating. Clearly, they'll be pitching you to some extent, but it's still a worthwhile conversation (and one that far too few grad students actually have before enrolling).

When you're going through this research process, bear in mind that it's not a simple "X degree = Y job" equation. For example, if you want to work in education (see page 169), you could get a Master's of Arts in Teaching (MAT), a Master's in Education (MEd), or a master's in a specific form of education (e.g., Social Studies Education, Special Needs Teaching). If you want to be a counselor, you could get a master's in social work, a psychology degree, or a specialty certification (or you could go to med school and become a psychotherapist). And if you're interested in public health, you might consider a Master's in Public Health (MPH), an MS in Public Health, a PhD in Epidemiology, or a number of other options. Bored yet? You get the point—there are many ways to get to where you want to go professionally, and as scary as it sounds, figuring out the right path will require getting a little more specific about that endpoint. The conversations you have with professionals and schools will be invaluable as you consider various options.

Popular Fields of Study (and the Industries Where They're Useful)

Business: Finance, accounting, consulting, marketing, entrepreneurship, economic policy, and economic development

Law: Law, business, politics, government, and nonprofits

Medical: Private and public medicine, health-related business, and academia

Education: Teaching, administration, policy, and research

Engineering: Specialty engineering (automotive, biomedical, robotics, nuclear), consulting, teaching, manufacturing, government work, R&D, product design, systems management, and energy

Sciences: Clinical laboratory work, veterinary work, environmental science and/or policy, pharmaceuticals, biotech, etc.

Library and Information Studies: Academic and public library work, archiving, system analysis, database maintenance, web development, webmastering, and LAN coordinating

Social Sciences: Administration, business, corrections, counseling, education, investigations, journalism, politics, public relations, market research, and social work

Career Options

Popular Fields of Study continued...

Humanities: Almost anything, from industrial design to advertising to publishing to nonprofits

Health: Public or private medicine, physical therapy, pharmaceuticals, NGOs, public health in developing countries, and policy

Fine Arts: Design (fashion, interior, graphic, etc), art, museums, gallery work, and art dealing

Technology: Software engineering, information security, and database administration ■

Finding the Right School

Once you've decided on the degree, it's time to get down to the nitty-gritty work of comparing the offerings at different schools. The first step, of course, is figuring out which schools have good reputations for what you're trying to do. In college, your degree is often measured by the overall "ranking" of your school, which is pretty easy to find. But when it comes to grad school, the most random school you can imagine might just have the country's strongest program for some esoteric degree. The best place to start is *U.S. News & World Report*—each year it ranks basically every program out there, down to the most niche specialties (e.g., Digital Librarianship). If you're looking at a more common degree, you should also check out *The Princeton Review*'s rankings. These don't cover as many fields, but they go deeper into the main programs (e.g., MBA programs get ranked by several different criteria). You have to register to see the results, but registration is free. Finally, industry magazines like *BusinessWeek* tend to have rankings related to particular fields.

Once you've vetted a reasonable list of options, you'll need to consider some more specific criteria to narrow down the field:

What type of study appeals to you? Having successfully navigated an undergraduate degree, you should now have a better sense of your learning style. Would you like a theoretical or practical focus? Do you enjoy doing research? How much flexibility would you like to determine your own course of study?

With whom would you like to work? There may be professors who are particularly renowned in your field that you're dying to study under. Also, certain programs may be strong feeders into the specific things you want to do. Ask faculty at your college for recommendations of good programs and professors in your chosen field.

How strong is the alumni network? Does your dream company or organization have strong alumni ties to a particular school? If so, going to that school might be a good strategic move.

How long? There's a big difference between a two-year master's and being in school for another eight years. Clearly, you can decide whether or not to pursue a PhD later down the line, but it's still worth giving some thought to the overall timeline of your further education.

How much does is cost? It's not just the tuition and the opportunity cost—don't forget to factor in years of living expenses, either.

Do all the things you did as an undergrad. Visit the campus and do your research. Connect with alumni. You know the drill. Consider location and size—if there's a program you like near home, is it possible to live with Mom and Dad? (See page 23 for more on returning to the nest.)

The Three Elephants in the Room: Business School, Law School, and Education

Why are these elephants in the room? Not because they are necessarily the three most popular graduate school options, but because they're the ones that we hear questions about most commonly when working with seniors and recent grads (an MD is amongst the top but we figure if you're taking that route you probably already have everything planned). If you're considering one of these three routes (or you're wondering why so many others are interested in them), here's a quick and dirty overview to get you started.

Law School

You put in your hours watching Law & Order, and now you think you're ready to be the next Sam Waterston. We don't need to tell you that the reality of a legal career is quite different from the reality of watching courtroom dramas on TV. However, looking at President Obama and his cabinet, it's clear that JDs tend to wield a lot of influence in this country, and that's not a coincidence. However, not every law school graduate ends up as president. Some lawyers will tell you that unless you are able to get into a top 30 law school, it's probably not worth your time. Lower-tier schools can cost just as much as Harvard and Yale, but the benefits are murkier, since top legal firms rarely get filled from this pool. Of course, you can still leverage a JD from a lower-tier school in many ways, such as opening up your own practice. But you could also take the $200k you would spend on tuition and buy a house instead. It's all a matter of weighing risk and reward.

Who goes, and why? There are three predominant "types" you find at law school. First, there are the people who want to go into the legal profession and/or politics and are attracted to the philosophical and political ideals of studying the law. Then, there are the people who maybe studied economics as undergraduates, enjoyed economic analysis of the law, and want to understand the role of the law in business. Finally, about 50% of law students are just there because they thought it seemed like a good "next step." (If you're in the last group, we would suggest clarifying your reasons for going before you commit yourself to three years of potentially mind-numbing toil and a mountain of debt.)

You may therefore not be surprised to learn that, just five years after graduation, over 50% of law school grads are not practicing law. Many find that practicing law isn't a good fit. Thankfully, a law degree can be applied to jobs in a range of industries if you position yourself correctly. The ability to read and write contracts comes in handy in many contexts (though if your job is reviewing contracts, well, you're a lawyer). Government work is a popular route, especially with branches like the Department of Justice and the Department of Labor. In short, knowing the law can be applicable to a wide range of careers that don't actually require practicing it.

Of the people who do stick it out as lawyers, many end up working for companies in their legal departments, often after starting at a law firm and getting cherry-picked by a client who can offer a better work-life balance.

Tuition versus salary? Tuition varies widely, with the top private schools charging between $30,000 and $40,000 a year, and the top public schools running around $20,000. Financial aid is generally available for a portion of tuition, but you will probably have to take out loans to cover the rest. If you snag a job at a top firm, starting salaries of $160,000 a year plus bonus will make paying off loans a lot easier. However, the recession has hit top law firms particularly hard. It's unclear whether these firms will continue to provide lucrative positions in the same numbers to law school grads. Moreover, the median starting income for law school grads is "only" $59,000, so a JD is not a free pass to Ballerville.

How do I get in? The LSAT is the required test for law school admission. Essentially it's a reasoning test, with a very strong logic component. It's administered four times a year and costs $123 to take. Once you have an LSAT score, you can pretty much match it up with your GPA and find a chart online that will show you which schools are in your range (e.g., "The Boston College Law School Locator"). Essays, recommendations, and the water well you built in the Serengeti may be able to give you a slight edge, but it's mostly a numbers game.

Bottom Line: If you want to be a lawyer, you have to go to law school (so don't try to be a renegade and take the bar cold turkey). Be warned that many lawyers don't wind up enjoying practice. Having a law degree can open doors outside of the prescribed "legal track," but it's good to go into law school with a focus and plan what you'd like to do once you graduate. Three years and a life-altering pile of debt are a high price to pay if you're not sure what you want to do.

Business School

A lot of people think "B-school" is just a place you go to network, skip ethics lectures, and attend tons of theme parties. It is that, but it's also a launching pad to many different career paths. Whether you're a bio major that wants a business background or a finance jock that needs a degree to climb the corporate ladder, getting an MBA could be a smart move. Applying is an involved process, and competition becomes particularly fierce in down economies, as many people view B-school as a place to take shelter (and gain credentials) while they wait for the storm to pass. In 2008, after news of the recession made the rounds, the Graduate Management Admission Council (GMAC) reported that 77% of business schools had received an increase in application volume since 2007, and some of them saw individual increases of 25–40%. Nonetheless, recession or no recession, business school is worth considering for many reasons.

Who goes, and why? There are two different groups of people who attend business school. Most common are those who need an MBA to advance in their job or industry. The other group is composed of individuals who want to reset their careers, whether that means switching from a nonbusiness field or changing focuses within the business world. Oh, and there are plenty of folks who just want to go back to school and "take a break from it all." It's surprising that these people get in, because that's not a sound business decision. However, they are usually the ones who have the time to plan the best parties, so they round out the student body nicely. Members of all groups are interested in building their business networks. You never know, the guy timing your keg stand could end up being your start-up's angel investor ten years down the road.

How do I get in? In order to apply to business school, you need to take the GMAT, fill out an application that includes a soul-searching "personal essay," and gather two to three letters of recommendation. Many business schools also require some work experience (even if it's just two years), though it's not unheard of to jump straight in from undergrad. Assuming you have decent grades, the most important part of your application is your GMAT score (a score of 650 is competitive for the top twenty schools and 700+ will dramatically increase your odds of acceptance), so it's incredibly important not only to prepare thoroughly (see page 170), but also to use your GMAT score as a guide for where you can apply. *Business Week* publishes an annual report on the best 70 U.S. business schools and includes average GMAT scores and other pertinent information for each. When you're talking to b-school hopefuls, you'll probably hear people reference the business school application cycle. Certain schools have unique admissions practices, and just as with undergrad, there are some schools with early action, rolling admissions, and so on. But the basic idea of the business school cycle is that most schools accept applications at three points throughout the year—usually October, January, and April. All sorts of strategizing goes on about the optimal time to ship off your app, but the only reliable rule of thumb is that the last possible date is the worst. So if you're going to do this thing, try to get on the ball early!

Bottom Line: Business school is a worthwhile endeavor if you go for the right reasons. For the wrong ones, it's at least $60,000 out the window that you could have put towards starting your own ferret-grooming business. If you're determined to go, make sure to seek out the schools that best suit your needs. Some schools excel at finance, some focus on entrepreneurship, and others have great all-around programs. You'll also have an option between full-time and part-time classes if you need to keep working to bankroll the endeavor (see page 176 for more on balancing school and work). Regardless of why you're going, make sure you reap the benefits: either a job in the business world, promotions and salary increases in your current line of work, or the business skill set you need to pursue your dreams of running a nonprofit or starting your own company.

Education Programs

When it comes to recession-proof industries, education is about as good as it gets. The Obama administration has clearly articulated its intention to add teaching jobs in order to meet the growing enrollment in grades K–12. In addition, many current teachers are reaching retirement age and will need to be replaced in the coming years. As a result, it's no surprise that the National Center for Education Statistics predicts that in the next eight years, 2.8 million new teachers will join the existing 3.2 million teachers in the United States. Of course, not every teacher needs an advanced degree. But while some states only require a certification to teach (which is different from a degree and easier to attain), master's programs will give you a big leg up—and, in some cases, the school you work for will even help fund your continued education.

Who goes, and why? Teachers and education professionals of all types get advanced degrees in education, so the field of applicants—as well as the specific programs—is as varied as the jobs that exist in a school.

What are the degrees? The two main advanced education degrees are the Master's of Arts in Teaching (MAT) and the Master's in Education (MEd). In addition to being required in many states, the MAT plays a role in the competition for the more desirable and lucrative classroom teaching opportunities (e.g., cushy private school gigs). If you're more interested in the administrative, policy, research or leadership side of things, then a MEd is the way to go. Some schools offer a master's in a specific form of education (e.g., Social Studies Education, Special Needs Teaching), but that alone won't always provide you with all of the qualifications you'll need to teach. As far as the actual teaching certification goes (again, different from a master's), each state has different guidelines, so you'll have to check in with the Department of Education in the state where you want to teach in order to make sure you're ticking all the required boxes. The good news is, most degrees will include your certification, so it often makes sense to attend a school in the same state where you want to teach (or at least in a state that has reciprocity with that state).

How much does it cost? Education degrees can range from $20,000 all the way up to $50,000. State schools tend to be on the less expensive side and private schools tend toward the ludicrous (and it's not like you'll be paying back those loans super-quick as a teacher). Thankfully, many states and indi-

Career Options

Tips & Tricks: D.I.Y. education

At some point someone probably told you there are "no do-overs" in college, but that's not really true at all. If you squandered your days playing Ultimate or wish you'd gone to a different school, don't worry—there are tons of free college courses and resources available via the Internet. You can watch Harvard's famous "Justice" philosophy class for free online, teach yourself new skills like computer programming, or check out free lectures and cultural events in your city. For more ideas on free and low-cost ways to grow as a human being, check out Chapter 9.

vidual schools provide scholarships that will cover a portion or all of the tuition if you commit to teach in the state/school for several years after graduation. It's also worth noting that if you end up doing a program like Teach for America, it will provide you with some level of teaching certification for free, but it isn't always strong enough to qualify you to teach in every school (as a MAT would).

How do I get in? Most programs will require you to take the GRE. However, because there are so many specialties and different kinds of degrees, it's advisable to figure out what type of teaching position you want and then work backward to the degree, the programs, and finally the requirements for admission. Check out TeacherDegrees.com for a comprehensive list of all the options out there. Once you've settled on one, call the schools you'll be applying to and ask what tests and materials are required of applicants.

Bottom Line: With an average base salary stopping just short of $50k a year, full-time teachers don't necessarily live large. But when it comes to respected professions, teaching is second only to firefighting. So unless you plan to hook up with your students like Cate Blanchett in *Notes on a Scandal*, you can be proud to know you'll have a positive impact on the lives of many kids—rumor has it they're the future.

Studying for the GMAT, LSAT, and GRE

Welcome to the trifecta of graduate school standardized tests: the GMAT, LSAT, and GRE. The thought of taking these tests (let alone studying for them) fells many recent grads before they even begin the graduate school admissions process. But if you really want to re-enter academia, you'll have to deal with this annoyance. And the good news is, studying actually helps. As with the SAT, there are strategies that can be learned to conquer these exams, and one of the best is just knowing the format and content of the test inside-out. To tackle this process, you have four options: Study alone, sign up for a prep class, hire a private tutor, or pursue some combination of the three.

The Diagnostic Test

Before you decide on a prep strategy, you need to know where you stand. Enter the diagnostic test. It will provide you with a proxy for how you'd do on the actual test if you took it that day. This score is important for two reasons. First, you can use it to determine whether it's realistic to be applying to the schools you're hoping to attend. Just bear in mind that you should be able to increase your score before the official test, but don't expect a miracle (i.e., you might reasonably expect to move from a 160 to a 170 on the LSAT, but not from a 130 to a 170).

Another reason for taking a diagnostic is to help you create a study plan to improve. After taking the test, you'll determine whether you need help on verbal, math, and so on. And if you score high, that doesn't mean you're off the hook yet. The key is to consistently achieve your target score, so you should continue to take practice tests (which can be found in test prep books or online).

Diagnostic tests are easy to come by. The companies that write the tests (e.g., GMAC, LSAC, and ETS) provide free diagnostics on their websites. In addition, you can usually find diagnostics in test prep books. To ensure that your diagnostic is an accurate representation of where you stand, try to simulate a real test-taking environment. That means no phone calls, no napping, and, obviously, no Googling answers.

Studying Options

After determining where you need help, it's time to practice like whoa. Test prep books and practice tests should be your new best friends—going through sets of questions over and over really is the best way to learn each test's patterns. When it comes to learning test-taking tips and tricks (that make a real difference), you can choose the approach that works best for your learning style and budget.

Going It Alone

Pop quiz: Take the 20th practice test of the month or watch *Wet Hot American Summer* again? If you chose the former, then you're a self-motivated freak of nature and you'll probably be fine going it alone. Check out the websites of

Career Options

testing companies (e.g., ETS) for free test prep material and pick up a few books. It's usually best to get a book of practice tests compiled by the company that writes the test, and then a couple of books from test prep companies to cover tips, tricks, and winning strategies. Books cost around $12 to $25, so this route shouldn't break the bank. Once you're consistently reaching your target score, it's time to take the actual test. If you falter when it's game time, it might be time to turn to a class (or even a private tutor).

Attending Classes

This is a more regimented way to go about studying for the test (and it's cheaper than private tutoring). Classes are offered by companies such as Kaplan, Test Masters, Princeton Review, Manhattan GMAT, and Atlas LSAT.[1] They all provide a solid overview of the test material, along with helpful tips and techniques for all question types. They also offer opportunities to take practice tests in a more realistic setting than you can recreate in your living room (though if you can focus with your roommate sitting next to you in his Snuggie, you're golden). Prices range from $800 to $1400+ for a test-prep package, which usually consists of approximately 25–30 hours spread over 7 to 10 sessions. Class sizes max out at between 15 and 60 people, depending on the company. The problem with big classes is that your specific needs may not be addressed, so some companies offer "small group tutoring" as a compromise between classes and private tutoring.

Getting a Private Tutor

Ready to pay to play? If the previous strategies really aren't working for you or you're the type of person who learns best with a one-on-one dynamic, a private tutor might be necessary. The companies previously listed, as well as reputable companies like Advantage Testing, can hook you up with a tutor who probably aced the test you're taking. While these tutors can run from $100 to $200+ per hour, they may be able to push you to your highest potential. You've got to weigh how important those extra points are in the grand scheme of things (this is where looking at the average scores at schools you want to attend comes into play). When choosing a tutor, the most important thing to look for is experience; we recommend finding one with at least five years of tutoring

---

1 Full disclosure: MG Prep, Inc., parent company of Manhattan GMAT and Atlas LSAT, is our publisher. But if we didn't think their test prep materials and strategies were awesome for recent grads, we would have told them to take the million dollar checks and iced-out chains they offered us to publish this book and stick them where the sun don't shine. [Visit www.gradspot.com/mgtestprep for special discounts.]

experience under his or her belt. Most companies either sell tutoring packages in ten and twenty hour increments (so assume you'll be shelling out a minimum of $3,000 bucks for less time than you'd get in a class setting), or on an hourly basis. It's crazy money from one perspective, but who knows—down the line a cool $3,000 might feel like Monopoly money after you've been to a great school and snagged a sick job.

A Word of Warning: The Cost of Grad School

We'll be blunt: many graduate schools are expensive, and having an advanced degree is not always worth it (financially or career-wise). That might sound like an annoying thing to say, and we don't want to suggest that the only reason to go to grad school is to cash in once you're done. If you want to study Plato for the next ten years because that's what you think you were put on this earth to do, by all means go for it! But to take you back to Economics 101, do consider the "opportunity cost" of grad school. The money and time you put into your studies will require a tradeoff in terms of "what you would be doing otherwise." Of course, it's impossible to know exactly what the road not taken would look like, but just keep in mind that there are many roads, and not all of them lead to grad school.

If you don't want to spend the next ten years repaying loans, you need to anticipate what your career might look like once you've earned your degree, and then do some research into the risks and rewards of pursuing a career in that particular field. Does that mean mapping out *exactly* how much a degree is going to cost and predicting *precisely* how much money you'll be making as soon as you graduate? Of course not—life doesn't work that way. But is it worth ball-parking just to know what you're getting yourself into? Certainly. Marc Scheer, author of *No Sucker Left Behind: Avoiding the Great College Ripoff*, offers the following rule of thumb for identifying less risky programs:

> *"First and foremost, grad school candidates should verify [the type of starting salary they can reasonably expect] when they graduate, and that their student loan payments will require less than 15% of their monthly salaries to pay (even better if this debt takes up less than 10% of salaries). In addition, students can take these steps: ask schools where their recent grads are now employed; ask to talk directly to recent grads; ask employers about the quality of the programs and if they would hire someone from them; verify graduation rates and actual number of years until graduation at each program; and talk with people in the field right now to see if they think the program offers good value. Every gradu-*

Career Options

ate program should be required to provide this information to students, but right now students need to do their own homework."

You want the scary facts? Scheer happily obliges: "The average graduate or professional student leaves school with a grad school loan debt burden ranging from $27,000 to $131,000, or a total loan debt burden ranging from $50,000 to $154,000 (including the average college loan debt of $23,000, but credit card debt is excluded.)" Thankfully, several different sources can offer you some help.

But scary facts aside, in the end, graduate school is about advancing your career story and putting yourself in a position to grow and excel. If you're really excited to go back to school and know why you want to go, then we hope that financial limitations won't stand in your way.

Funding Grad School

So you got in! We believed in you all along. Now, let's figure out how to pay for this thing. Besides selling organs, there are many ways to ease the financial burden of going back to school in your twenties.

Free programs. Believe it or not, some graduate programs are actually free. Many PhDs, for example, are fully funded by the university where you earn your degree, and if you teach on top of doing your own coursework/research, you can actually make money overall. In addition, some master's degrees (e.g., certain MFA programs in creative writing) offer full funding to students, regardless of financial need. Clearly, you should not pursue a degree just because it's free, but if there are strong fully funded options within your field of interest, count yourself lucky and take advantage.

Grants. When you apply for an undergraduate degree, the school checks out how much money Mom and Dad have in the coffers before doling out any financial aid. But now that you're all independent and broke, you can definitely apply for federal and state government grants, each of which are worth thousands of dollars and distributed to students based entirely on need. To start the process, all you have to do is go to fafsa.ed.gov and fill out a Free Application for Federal Student Aid (FAFSA). Completing a FAFSA also makes you eligible for several federal loans and is used by schools in awarding basic work-study positions.

Scholarships. This time around, being awesome at softball isn't going to help you out. It's all about academics, and there are two basic types of scholarships up for grabs: national awards (both need- and merit-based) and university-specific awards. The benefit of national awards is you don't need to know what school you want to go to before applying (and receiving one might make the decision for you). FastWeb.com and FindTuition.com are two great places for you to start. Try to pick awards that cater to your strengths or background (i.e., if you're Cuban, go after scholarships for Hispanic students). If you're interested in pursuing a degree in education (p. 169), note that many states offer financial incentives for students willing to work in hard-to-staff subjects or geographic areas after graduation (e.g., the Kansas Teacher Service Scholarship offers $5,000 toward each year of graduate school). As far as offerings at specific universities go, sign up for department newsletters, visit their offices, and check out different schools' websites.

Fellowships, assistantships, and work-study. Welcome to Valhalla, scholars! Fellowships are about as good as it gets, offering tuition (often a full ride) plus a stipend and sometimes even health benefits. Assistantships and work-study positions are similarly sweet, though the catch is you've got to help with research or teaching a class. The same websites mentioned for scholarships also list national fellowships, though the real trick is to track down department offices at private universities that have the endowments to cover these awards.

Working your way through school. If you can't land a job working for the university you attend, that doesn't mean you can't work elsewhere to defray costs. Check out page 27 for a list of ways to make extra money. In particular, the flexibility of tutoring (p. 27), temping (p. 38), being a waiter/waitress (p. 33), and working in retail (p. 34) can work well when you're juggling schoolwork. And while it's certainly a tough road, there are some instances where it's possible to pursue a part-time degree while holding a full-time job (see below).

Getting an employer to pay. Business-related fields (e.g., business, marketing) are the

> ### Tips & Tricks: Don't try to hide what you're doing at work or at school
>
> One successful worker-cum-grad student we spoke to said, "The most important part of working while in school is to make sure that the employee has a healthy understanding with the employer. The employee/student needs the flexibility to do his/her schoolwork—even if it means doing some while at work." Without this flexibility, it's easy to get burned out or to fall behind on school, your job, or both.

Career Options

most common sources of employer-subsidized education. Architecture, engineering, journalism, and scientific employers also sometimes offer continuing education expense reimbursement. Some programs allow you to both work and go to school part-time, while others allow a full-time leave of absence from the office. Don't ask for education subsidies until you've worked at the company for at least a year (it's a serious investment for your employer and they want to make sure you're worth it), and, when you do, be sure to ask questions about the stipulations. For example, will the employer pay initial costs, or reimburse you? What are the dollar limits? Will low grades affect your reimbursement? How long will you have to work there after you earn your degree? (Three years might be worth it, but ten is a big commitment to make).

Join the military or get a government job. You've seen the commercials, but you may not know the drill. Look into the Military's Tuition Assistance Program, which pays "up to 100% of the cost of tuition or expenses, up to a maximum of $250 per credit, and a personal maximum of $4,500 per fiscal year per student." Other government jobs offer tuition assistance and loan repayment programs as well, so do your research and check out our government jobs primer on page 141.

Loans. Needless to say, accruing more debt is not ideal, but sometimes it's the only option. Figure out how to pay it all back (or even get it forgiven) on page 290.

Is It Possible to Balance Full-Time Work with Part-Time Grad School?

We've received this question via our Twitter account, @gradspotguru, as well as at some of the campuses we've visited. And we always respond by asking: What type of degree are you talking about? While part-time MBAs are quite common, part-time medical school is not something you hear of very often (if ever).

Before you even consider pursuing a degree part-time, make sure that it is a viable option. Then, do some research into specific programs to determine how flexible they are and whether there are hidden drawbacks to not enrolling full-time. For example, are night or weekend classes offered? Are the faculty members the same for full-time and part-time students? What resources, such as libraries and labs, are available to part-timers, and do the hours fit your schedule?

Another point worth considering is that it's unlikely that you'll be able to snag full grants and scholarships if you're not a full-time student. And if getting a free education means committing full-time, that's probably your best bet.

Pros to Full-Time Work

If you've got the gumption to pull it off, there are many benefits to working full-time as you pursue your studies.

Avoiding debt. We've all heard the horror stories of grads crippled by debt. Heaping on grad school bills before you've paid off your undergrad tuition is not an attractive option for anyone. Having a full-time job will obviously ease the burden significantly, and if you're lucky, you may even be able to afford to live in a real apartment and eat food that doesn't say "just add hot water" on the instructions.

Improving your marketability. Diversifying your skill set and creating a story are essential to standing out to employers, so staying in the job market and gaining career experience while you accrue further academic credentials will certainly benefit you in the long-run. And since no degree can guarantee you a great job when you're done, staying employed provides a nice safety net.

Getting tuition benefits. Depending on the type of program you're enrolling in, you may be able to work for the university you're attending as a researcher, lab assistant, teacher, and so on. In many cases, this work will garner tuition benefits—not a bad way to finance your degree. Also, if you are in a job that encourages a graduate degree, inquire about ways in which the company can help you pay for school, and find out whether or not it's encouraged to continue working while you get your degree.

Cons to Full-Time Work

This isn't going to be a walk in the park. Your professors don't care that you couldn't hand in your paper because you had to pull an extra shift, and your manager won't care that you have a paper due when he or she

Career Options

Is It Possible to Balance Full-Time Work with Part-Time Grad School? continued...

needs you for that shift. Here are some drawbacks to juggling work and school.

Burnout. If doing your schoolwork means that you risk getting fired, you're in trouble. If doing your job means you can't keep up with your schoolwork, you're not getting the most out of your degree. Many say that working full-time while going to school is the equivalent of holding two full-time jobs, so you had better be prepared for a tough slog. (Note: Many graduate programs, including some law schools, require students to take classes through the summer, so you may not even be able to get a break from the double-grind during those months.)

Bad work-life balance. On a similar note, working and going to school is almost certainly a recipe for zero social life. And while we don't suggest that anyone should ever go to grad school to relive their undergrad glory days, meeting new people and networking with those in your field of

choice is all part of the graduate school experience. Not only will your networking be hamstringed (though contacts from your job may balance out this sacrifice), but you'll also limit your ability to attend symposiums, go to conferences, and participate in other events. This may hurt you in an academic field, but could be less relevant if you're getting a more vocationally-focused degree.

Losing a job. If you really like your current job and have the potential for advancement, it's worth considering how juggling school will affect your prospects. On the flipside, if you're going to school as part of a career-shifting move, throwing yourself into it full-time program is advisable. (Bonus: During summer breaks, you can pursue internships that may eventually lead to full-time jobs.) ∎

Chapter IV: Getting Hired

Getting Hired

The job hunt can be the most trying of all post-college obstacles because it distills so many doubts and challenges into one seemingly all-important process. Once you've tackled the process of deciding what you even want to do (not always a simple task), you then have to address the thorny issue of actually landing a job. According to outplacement firm Challenger, Gray and Christmas, the average job search lasts four months, so don't be discouraged if nothing falls into your lap immediately. Just remember that the job hunt is a rite of passage, and like all rites of passage, it will probably be sort of uncomfortable and humiliating at the time, but one day you'll either romanticize it into a great yarn or block it from your memory entirely.

For most recent grads, one of the most frustrating aspects of the job market is the lack of clear-cut expectations. In college, you pretty much knew what you had to get a good grade, and if you messed up your teacher told you what you did wrong. During the job hunt, you will almost never get any explanation of why you didn't get a job. In many ways, it's more like the college application process than actually being in college—no matter how stellar your credentials are, sometimes the other kid's grandfather donated a building.

Needless to say, inexplicable rejections, unanswered emails, and botched interviews can take the wind out of anyone's sail. But letting these setbacks fester never helped anyone. Instead, realize that while there are no "rules" to the job-hunting game, there are *plenty* of best practices that will help you stand out from the pack. Trust us: Being in the dark about why you didn't get a job feels a lot better than knowing you got cut for making a simple resume error or failing to dress appropriately for the interview.

In this chapter, we'll debunk the mysteries of the job hunt and give you the tools you need to tackle the process with confidence. This isn't *The Secret*, so you're not going to learn how to take over the world simply through the power of thinking you're the bee's knees. Instead, you will learn things that are actually useful, like how to effectively clean up your online identity, ways to nail your resume and cover letter, and tips for networking your way to interesting people and places. We'll also provide you with the best strategies for acing interviews and what to do once you actually receive an offer. Enjoy yourself—this is where life after college really starts to heat up!

Cleaning Up Your Online Identity

First things first: Before you begin networking and applying for jobs, make sure your online persona is up to snuff. This doesn't mean your past has to be picture-perfect. Companies are not so naïve as to think that none of their potential employees has ever had a few too many cheeky tequilas or lit a fart on fire in a crowded space—it is corporate *America*, after all. Everyone knows you went to college and probably got caught on camera acting a fool. The point of cleaning up your online identity is simply to ensure you are putting your best foot forward and avoiding giving a potential employer an excuse to reject you—using a profile picture of you rocking a keg stand in your underwear or picking up M&Ms with your feet at a sorority pledge event is not a good move. You don't have to censor all personality out of your online game; just use some common sense and avoid shooting yourself in the foot for no reason at all.

Okay, enough of that sermon—let's get down to business. For most recent grads, protecting your rep online is mostly about rethinking your Facebook profile, which basically boils down to two words: privacy settings. (A similar process can be iterated across other networks like MySpace, Bebo, etc.) Conveniently, even after the brouhaha over the most recent privacy settings update in 2009, Mark Zuckerberg & Co. actually provide users with pretty granular control over what people can and cannot see. (Note: Facebook often changes privacy settings and while this section should provide a good general overview of the topic, it's worth checking http://www.facebook.com/privacy/explanation.php for any updates before you end up making changes.)

There are four aspects of your Facebook presence you can control through the privacy settings page—profile (which includes photos, status updates, posts, etc.); contact information; applications and websites; and search. For each of these areas, as well as the subsections within them, you can select who sees what. Will you let everyone see your goodies? Just your friends? Perhaps friends *and* friends of friends? Or maybe even an entire network? You can even create customized lists (e.g., previous co-workers, camp friends, networking contacts, etc.) to provide access to specific portions of your account and block specific people—or everyone—outright. Then, when you post a piece of content (like a photo or a note), Facebook will allow you to assign settings to that specific post right before you submit it.

Profile Information. Facebook allows you to make different parts of your profile available to each of the groups discussed above. For example, you could make your "About Me," "Birthday," and "Education and Work," available to everyone, but limit your "Photo Albums" and "Posts by Me" to only your friends and friends of friends. Of course, you can also go all out and **block** everyone from everything, which we think is really the only failsafe move. This is because it's important to realize that even if you make this stuff available only to a select group of people, your

---

Tips & Tricks: Cleaning up your Google search

Affecting Google rankings is no easy task. Whole books are devoted to improving search engine results, and companies spend millions of dollars each year on search engine optimization (SEO). Before you even think about going into battle with the rankings, make sure it's worth your time. Google all variations of your name and nicknames (with quotation marks and without, etc.) and see if you find anything you're not happy about. If there is nothing unsavory, or if your name is common enough to render you anonymous for search purposes, then you are in the clear. Otherwise, the best you can usually do is to make your Facebook and LinkedIn profiles public (assuming you've cleaned them up), and contact webmasters to request they take down anything that you'd prefer not to have on the 'net. The latter tactic may be useful when your friends tag your name and the phrase "superman that ho" on pictures they posted at Urban Dictionary. But if the *Waterloo Courier* ran a story about the time you were arrested for streaking through the mall, there's not too much you can do about it.

---

data will probably still get out (we've heard stories of sneaky employers finding people with connections to their potential hires in order to be able to see what they marked as private—hopefully you don't know any snitches). Of course, employers aren't out to get you, but if you're really paranoid, you might consider making everything except your most basic information private during the course of the job hunt.

Contact Information. This is pretty straightforward. You can choose who can see your email address, phone number, and so on. You're not going to lose a job opportunity or get fired as a result of hiding or showing your cell phone number, so just select whichever privacy settings you're comfortable with.

Applications and Websites. With the advent of applications and Facebook Connect, you may be releasing your private data to websites and/or applications without even knowing it, and they in turn may be making it publicly available. In fact, your friends can even share some of your information without your knowing it. Just be aware of what access applications and websites have to you. Also, don't forget all of the status updates and posts they can make on your behalf —while it might be difficult to wean yourself off of Mafia Wars for the few months until you snag a job, do you really want a potential employer knowing you just shot Little Jonny and stole his coke stash?

Search. Unlike the old days when you had to construct insanely complex advanced searches to find the person you made out with the night before, it is now extremely easy to search Facebook. As a result, the floodgates have opened and people can search almost anything you make available. It's important to check your "search" privacy settings to make sure you block what you don't want the community to see. In addition, Facebook can make your profile public via Google, so you should consider whether you want to create a **public search listing** or not. On the one hand, this makes it easier than ever for employers to track you down (which could be good or bad depending on what you make public). On the other hand, if you're concerned about what people find when they search for your name using Google, a public search Facebook profile will show up on the first page and may help to "bury" less desirable hits for your name (like that in-depth tutorial you published about how to steal cable).

When reviewing the above settings, pay close attention to the four basic types of content that could get you in trouble: your personal profile, photos/videos, status updates, and wall posts. In other words, the places where you're most likely to crack a risqué joke or "reveal too much." The trick is to decide who you want to see what and then adjust your privacy settings accordingly, even if that means just blocking someone during the duration of your job hunt.

Needless to say, it's really up to you to decide how private you need (or want) to be. If you're angling for a government job or for one in a very conservative company, you may have greater concerns than others about potential employers viewing your profile and pictures. Moreover, job hunt aside, some people just don't feel comfortable being easily stalkable, while others derive great pleasure from online exhibitionism.

Oh, and one last thing: Just to make sure you read this chapter thoroughly, we'll be systematically Facebooking each and every one of you. Watch your back!

Compiling Your Life on Paper

Once you've cleaned up your online act, it's time to get your job-hunting ducks in order so that you'll be able to strike when the iron is hot. For most positions, you will need to present a resume and a cover letter. If you're applying for a creative position or media job, you may be required to submit some samples of your previous work (e.g., a portfolio in creative fields, "clips"  in journalism). And for some jobs, you may have to take a skills, grammar, or knowledge test. Certain jobs will also require references, and while they typically only request them once you've interviewed and are being seriously considered for the position, it's a good idea to plan ahead and line up your references before you apply (see page 197).

As you get started, remember that "attention to detail" isn't just a skill you'll need on the job—it's a skill you'll need during the job hunt as well. A sloppy resume or typo-riddled cover letter will leave you grounded before you even get a chance to take off. Put some time into nailing these items down—they will not only be crucial in helping you snag interviews, but they will also give you confidence as the search progresses and things start happening quickly. When someone calls and says, "Meet me for coffee in half an hour. Bring your resume," you don't want to be scrambling like an idiot. Preparedness is the cousin of "getting a job." And they are cousins that actually like each other.

Keep in mind the different purposes of these documents when preparing them—a resume basically lists your background and skills, while a cover letter ensures that you have "intangible qualities" like a personality and an enthusiastic approach to work. It's often said that an employer should be able to glance at your resume for 20 seconds and have a strong impression about whether or not you're a good fit for the job. Here's how to make sure you make it past those 20 seconds.

Resume

Resume. Curriculum vitae. Autobiography.

Surprisingly, these words are not synonymous. In this section, we'll discuss the differences and give you some tips on how to craft the perfect on-paper identity.

When someone says that various products, ideas, and people "look good on paper," they are invoking the concept of a resume. When writing your own, the idea is to elicit this response right off the bat. During the interview, you can prove that you look good in the flesh as well.

To download a resume template, visit gradspot.com/book, then read through the guidelines provided below as you fill it in.

Contact Info. Make sure your name is displayed prominently at the top of the page and all of your contact information is up-to-date. You want to make yourself accessible in the long run, so don't give the landline number in the apartment that you might move out of next month. Even if you don't get a job immediately, a company may keep your

> ### Tips & Tricks: Customize yourself for each job
>
> Different jobs (and sometimes similar jobs within different industries) expect different things from new hires. Consider reworking your resume and writing a variation of your cover letter for every position. When putting together an application, always check the original job post and the career section of the company's website to pick up keywords and figure out what the employer is looking for. Then, tailor your skills and experiences to show that you are the ideal candidate for the specific position. This approach should trickle down through the entire job-seeking process—from the resume and cover letter right through to the interview. To help customize your pitch, we've polled professionals across many industries to see what traits they look for in prospective hires. For a list of skills to stress by industry, visit gradspot.com/book.

resume on file for a later opening, so don't sabotage yourself by disappearing off the face of the earth. And if you do keep your number at home, you never know who might pick up. It could be your senile grandfather who says that you have moved to the family's native Deutschland. In most cases, it's ideal to use a cell phone number. Furthermore, give a professional email address (sk8Rchick86@yahoo.com won't impress anyone). Make sure it is permanent (e.g., Gmail) and will not expire when you leave school or a job.

Be Clear, Concise, and Honest. Don't get bogged down in jargon because you think it will make your duties sound more official. While it's acceptable to candy-coat tasks like coffee-making and photocopying with phrases like "performed administrative duties," there is no reason to pack your resume with white lies. Use action verbs (e.g., administered, built, reviewed) and articulate each task in one or two phrases. If anything comes up in an interview, you should be able to expound upon it without having to say, "I guess by 'managed the books' I meant that I opened the mail, and my boss often received a lot of books." Similarly, don't be dishonest about your skills and background. Even if you pull the wool over an employer's eyes by saying you are proficient with InDesign or Excel, they are not going to be too pleased when you arrive on the first day and suddenly need training. That said, you should certainly emphasize your skills when applicable and make an effort to be as precise as possible in your resume descriptions. Lastly, in today's age of Monster.com-type websites and massive HR departments, you need to make your resume highly searchable online by packing it with keywords. This technique is particularly important when applying to government agencies, many of which use a system called Resumix to automatically sort through resumes. (For tips on getting past the resume robots, see "Tips & Tricks" on page 147.)

Objectives. This section is optional, but may be useful if you need to fill up space or you are applying for a job that doesn't obviously align with your experience. State your objectives in one or two tight sentences and make them as specific and compelling as possible. If you are applying to a range of places, tweak this section for each version of the resume that you send out. "Stacking cheddar" and "getting out the house" are not great reasons for wanting a job. Understand your audience and let them know exactly what you hope to get out of the experience. Also, if you are applying in an industry where you have no experience, tell a story (the extreme CliffsNotes version) of why you want to go from finance to nonprofit work, for example.

The Power of One. Keep it to one page. Most employers of recent grads are dealing with a high volume of resumes, so HR managers don't have time to wade through multi-page documents. But more important, the resume is the first test to see if you can present information clearly and concisely. If it takes you more than a page to outline yourself, then you are effectively outlining your professional aspirations in chalk. Ya dig?

> ### Tips & Tricks: Change your voicemail recording
>
> It's a huge turn-off for a potential employer to call your cell phone and be redirected to an absurd voicemail recording. ("Hey, this is Dylan. You know the drill," may have worked on *90210*, but it won't work now. Trust us.) Be brief and professional. Go with something along the lines of, "Hi, you've reached Megan Werner. I'm unable to answer the phone right now, but if you leave your name and number I will get back to you as soon as possible." You'll sound like a dingus to your friends, but it's a small price to pay for a sweet job.

Getting Hired

Tips & Tricks: What did I do for the last year?

If you get to the end of an internship or leave a job and are having trouble articulating what exactly you did there, check the job posting for the position you are leaving and see what the description is. Hypothetically, it should cover what you did (or were supposed to do).

Prioritize. There are no set rules for chronology or layout on a resume. However, you want to prioritize the most relevant information so that it appears near the top of the page. Generally it makes sense to start with your educational background (if you need to save space, consider nixing your high school—it is obvious that you went to one, and it's unlikely the employer will know the school) unless it happens to be local or well-known. Then move on to your relevant work experience (including internships). Under each entry, the bullet points describing your duties and achievements should be prioritized as well. Save activities and interests for the bottom.

Design. Unless graphic design is essential to the job you're applying for, having a slick-looking resume is not going to help you, and it certainly won't gloss over a lack of relevant experience or skills. Avoiding a lot of white space on the page will help you fit more information, but in general, don't get hung up on aesthetics. Just make sure your resume looks neat and, if possible, spatially balanced.

What if I have never done anything? Recent grads are often sorely lacking in the "Work Experience" category. If this is the case for you, emphasize your skills in other ways. Maybe you led a team on a semester-long project or organized a charity race in your town. Feel free to mention something from school or activities you have done in the past. The bottom line is that you are trying to sell yourself as trustworthy and capable. If you don't have a job or internship to speak for you, that doesn't mean your relevant talents shouldn't be noted.

To include my GPA, or not to include my GPA. In the realm of resume quandaries, this is one of the trickier situations to navigate. Everyone wants a rule of thumb, and the one that gets invoked most often is that you should include your GPA if it's over 3.0, or include only your GPA within your major if it's significantly better than the overall number. But every thumb is different, just like a snowflake. Generally, technical jobs (think engineering, Google, etc.) will definitely be interested in your GPA, and if you don't include it they will ask for it in the interview. In this case, leaving a GPA off your resume will read like an admission of guilt, so you'll have to decide whether it's really bad enough to try to keep under wraps. If it is particularly low and there is a good reason (e.g., you worked a job while going to school or held multiple leadership positions), be sure to address this in the cover letter and/or interview. Finally, specify the scale used—different schools have different ways of expressing GPAs, and 3.5 out of 4.0 is quite different from 3.5 out of 15.0. If you're lucky, you went to one of those "progressive" schools that doesn't have GPAs.

Proofread. Proofread. Proofread. The administrative staffing service Office Team reports that 47% of executives said they would throw out a candidate's resume for just one typo. This statistic might seem a little harsh. Should a typo really be that big of a deal? But you've got to think about it from the perspective of the employer: HR departments have to wade through a huge amount of resumes, so separating out the typo offenders is a quick sorting device to make their job easier. Furthermore, a typo on a one-page document does not really scream "detail-oriented" or "professional," which are two qualities that you should be shouting about. In particular, make sure that you don't mention the wrong position or company in your materials—an easy mistake to make when applying to numerous jobs. Basically, don't give a potential employer an excuse not to consider you.

Read This, It'll Knock Your Socks Off. Once you feel confident about your resume, run it by as many people as possible. The extra eyes will help weed out the typos and also provide you with feedback about how well you're selling yourself. It's ideal to get some feedback from someone working in the industry you're interested in, because he or she will have a sense of what specific employers will want to see.

Curriculum Vitae

You're probably thinking that this is just a fancy way of saying resume. It's a pretty fun phrase to toss around, no doubt. But the reality is that CVs and resumes are quite different documents. Whereas a resume is a sort of "highlight" reel of educational background and relevant experience/skills, a CV is the uncut version—the uncircumcized junk of resumes, you could say. And like uncircumcized junk, CVs are more popular in places like Greece than they are in America. They detail your entire educational background and list every single job—dating back to your high school camp counseling days—in chronological order with a description of job duties. They are presented in paragraph form. And they include "vital statistics" like date of birth, nationality, height and weight, and sometimes even a photo.

Getting Hired

When to use a CV: International jobs; academic, education, scientific or research positions; and in applications for fellowships or grants.

Autobiography

This is something else entirely. For examples see *The Autobiography of Benjamin Franklin, It's Not About the Bike: My Journey Back to Life*, and *Confessions of a Video Vixen*.

Sample Resume

JANE DOE
1234 Pine Avenue, Apt. 1 • Beverly Hills, CA 90210
(301) 555 5555 • jdoe@gmail.com

OBJECTIVE [Optional]

Detail-oriented Computer Science graduate seeks position as member of a software engineering team in a fast-paced, challenging work environment [Highlight relevant skills or strengths]

EDUCATION

University of California, Los Angeles (2007 – 2010)
Bachelor of Science in Computer Science, with Minor in Electrical Engineering
GPA in Major / Overall GPA: 3.79 / 3.54 [Show GPA in Major if higher than overall GPA]

Relevant Coursework and Projects
- Coursework heavily focused on practical aspects of Computer Science, including *C++ for Programmers, JAVA for Programmers*, and *Machine Structures* [Technical skills]
- Head of the Berkeley Machine Learning Project Group, leading a team of eight undergraduates in the design and development of an original machine learning algorithm [Leadership, Intelligence, Passion]

Redondo Beach High School (2002 – 2007) [Optional]
Valedictorian, June 2007

WORK EXPERIENCE

[Focus time spent on relevant jobs and qualities]
Google Inc., Mountain View, CA   2010 - Present   2006 – Present
Intern
[Describe the company and position, especially if it is not well known]
- Selected as one of 100 summer interns in the highly competitive Search Media Group at the world's leading internet search company
[Projects & Accomplishments – Focus on relevant responsibilities]
- Designed and developed source code for a variety of projects focused on search-based product offerings [Relevant programming experience]
- Built large scale distributed file systems and other infrastructures to reliably and efficiently manage and process hundreds of terabytes of information [Technical skills]
- Part of a team of six software developers responsible for optimizing performance of major database containing over 10 billion cached websites [Teamwork]
- Achieved proficiency in COBAL without any prior experience and successfully tested and debugged over 60,000 lines of legacy software code [Fast learner, attention to detail]

[Do not spend too much time on less relevant work experience]
Reborn Computers, Los Angeles, CA   2009 – 2010
Computer Repair Technician
- Repaired all brands of desktop and laptop computers and performed diagnostic services on computers and peripherals [Technical skills]

SKILLS
- Sun certified Java developer and fully proficient in a wide variety of other programming languages including Unix, Linux, C, and C++ [Technical skills]
- Fluent in English and Spanish, proficient in French [Be careful not to exaggerate]

INTERESTS AND OTHER
- President of the UCLA Computer Science Student Association (CSSA) [Leadership responsibility]
- Vice-captain of Barrack House softball team [Teamwork]
- Avid scuba diver with Advanced PADI Openwater certification [Include something interesting!]

Cover Letter

Cover letters involve a curious mixture of personality and homogeneity, as well as confidence and humility. In many cases, writing a cover letter is harder than actually performing the job you are applying for. Though the cover letter should logically be an introduction that says, "Hi, here are some things to know about me before you look at my resume," the reality is that it's probably going to be the reverse. Most employers just don't have the time to read a bunch of cover letters. Thus, the cover letter is the icing on a well-baked resume.

With that realization in mind, the main objective of a good cover letter should be to explain why you should get the job. It should tell a story of where you've been and where you are hoping to go, so you should spin your experiences specifically toward the job in question. This is particularly important if you appear to be shifting gears (e.g., you're a chemistry major interested in PR or you're dropping out of med school to do finance). A cover letter is a test of your personality and your written communication skills, but mostly it's a personal sales pitch. Stay focused—anecdotes and tangents, no matter how hilarious, should be kept to a bare minimum.

Thankfully, there is a basic formula for a strong cover letter. Follow these guidelines to ensure that you make a good first impression on paper.

Length: One page, including any headers, footers, or whatever other design flourishes you include. (No negotiations here.) The standard cover letter follows a three-paragraph formula.

Heading: Whenever possible, you want to address your cover letter to an actual human being. Headings like "To Whom It May Concern" and "Dear Sir or Madam" should be used only as last resorts. If you aren't given a name off the bat, do a little research. Applying to a magazine? Check the masthead for the editor's name. If it's a large office, try calling HR, telling them what job you're applying for (you don't have to say who you are), and ask-

> **Tips & Tricks: Naming electronic files**
>
> When naming your resume and cover letter files, make sure they are distinctive. Recruiters get hundreds of documents via email titled "resume10.doc" or "myresume.pdf"—make it easier for them to find your information later by saying who you are in the filename (e.g., "Jacob_Sills_Resume.pdf"). It will be more searchable and your name will be more memorable.

Tips & Tricks: Show, don't tell

Your cover letter should not be a laundry list of your traits and skills. Rather, it should be a place where you demonstrate how you actively put your traits/skills to use to do something awesome in the past. Saying, "I'm resourceful," isn't going to convince anyone, but describing how you took initiative to design and implement a database where all of your company's information could be consolidated *proves* that you're resourceful. Go you!

ing for a specific name within the department. The personal touch will show that you're resourceful and that you care enough to figure out whom you are dealing with.

Paragraph One: What are you applying for and why? The cover letter is, in essence, an introduction to a stranger. So what do you do when you meet a stranger? You find some common ground. You announce your purpose for addressing him or her. You figure out if you "know the same people." This doesn't mean that you find out your potential boss went to Stanford and say, "OMG, do you know my friend Brittany?" It means covering a few basics:

1) What position are you applying for?

2) How did you find out about the job?

3) Do you have a networking connection? (If so, mention this as early as possible.)

4) Why, in a sentence or two, are you interested in and a good fit for the job? (This is like the thesis statement of your cover letter that will be illuminated in the subsequent paragraphs.)

Second Paragraph: What have you accomplished in your life that is relevant to this job? You'd like people to "read between the lines" of your resume and realize you are a wonderful person with great perspective. But if they didn't even realize that Dumbledore was gay, you've got to keep your expectations realistic. Here's where you expound upon your experience and spell out the subtext for them. For example, you can talk about a specific project that you handled well but weren't able to fully convey in a simple bullet point on your resume. Or you can talk about the type of feedback you got from your boss and coworkers. Remember to be specific: Only highlight things that are relevant to the position you're applying for. This is one occasion where you can toot your own horn. That doesn't mean you should sound arrogant, but you should sound convincing.

Third Paragraph: How do you match up, why do you want the job, and why should you get it? If you were playing *NBA Jam: Tournament Edition*, this is where the announcer should be yelling, "That's the nail in the coffin!" Tie up your experiences and interests to convince the reader that you are the woman or man for the job. Show the employer that you are enthusiastic and passionate. Don't say, "If I don't get this job, I will literally kill myself!" But do give a strong indication of why the job interests you and what unique contributions you would bring to it.

Closing Statement: Mind your Ps and Qs. When closing out a cover letter, remember a few key things:

- Reiterate your contact information.

- Thank the reader for taking the time to consider your application.

- Sign your name if you are not sending electronically.

Sample Cover Letter

JOHN DOE

8888 W. 16th St., Apt 5B · john.doe@gradspot.com · (215) 555 5555
Philadelphia, PA, 19147, USA

Derek Anderson
Head of Undergraduate Recruiting
Diamond Group
222 Malone Street
Houston, TX 77007

Dear Ms. Anderson,

I am writing to apply for an Assistant Strategist position with the Diamond Group. After speaking with Daniel Kelly and conducting my own research, I know that Diamond would be a perfect match for my talents and aspirations. I recently graduated from the University of Michigan, where I maintained an overall GPA of 3.85/4.00 with a major in Marketing and a minor in English Literature and Language. Through a diverse range of professional experiences, including internships at *The Milwaukee Journal Sentinel* and Morgan Stanley, I have consistently been intrigued by the way in which companies both predict and shape the desires of consumers as they build their brands. By joining the Strategic Planning team, I hope to pursue this interest and further develop my knowledge of the industry as a whole while producing for your company.

While working on the arts desk at the *Sentinel*, my coverage of commissioned music in Nike's viral marketing campaigns garnered the interest of the business editor, who asked me to write a piece about the role of authenticity in the company's branding strategy. I continued to follow this trend on my blog, eventually leading to a successful pitch to Slate.com last year. Meanwhile, my internship last summer at Morgan Stanley offered me an intense immersion in the basic mechanics of M&A corporate advisory, as well the investment banking industry in general. I acquired a great deal of business acumen from being part of such a hard-working environment, and I greatly enjoyed researching the potential for market growth in a variety of industries. However, while I received encouragement from my supervisors to pursue a full-time position with the company, I did not find that the job played to my creative strengths.

At Diamond, I hope that I can pursue my passion for corporate branding and marketing strategy within the context of a more focused and creatively challenging environment. My background in print and online media provides me with a lens through which to analyze a brand and assess its marketability, while my investment banking experience has helped me develop a high level of professionalism, attention to detail, and analytical skills to review businesses. I especially hope to apply these skills to aid Diamond's shifting focus toward digital advertising. I am extremely excited by the prospect of translating my skills into a market strategy role, and I look forward to speaking with you about the possibility of joining your company. If you have any further questions you can reach me by email (john.doe@gradspot.com) or via phone at (215) 555 5555.

Thank you for your time and consideration.

Sincerely,
John Doe

Salary Requirements

Many jobs will ask you to include salary requirements with your application. While it might sound awesome to say you require, "Cheddar, gouda, and other denominations of cheese," this is actually sort of a no-win situation. On the one hand, the company may be using the salary requirement as a screening process—if you are too high, you might not be considered. On the other hand, it might be trying to save money by finding people who will work for cheap.

Unless you're Criss Angel, you don't want to dig your own grave, because you may not be able to get out of it. There is no cure-all to this irksome malady, but here are a few suggested remedies:

Do your research. Look into the industry in which you're applying for a job and find comparable positions. Visit Salary.com to gauge ballpark figures, talk to people you know in similar positions, or cold call a competitor and try to find out what they offer. The compensation should be pretty standard across the board. If you think you can get away with it, you might consider writing something like, "I hope to receive a competitive salary," but you're dodging the question, which is not what you want to do in the face of a potential employer.

Give a range. You really don't need to say, "I hope to receive $34,553.78 per annum." Figure out the industry standard and say something like, "I hope to receive a salary in the low- to mid-thirties." Covering the basics without being evasive shows that you are a diplomatic wizard.

Stall. Say you would prefer to discuss compensation in an interview, but you don't imagine it will be a problem.

Don't forget benefits. Make sure you know what benefits are offered, such as health care and 401(k) plans. When the time comes, it may be easier to negotiate for wider benefits than a higher salary. Assess your own needs to figure out if a $35K salary with full benefits is better than $40K with none (hint: it probably is).

Emailing Your Job Application

An HR professional once said, "The three most important factors in screening an application are delivery, delivery, and delivery." But that's absurd: We all know that it's not delivery. It's DiGiorno!

In this day and age, it's rare to physically mail in an application. Often there will be an online application where you simply plug in your info and upload your resume and cover letter. However, sometimes you will be asked to email your materials. While this system is supposed to make things easier and more efficient, it also adds new trauma-inducing variables to the equation. What do

I put in the subject line? What do I put in the body? Take a deep breath, young grad. It's basically a matter of common sense and following directions.

Sometimes HR will tell you to put a job code or phrase in the subject line so that they can easily sort applications (see "Tips & Tricks: Naming electronic files" on page 191). If so, follow directions, attach your resume, cover letter, and any other relevant materials, and then write a quick note in the body saying that you have done so. In general, you will not be penalized for sending documents as Word files, but sending them as PDFs is preferable because they will look the same across all operating systems and computers. The format you choose is not a huge issue, but just remember that if a company receives a lot of applications and they can't open your resume, they probably won't ask you to resend it—you're out of the running.

If there are no instructions for the subject line, include your name and the title of the position. A catchy or offbeat subject line (e.g., "Will Work for Food") is rarely appropriate, though it's up to you to judge the attitude of the organization. As a final point, don't be afraid to paste your cover letter directly into the body of the email as well as attaching it. This is the one document you really want someone to read, so serve it up on a platter.

Sample Application Email

From: Samuel Bentley <sbentley@gradspot.com>
To: Mrs. Daniels <Mrs.Daniels@fakeweb.com>
Subject: WX957 – Production Assistant
Attachment: Sam_Bentley_resume.pdf,
Sam_Bentley_coverletter.pdf, Sam_Bentley_clips.pdf

Dear Mrs. Daniels,

I am writing to submit my application for the role of Production Assistant, which I learned about through your listing on Media Bistro. Attached you will find my résumé and cover letter, as well as a PDF of my writing clips. For your convenience, I have also pasted the text of my cover letter below.

If there is any other information I can provide, please do not hesitate to contact me by e-mail (sbentley@gradspot.com), or by phone at 646 555 5555.

Thank you for your consideration,
Samuel Bentley

References

Hiring is always about trust. Unfortunately, the prevailing code on the streets is "don't trust anyone," so you'll often need to bring in some backup to vouch for your good name. The good news is you usually won't be asked for references until after you've applied and are being seriously considered for a job. The bad news is you have to ask yourself a tough question—who thinks you are the bee's knees other than your mother? Hopefully one of these people:

- A former boss
- A professor or a dean
- A coworker
- A coach
- A family friend in the industry
- Someone who already works at the company you are applying to (money in the bank)

Here are some tips for providing references during your job search.

Choosing Your References

The most important thing to note about references is that a personal relationship speaks louder than a fancy name. If you had a great rapport with your thesis advisor and never spoke with the dean, go with the thesis advisor—he or she will know a lot more about your strengths and will have a genuine interest in promoting them. Maybe you want to get into trading and your second cousin's great uncle is T. Boone Pickens—utilize this connection for networking, but don't ask for a meaningless reference. You don't want HR calling up someone who barely knows you. This makes you seem like you haven't cultivated meaningful relationships with people who are willing to vouch for you.

Building a Reference Network

A good rule of thumb is to ask for a written reference from a supervisor or coworker whenever you leave an internship or a job (and ask as early as possible so you are not putting them on a ridiculous deadline to help you out). This way, you'll have a nice little stash of kind words to deploy at will. But playing into the whole theme of mistrust, most employers won't be interested in written recommendations because they can easily be forged. Instead, you will provide contact information so they can get a reference on the phone and ask hard-hitting questions like, "What is Teddy's greatest strength? And, as a follow-up, "What is his deepest, darkest secret?" In this case, always get permission by asking a potential reference if he or she would mind being listed.

Maintaining a Reference Network

While you can't give out your home phone number and have your little brother pretend to be the CEO of General Electric, you can definitely take steps to ensure your references aren't burning your bridges. The first way to achieve a little editorial control is to choose your references wisely. Once you've done that, keep them in the loop about the status of your job search. If a company recently asked you for references, contact your people to tell them they should expect a call. While you're at it, describe the position so they'll know how to pitch you. Never forget that they are doing you a huge favor. Thank them often and stay in touch.

While you should line up your references before applying for a job, you don't need to include them in your initial application (unless specifically instructed to do so). Generally, references come into play once you are being seriously considered for a job. Upon request, provide a Word document with the name, title, company, and contact information (work phone and email) for each of your references (usually three to four). No major formatting is required, but make sure the file name is easily identifiable, and remember to list your name and contact information on the page. In addition to the attachment, it is appropriate to paste this information into the body of an email.

Networking

Once you've got your career story down on paper, it's time to put yourself out there in order to leverage any connections you may have to potential jobs and to create new ones. No matter how great a candidate you are for

a position, you may never get an interview without the help of someone on the inside who can make sure your application finds its way to the top of the pile. And you might not even know about a job in the first place until you meet the right person who thinks you can do it. In fact, far more positions are filled through referrals than through a job hunter applying blindly to a posting. Thus, it's no surprise that just about everyone on the planet—from corporate execs to skateboarding pros to acupuncturists—ranks networking as one of the most important parts of career building.

To understand how the real world works, consider the following situation: You're applying for a job and are up against one other candidate. The two of you have the same credentials, and you both come off well in social situations. But now for the X-factor: The other candidate is best friends with the interviewer's daughter. Peace out! Another of life's bitter herbs, but that's just the reality of the job market. Rather than crying about nepotism and pursuing some sort of proto-Marxist vendetta, get out there and network. As annoying as it is to get passed up for a job because someone else has a relationship that you don't, it's awesome when *you* are the one with the relationship. It's not a perfectly meritocratic system, but you have to accept that companies are much more inclined to go for a known entity than a wildcard (so much so that many pay employees for referring friends to fill new positions).

This is not a *carte blanche* to shamelessly social climb your way to the top. In fact, networking is not actually all about kissing butt and taking names. Good networking essentially involves being friendly, polite, proactive, and reasonably adept at expressing your interests to people. You do not have to be a slimy, shallow a-hole. At the end of the day, the more you network, the less "net work" you will end up doing in life. Doors will begin opening for you. Exciting opportunities will materialize out of thin air. And you'll have a lot of coffees with semi-interesting people.

Networking doesn't start with your dream employer. If you were talking to the employer of your dreams, then you wouldn't need to be networking in the first place. Networking starts by interacting with anyone. The key is to understand that just because you aren't talking directly to the CEO of the company you hope to work for doesn't mean that another person can't help you get your foot in the door. Ironically, the CEO is probably not the one who would ultimately be making the decision to hire you, so shoot for the people who would be your immediate superiors or coworkers.

Leave no stone unturned. Networking is a 24/7 endeavor. You're just as likely to find out about a potential job while socializing as you are while seeking advice from professionals. That doesn't mean you should only befriend rich kids with powerful parents, but it does mean you should look for networking opportunities all around you. Meet up groups, recreational sports teams, and volunteer activities all provide settings in which you could meet someone who might know of a job lead. Chat up that guy in the corner of the café where you

Getting Hired

hang out—while he may just be a wannabe screenwriter, he might also be the favorite nephew of Steven Spielberg.

Don't underestimate the influence of other recent grads. Don't turn your nose up at networking with people who are one to three years out of college. They are often asked to review resumes submitted by applicants from their alma maters.

Don't expect to get a job right away when networking. While networking is the art of getting the job before the interview, that doesn't mean you're going to get the job immediately. In fact, the first step in courting a contact should just be asking questions about the industry you're seeking to enter, the company you're hoping to be employed by, and any advice in general. Ultimately, this is a soft sell and you'll learn something. If you impress someone, they'll remember the conversation even if you haven't asked them for a job—maybe they'll connect you with someone else or even employ you later themselves.

Networking isn't brown-nosing; it's about finding commonalities. Many people pursue the following tactic when networking: Locate backside of powerful human. Implant nose in said backside. Repeat. But no one likes a brown-noser, so try to be a bit more genuine. Don't launch into a conversation with people you're networking with by asking them whom they know or if they can help you land a job. Also, don't just agree with everything they say or talk about how great the company they work for is. Instead, be completely candid (and somewhat subtle). Ask them about their job and their interests. Share your genuine passion for the industry with them. Try to find some common ground—if need be, feel free to talk about something completely non–work-related (e.g., current events, sports). If you establish rapport first, the conversation will eventually turn toward what you want to do (or you can politely nudge it in that direction). And when that happens, you're effectively networking.

Informational interviews = good networking. Informational interviews are the perfect way to get your foot in the door because they're easier to score than job interviews. An informational interview is an opportunity to talk with someone in an industry or at a company you find interesting. It's not an interview for a job, but rather a way to become more informed about potential opportunities and to make yourself known. This approach will provide you with two advantages: It will enable you to be more knowledgeable when the real interview rolls around, and it may actually turn into an interview. Remember that anytime you're talking with an employee of a company you one day hope to work for, you're being interviewed (even if they don't say so), so look alive! For a sample informational interview request, see the next page.

Where to meet for a networking meeting. Assuming it's not someone you have a prior relationship with, don't ask to meet over dinner or "drinks," unless they offer. Instead, ask if they would be willing to talk over a cup of coffee, or during a quick breakfast or lunch. Other options include meeting at someone's office, or finally, talking on the phone. Of course, an in-person conversation always has more impact, but you should always meet at a time and place that is convenient for the other party.

How to prepare for a networking meeting. We can't stress enough that you should prepare for any networking meeting as if it's an interview. This means reading up on the person whom you're meeting with, the company they work for, related recent news, and the industry as a

> **Tips & Tricks: Networking to recruiters**
>
> Some industries never use recruiters for entry-level jobs, but many companies that hire a lot of recent grads each year use recruiters as a filter between the company and the field of potential candidates. "The best place to start at a large company is with a recruiter," says Holly Paul, the National Sourcing Operations Leader for Campus and Experienced Recruiting at PricewaterhouseCoopers. If you're lucky, a recruiter from a company where you want to work visited your school during a job fair. But even if you didn't encounter one through campus recruiting, you can still use them to get a foot in the door. You can find company recruiters through networking or you can ask your school's careers services office if it has hookups. You can even just call the company and ask. Within the recruiting industry, however, there's also an allure to going out and finding great candidates. And guess what? From our conversations with people in the industry, it's clear that Facebook (p. 212) and LinkedIn (p. 206) are very much on the radar, so be sure to maximize your presence on those platforms.

whole (thank you, Wiki-Google). This will help with conversation topics, and your preparation will convey your enthusiasm. That said, don't go wild with displaying your knowledge of someone's personal history—you don't want to transform from "job candidate" to "restraining order candidate."

What to bring to a networking meeting. Always bring some type of notebook and a pen. If you can do so discreetly, bring a resume in the event the person you're meeting with asks for it—though you can always email it afterwards. If you are networking over the phone, you can compensate for the lack of face

Getting Hired

time by being extra organized. Spread out your notes in front of you or keep a Word document open—the person you're speaking with will never know and it can make you look extremely knowledgeable.

Don't forget etiquette. You'll never get yourself in trouble by being too polite (at least at first). Call people Mr., Ms., Mrs., etc. Always meet/speak with people at their convenience. If you're getting coffee or food, offer to pay even if you think they'll insist on picking up the tab. If they do insist, you can give in and let them pay at that point. (Check out page 267 for a whole discussion of meal etiquette.) As your interactions move along, you can get a vibe from the other person and loosen up accordingly. For example, if they tell you to call them by their first name, it's most likely not a "test," so go ahead and do it. If it is a test, they're creepy and you may be networking up the wrong tree.

Always send a thank you note after every networking meeting. So, you've spent an hour talking with someone about a job, and that person has been kind enough to share her career insights with you. She did you a favor. Acknowledge it by sending a thank you letter (or email, as the case may be these days). Depending upon your relationship with the person with whom you just spoke, the letter can be formal or just a few sentences. Referencing something you discussed during your conversation goes a long way. You can even ask a follow-up question, and if the person requested to see your resume, this is an opportunity to send it along. For more information on crafting your resume, see page 185.

Professional karma. Networking never ends. Even after you've gotten the job, you should make sure to inform the people who helped you, and also stay in touch with them (as well as anyone else with whom you networked along the way). Who knows when you'll need your next job? Or better yet, when you can help someone else? Because when it comes down to it, networking is a pay-it-forward game. Sometimes the student doth become the teacher, and someone you help may also be able to reciprocate down the line.

Sample Informational Interview Request

The first sentence of your request should both introduce who you are and explain your connection to the individual you are contacting. Maybe he or she is a friend of a friend (as per the example below). Or maybe you found the person in your alumni network. Or maybe this is just a cold call and you pulled the name from a newspaper article.

From: Michael Humphrey <mike@gradspot.com>
To: Mrs. McGregor <McGregor@fortune500.com>
Subject: Interview Request

Dear Mrs. McGregor,

I recently graduated from the University of Miami, and after my good friend, David Johnson, learned that I was interested in a career in marketing, he suggested I contact you to request a brief informational interview.

While at the University of Miami, I majored in marketing. In addition, I had an internship last summer at Razor Corp, where I assisted media buyers on several high-profile interactive marketing campaigns. I now plan to apply both my education and my work experience to a career in marketing. At your convenience, I was hoping to learn what types of positions you suggest for a recent college graduate, and also to hear your thoughts on the future of the industry as a whole.

Thank you very much for your time. If you are available to speak with me, we can talk over the phone, or I can meet you at a location of your choosing. I can be reached at 305 555 5555 or by e-mail at mike@gradspot.com.

Appreciatively,
Michael Humphrey

Phone Message Script: "Hi, my name is Michael Humphrey. I was fascinated by the recent article about you in the *New York Times*, so I thought I would get in touch because I'm very interested in pursuing a career in marketing. I was hoping you might be willing to spend a few minutes talking on the phone or in person to provide me with some advice based on your experience. Would it be possible to set up an informational interview at your convenience? Thank you very much for your consideration. You can reach me at 646 402 5557 or via email at mike@gradspot.com."

Top Networking Targets and Opportunities

- Family

- Friends and fellow students (don't forget about their parents)

- College alumni networks

- College professors or deans (depending upon your relationships)

- Career services office

Getting Hired

- Facebook, LinkedIn, Doostang, and other online communities (see next page)

- Charities

- Teams

- Organizations

- Trade conventions (many are free)

- Social events (parties, weddings, reunions, etc.)

Set Up a Networking Spreadsheet

If it sounds dorky, that's because it is. But you want to know what's not dorky? Getting a job! It's easy to keep track of your contacts at the beginning of your professional career, when you tend to peg all your future hopes on the first person who tells you they "may have something coming up soon." But before you know it, you'll be wheeling and dealing all around town with a stack of business cards on your desk that resembles the Leaning Tower of Pisa. And the thing is, sometimes you will need to follow up with someone a couple months or even a year later. In order to keep track of all those contacts, it's worth making a simple "Networking Contact Spreadsheet." Here's how to do it.

1. Set up a spreadsheet. This will serve as HQ for all networking you do. In our opinion, the best way to do this is to create a Google Doc so that you'll have access to it wherever you are. Along the top of the spreadsheet, create the obvious columns—"name," "company," "contact information," "how we met," and "correspondences/meetings." However, you can really stand out (particularly when networking with someone you've only met once or twice) by remembering specifics about your discussions. So also add a "notes" column for details (e.g., "Mary loves *Curb Your Enthusiasm* and started out as a waitress before she got into the PR biz").

2. Fill it out every time you make a contact. After you meet someone (whether it happens randomly or at a networking event), try to immediately take notes on things such as what the person does, what you talked about, where you were, contacts you have in common, interests, and so on.

A convenient place to write this info is on the back of his or her business card. Then, once you can get in front of a computer, sit down with your business cards and spreadsheet for a few minutes and enter the info. If you don't, you'll eventually forget everything about that really interesting person you met, and you'll probably lose the cards and kick yourself for it.

3. Keep track of correspondence. Put things like, "Sent resume 7/19/10. Told to follow up 9/1," in the notes column. This way, you won't forget anything or annoy people with multiple or ill-timed messages. Of course, there are many other ways to make this system more complex (e.g., color-coding by industry). But then you really *would* be a dork, more likely to be given a swirly in the toilet than a job offer! (Only joking—in this game, dorks rule the roost. Just look at Bill Gates.)

Once you start a networking spreadsheet, the most important thing you can do is to keep it up. The people you meet today may be the people who help you in five years (or vice versa), so don't think of this as an exercise that's useful only during your initial job hunt. Continue to add contacts at your first job, your second job, and beyond. It could easily develop into the most valuable arrow in your career quiver. And if not, you can attempt to sell it to some naïve recent grad for $25. ∎

Professional Networking Sites: The Anti-Social Solution

While it's wise to protect yourself from prying employers online (see page 182), the Internet is also a great place to self-promote, get your name out there, and network your way toward great jobs. Online career networking is growing rapidly as the first web-savvy generation of workers begins to make its mark on the professional world. Needless to say, it will only get more relevant with time, unlike other Internet phenomena like Tay Zonday.

The two biggest players in the arena of career-oriented social networks are LinkedIn and Doostang. As an increasingly multi-purpose platform, Facebook has its place in the hierarchy as well. If you decide to take the online career networking route (and we suggest you at least give it a shot), ditch whatever hab-

---

Tips & Tricks: The point of online networking

While online career networking can feel more casual and less intimidating than striking up conversations over cocktail wieners, remember that it is a means to an end, not an end in itself. The key is to turn your online contacts into offline phone calls, meetings over coffee, and interviews. Nothing can replace face-to-face contact, but online networking can broaden the scope of your search and help you connect with people even if you're from the middle of nowhere, attended a tiny school, and have no friends.

---

its you've developed in your prior *social* networking and keep your profile purely professional and the privacy settings conservative. As a rule of thumb, treat it as you would a resume: List all of your accomplishments, but don't lie or exaggerate. Keep in mind that you're not just friending people to share party pics or appear popular anymore; you're attempting to connect with specific recruiters and future employers, many of whom are now online. They will catch you in a lie quicker than a jealous ex. Well, maybe not quite that quickly. Either way, there are plenty of tips and tricks to getting the most out of online career networks.

LinkedIn

LinkedIn.com was the first online career network to gain widespread popularity, and today it boasts a user base of 48 million "professionals." Basically, it's like one massive cocktail party, minus the cocktails and the human interaction. (If you want to set the mood, however, just whip up a gin and tonic and play some light jazz on your computer.) All online career networks have the basic features you'd expect, so we're going to assume that you can figure out the basics. What we want to explore here are ways to make your profile stand out and get exactly what you want from the site.

- **Make your profile public.** This means anyone can view it, and Google will even display it as a search result when people Google your name (see page 183). To do so, go to your account section and edit your "full profile." While you're at it, choose a custom URL (e.g., linkedin.com/in/sarahpalin). One caveat: Before you plaster your name all over the 'net, make sure that you've fine-tuned every part of your profile.

- **Utilize the "Advanced Search" feature.** Instead of just browsing for people by industry, search for specific companies or positions as well. You can even use Boolean searching, the most comprehensive search technique of them all. You might recall from 5th grade library sessions that these searches use AND or OR to tailor your result—for example, you might search "IT Department AND Apple." When searching for a phrase, make sure you enter it within quotation marks (e.g., "IT Department," not IT Department).

- **Dig deep for connections.** Found someone who works at the company of your dreams but don't want to cold call? Check his or her LinkedIn profile to see if you have any connections. LinkedIn shows connections that have up to six degrees of separation—you could probably even find a way to holler at Kevin Bacon! In a bind, you can have your friend ask her friend to put you in touch with a friend's friend. Again, it may not sound ideal, but it's better than sending a random email to a potential employer before you've laid any groundwork

- **Ask questions.** LinkedIn enables you to send a message to your entire network in the form of a question. So, once you've built up your LinkedIn buddies, ask a question like, "Is anyone connected with a friend who works at Macy's?" to start the ball rolling on your job search. You may be surprised to find several responses from friends who know someone who knows someone else who works at Macy's. Even if you only have a second-degree connection, it's better than blindly submitting a resume.

- **Post a status update.** Just like with Facebook, you can post status updates that will appear on peoples' LinkedIn news feeds and your profile page. Just remember to be careful what you post, particularly if you've set your profile to be publicly accessible.

- **Consider going "Business" for even more connections.** Once you find someone you want to talk to, you can't directly message that person unless you are connected. However, if you sign up for a "Business Account" (starting at $24.95 at time of printing), the floodgates will open and you can contact whomever you like. The best way to holler at someone out of the blue is through the option called "Expertise Requests" (a.k.a., informational interviews), in which you appear to be asking for advice rather than a job. (Don't worry, these interac-

Getting Hired

tions can often turn into interviews if you impress the contact and the company is hiring.)

- **Don't stop short of the finish line.** Remember that networking isn't just about getting an interview—it's about getting a job. If you manage to land an interview, take things one step further and see if you can network to your interviewer ahead of time. Even if you can't, check out his or her LinkedIn profile to see if you have any commonalities (e.g., you're from the same state or previously worked for the same employer). This way, you can enter any interview strapped with ammunition.

- **Scour the job boards.** LinkedIn has job boards, and while we've heard mixed reviews about the listings, it doesn't hurt to look. Keep in mind that most employers on LinkedIn would probably prefer to network to a job candidate than have someone respond through a job listing.

- **Don't be shy about asking people for LinkedIn recommendations.** LinkedIn enables former bosses, coworkers and other connections to add letters of recommendation to your profile, similar to traditional references. There's nothing better than an objective source lauding your talents. And don't forget about karma—you may need to return the favor one day, so be careful about whom you ask to recommend you and whom you're recommending.

- **Don't accept everyone and every offer you get at face value.** More and more, recruiting companies are popping up on LinkedIn. When you think you're networking your way to a job at Nike, you might just end up networking your way to a chat with a recruiter. This isn't necessarily a bad thing—just something to be aware of.

- **Expand your network.** If you don't opt for the "Business" account, the best way to leverage LinkedIn (aside from optimizing your profile so that a recruiter can find you) is to grow your network. The easiest way to do this is to import your contacts from your Gmail or other email account. You can do this when you first create an account or by going to the "Contacts" section.

- **Stay informed.** There are blogs that follow career networking as well as entire books written on the ins-and-outs of LinkedIn. Try to keep up with the newest networking techniques.

Interview: LinkedIn Tips for Recent Grads

Lindsey Pollak is one of our favorite career gurus for recent grads. She's the author of Getting from College to Career: 90 Things to Do Before You Join the Real World *and a frequent contributor to FastCompany.com and the Huffington Post. She also happens to be a Campus Spokesperson for LinkedIn, so we figured we'd pick her brain for some insider tips for recent grads dipping their feet into the career networking pool.*

What one LinkedIn feature should every recent grad job hunter know about and leverage?

Though it may seem obvious, the most important LinkedIn feature is your profile—specifically your use of keywords, profile picture, and recommendations.

It's extremely important to include keywords in your summary statement. The summary portion of your profile provides a chance to share the highlights of your bio in your own words. It's also a place to include keywords and phrases that a recruiter or hiring manager might type into a search engine to find a person like you. The best place to find relevant keywords is in the job listings that appeal to you and the LinkedIn profiles of people who currently hold the kinds of positions you want.

Keep in mind that you should list *all* experience (including unpaid or volunteer work) in your summary, as it provides a full view of your experience and will help former colleagues and classmates find you on LinkedIn. If you are a current student or recent grad, you can include relevant coursework and extracurricular achievements as well.

Finally, nothing builds credibility like third-party endorsements. The most impressive LinkedIn profiles have at least one recommendation associated with each job a person has held. If you feel awkward soliciting recommendations try recommending someone else's work first—in hopes that he or she will kindly return the favor.

Interview: LinkedIn Tips for Recent Grads continued...

Is there a best practice for cold-connecting/emailing people on LinkedIn?

Once you've connected with people you already know from "the real world," LinkedIn provides you with tools to connect, degree by degree, with the connections of your connections for mutual benefit.

Note that the way LinkedIn is set up, you can only connect to someone via an introduction from a mutual connection. This ensures that the connections on the site are trustworthy and there is very little spam. Other than paying for a "Business" account, the best way to connect with people you haven't met is to ask for an introduction through a mutual connection. If you don't have a mutual connection but belong to the same Group, you can send a message to a fellow member.

If you do ask a mutual connection for an introduction to someone new, be sure to be polite, professional, and proactive. Customize the message and use proper grammar and professional etiquette. If you demonstrate your interest in the person's career and show that you've done your research, the cold connecting won't feel quite so frigid.

Should I join groups? Any recommended groups for recent grads?

Absolutely! Groups are at the heart of LinkedIn and are a great way to become active on the site. LinkedIn Groups are communities of professionals based on common interests, experiences, affiliations, and goals. University alumni groups are among the most popular and active on LinkedIn. I definitely recommend that recent grads join their alumni group to get access to interesting members, discussions, job postings, news postings, and more. If you're part of a professional organization or a Greek organization (business or social), it's a good idea to join these groups too. There may be national or regional groups as well as groups for your school's alumni. LinkedIn groups—especially the well-established ones—can serve as an additional communication tool, a community builder, and a research tool to boost your job search and expand your network. ■

Sample LinkedIn Profile

Summary

Versatile writer/editor with experience in both print and online media. Particularly interested in entertainment coverage and reviews.

Specialties

Restaurant and bar reviews; music coverage; copywriting; CMS administration; Search Engine Optimization; and HTML

Experience

Associate Editor

Hang Ten Media
Writing and Editing industry
June 2009 – Present (9 months)

* Review bars, restaurants, and live music shows

* Develop story ideas with editors and freelancers

* Copy and style edit online and print submissions in preparation for publication

* Manage database of establishments

Doostang

The "Doo" is a lot like LinkedIn, except with a much smaller user base (it began as an "invite only" network and still maintains a certain air of exclusivity). Initially, Doostang leveraged its "high quality" users to attract companies that did not list jobs on other sites. Now that it is an open network, most of its cachet has worn off, but its job listings still contain a higher percentage of the more sought-after (and thus competitive) positions. So while LinkedIn is larger and will afford you access to more people and companies, Doostang may very well provide access to a gem that you won't find on LinkedIn. The only kicker is that in order to apply to Doostang's premium jobs, you have to pay $39.95 per month (which to be fair, is a small price to pay if you actually land one). Savvy job hunters might consider using LinkedIn to build a large network and Doostang to search for diamonds in the rough.

Facebook as a Career Networking Tool

Don't forget Facebook (as if you would, you Facebook FREAK). Although not focused exclusively on career networking, Facebook has over 300 million users, many of whom list their employer. Expand your network and scan it to find people in the industries that interest you or, better yet, people who work for the companies you want to target. In 2009, they opened up their search feature and now it's easy to find people who work at a specific company or mention a phrase that might resonate with your job hunt. Facebook is also useful for letting people know what you are after. For example, you can post notes or use your status to alert your friends to the type of job you want; with any luck, they'll holler at you when they come across something they think might be of interest. Just don't sound too desperate—networking, even online, is a lot like dating. "Why are you still single?" and "Why don't you have a job yet?" are questions that go hand in hand—in fact, sometimes the response to one can answer the other! When using Facebook (or any other social network) during your job hunt, just make sure to review your privacy settings so that nothing ridiculous gets out to a potential employer. For more information on cleaning your online profile, see page 182.

Twitter: It's (Not Just About) What's for Breakfast

Love it or hate it, Twitter has arrived as a major player on the social media scene, driving the discussion on issues as far-reaching as the Iranian revolution and whether or not Ashton Kutcher is actually the man. (He isn't.) For those who haven't given it a try, it's easy to pass off as a lame website where people just tell each other the boring minutiae of their lives. But like any tool with this type of scale (more than 6 million users as of this writing), Twitter has a lot of uses beyond the relating of mundane details. And while it would be insane to say you can get a job on Twitter by doing X, Y, and Z, creating a presence on the site can be another effective weapon in the twenty-something job hunter's arsenal. The reasons are twofold. First, it's a great networking tool with one advantage over Facebook: Because it's more public, it's easier to connect with new people and even gain access to brands and companies. Second, because of the combination of individuals, websites, and companies using Twitter to communicate, you can essentially use it like a news feed to stay on top of industry chatter.

Getting Started

If you're already a Twitter disciple and just want some tips on how to leverage it as a job hunter, jump to the next section. But if you're a newbie, here are five simple steps to get you up and running.

Step 1: Understand what Twitter is. If you could explain Twitter flawlessly, you'd probably win a Nobel Prize. But at heart, it's pretty simple: Twitter is a social network where you can share and read messages called "tweets"—short text updates containing a maximum of 140 characters. Some people call it a "microblogging" or "microsharing" platform, because instead of writing full blog posts, you're forced to keep every post short and sweet. They're almost exactly like Facebook status updates, but Tweets are much more public; they are presented in a more streamlined-fashion; and (here's the part you should be paying attention to) they can have a lot more reach, since anyone can "follow" you.

Step 2: Create an account. Go to Twitter.com and follow the straightforward instructions for starting a new account. When choosing a username, remember that your Twitter page will get its own URL (e.g., twitter.com/gradspotguru), so make sure you choose a good nickname, or even your full name if you plan to use the account primarily for job-hunting purposes. If you can, keep it short. As tweets are 140 characters or less, the shorter your name, the more people can say to you when they're tweeting you directly. Also, be mindful that many professionals use Twitter on their mobile devices, so try to forgo any punctuation or weird characters. After you get past the sign up page, you'll be given the option to pull in your contacts from Gmail, Yahoo, and AOL, to see if anyone you know is already using it. You'll also be given the option of following a random grab bag of celebrities and mainstream media sources—we suggest skipping this part and going straight for our favorite celeb accounts, @OGOchoCinco (Chad Ochocinco) and @stephenfry (Stephen Fry).

Step 3: Learn the lingo. Just as Facebook brought us "poke" and "wall," Twitter has its own lexicon. You'll want to know these terms and functions in order to use the platform effectively.

- Follow/follower—This is sort of the equivalent of "friending" someone on Facebook, but with a twist: People you follow don't have to "follow" you back. When you follow someone, his or her tweets will show up for you to read in your Twitter feed that is displayed on your twitter home page (i.e., the screen that you are greeted with after logging in, which is different from your user page). Note that when people go to your user page, they only see all of the tweets you yourself have posted, not tweets from your "followers." Just a heads up: Some users protect their updates so you have to be authorized to see them, but the default setting for all accounts is public. In other words, you don't have to "confirm" someone in order for them to follow you— but you will get an email in your inbox alerting you each time you get a new follower.

  e.g., "I'm following 546 people but I only have 26 followers. Am I a loser?!"

- @—The "@" symbol is just shorthand for a Twitter account, so when someone says "at me" or "follow me, I'm @joeblow," he just means to check him out on Twitter. When you're writing tweets to (or about) a specific person and you use the "@" symbol, it will alert the person to the fact you're talking about him or her. People often call this a "reply" or "@-reply," as it essentially creates a public conversation between two users. In addition, using the "@" symbol will turn the username into a link so anyone reading your tweets can then go check out the user you're mentioning.

  e.g., "Hey @gradspotguru, what's the best way to tell my coworker he needs to wear deodorant?"

- RT ("retweet")—If you are posting a Tweet someone else wrote, the proper etiquette is to precede it with the letters "RT" (sometimes "R/T") and the original tweeter's name or to just click the retweet icon.

e.g., "RT @rustyrockets: I am transcending the material world by ac-knowledging the eternal light within. Then I'm gonna watch some porn."

- DM (Direct Message)—If you and another user are mutually follow-ing one another, you can exchange private messages. Use this func-tion as you would a Facebook message—this can be done via the Direct Message link on people's user pages, or from within the Direct Messages section on the right-hand navigation pane.

    e.g., "I've really enjoyed following your tweets and notice we live in the same area and have the same professional interests. Would it be terribly creepy if I suggested getting together for coffee?"

- Hashtags (#)—These are the Twitter equivalent of tagging a blog post. Don't know what that means either? No worries: It's just a way to categorize tweets so that other people can track certain topics using Twitter's search engine (see below). You just put the "#" symbol in front of any keyword(s) you want and Twitter will make them links for you.

    e.g., "Anyone know the best sites to check for jobs in #government? #job-hunt #career

- Truncated URLs—Since Twitter restricts messages to 140 characters, a lot of people shorten lengthy URLs when sharing links. You can cre-ate shortened URLs at a number of sites including tinyurl.com, bit.ly, and is.gd.

    e.g., "LOL there's nothing cuter than a sneezing panda! http://is.gd/45uSQ"

Step 4: Find people to follow and search for what you want. Once you've found all your real-life friends, the Twitterverse can seem pretty overwhelming. Thankfully, there are a bunch of useful tools for tracking down the people and discussions most relevant to you. Start out with the "Find People" tab on the top navigation and use the tool to find people and companies that you think might be interesting. This tool will sift through user names and Twitter pro-files for you, so if you're inclined to work for a skydiving company, search for "skydiving" and see who (and what) comes back.

In addition to skydiving resources and companies, you can also find a whole slew of individuals who might be interested in the same things you are,

Getting Hired

professionally and otherwise. Head on over to search.twitter.com and you can search individual keywords as well as any user-generated hashtags as discussed above. If "#career" proves too broad (and it will), try narrowing down to specific industries (like #skydiving, #basejumping, #parachuting), companies you want to know about, or even specific people who work at those companies. You might find someone who works for the company you've just sent your resume to but who doesn't list their company inside of their biography or name but does have it in their tweets. (Otherwise, they would have appeared in Twitter's "People Search" tool.)

Another way to find relevant tweeters is to search an external Twitter directory like Twellow.com or Wefollow.com. When you find people talking about the topics you're interested in, start following them (when you're signed in, a big "follow" button will show up under their names). Take note of whom they tweet at, and follow those people as well.

Step 5: Get involved. As with any social networking tool, the mountain won't come to you just because you created an account. There's no need to become a Twitter fiend who can't sit through your cousin's rehearsal dinner without feeling the need to post 35 updates detailing the chef's choice of garnish on the baked potatoes; but, you will need to spend a little bit of time with it if you want to see the benefits. When someone asks a question you think you have a good response to, "@" them and respond. They'll likely write you back to thank you, or ask for more information.

Most importantly, post good content. The better the content, the more likely others will re-tweet it—providing useful links or saying funny things tend to be the most successful approaches. You should also re-tweet other posts—it feeds people's egos and makes them like you! Of course, you can also just follow a bunch of people in silence and use the site like an RSS reader, but if you want to garner any attention, you'll have to contribute to the "conversation." At the very least, it's worth spending five to ten minutes a day checking on what the people you follow have to say. You never know—they may mention a job opening that hasn't been formally announced yet!

Our friend Michael Gruen (who co-authored the *Dummies Guide to Twitter*) helped us to further understand the ins-and-outs of extending your job search to the Twitterverse. Here are some more savvy maneuvers to get you started:

- In your Twitter bio, link to your LinkedIn profile, your personal website or portfolio, or anything else you'd like people to see when they check out your Twitter feed.

- Before you start following people, make sure your profile is as refined as it can be (i.e., has a link to your resume, includes a compelling description, has a good nickname, uses a neutral background or one appropriate for the type of job you want).

- The #tweetmyjobs hashtag is a great source of job listings (and it also has an accompanying website at tweetmyjobs.com).

- Twitterjobsearch.com is a pretty good search engine to find job tweets.

- Follow the right people—in addition to the techniques already mentioned, search Twitter and Google for headhunters and recruiters, and check out the Twitter accounts listed below.

Bottom Line

Ultimately, Twitter is just another (albeit powerful) method for gaining access to people you might not otherwise know about. Start looking for people you think you'd want to connect with, and it just may happen that they'll be interested in connecting with you too. Who knows—they might help you find a job that you like a lot more than one you would find on a more traditional site like Monster.com.

Whom to Follow

Start with these useful Twitter feeds for recent grads:

- @freelance_jobs—tons of random projects, ranging from technical gigs to research to translations

- @heatherhuhman—the career guru from Examiner.com frequently tweets job opportunities and helpful links, as well as advice

- @project4hire—freelance programming / design jobs

- @jobangels—job listings, advice, networking, employment statistics and inspiration, all from a site whose mission is to help people find jobs (and motivate other people to help out as well)

Getting Hired

- @jobshouts—job posts from all over the country

- @simplyhired—job statistics, employment trends, and infrequent job postings

- @jobsforkarma—lots o' job postings

- @StartUpHire—a good source for start-up jobs

- @wFreelanceJobs—creative/design gigs

- @mediamatchjobs—film/TV production gigs

- @Hcareers—hospitality gigs

- @media_pros—media jobs

- @journalism_jobs—journalism jobs (in the U.S. and abroad)

- @kellyjobs—listings from the well-known staffing firm

- @manpower—another huge staffing firm

- @resumebear—solid advice for hunters

Interviewing

Now that you've prepared your application materials (see page 185) and mixed and mingled (both online and off), the real fun begins. It's time to show your face at the companies that would like to interview you. But keep in mind that there may be a bit of a lull between sending in your application materials and actually being summoned for an interview. One of the most frustrating parts about applying for jobs is that sometimes (quite often, in fact) you never hear back. Even though you spent six hours perfecting the cover letter and sent an extremely gracious follow-up email a month later, you might get straight up blanked. Companies receive too many applications to muster the humanity it would require to respond to all of them. For this reason, it's advisable to cast a wide net—you may catch some unwanted things like diseased crustaceans and discarded diapers, but you'll also increase the odds of finding something you want.

The best advice we can give, particularly for newcomers to the job market, is to accept every interview you're offered. Even if you are 99% sure you will not want the job, interviewing is an acquired skill, and any chance to practice will pay off down the line. Each time, you'll learn how to manage your nervous tics, expose yourself to new questions, and perfect your handshake until it hovers playfully between dead fish and vise grip. You might even learn that you do actually want the job. The whole process of interviewing can be extremely nerve-wracking for some people, but it's also the part of the game where you can really stand out from the hordes of other applicants with comparable credentials. We hope our tips will help you shine with the intensity of a thousand suns.

Prep Work

Prepare for an interview as you would prepare for a test. That doesn't mean drink a sixer of Red Bull and stay up all night playing online cribbage. It means anticipate what's coming and make sure you are ready to knock it out of the proverbial ballpark. Research the company, the industry, and the interviewer beforehand. Start with the company website: Pay close attention to major divisions of the organization, highlighted products or services, press releases, vocabulary, and who's who within the company's hierarchy. Search Vault.com for company profiles, employee surveys, diversity statistics, and more (see page 134 for more resources). Find out if the company has been in the news using Lexis Nexis (often available through your college library) or by searching the archives of major papers like the *New York Times*, the *Wall Street Journal*, or the *Washington Post*. Finally, don't forget to do some Googling, and consider checking out online career networks like LinkedIn and Doostang to find the interviewer and see if you have anything in common. (For more on online career networking, see page 205.)

After you've done your background checks, write up a list of potential questions that might pop up, including both general personal questions and those specific to the firm. Ask other people who may have interviewed with the same company or similar companies for advice on what to expect during the interview. Also, refer back to the job description to remind yourself of exactly what skills they are looking for so that you can stress them throughout the interview. Finally, know your resume and cover letter inside out; sometimes, the information on your resume is the only thing that the interviewer will know about you, so be prepared to defend its honor to the death.

Getting Hired

Interview Dress

One of the most anxiety-inducing elements of the interview process is figuring out what to wear on the big day. The corporate culture of the company you're interviewing at plays a large part in how you should dress for your interview, but gauging this culture ahead of time is not always easy. There are however a few things you can do to prepare. First, if you know people who work at the company (or at a similar company/in the same industry), ask them what they wear to work and what they think would be appropriate. Second, scan the company's website for photos. If there are images of employees happily working away, take note of what they're wearing. And if those two routes fail, call the company and ask the receptionist what the standard dress code is. You don't have to reveal who you are—just say you have a meeting coming up (or, if you're really paranoid, have a friend call up for you…from a payphone…in a different state).

Golden rule: No matter what you decide to wear, make sure that it is clean, pressed, newish looking, and well-fitting. For advice on wardrobe staples and where to get them, see the "Office Dress" section on page 254.

Women. If you're interviewing at a more traditional company or corporation (e.g., a bank, a law firm, or a company's corporate headquarters), a conservative pant or skirt suit should do the trick. Wear closed-toed shoes and, if

you wear heels, make sure they aren't distractingly high. Tripping down the company stairs will make an impression—but probably not the one you were going for.

If you are interviewing at a more creative or casual company, a suit is probably overkill, but you should still look like you made an effort. A conservative dress or knee-length skirt with a nice blouse and/or nonmatching blazer is a safe bet. When in doubt, err on the side of formality. And no matter what you wear, remember that carrying yourself with confidence makes *any* outfit look that much better.

Keep flashy accessories and colorful pieces to a minimum during the interview. Once you land the job, you can start to live it up. Same goes for handbags: If you tend to carry a bag with a blatant brand logo, be aware that it will be noticed (for better or worse).

Guys. The same basic ground rules apply for guys. If you're interviewing in a more conservative industry (or in an industry where you will be in the public eye, like hospitality or sales), you should wear a suit. Navy and grey suits are flattering and work well with accents, such as pastel-colored collared shirts or colorful ties. Just remember that anything too flashy will distract—and you don't want to be remembered as the guy with the blindingly bright shirt, or the guy with the novelty tie that plays "Take Me Out to the Ballgame," for that matter. The safest bet is always a dark blue or grey suit (two or three buttons with the bottom button always left unbuttoned), a white shirt, and a conservative tie. If your suit doesn't fit well, it's worth spending the money to have it altered ($25 to $150 depending on how much of a disaster it is). Wear dark socks and invest in a nice pair of (recently polished) shoes. For other types of industries such as IT or publishing, business casual attire will be sufficient. This generally means nice pants, a belt, a collared shirt, and a sweater or non-matching blazer.

One frequent trap male interviewees fall into is being poorly groomed. This is a huge issue and one you can easily avoid with some basic prep work. We don't doubt that you look sexy with three-day scruff, but you also look a little bit like a caveman. And unless you're interviewing at Geico, that's probably not the look you want to achieve. Shave, shower, and do multiple mirror checks before marching into the line of fire. You're more likely to nail the interview if you're confident that you've nailed your look.

Day of the Interview

If you played sports in school or were on the debate team you know how nerve-wracking it can be to anticipate an event where you have to be 100% on the ball. Game day readiness is all about routine and preparation; quell anxiety by avoiding last-minute problems. Print out multiple copies of your resume and any other materials the night before and put them in a nice folder. Make sure your outfit is pressed and looking sharp. Don't eat anything that will upset your stomach, pop an Icebreaker, and don't drink too much caffeine if it will make you jittery. Finally, make sure you know how to get to the interview, and plan to arrive early. A late showing is a surefire way to ruin your shot at the job. If you *are* running late because of an Amtrak strike or legitimate emergency (catching the end of *Pirates 3* on TV doesn't count), call ahead to let them know what is going on and when to expect you.

Getting Hired

In the War Room

When the moment of truth arrives, be prepared to cock back a fully loaded clip of wit, charm, and illuminating-yet-humble tales about why you are awesome. Here are some things to remember:

Check your body language. Along with being well-dressed and well-groomed, body language can make a big difference in how you are perceived by your interviewer. Sit up straight, avoid nervous fidgeting, and make eye contact (though not to an awkward extent). If you are not a very expressive person, try your best to smile and display enthusiasm—someone who does not know you may mistake your demeanor for boredom or apathy.

Go in with a game plan. You know what skills they want, and you know what experiences and achievements you can offer to prove that you are the best fit. Figure out how you are going to pitch yourself for the job at hand, and know what talking points you definitely want to hit. Even though the interviewer is asking the questions, you can still "topsy-turvy" the situation and put yourself in the driver's seat. If they ask if you can follow directions, don't just say "yes." Use this as an opportunity to segue into the story of that time you followed directions mad well!

Speak slowly and clearly. Unless you are interviewing to read off the side-effects at the end of a Lipitor commercial, speaking a mile a minute will make you seem insane, incomprehensible, or nervous—in any case, not the impression you want to make.

Tips & Tricks: Phone interviews

Phone interviews are often a critical first step toward landing an in-person interview. In rare cases, they can be the only interview you'll get. Since you can't read the various social cues of a face-to-face conversation, you have to rely solely on what you say and how you say it— use enthusiasm and intonation to sell yourself, and avoid chewing gum, smoking, or eating. Be prepared for the call, find a quiet place where you feel comfortable chatting, and find a landline to avoid a cell-related snafu. Tell family members or roommates they are forbidden to touch the phone while you're interviewing. Finally, take advantage of the best part of phone interviewing—no one can see you, so you can lay out all of your notes in front of you and nail all your talking points. You can also wear your pajamas—score! Some people feel that standing up during a phone interview helps them feel (and sound) more energized. Just remember that standing does not mean running laps around your living room. Being out of breath will make you sound frazzled, creepy, or both.

Before fielding each query, steady yourself with a deep breath, which will have the added benefit of making your answers seem less rehearsed.

Don't panic. If a question throws you off, don't stare at your feet for five minutes or go into an epileptic fit of "uhs" and "likes." Getting truly stumped is more likely in finance or consulting interviews where you have to address case studies or logical dilemmas, but you never know when you might just draw a blank under pressure. The trick is to be prepared for this eventuality. Utilize stalling techniques like repeating the question out loud or asking for a clarification. If you are offered a drink at the beginning, accept even if you're not thirsty—a well-timed sip can be a lifesaver when you're flummoxed. When all else fails, thinking out loud is always better than silence, no matter how much you think you're bombing.

"What is your biggest weakness?" You will almost always be asked this question, because everyone in the world thinks it's revealing, when in fact it is not at all. Most applicants pursue the same tactic: Take a strength and then frame it as a weakness. This approach can work, but realize that "I'm a perfectionist" is getting a bit tired. Instead, you might try an honest yet strategic approach: State an issue that is not horrendous, explain how you confronted the issue, and show that you have taken proactive steps to improve. Something like, "I have gotten bogged down in the details of large projects in the past, but after realizing this about myself I have been consciously stopping to take a step back and look at the bigger picture." Never say you are lazy or tend to make mathematical mistakes, even if it's true.

Don't be negative. Badmouthing ex-bosses or past experiences makes you sound high-maintenance and pessimistic. Rather than talking about what you hated about your previous jobs, find a way to describe what you learned and what your new goals are.

Ask questions. It's safe to say that 99% of interviews end with an invitation to ask questions about the job and the company. The ball is nominally in your court, but you are still being tested. The questions you ask should demonstrate your enthusiasm and knowledge of the company and industry. Utilize the research you did to go in with a solid list of questions. An original question will demonstrate that you've thought deeply about the job/company/industry and will make you stand out from those other drones being interviewed. Refrain from asking about salary, benefits, vacation time, and so on. You can handle that with HR, or after you actually get an offer. For some example questions, see page 226.

Getting Hired

Tips & Tricks: Clean up your online profile

Just as you will research the company, industry, and interviewer prior to the interview, odds are they will also look into your background. First place they'll start? The Web. So, be sure to clean up your online profile before starting the interview process. Check out page 182 for a full breakdown of how to streamline your online identity for the job hunt.

Request a response. To give yourself peace of mind, don't hesitate to ask when you can expect to hear back. Ideally, doing so will save you some sleepless nights spent worrying why you haven't received a response yet. Be aware, however, that sometimes hiring schedules can shift. If you haven't heard back within the time-frame indicated, feel free to send a polite follow-up email.

Ask for business cards. Request a business card from each person you meet during your interview, otherwise you'll be kicking yourself when it comes time to send thank you notes and you can't remember anyone's name. If possible, make notes on the back of each person's card about specific points you can reference when you write to thank them (see page 226).

Sample Interview Questions

Thankfully, not every interviewer is as creative as Jimmy Fallon, so it's not uncommon to hear the same general questions time and again. No matter how suave you are, it's worth taking a moment to prep your answers. Grab a friend and run through the list of questions to expect to think about how you'd answer them at each company where you plan to interview. You don't need to memorize your answers (after all, you have to be able to think on your feet), but after this exercise, you'll have plenty of coherent thoughts in the chamber. And don't forget to come up with some questions to ask your interviewer to demonstrate your interest in the company. When constructing these questions, go to the company's website, browse the recent news, and develop a question from there. For example, you could ask, "How is this company taking advantage of new opportunities in digital media?" However, it's probably safer to steer clear of asking about salary (see page 194) and benefits unless the interviewer broaches those topics.

Questions You May Be Asked

- Tell me about yourself. (Another variation: Walk me through your resume.)

- Can you share some experiences that you think prepared you for this opportunity?

- Why do you want to work here?

- What interests you about this industry?

- Describe some experiences in which you had to work as part of a team. What was your role? Did you like it?

- Can you describe a situation in which you successfully multitasked?

- Can you remember a situation in which you held a lot of responsibility? Solved a problem? Rose to a challenge?

- What are your goals in pursuing this job?

- What are your interests outside of work?

- Do you consider yourself detail-oriented or more of a "big picture" person?

- Traditionally, what does your decision-making process entail?

- Can you share a situation in which you had to make an ethical choice?

- Share with me a time when you were disappointed in yourself. How did you improve?

- Describe a situation in which you had to be insistent to make your point. How did you make sure your voice was heard?

- Are you self-motivated or do you prefer to follow directions?

- Have you ever had to resolve an issue with a superior? If so, how did you do it?

- How do you manage your time?

- Do you have any questions for me?

Questions to Ask Your Interviewer

- What is the most rewarding thing about working here?

- Can you tell me a bit more about the company culture?

- How is success measured?

- What are the opportunities for advancement for the position I'm applying for?

- How many people work in the department where I would be, and how is the department structured?

- Is there a "typical day" for the job I'm applying for?

- What's a typical first-year assignment?

- What are the organization's plans for change and or growth in the future?

- What are you looking for in a new hire? ∎

Follow-Ups

A follow-up thank you letter is not just polite; it is also a chance to reiterate qualifications, reemphasize your interest in the position, or bring up something you didn't get to mention in person. Within 24–48 hours of interviewing, write a brief note to each individual who spoke with you. If there is any doubt about correct names, spelling, or titles, check the business card or call the office to double-check. After that, wait until the timeframe that you were given for a response before calling or emailing again. An overly eager beaver is no one's favorite type o' beaver.

Sample Thank You Note

> Dear Mr. Alexander,
>
> Thank you for taking the time not only to interview me, but also to share your insights into and experiences at Smithfields with me. It was exciting to hear you discuss how the meritocratic culture truly pervades every facet of the firm. I also enjoyed learning about the lean project teams that enable new hires to assume lots of responsibility very quickly. After meeting with a number of employees on Monday, I feel certain that I would like to become part of the Smithfields community. Thank you again for your time and I hope to be hearing from Smithfields soon.
>
> Sincerely,
> Blair Stevenson
>
> *Blair Stevenson*

Making a Decision

Congratulations! After months of begging and pleading at the feet of employers, the offers are rolling in. Now you've got some swagger! If you get two or more offers, all we can say is take into account all of the issues we've brought up throughout the last two chapters: geography, salary, benefits, office vibe, and so on. Go with your gut, and if you got job offers in different industries, don't feel that by choosing one you have to stick with it forever.

So there you have it, the Gradspot guide to landing your first job. Before we move on, there's just one more set of demons to lay to rest...

Settling: Should I Take a Job I'm Not 100% Sure About?

We won't go so far as to say that starting your first job will cause another existential crisis, but let's be honest: it could. Taking a job that you don't feel is perfect for you can be a tough pill to swallow. Like the pilgrims of yore, today's "settlers" may wonder why they gave up a mediocre life of unemployment and mild persecution for "the New World." But if you are stressed out about settling, we suggest that you settle down. Just look at America—400 years down the line and it's not half bad.

We're joking, of course—America is so screwed up! But settling is all about perspective. On the one hand, there's a dark storm cloud in the post-grad forecast: 99 times out of 100, your first job is not going to be your dream job. But there's a silver lining as well: The majority of recent grads hold three or four jobs in their first five years out of college, so you don't have to stick with anything you hate for long. Still, feeling like you've sold yourself short can definitely keep you up at night. There are no simple answers, but it's important to develop a more holistic view of your entry into the work force. (See our interview with Alan Pickman on the next page for thoughts on "false feelings of irrevocability.")

Why Do You Feel Like You're Settling?

There are a lot of factors that go into the decision to settle for something that isn't fully "you"—your economic situation (often based on how long Mom and Dad will pay your way), the difficulty of entry into a given industry, and the likelihood of other opportunities arising. Not even the great mathematician Leonhard Euler could reconcile those variables, so you probably can't either. Try to pinpoint exactly why you feel like you're settling—by necessity (you need to pay the bills or take a job in Wichita to be near your sick grandmother), by ambition (you have big dreams and will not be satisfied until you run your own company), because it's the easy option (laziness), or because you don't yet know what your dream job is (lack of clarity at this point is totally normal).

Make a Commitment

Once you've made a decision, it's important to commit to it rather than constantly wondering what could have been (at least at first). As the old saying goes, "Finding a job is a job in itself." It's sort of like how finding a boyfriend or girlfriend is as annoying as having one, but at some point, you have to stop playing the field and commit (for a bit). You may be surprised—what seemed like trivial busy work could evolve into real responsibility (in the same way that a one-night stand could evolve into a meaningful relationship). In addition, you can look for other jobs/partners while you're at it, but your hands are going to be tied because if you get caught, it's pretty awkward.

Okay, this analogy is pretty much aces so far except for one important fact: Getting out of a relationship sooner rather than later will make things easier, but when you start a job, a certain level of commitment is expected (it varies, but generally a year is considered the minimum, and two demonstrates a strong commitment). Here's the thing, though: Just as being in a relationship makes you more attractive to other people (the old "I want what he/she has" phenomenon), holding a job will boost your status in the eyes of other employers, as well as provide you with new skills and experiences. Moreover, if you perform well, they'll be more likely to speak highly of you to others when you move on (rather than badmouthing you 'round the block and on the Interweb).

Should I Take a Job That Pays Less than I'd Hoped For?

This is a whole different type of settling—forgive us for not feeling bad for you. Presumably, you can either slave from "8 'til late" every day doing something you don't love, or make a significantly smaller salary doing what you really want to do. Either way, it's nice to have options. We'd like to say go with your heart every time, but we realize that things like student debt and rent are real concerns. If you are fortunate enough to have a little bit of financial cushioning, think twice before buying into the allure of a six-figure salary. Even though parents and grandparents love to recount their days of "paying dues" in terrible first jobs, it's a slippery slope toward a breakdown when the only thing getting you out of bed in the morning is the paper chase.

See page 277 for more information on deciding when to move on from your first job.

Interview: To Thine Own Self Be True

Admittedly, it's more than a little daunting to consider planning an entire career when you don't even have your first job yet. To help keep the demons at bay, our friend Alan J. Pickman, a career management professional and psychologist, shared some wisdom about how recent grads can channel their skills and interests into fulfilling work lives.

I graduated. What do I do with myself now?

In terms of self-assessment, you should not only consider your skills, strengths, and interests, but also your values, hopes, dreams, and drivers.

Getting Hired

Interview: To Thine Own Self Be True continued...

To get to know the job marketplace, you can gather information from electronic and printed sources, but at some point, you must talk to people who work in the fields that interest you to explore what different working environments are like, what the people are like within a given profession, how they are rewarded, and how their careers have developed.

Slight problem—I didn't do so well in school. Am I doomed as a professional?

If you didn't do well in school, it doesn't mean you don't have interests, values, and things that you're good at; you simply have to be self-aware and mindful of those other elements. In thinking about a career, you should consider the activities you were involved in, clubs you might have joined, things you did during your summer vacations, and the type of people you surround yourself with. These are all indicators of what's important to you; academic excellence is only one piece of the larger puzzle.

What if I make a mistake?

This worry is often based on a false sense of irrevocability—"if I choose Path A, I am saying goodbye forever to Path B." Today, it's appropriate for young adults to hold a number of different jobs in the years after they graduate. Your early jobs are really mechanisms by which you can help to form and sharpen your sense of career identity, so as long as they are increasing your self-awareness, they are useful. If you don't go through this exploration as a young adult, it's very possible that you'll end up needing to go through it much later in your career.

What are some common traps I should avoid?

The biggest trap I've seen among young adults is that your own voice may be less clear (and given less weight) than the voices of those around you. Whether it's peers or parents who are influencing you, it's often difficult for young adults to have a high degree of self-knowledge and the courage to attend to their own voices. I would strongly advise you to run with your interests and passions when you're starting out, because there will never be a better time to do so. ∎

Chapter V: Working Life

Working Life

When you get that call or email telling you that you've got a job or internship, relief will wash over you in an awesome wave. Maybe you'll have a celebratory drink or go to Six Flags. But as the big first day draws nigh, a creeping sense of dread can begin to sully even the most buoyant of dispositions. "What if I am bad at the job? What if it is miserable? Is this really what I want to be doing? Are they going to find out that I don't technically know how to use Excel?"

First order of business: Give yourself time to bask in the triumph of employment and enjoy the excitement of starting something new. Save the stress for when you actually have some work to do and don't get too worried about whether you chose the "right" job. The thing about the "right" job is that it's a myth, sort of like El Dorado or the claim that if you put a steak in a tanning booth, only the inside will get cooked. You'll soon see that aside from unisex bathrooms, the workplace and college have very little in common, so you need to give yourself time to adapt and develop a sense of what you value in your working life. (For example, you may find working in a fun office with interesting people can be much better than doing "what you want" in a miserable environment.)

As you set forth into the world of paid labor, remember that this first job is a stepping stone, not the defining moment of your career. According to *Young Money*, recent grads hold their first position for an average of 1.6 years. Chances are you'll be out the door before you even know it, so treat it as an opportunity to build your story and develop a sense for where your personality and talents fit into the mix. Whether the job ends up as the launching pad for your career or the butt of a joke, the important thing is you are putting yourself out there, picking up new skills, and learning just how little some people can accomplish in an eight-hour workday.

In this chapter, we'll help you ace your first day, avoid the booby traps of office politics, dress the part, instant message with old people, and much more. Office life is not always intuitive, so it's important to prepare yourself. You'll be running the place in no time, we know it.

First Jobs of Famous People

Few careers begin at the top, and many of the people we now idolize started their working lives with some pretty suspect first jobs.

First Jobs of Famous People continued...

Bill Gates: Congressional page

Bill Murray: sold chestnuts outside of a grocery store

Tommy Hilfiger: sold his jeans from the trunk of his car when no stores would carry them

Jerry Seinfeld: sold light bulbs over the phone

Madonna: worked behind the counter at a Dunkin' Donuts

Stephen King: janitor (inspired to write *Carrie* while cleaning a girls' locker room)

Walt Disney: ambulance driver

Coolio: fireman

Jeff Koons (artist): door-to-door salesman

Danny DeVito: hairdresser

Ellen Degeneres: shucked oysters, painted houses, sold vacuum cleaners

Rod Stewart: gravedigger

Sylvester Stallone: lion cage cleaner, porn actor ∎

Surviving Your First Day

Starting work can be one of the most awkward things you've ever done in your life. Waiting to be told where to sit, how to log into your email, and who (if anyone) is going to go to lunch with you can make you feel like a helpless infant waiting to suck from the teat of responsibility. The thing to remember is that adults in the workforce can be as awkward, lazy, and self-absorbed as the people you knew in college, and, unfortunately, not everyone is going to make an effort help the new person feel welcome. You have to slowly work your way into the fold—don't force it. Be polite, enthusiastic, and friendly to start out, and give yourself time to feel out the office vibe. Here are a few tips to facilitate your entry into the workplace.

Don't Be Late

The cardinal rule of your first day is to be on time. If possible, take the trip from wherever you're staying to the office beforehand to gauge how long it will take. Or at least time it out using HopStop.com or Google Maps. Then add an hour to that. If you're there early, grab a coffee. Maybe you'll have time for a few. But it's worth it, because being late will set a horrible precedent.

The Name Game

Most likely, you'll meet a bunch of people on your first day, from mailroom employees up to your boss. No one will fault you for taking a few weeks to get acclimated and acquainted with the office, but quickly learning people's names can help you make a great first impression. After you've been shown around, try making a quick chart of who people are and where they sit. If you do forget, don't be afraid to ask again—"I'm so sorry, I've been meeting so many people and managed to forget your name. Could you remind me?" Eventually, however, you will not be able to use this line anymore, at which point you'll find yourself in the extremely awkward situation of mumbling the name of someone you've seen every single weekday for six months.

State Your Purpose

Sometimes you will meet your boss or supervisor for the first time the day you arrive for the job. Don't go barging in with the wild ideas you came up with on the ride over, but do be forthcoming with your goals and expectations. Let your boss know what aspects of the company interest you most and where you'd like to get involved. If the response to that is, "Actually, you will just be buying me Frappuccinos and doing my son's homework," then

> **Tips & Tricks: The company cell phone conundrum**
>
> If your company is willing to pay for your cell phone plan, why not let it? Low-balling it, that's $600 per year of extra cash in your pocket. It would be a no-brainer, but, of course, all corporate generosity comes with baggage—in this case, full disclosure of your minute usage and call logs. The company is compensating you for all the business calls you are hypothetically making, which, believe it or not, does not include calling your boyfriend in London. Some people take the company plan and then get an additional phone with a scaled-down plan for their personal use. However, many companies probably don't really care what you do with the phone, so talk to coworkers to find out how lenient things are before running in fear.

go with the flow. Nonetheless, it will still be useful to give your boss a sense of your aspirations, even if he or she appears to ignore them. For more mundane run-of-the-mill issues like hours, vacations, and reimbursements, it may be more prudent to check in with HR. However, feel free to bring these topics up with your direct superior (not necessarily the boss of all bosses) if there is confusion, but don't do it during your first day and make sure you take an approach that does not bear hints of an "I want to work as little as possible and go on vacation next week" attitude.

Start Strong

You know how whenever you meet people you immediately size them up and sometimes text your best friend about how they have a big forehead or super wet hands? Well, that's admittedly a bit superficial, but everyone makes those snap judgments. In the case of starting a new job, the point is not to try to be cool but rather to put your best foot forward in a professional sense, because each of your coworkers and certainly your manager will develop an impression of you early on—as hard-working or lazy, smart or not-so-smart, and so on and so forth. Impressions stick, so be ready to go the extra mile while it really counts.

Get Your Bearings

At larger companies, offices can be like labyrinths, with more barriers to entry than Cuba. If no one shows you, be sure to ask around to locate the following essentials: bathroom, fridge/coffee machine/kitchen, mailroom, office supply cabinet, and the fire exit. You may also need to get an ID card made, so try to look presentable (though the photo will be terrible anyway). It is advisable to get on the good side of the security guards, who are like the Minotaurs of your office. If they decide that they don't like you and you forget your ID, they'll pretend they've never seen you and make you contact your supervisor to get in, thus causing embarrassment and annoyance all around.

Write It All Down

During the first weeks and months on the job, you will be the recipient of a nonstop deluge of information, ranging from the menial (e.g., how to sign in guests, where to find post-it notes) to the monumentally important (e.g., how to get paid, who is your manager). Even if your superiors don't expect you to take it all in the first time around, you will come out looking on the ball and ready if you do. For this reason, it's important to take copious notes about the who, what, why, when, and how of the office as you go along. You might feel silly writing down something as simple as "BCC Geraldine on all client emails," but you will feel even sillier if you mess it up. As a general rule, always bring a pen, pad, and potentially a calculator to all meetings—even if you just draw pictures of beagles wielding grenade launchers; at least it will look like you are trying.

Be Prepared to Fill Out Forms

Over the course of your first few days you will probably be presented with a number of forms to fill out, many of which will require your Social Security number (worth memorizing if you haven't already). They include:

W-4 form. This will allow your employer to determine the correct amount of withholding tax to deduct from your wages. Don't want them taking any of your money? Unfortunately, it doesn't work like that. If your employer did not withhold these taxes from you, then you would have to pay them all in one enormous lump sum at the end of the year anyway—better to just play it by the books and avoid extra hassle. When filling out the form, you will have to note any tax deductions that you will be eligible for that year. But since most of us are unmarried with no kids or house, it's pretty straightforward—you'll just file as a single person with no dependents. If you think you may be eligible for any deductions, check out the "IRS Withholding Calculator" online (IRS.gov) before your first day

Tips & Tricks: Reimbursements

While no one complains about a free dinner at work, it's important to realize that the proverbial "free lunch" is still elusive. Sure, you can get a filet on "the Man" every now and then. But if he's paying, that only means that it's late at night and you're at the office eating dinner when you could be home or out with friends. Nonetheless, don't look a gift-horse in the mouth. Get anything and everything reimbursed: cell phones (p. 235), transportation, food, and whatever else the company is willing to cover. Most likely, you'll have to spend cash up front, and then your expense department (after approval by your boss) will reimburse you. But there's even a silver lining to this cloud. If you pay for everything on a rewards credit card (p. 304), you're banking the points without spending any money of your own. Jackpot! Usually, to get reimbursed, you'll just have to hand your receipts to someone in the back office. One caveat: The reimbursement might not come immediately, so make sure you will have the money in your account to pay your credit card bill when it's due.

of work. It provides a series of simple prompts that will help you figure out your filing status.

Benefits. Landed a job with a 401(k) plan and health care coverage? Back of the net! Choosing a doctor or deciding how much of your monthly paycheck you want to put into savings can be confusing (particularly if you've never done it before), so don't feel you have to pick on the spot. Take these forms home so you can do some research and seek advice from parents and friends. HR's job is to help you understand your options, so feel free to schedule as many explanatory meetings as you want. Believe it or not, some grads feel timid about taking advantage of benefits when they know they don't plan to stay with a company for very long—don't be! You are working hard and they're part of your compensation; they are meant to be used. (For more on retirement funds see page 328 and for more on health care, see Chapter 7.)

Direct deposit. Assuming you have a bank account, sign up for direct deposit of your paycheck so they will be dumped straight into your account and you won't have to worry about losing checks or waiting for them to arrive in the mail. To do this you will need to bring a voided check to the office. (To learn how to void a check, see page 303.)

Noncompete and non-disclosure agreements. If you are working at a start-up or a company that deals with proprietary information, you may be asked to sign legal documents stating that you won't share confidential information or offer your services to other companies that are deemed competitors. Often, you either sign or don't take the job and that's the end of the story. However, sometimes there is some wiggle room, and at any rate it is advisable to at least take some time to review the documents (and ideally show them to a lawyer) so you know you are not shooting yourself in the foot. The last thing you want is to finally get a job at the company of your dreams, only to realize that you have agreed to not work in the media industry for at least two years after leaving your current gig.

School vs. Work: What's the Difference?

There's a natural inclination to think that whatever job you take will be a lot like school. If you were a good student, it's logical to assume you'll be good at work. Unfortunately, school and work bear very little resemblance to one another, and the recent grads who enter the workforce each year thinking otherwise are pretty much responsible for our generation's bad rap as entitled know-it-alls. So what's the difference? For one thing, you pay schools money so they have to pretend to care about you, whereas companies pay you money and are more inclined to be bitter if you don't live up to expectations. But beyond that obvious fact, there are many differences that can be leveraged to your benefit if you're ready for them. To help you prepare, we've laid out some of the key aspects of college that will probably no longer apply on the job, as well as tips for acing the transition.

In college... It didn't matter if your professor liked you. Sure, you might have brownnosed your way from a B to a B+ a couple of times, but more often you barely interacted with your professor, and he or she may not have even known your name.

In the workforce... If your direct boss doesn't know your name, you're in trouble.

Tip: Make sure your boss likes you. If he or she isn't on your side, making your way up the ranks will be infinitely more difficult.

In college... It didn't matter what your classmates thought of you (at least in terms of classes—social life was a whole different viper's nest). As long as you had a friend or two to mess around with in the back of the lecture hall and some poindexters to crib notes off of for the final, you were fine.

In the workplace... If you don't get along with your colleagues it's tough to succeed, especially since there are many more buses you can get thrown under at work than in school.

Tip: Be nice to your colleagues, even the ones you don't like.

In college... You could get your work done by yourself most of the time, aside from the infrequent group project.

In the workplace... You'll likely find that much of your work relies on other people in some way (e.g., boss, colleagues, supporting departments/staff, vendors, clients). Teamwork is critical in most professions—not just for getting the job done, but also so you've got soldiers who will ride for you when things get real.

Tip: Don't hesitate to take up the slack of another team member; it will help you in the future. And don't be critical of other people's work. Be constructive.

In college… There were long periods of chilling punctuated by short and unhealthy bursts of intense effort.

In the workplace… The "daily grind" says it all. Not to suggest you won't love what you do (hopefully you will), but there's definitely a Sisyphean element to a full-time job. You work like a maniac on a big project, then as soon as you're done, another shows up. Then another. Then another.

Tip: Again, if you're going to work hard at any point, put in a strong effort for the first three months immediately after arriving at a new job. Everyone will form an impression of you as a hard worker, thus buying you padding to slack off later down the line.

In college… You receive months-long breaks.

In the workplace… You pretty much have to lose your job to get a break that long (unless you're a teacher/professor-type).

Tip: Plan vacations strategically and become a vacation magician: Turn three-day weekends into four-day weekends and weeks off into ten-day vacations with the aid of major holidays. Also, it's key to take full advantage of any free time you have before finding a job, or when you're in between jobs. Once you're working, you'll daydream endlessly about having that kind of free time. Check out page 47 for travel ideas, as well as jobs and volunteer opportunities that allow for travel.

In college… There are grades and clear feedback cycles for your work.

In the workplace… It's often somewhat difficult to figure out precisely how you're doing, where you stand, and where you're going, even if the company makes an effort to schedule regular reviews.

> ### Tips & Tricks: You didn't have to be an "A" Student
>
> It's clear that job success and school aren't perfectly correlated because research shows that "B" students wind up making more money than "A" students. So if you're a "B" student, congratulations—you hit the money spot! If you were a "C" or "D" student, act as if you were a "B" student. And if you were and "A" student—settle down, morning glory!

Tip: Every once in a while ask your superior how you're doing, particularly if you've just delivered on a project or task. Don't overdo it though, as you can easily be marked as high maintenance.

In college... You knew you had four years, and most people stuck it out in the same place without transferring.

In the workplace... People come and go all the time, especially at our age.

Tip: Try and figure out how long you want to be somewhere, and plan accordingly. But remember: Best-laid plans don't always work out, so you should act like you're going to be at your job forever until the day you actually leave. When you do bounce, try not to burn any bridges on your way out—unlike some of the less savory characters at college, your workmates could be useful networking contacts down the line (and they might even be called as references).

In college... Dropping out wasn't much of an option.

In the workplace... Quitting is *always* an option.

Tip: Here's a good test to run: If you look around and there's no one in your workplace with a career and lifestyle that you'd like for yourself personally and professionally, that's a great sign that you're not a long-term fit for that organization. If you see someone who fits that description, that's awesome. Go make friends with that person now!

In college... Literally everyone was fair game to hook up with on any given night (hypothetically).

Tips & Tricks: Never stop looking for opportunities

When you finally land a job, there's something to be said for giving it your full attention and not being distracted by the "what if" demons. Better jobs than yours certainly exist, especially when you are young and inexperienced, but doing well now will help you get to those eventually. That said, working hard shouldn't put up the blinders on career opportunities. Take an hour each month to scroll through some job sites (while at home, never in the office!), check up on openings at your dream companies, have coffee with an old boss, or read up on your industry to see what's new and exciting. Networking doesn't just have to be done a few weeks before you apply for a job—building contacts will always come in handy when you decide to make your next move.

In the workplace… Every cutie is a potential landmine.

Tip: Tread very, very carefully. For more tips on office romances, see page 251.

On Work and Boredom

According to *The Quarterlifer's Companion*, well over one half of recent grads in the workforce complain about severe boredom on the job. In fact, that number is far higher than those who complain that they are stressed out by their workload. Since fresh-out-of-college employees lack experience, many supervisors are careful about putting too much on their plates. However, sometimes whole offices are just sluggish and inefficient. If Internet caches could talk, they would weave a tale of monumental inefficiency across the Webisphere. According to a survey by AOL and Salary.com, the average American worker wastes 2.09 hours per eight-hour workday, mostly by hanging ten on the 'net, socializing with coworkers, and attending useless meetings.

The point is, being bored at work is normal, but you need to figure out whether it's the job as a whole that bores you or the fact that you're not getting enough challenging work. The latter situation can be rectified if you are proactive. Ask bosses and coworkers if they have any side projects that you could help out with, or pitch your own ideas when given the opportunity. Don't expect everything to come to you—go out and get it, and eventually you'll earn people's trust and they will feel comfortable giving you more responsibility. And then you will be extremely busy, and you'll probably complain about that too!

If, however, the whole place just feels like somewhere that dreams go to die, perhaps it's time to start putting out the feelers for something new.

Tips & Tricks: When to admit you hate your job

Does it feel like work is throwing you into an emotional rut? Be sure to assess the source of any negative feelings about your job. If you are just frustrated because you think you should be running a company, dating a model, and vacationing in Bora Bora, then give yourself time. However, if every day fills you with dread and you often consider staying in bed instead of going to work, maybe you are in the wrong job. If you've been there a year and feel discontent, now is the perfect time for a change. For tips on switching jobs, see page 277.

Women in the Workplace: A Recent Grad Perspective
by HANNAH SELIGSON

Hannah Seligson is a recent grad after our own hearts. In her book New Girl on the Job, *she addresses the difficulties of being a young woman in the workplace from the Gen Y perspective. It's a great supplement for any females reading this book, as well as males who want to appear sensitive to their friends or romantic prospects. Here, she provides some essential tips for "new girls" trying to find their footing in a first job.*

As a Gen Y, I've grown up with the protection of Title IX, witnessed women make inroads in every imaginable field and profession, and have never been told I couldn't do something because of my gender. In fact, it was quite the opposite. So why, with all these doors swinging open, did I write a book offering advice to young working women?

Because, distressingly, there is very little advice directed toward young women about how to "make it" during their formative years of employment. As both the AAUW's "Behind the Pay Gap" study and NACE's "2007 Graduating Student Survey" confirm, workplace inequities don't settle in five years after graduation, when you've bumped your head on the glass ceiling for the first time, or even once you've reached the executive suite— they kick in immediately.

The good news is that Gen Y women have the power (we are 35 million strong) to exact some real change in the workplace. Here's how we can make it happen.

Think career, not job. When people talk about what you are going to do post-graduation, the question is typically framed in terms of "finding a job." You don't hear people say, "Julie, find a career." But they should. While it might be daunting to think that way in your twenties, it's imperative. Jobs are not as lucrative or satisfying as "careers." In practical terms, think about how your first few jobs will help you achieve your career goals. Map out where you want to be in five years and work backwards in terms of the steps it will take to get there.

Don't get assistant-ized. Tory Johnson, the CEO of Women for Hire, puts it like this: "It's very easy for young women to get stuck in support roles... After a year or so you become pegged and it's more difficult for

Women in the Workplace: A Recent Grad Perspective continued...

your employer to see you in a different light." Ilene H. Lange, president of Catalyst, attributes the glaring absence of women at the top to the fact that women are two and half times more likely to be channeled into staff jobs like Human Resources and Communication than into operating roles where they would generate revenue and manage profit and loss. So use an assistant position as a springboard to bigger opportunities, not as a place to incubate.

Self-promote, because no one will do it for you. Too often, working women's desire to "please" and to "be liked" prevents them from receiving recognition for their hard work. A recent survey by Women Unlimited found that 56.4 percent of women took credit for their work "rarely" to "sometimes." This, unfortunately, doesn't jibe with the advancement paradigm in the American workplace. Whether you are a man or woman, just putting your head down and doing a good job won't put you on the path to advancement.

When you get accolades from a client (or anyone for that matter), make sure to inform your boss. Keep a work journal and note your contributions to projects so you'll have a concrete list (read: bargaining power) when you need to negotiate for a raise or a promotion, and always take credit for your work—or someone else will!

Grab a mentor, or a few. According to a 2002 survey by the Simmons School of Management, women who had informal mentors reported greater numbers of promotions and a higher promotion rate than those without mentors.

Think about it as if you are building a team. You want to seek out relationships with a broad range of people, both within and outside of your office, so you can strengthen different skill sets. Don't ask a would-be mentor, "Will you be my mentor?" It's the office equivalent of, "Will you be my boyfriend?" Instead, approach him or her with specific requests and questions. For example, "I really admired the way you pitched that client on. Can we sit down for ten minutes on Thursday and go over the client presentation I'm giving next week?" And when you're in a position to mentor, you can pass the favor on. ■

Office Politics

Office politics are one of the mythical aspects of working life that most people cannot truly appreciate until they have experienced their effects first hand. They are the basis of huge debacles like Monica Lewinsky giving the "Head of State," as well as great works of art like *The* (British) *Office*. Indeed, as long as you stay out of hot water, office politics are one of the best parts of a job, if only because a classic workplace faux pas can be pretty hilarious. Just think about it—unless you are one of those overly braggadocio types, you probably don't go around telling people about what a

"dope spreadsheet" you made at work last week (because you have correctly assumed that no one cares). But when that guy who works on your floor accidentally sends out a company-wide email about his Quiznos-induced gas, you will regale anyone who will listen.

Despite their mystique, office politics can be easily navigated with a bit of common sense, confidence, and composure. At the end of the day, most disasters boil down to ambiguous power structures, judgment lapses, and the general awkwardness of human beings. Here's a quick field guide to social and professional interactions in the workplace.

Gossip folks. If office romances are a "play it by ear" situation, office gossip is firmly in "don't play it at all" territory. Listening to the resident gossip-mongers dish the dirt is all very well and good, and you should feel free to take that information home and laugh about it in private. But once you start soliciting or dispensing gossip yourself, Pandora's box will creak open and unleash a minefield of potential hazards to your good standing in the office. As with life in general, your safest bet is to employ a "don't trust anyone" strategy. Even if others are making fun of your boss or sending around incendiary emails, resist the urge to join in with a zinger of your own. Some people talk recklessly, while others consciously backstab—either way, whatever you say will mysteriously find its way back to you.

Bringing baggage to the office. Everybody has problems. But if you don't hear grown folks complaining about divorces and mortgages, why do you think it's appropriate to whine about your boyfriend or messy roommate? Water-cooler chatter is one thing, and if you make a friend at work who is willing to listen to your moaning then all the better. Just don't let non–work-related issues affect your productivity or attitude. "Professionalism" means ignoring your emotions and acting like work is literally more important than your own life. (Also, unless people know you are going on vacation, don't bring literal baggage to the office, either. It will be a dead giveaway when you call in sick the next day.)

Socializing with coworkers. The sociability of an office varies quite significantly from place to place (and, often, from industry to industry). Some investment banks have a fratty "work hard, play hard" approach that is fueled by popping bottles and sometimes ingesting class-A drugs. Other offices have training programs or "class" systems that attempt to foster strong bonds between coworkers through retreats, volunteer outings, and parties. And, once in a while, people befriend coworkers at normal offices because they actually like them or are just very bored. The thing to remember is this: Just because you work with someone does not mean you have to be best friends. Nor does it mean you have to invite him or her to your birthday party. Pay attention to the social dynamics of your office, but realize that you are free to set your own standards and boundaries. Once you've proven to be a good worker, only a huge jerk will begrudge you for having your own life outside of the office.

Pushing back on your superiors. The first time you feel you are disrespected or mistreated in the workplace can be a shock to the system and make you want to run to your mom crying. But, depending on the severity, it might be advisable to let it slide before you've gauged your boss's style and expectations. If it becomes habitual and makes you feel uncomfortable, then it is time to talk to HR or speak with a superior. We understanding how it can feel like you are admitting weakness if you say your workload is too heavy. But again, there comes a time when your boss's expectations need to be in line with your own. At the end of the day, most people would rather you speak up and say that you are overwhelmed than end up with an unfinished or shoddy product when the due date arrives. Over time, you'll get a sense of who will value and reward your hard work and who is just looking to pawn off all the dirty work on you. But when you're a newcomer, the best course of action is to stiffen that upper lip and work hard enough to earn a good reputation. A good rep, in turn, will allow you to push back down the line without being looked upon suspiciously.

Office parties. The company Christmas party is a tried and true tradition in most offices around the country, but it is just one beast in an odd menagerie of social events at work. Whether it's a holiday shindig, Friday happy hour, or a farewell party for a retiring fossil, the same rule applies: Don't get wasted. It seems as though it would go without saying, but you'd be surprised at how many bright, hard-working recent graduates embarrass themselves by going hard on mixed drinks or failing to gauge their limits. You can drink, and in some cases even get a little bit tipsy if that's how other people in your company get down, but just don't overdo it because it's not worth the risk of saying or doing something that will affect your standing in the office. Once you've passed the "are you an alcoholic?" litmus test, office party etiquette pretty much boils down to basic standards of sociability. Avoid the obvious taboos in conversation—sex, religion, politics, and off-color jokes. However, don't feel that you have to only talk about job stuff. Office parties are a great opportunity to interact outside of the structure of work, which is often not very conducive to getting to know people. Being sociable at a work party can put you on the radar of someone you don't know very well or help you impress your boss, both of which can pay dividends back in the office. (If the party involves a meal, see page 267 for more on business meal etiquette.)

Taking responsibility and getting credit. At school, you hand in a paper and you get a grade. Sometimes you do group projects and end up doing all the work while your pothead partner reaps the benefits, but at least you still end up with the results on your report card. At work, there is a lot more ambiguity not only in terms of the feedback you receive, but also in who takes credit for what. Sometimes a boss might simply make a false assumption about who has completed the work that he or she is receiving, while at other times your superiors will just take credit for your labor in order to make themselves look better. Either way, you've got a tricky situation on your hands. Demanding credit for everything you do might not be realistic or even necessary. However, if you are being systematically overlooked, you may want to address the issue head-on. If you go this route, do so calmly and don't storm in with guns blazing. Ask a mentor or a senior person you have a good relationship with for advice. Meanwhile, don't be the perpetrator of poor professional etiquette—give credit where credit's due, and take responsibility when your work is queried instead of passing the buck.

Business Speak 101

Sometimes walking into an office can be like touching down in a foreign country. The local uniform is borderline fascist, and people speak a dialect

Business Speak 101 continued...

that you've probably never heard before. But while the garments are unnecessarily uncomfortable and expensive, the language has fewer words than Esperanto and is pretty easy to pick up. Here's a crash course:

Chicken and egg situation
- Corporate meaning: There is an unclear causality at work.
- What it really means: There is probably some sort of logic to the data that you are presenting to me, but it would require too much thought to figure it out. I will just artfully dodge the entire issue with a meaningless cliché!

Grab the bull by the horns
- Corporate meaning: Take control of the situation.
- What it really means: No one grabs the bull by the horns, not even a bullfighter. It's just dangerous. The better move is to wave a colorful sheet around to annoy it then jab spears into its spinal column.

Golden goose
- Corporate meaning: A cash cow, but in avian form; an idea that will produce high returns.
- What it really means: Now that things are going well, I no longer worry about whether eggs come before birds, or vice versa. When the egg is golden, don't ask questions.

Compare apples to apples
- Corporate meaning: When doing analysis, only compare like things.
- What it really means: Apparently, it would sound too negative to say "don't compare apples and oranges" like a normal person would. That said, we'd love to meet the person who can objectively compare a Granny Smith to a Red Delicious.

Don't reinvent the wheel
- Corporate meaning: Let's not try to fix something that isn't broken or come up with new solutions to problems that have already been solved.

- What it really means: I am far too lazy and uninspired to think of a creative solution. (Unfortunately, this fear of taking on the wheel has slowed GDP growth by at least 10% per year. Maybe there really is a better solution.)

Deliverable
- Corporate meaning: A tangible piece of work that can be handed in and reviewed.
- What it really means: I don't trust that you are actually doing any work so I will force you to waste time by turning it into a grown-up homework assignment.

Baked In
- Corporate meaning: The assumption is already included (e.g., continued sales growth is "baked into" the projections for next year).
- What it really means: Mmm, brownies.

Drink the Kool-Aid
- Corporate meaning: You have to buy into the corporate culture and believe in the company.
- What it really means: Working is miserable, so you must trick yourself into thinking that it is awesome, mostly by pretending that Ultimate Frisbee outings and happy hours are better than not doing those things. This phrase originated from a mass suicide orchestrated by Jim Jones—the zealot, not the rapper. Baaalllllliiiiinnnn'!

Suboptimal
- Corporate meaning: There is a better path or solution.
- What it really means: Whatever we're talking about is terrible.

It is what it is
- Corporate meaning: We're all underwhelmed by the situation at hand, but I have no intention of fixing the problem.
- What it really means: Literally the most meaningless phrase in the world. ∎

The Importance of Mentors

We've established that the working world is a lot different from college, but one thing that remains the same is that it's useful to have someone older and wiser on hand to help you navigate tricky situations. In college, an advisor or dean probably helped you (or at least should have helped you, theoretically) when your roommate urinated on your term paper or you needed guidance on which major to choose. In the "real world," however, an adult whom you trust and who cares about your career development can be a godsend. Holly Paul, National Sourcing Operations Leader for Campus and Experienced Recruiting at PricewaterhouseCooper, puts it bluntly: "If you don't [have a mentor], you need to find one as soon as possible. Someone who knows you well and who you can trust to give you candid feedback is indispensable when you're starting your career." So unless you've got mentors flying out the wazoo already (lucky you), check out these tips for tracking down that special someone.

Two Mentors Are Better than One

A mentor doesn't have to work in the same office as you—indeed, it's often better to have a third party you can address freely without stepping into the mire of office politics. Different people can help you with different aspects of your professional growth, so don't feel you have to limit yourself to one all-encompassing mentor. That said, sometimes it's useful to have a mentor within the office as well, since every company has its idiosyncrasies, and you may need someone who understands the specifics of your situation. Also, if you have someone looking out for you in the office, it can make a huge difference with regards to decisions like year-end bonuses, vacation time (when someone else wants the same days), and getting staffed on good projects.

How to Find a Mentor

Whether you gravitate toward your Uncle Larry or a woman you met at your first internship, the trick is to find someone with whom you share common ground (e.g., you grew up in the same town, went to the same school, share similar interests). Lots of people are happy to help a young person just beginning his or her career, but the right person is one you feel comfortable with and who has experience in your industry of choice. As Paul explains, "You can also try to find alumni through your school, or if you've been hired, you can reach out to people at your future employer via LinkedIn. The trick is to start asking proactively for targeted guidance, since it's unlikely that someone will just suddenly want to be your mentor." Another strategy is to utilize your company's mentorship or "buddy" program, if it offers one. Also, how about contacting old professors who might know someone in your field? Along the path to the perfect mentor, gather advice from anyone with whom you develop a friendly relationship. It's free, so why not listen, right?

What Do You Hope to Gain?

It's best to ask for your mentor's advice on a particular topic, such as the pros and cons of getting an MBA or figuring out how to ask for a raise. Furthermore, the more you share about yourself, the easier it will be for mentors to specifically address your personal goals, interests, motivations, and background. A mentor who really knows you can give the most meaningful advice during times of transition, especially if you are struggling to figure out what it is you really want to do or how you can best grow in the industry you've decided to focus on.

Make It a Commitment

Once you have found your mentor(s), establish a specific time commitment from the onset that you're both willing to make, because without a schedule, you're less likely to have regular contact with each other. Will you be meeting monthly for coffee? Catching up on the phone every couple of weeks? Be sensitive to your mentor's schedule and make it easy for him or her. Investing time and energy into your mentor relationship could potentially have a positive, lifelong effect on your career and your life, so take advantage of those who want to help you—you never know when you'll need sage counsel. And if there's one thing that's really hard to track down at the last minute, it's sage counsel!

Office Romance

Ah, the fresh hunting grounds of a brand new office.... Excited to hook up with all your colleagues? You should be. But you need to tread carefully—no matter how "progressive" companies claim to be, some HR departments will still come down on you like a ton of bricks if they think you're using the terms "spread" and "sheets" in a context that doesn't involve Excel. Some may even fire you.

That said, the taboo of the office romance is fading to some extent. Yes, there was a time when a little cubicle copulation was considered anathema to a successful career. "Business and pleasure don't mix," said the conventional wisdom. "Sex in the office is harassment, even if it's consensual." But while many people profess a "don't poo where you eat" philosophy with regards to a little flirty flirty in the workplace, the stats show that at least 40% of workers have tried it.

Young people are working longer hours, and as the work-life balance shifts further toward the "work is life" end of the spectrum, the office has become the new bar (with the only difference being that you have to wear headphones when you listen to "Living on a Prayer"). Before you dive in head first, consider a few crucial questions: Will an *affair de cubicle* alienate you from the rest of the office? Can you hide embarrassingly red cheeks with some concealer? Will your suit accommodate a surreptitious Texas tuck when the CEO rounds the corner? Do you really have no other prospects?

If you do decide to play with fire, here are the different scenarios you might run into:

- **Dating an Equal.** If you are dating another newb, it's mostly up to the two of you to decide if competing for the same promotions, raises, and projects will breed ill will. Most other people won't care as long as there's not too much repulsive canoodling in the break room. However, think about your work-life balance—at the end of the day the last thing you want is a reminder of work, even if that reminder has great abs.

- **Dating a Superior.** Let's be blunt: Sexing your boss is almost always a bad idea. Even if you successfully pull off an unethical plan to get ahead through sexual favors, the rumor mill is quick to spot an unjust promotion. If you really "like" your boss, check your feelings to make sure they are genuine. Then check his or her hand for a wedding ring. Then quit the job and pray it works out.

- **Dating an Inferior.** Most of us don't have to worry about this right now because we are the inferiors. But again, the issue that arises here has to do with maintaining "professional integrity." Of course, the interns are always fair game, regardless of age—they can't find the paper for the printer, let alone HR! Just kidding. In all seriousness, this is also a horrible idea, as the last thing you want to be known as is the manager who hits on subordinates. Check yourself before you wreck yourself, because those texts you thought were "playful" could quickly get you sued.

- **Dating a Client.** If your job involves going to a lot of dinners or entertaining clients outside of the office, you never know what might develop once the vino starts flowing. Know your own limits and remember that your job is not to jump people's bones (at least we hope not). If your boss finds out, your actions will not be looked upon favorably. If he or she is the one cajoling you to flirt for business, ask yourself why you decided to work for Don "Magic" Juan.

- **Dating Someone in a Different Department.** "Cross-pollination" is probably the safest bet, but remember that it has also bred some of nature's biggest freaks, like the liger. Lindsey Pollack, author of *From College to Career: 90 Things to Do Before You Join the Real World,* flies a cautionary flag: "When I was working at a dot com several years ago, I went on a few dates with a cute guy in the IT department. After it ended, I was too embarrassed to call IT support again, even when my computer got a serious virus!" The lesson is simple: Never date someone who has access to your computer.

- **What about the Janitorial Staff?** The janitor has access to three important things: keys to the supply closet, a late-night schedule, and the wherewithal to quickly clean up the "scene of the crime." Worth considering, perhaps.

- **Final Precautions.** In all cases mentioned above, avoid P.D.A. like the plague. Petting, kissing, and even subtle hand-holding will alienate both of you and make work uncomfortable for others. Be wary of swapping love notes over company email or treating the Christmas party like Freaknik. And finally, always be prepared to deny everything when the crap hits the fan. An office tryst may literally be against company rules, so you'd better check that employee handbook to know how serious the situation could get.

At the end of the day, office romance is a Pandora's Box that's probably not worth opening. But when the juice is worth the squeeze, you'd better believe that no pantsuit or necktie is going to stop nature from taking its course. Just remember that work is stressful enough without exes lurking in the corridors and people asking why you "never call IT" anymore. Be smooth, be smart, and always protect your assets.

Office Etiquette

The office is a minefield of potential faux pas waiting to happen. Let us take a moment to guide you through this jungle and pinpoint potentially explosive situations. No capri pants please—in spite of the ostensible dangers, this "jungle" has a dress code and is very well air-conditioned.

Office Dress

Unless in college you were a certain type of person (i.e., a terrible one), you probably didn't roll around campus on the business casual tip. More than likely, you dressed in the collegiate uniform of sandals, hoody, jeans, sweatpants, Uggs, or some combination thereof. We forgive you for the Uggs (and Muggs, if you were *that* guy), but it's time to step up your wardrobe. Now that you're employed, you've got to figure out how to dress the part. This is no simple task, as today's office dress code is not as clear-cut as it once was. Hipster chic? Creative corporate? What does it all mean? The diversity of industries and office cultures means that dressing for work can become a job unto itself. From ultra-corporate to totally laidback, different jobs demand different looks. Not surprising, in addition to non–gender-specific tips, each gender (turn to page 256 for men and 258 for women) has its own style cues. Still, there are certain rules of thumb that will help guide you in the right direction.

> ### Tips & Tricks: Dressing for the first week
>
> If you're completely unsure about the dress code before starting a new job, call HR and inquire about appropriate attire. Then, make sure you have enough clothes to get you through the first week, but wait until you've seen what other people wear before going on an all-out shopping spree. If it turns out things are a lot more casual or formal than you'd expected, you don't want to be left with a pile of clothes that you won't actually wear to work and probably don't want for your personal life.

General Style Cues

Some companies have explicit dress codes, while others may not. Megan Schuster, a Public Relations Associate at Gucci, notes that even in her chic industry, it's important not to try too hard. "Office fashion is about having personal style; there is no need to look like you fell out of a page in *Vogue*. Be comfortable. The key to looking good is feeling good."

But be savvy about the impression you're giving and what's expected in your industry. If you're a government worker, for example, you'd best leave your Louboutins and Ferragamos at home. As Amy Levenson, who works in book publishing, explains, "There's some strategy [when it comes to dressing for work]. You can't walk in there every day with really nice clothes, cause then they'll think they're paying you too much. You have to walk a fine line to evoke just enough pity but still have respect for yourself and your appearance." And bankers—do without the monogrammed cuffs. Please.

In building your work wardrobe, versatility, comfort, and style should be your top priorities. (Remember, you have to wear these clothes for an entire eight-hour work day, if not longer.) Choose fabrics you can wash at home to save on dry cleaning costs (wool and cashmere are comfy, but they will definitely run up the bill). And, at the beginning, err on the side of conservatism to avoid a misstep.

If you're on a tight budget, try to choose colors that you can easily mix and match (black, white, and neutrals) so you can maximize every piece of your wardrobe. Owning one or two really nice pieces (e.g., a blazer and a pair of shoes) that you can mix and match with less expensive articles will give you the air of dressing well without having to spend a lot of cash to get there.

Finally, there's the joy (or trap, depending upon if you pull it off correctly) of Casual Fridays. They may seem like an excuse for grown men to wear Crocs and women to wear liquid leggings, but don't let these outliers fool you into a false sense of security. As a young employee, you are constantly fighting to make sure people take you seriously, so avoid the temptation to roll to the office with bed-head and a COED NAKED TRUCKING T-shirt ("We go all night!"). Instead, make sure that whatever office attire you choose is something you'd be comfortable wearing when meeting, say, your girlfriend's or boyfriend's parents. In addition to retaining your sense of propriety within the office,

> ### Tips & Tricks: Dress for the job you want
>
> Have you ever heard someone say, "Dress for the job you want, not for the job you have?" That doesn't mean you should come into work dressed as an astronaut, nor does it mean you should cultivate a rotation of Nancy Pelosi–inspired red power suits. It does mean you should show up prepared for any situation that might arise—even if you spend most days daydreaming at your desk. You never know when a last-minute meeting might come up, and your chances of being asked to attend will skyrocket if you're looking sharp. If you plan on having a successful career, take pride in your appearance and the people that matter will notice.

remember that "Casual Friday" is not a government-sanctioned event, so not everyone else you do business with will understand why you are wearing ripped jeans and flip-flops. If you have meetings with clients outside of your office, plan accordingly.

Industry Norms

Different industries have different norms when it comes to office fashion. Here are some basic industry-specific guidelines for looking your best.

- **Corporate Environments (Law, Consulting, Banking).** Keep it conservative. You don't have to wear a suit (unless you have a meeting or dress code that requires one), but choose classic pieces that say, "I mean business."

- **Advertising/PR/Publishing.** Keep it classic and professional, but feel free to mix in some trendier pieces, colors, or accessories.

- **Fashion/Retail.** If you work for a specific brand, you will likely be expected to wear pieces from the brand. Otherwise, try to incorporate the brand's style with classic pieces to remain fashionable yet professional. Just remember, it's an office, not a runway.

- **Media/Creative Arts.** If it's a less traditional environment, jeans may be okay, but make sure your overall look is neat and put-together.

- **Education.** Remember your crazy sixth grade drama teacher who wore denim skirts hiked up to her boobs and floral-patterned blouses with lipstick stains on the collar? Don't dress like that. Instead, aim to wear classic, comfortable clothes that won't distract horny adolescents.

Work Dress for Guys

Work dress for guys is not that complicated, though there are some rookie mistakes that are easily avoided. Where many recent grads stumble is not so much in figuring out *what* to wear, but more so in failing to adjust their standards for "put-togetherness." Perhaps the biggest source of blunders is in fit—a lot of guys come out of college with no sense of what fits well and what doesn't, so it's worth making an honest assessment of any "dress clothes" you already own and deciding whether or not they really fit well. Baggy pants and over-sized shirts can easily make otherwise suitable items look a bit sloppy. Another common pitfall is mistaking "going out" shirts for nice shirts. The difference is sort of difficult to describe, but if it's black or has extremely colorful stripes, you might want to reconsider. Finally, it's time to invest a little bit of that salary into dry-cleaning. Peeling clothes off the floor and giving them a quick *eau de toilette* misting won't cut it anymore. Keep items freshly laundered and pressed. Brooks Brothers makes great no-wrinkle shirts that can ease a lot of the hassle.

Men's Staples. According to Michael Williams, a fashion PR pro and author of the men's style blog AContinuousLean.com, anyone who works in a professional office environment should start building the following staples into his wardrobe: "Two grey suits (a summer weight and a winter weight), two sport coats (corduroy and wool), seven collared woven shirts (white, blue, yellow, etc.), five pairs of non-denim trousers (khakis, wool, etc.), ten white tee shirts, ten pairs of dark socks, a khaki rain coat/trench coat, a dark overcoat, and three pairs of shoes (brown, black, and boots for winter)." Clearly, you won't buy all of these things at once. But if your office is on the formal side, a good start would be one pair of dress khakis (no cargo pockets!), grey wool slacks, a dark suit that's been tailored, four or five long-sleeve button-down shirts, and dark shoes. A good black belt will go a long way, as will a couple of versatile blazers and ties.

Grooming. At the beginning, you should assume you need to be clean-shaven. No goatees, no two-day stubble—not even a subtle flavor-saver. A fresh haircut is also a worthwhile investment before your first day. Once you get a sense for what's acceptable, you may be able to throw a little facial hair into the mix, but keep it clean and neatly trimmed. Also, while it should go without saying, brush your teeth before going to work—you may have brushed once a month in college, but it's no longer optional when you're working closely with people in the office.

Shoes. "Comfortable and classic is the way to go," says Williams, but don't think that means you can wear your "fancy" sneakers. "Footwear is the one place that it really pays to invest in. Buy well-made Goodyear Welted shoes in brown and black (this means that the upper and the sole are two separate pieces that can be easily resoled). Break them in once and then have them re-soled again and again, thereby saving money and still looking smart."

What the hell is business casual? No one really knows, even if he pretends to. A good rule of thumb is to err on the "business" side rather than the "casual" side. Better to look a bit stiff but respectable than to stand out for being overly relaxed. If you're looking for a general sense of what a business casual outfit might look like, it's basically somewhere between wearing a suit and wearing jeans and sneakers. Think wool pants, a collared shirt, and leather shoes. Maybe a blazer without a tie if you want to be extra spiffy.

Further Reading. If you want to make the jump from professional to dapper and sophisticated, check out Russell Smith's *Men's Style*, which sets a clear and at times hilarious blueprint for the dos and don'ts of menswear. Throughout the book, he provides sensible advice such as, "Start with basic black close-lacing oxfords. These will double as your formal shoes for black tie," and, "When you go shopping for suits, wear clothes that will match suits." He also notes, rather insightfully, that, "It is fear of unmanliness, fear of childhood or perhaps of old age, that drives so many men to the athletic sandal, to the kayaking shoe made of recycled rubber, with its bright nylon straps and plastic snaps and Velcro closures." Quite right!

Where to Go: J. Crew, Banana Republic, Brooks Brothers, Gap, and Men's Wearhouse. Department stores are good for variety, and you can always look for discounted gear at Target, T.J. Maxx, Ross, and Marshalls.

Work Dress for Girls

Office dress for the ladies is a whole other box of chocolates—the options for girls are both more fun and more nuanced than those for guys, but as a result they're also more overwhelming. The key is that you're not Lady Gaga, so you probably don't want to be defined by your clothes (or lack thereof). Instead, strive to be age-appropriate, office-appropriate (i.e., stylish but not sexy), and industry-appropriate. Not an easy balance to strike, but it can be done!

Depending on what industry you work in or what your work environment is like, the norms of office dress can differ quite drastically. A good rule of thumb is to take your style cues from your female superiors and co-workers. As you become more comfortable in your job, you'll get a feel for how much leeway you have when it comes to office dress. Just remember: Looking put together should trump any attempt to be "stylish." Not to get too Emily Post on you, but nicely styled hair and nails can take you from "presentable" to "chic" in no time flat.

Women's Staples. Do as the French do and come up with your own "uniform" that you don't have to think too much about. Here are a few key pieces that will get you through the workweek:

- Dress pants (black or grey)

- Pencil or A-line skirt (no minis)

- Tights (a great way to extend the life of your skirts into winter)

- Blouses or collared shirts (avoid "going out tops," or anything low-cut)

- Cardigans to pair with skirts or pants

- Office-appropriate dresses (nothing too short or sleazy)

- Blazers

- Pant or skirt suit (if necessary)

- Shoes: flats, reasonable heels, non-clunky boots

Shoes. Stylish shoes can dress up a very basic ensemble, but make sure you can last the whole day in them. Hobbling is never a good look, and your five-inch stilettos will likely be more of a distraction than an asset, so save them for your post-work cavorting. Instead, pick up some cute flats and comfortable heels you can wear with a variety of outfits. If you can wear jeans to work, low heels are a great way to dress them up.

Grooming. Accessories are another place to get creative, since it's easy to add a little flavor without drawing undue attention. As for hair, nails, and makeup, the best advice we can give is to keep it classy and observe what others around you are doing. If your boss is sporting this season's vampy nail polish, go for it, but stay away from acrylics or anything that needs to be glued or sprayed on.

Get Your Flair On. Even if you work in a traditional corporate setting, there's no reason why you can't have fun with your wardrobe and show off some of your personal style. Shoes and accessories are areas where you can do this, as well as occasionally whipping out your jazz hands. Adding colorful flats or some chunky jewelry to your black basics can provide you with that creative touch that will keep you from blending into your cubicle.

Where to Go: Banana Republic, Gap, J. Crew, Ann Taylor, Club Monaco, Old Navy, and Ross. Department stores offer a lot of merchandise all in one place, and many of them sell clothing manufactured under their own moniker, which can be cheaper than name-brand items. Stores to check out include Bloomingdales, Nordstrom, Saks, and Lord & Taylor. You can also score some great finds by combing the racks at Target, T.J. Maxx, and Marshalls. For more fun pieces and accessories, check out Zara, H&M, Anthropologie and Express. Visit BlueFly.com for designer items at discounted prices.

Internet, Email, and Phone

For most people, one thing that remains constant between unemployment and employment is that they spend most of their time online and on the phone. But while it used to be just Big Brother and "Net Nanny" on your case, you've now got to contend with company HR departments and nosy bosses. You're still surfing the 'net, but there are sharks in the water. Here are some tips for remaining above board.

Internet

Depending on what your job is, you may be able to explain frequent sessions on YouTube or TMZ, but sometimes your company will block certain sites. In general, let common sense be your guiding light and remember that you can surf to your heart's content once you get home. Also, be considerate of your friends who are starting new jobs: If you have unfettered access to the Web but know your bestie is heavily monitored, think before sending out links and be sure to add a lame but useful "NSFW" ("Not Safe For Work") caveat.

Email

First things first: If the company you work for doesn't block personal email sites (like Yahoo!, Gmail, etc.), then there's probably no reason to give your work email to your friends and family. Mixing business and pleasure in your inbox could be risky, and it can also garner you some incredibly weird spam. Worst of all, things that you don't even send can get you in trouble, so be wary of letting your friends recap your weekend behavior over company email. Bear in mind that anytime you use a company email account, you are technically representing the company in public and they can access your email at will.

Once you've figured out the conundrum of staying on top of personal email without getting too loosey-goosey in your work account, you've also got to deal with inter-office email etiquette. Here are some tips for switching up your email game to remain work-appropriate and professional:

- **Formalize your language and tone.** Once you get to know your boss and coworkers, you can gauge how they correspond over email and begin to adapt a bit. But part of professionalism is cleaning up the language and grammar of your emails. No IM abbreviations or other tics you might have developed!

- **Proofread, proofread, proofread.** Read over everything before you send it and check the spelling of names against the address you are emailing.

- **Don't inundate people with CCs.** If someone doesn't know why he or she is receiving a copy of an email, you have erred.

- **Beware of the reply-all.** One of the biggest pitfalls in the entire office environment is the "reply-all" button. Everyone from government officials to CEOs to interns can fall victim to an inadvertent "reply-all," or a reply that was supposed to be a forward. Usually, replying all is just annoying for other people, especially if you are replying to the entire office. But when you reply to an email that your boss wrote and you say, "WTF, does he really expect us to do that?" then you're flirting with job termination. Best to make a recipient list and check it thrice before sending an email.

- **Forward thinking.** Beware of forwarding confidential documents, even if it's to your dad or best friend to ask for help with deciphering them. A company could easily fire you

> **Tips & Tricks: Clean up your online identity**
>
> Remember, it's still important to keep your online identity respectable *after* you've landed a job. While everyone loves to scroll through hilarious pictures and "About Me" sections, there's just no way you'll be able to justify getting fired for something you posted online. Avoid blogging about confidential information or badmouthing your company/coworkers on the 'net, and be sure to check out our tips for reassessing your Internet presence on page 182.

for this, and someone on the other end could also get in trouble (especially if the FCC catches on).

- **Don't jump the gun.** Make sure you have read through all the replies to an email before adding your own commentary. No one likes to hear the same thing five times (unless it's "How You Remind Me" by Nickelback).

- **Step up your subject lines.** Titling every email "yo" will no longer cut it, not only because it is too informal, but also because most people receive an absurd amount of work email and need to be able to search their inboxes easily. Something along the lines of "January Expense Reports" is better.

- **Don't be a stick in the mud.** Socializing isn't what it used to be, and people have become accustomed to interacting almost exclusively via the computer even though they work 50 feet away from one another. This is not an excuse to be a recluse (on the contrary, it's important to have real contact with people). You can, however, use email to your advantage in the office. Send a link to a coworker if you think he or she will find it interesting. Email someone in another department if you'd like to grab coffee and learn about other things the company does. Or join in the joking around if you think it's appropriate— avoid racial or sexual jokes and other blatantly offensive things, but don't feel you have to be completely humorless.

- **Stay organized.** You will get crazy amounts of email at work from tons of different people. Some messages will contain tasks you need to complete right now. Others will pass along information that won't become relevant until three months down the line. If you're using "Outlook" (the most popular office email client), make some folders and figure out a system for keeping track of everything.

Phone

Being professional on the horn is something for which many recent grads are woefully under-prepared. Still, as the new kids on the block, many are forced to act as stand-in secretaries. Some positions have a specific protocol you need to learn, and if you work on a desk at a talent agency (think Lloyd in *Entourage*), you may even have a script that you have to follow to the tee. Get familiar with the standards expected in your office and learn to take down the necessary details. Few things are as embarrassing as calling back a client and asking them to remind you of their name and vital stats.

One rule that applies everywhere: Answer the phone by saying, "This is [insert name here]." Even if you're 100% sure you know who's calling you, answer like it's your boss (guaranteed, it will be sometimes). If you're in a conference room or somewhere other than your desk and you pick up the phone, say, "Conference room."

When it comes to personal phone use in the office environment, a certain degree of common sense and decorum is required. Ever wonder what it's like to have a wiretap? To find out, you can either sell drugs on a massive scale, or you can work for a big company. As messed up as it sounds, someone might be listening in (especially if you're in a sales position), so it's probably best not to talk about last night's deviance, unless you were doing your cousin's statistics homework. Even if the mysterious "HR" is not piped in, beware of coworkers lurking in nearby cubicles pretending to be listening to music—you know they surreptitiously mute it whenever you get a call. If you need to deal with a personal matter feel free to do it quietly and politely (time to master the always awkward "hushed office voice"!), but if you are going to complain to your mom about your roommates or plan a *Jersey Shore*-themed party with your friend, find the time to step outside and use your cell phone. Or wait until after work.

Instant Messenger

One of the most upsetting realizations about many offices is that IM is the prevailing mode of intra-office communication. It's sort of odd to IM with someone sitting literally a few feet away from you, and it is *very* odd to IM with someone 30 years your senior. While you may have grown up using IM to gossip and flirt with sexual predators online, your older coworkers were likely introduced to it solely as a business tool. Don't get caught in the trap of treating IM as a green light for being unprofessional. Here's how *not* to do it:

> **Tips & Tricks: Log all work-related chats**
>
> Since you are now chatting about work rather than cheating on your boyfriend or girlfriend, you shouldn't feel scared to enable "logging" in your AIM account (or whatever IM program you're using). People will send you phone numbers, figures, URLs, and other important information. By logging each chat, you save yourself the embarrassment of asking people to repeat themselves if you forget what they wrote or accidentally closed the window.

SeXyNeWb: wazzzzzuppppp, suckaaaa!!!!

LeRoyJenkins: Hello, could I ask who this is?

SeXyNeWb: im the new asst. can I ask u sumthin? i am so lost! LOL

LeRoyJenkins: Oh, hi Karen. I didn't know that this was your screen name. What can I help you with?

SeXyNeWb: i don't know where the stapler is. i would ask jon but he's sorta weird, right? LMAO! he smells like full-court basketball.

LeRoyJenkins: You can check in the supply closet in the hallway. There should be a few in there, but if not you'll have to order a restock. I believe your orientation packet has a map that points it out.

SeXyNeWb: yah i think i lost that! i am a little hungover ;)

SeXyNeWb: my boyfriend and I got in a big fight and I got a little frisky with the pinot... hehe

SeXyNeWb: brb... sum weirdo from my middle school is IMing me... wt fuuuu

SeXyNeWb: u there???? I still can't find anything!

LeRoyJenkins is idle (4:35pm)

SeXyNeWb: lataz

SeXyNeWb is away (OMG this is CRAZY guuurls!!! www. twogirlsonecup.com)

What went wrong? Ah, so many things. This conversation has more mistakes than Sinbad's Wikipedia page. Let's assess the damage.

- **Change your screen name.** Whatever you thought was hilarious in fourth grade is probably wildly embarrassing or inappropriate now.

- **Announce yourself.** Don't just jump straight into a question or a demand—write something like, "Hi, sorry to bother you. Got a second?" If you've never IM'ed a person before, say who you are. Figure out what screen names you will need in order to correspond with everyone in your department.

- **Avoid IM lingo.** If your coworkers are dropping "LOLs" and "brbs" all over the place, feel free to join in. But don't assume that everyone knows all the acronyms.

- **Be as clear as possible.** Take hormones and booze out of the equation and IM is still a hot zone for mixed messages—get to the point and say what you mean. Similarly, if you've got something lengthy to say, it's better to send someone an email, pick up the phone, or go talk to someone in person.

- **Do some buddy list housekeeping.** If you're rocking a screen name from way back in the day, you might want to change it or consider deleting some of the 400 buddies you've accrued since middle school. You don't want your past sneaking up on you in the workplace, so take precautions.

- **Show your status.** SeXyNeWb wasn't the only one making mistakes (though we can't blame LeRoy for taking a breather from that convo). If you are away from your computer, let people know. Word of warning: "I am here but am playing a computer game that takes up my whole screen" will not be looked upon favorably.

Interview: Do I Have Imposter Syndrome

When you are at the bottom of the age and inexperience pile, adjusting to the workplace can be particularly tough, and it's not uncommon for recent grads to harbor fears that they are not really as bright as their resumes suggest (and their coworkers assume). To get to the bottom of these feelings of inadequacy, we called Dr. Valerie Young, who studies a phenomenon that she calls "Imposter Syndrome."

What Is Imposter Syndrome? Imposter Syndrome is an often unconscious feeling deep down inside, the idea that [you are] not really as bright and capable and competent as everybody seems to think. People who typically experience Imposter Syndrome have achieved some measure of success, whether it's getting into college or graduate school, getting good

Interview: Do I Have Imposter Syndrome continued...

grades, and so on, but they just have a hard time internalizing that success. They kind of explain it away.

What would be the telltale signs that one is really suffering from Imposter Syndrome, as opposed to just general anxiety about life? I have heard people say, "I figure, if I can get a Ph.D. in Astrophysics from Cal Tech, anybody can." Constantly being sort of dismissive of your compliments—that would definitely be one sign. If there is a certainty that every time you do succeed you feel like, "Phew, got through that one, but the next time I'm not going to be so lucky," then that's something you need to pay attention to.

What do you suggest people do on a practical level to address it? I think the first step is to break the silence and realize that there is a name for these feelings. The problem is that people think that they are the only ones who feel this way and that's where the fear and the shame of stigma kicks in. Also, I think a lot of it is keeping entitlement in perspective. I think of entitlement as saying to yourself, "Aren't I entitled to make a mistake? And aren't I entitled to not know all the answers?" Finally, redefine competence not as knowing how to do everything yourself, but rather knowing how to identify the resources that you need to achieve the goal.

Is it possible to express to your superiors that you are feeling like a fraud and that it affects your job execution and/or enjoyment? You know, I don't think I would bring up to your boss that you feel like a fraud. Give yourself permission to feel really off base for the first six months or nine months, but recognize that this is how people feel when they start a new job because you are learning new systems, new acronyms, and a whole institutional history that other people know about and you don't. So, you go into this new job and you don't know what's going on and it's not like if you were any smarter you would know what was going on. It's not an intelligence thing, it's looking at it differently and saying, "Well, why would I know what's going on?" ■

Business Meal Etiquette

Once you arrive in the business world, your success will often depend on the way you present yourself. One of the most tricky work situations to navigate is the business meal, which could be anything from a "power breakfast" (who brought the multivitamins?) to a business lunch or an all-out formal dinner. Generally, you'll either be invited as a guest or as a potential hire, or you'll tag along with your boss/coworkers to meet clients. Whether you're the wooer, the woo-ee, or even if it's just you and the boss, the basic rules of engagement are pretty much the same. Here's some food for thought.

What to wear. If you're coming directly from work, then you may already be adequately outfitted (depending on where you work). Take wardrobe cues from your boss and, if you're unsure, ask beforehand what would be appropriate for the occasion. If you're rolling solo, consider swinging by the restaurant in advance or calling ahead to ask what the dress code is. In moments of uncertainty, err on the side of formality, but keep it subtle (you can foster your love of ascots and Madeleine Albright–style pins on your own time.) Check out the "Office Dress" section on page 254 for general rules about how to dress for professional situations.

Be early. It will give you time to compose yourself before the power players arrive. If you are the first to get there, wait for the other party to arrive before sitting down. (Note: This is *not* an opportunity to get aggressive at the bar.)

Navigating the menu. Lobster Thermidor may be delicious, but if it's the most expensive thing on the menu, you might want to steer clear. That doesn't mean you have to order "just an appetizer" (that would also be lame), but be reasonable. Essentially, you don't want your bizarre order to overshadow your great personality. Likewise, don't order something that is incredibly messy or complicated to eat. You're here to further your career, not to fling food chunks across the table. If you get put on the spot, politely ask the server to come back to you and then make a decision based on what others have chosen. If you want to play it really safe, you can always go with, "I'll have the same, please." Just don't be too overtly sycophantic about it.

Power down. Switch any mobile devices to silent mode, and then ignore them until you've left the restaurant. Even if others at the table are texting incessantly and checking BlackBerries, maintain your quiet dignity—they can get

Tips & Tricks: Understand "the waiter rule"

Knowing how to use a fork and knife is important, but don't get so caught up in the "rules" of etiquette that you forget to be a nice person. It's common knowledge that CEOs (and people in general) look at a person's social skills when making judgments about what he or she is really like. So when you're invited out for a business meal, it's not really about the food; it's about how you interact with the world and deal with whatever comes at you. How do you treat your waiter when everything is going well? And what about when he gives you your steak medium-rare when you asked for it medium-well? The answers to these questions could determine whether you land (or keep) the job.

away with it, but you might look rude or distracted. Double standards—deal with it.

Easy on the sauce. This is a no-brainer, but it's worth noting that business and booze mix dangerously. Some companies have policies against drinking in a business setting, while others are a little more relaxed. We're not saying you must abstain completely (if everyone's "trying the sake," there's no need to be prudish), but don't plan on spending the afternoon swilling martinis à la Don Draper. A good rule of thumb is never order a drink first, which ensures that you're never the only one drinking. (If you are, beware that you may come off as a total lush.)

Mr. or Ms. Congeniality. In essence, the key to etiquette is avoiding controversy and doing your best not to embarrass yourself. Fun, right? Set yourself up for success by dressing appropriately, being polite to waiters (see "the waiter rule" above), and generally going with the flow (i.e., don't throw a fit if they're out of pork belly). You'd also do well to avoid controversial topics in conversation (the time you pounded an entire bottle of Malibu is unlikely to impress a potential employer or client). Act as you would if you were out with a friend's incredibly intimidating parents, and let the host (or your boss) be the one to determine when the conversation turns to business.

Paying the bill. In most cases, you won't have to worry about this. For business meals, the rules are pretty easy: If you are invited, you should not be expected to pay, and it might be considered inappropriate if you offer. If you're just out with other coworkers bonding, offer to split the bill (they might pick it up depending on the age and status difference, but it's still best to ask). And if you're the host (e.g., you've invited someone out in order to network), you should offer to pay. For more information on networking etiquette, see page 202.

After the meeting it's the after-meeting. Going out with a boss or potential client can catapult the night into uncharted waters of business/pleasure awkwardness, and it is perfectly reasonable to gracefully decline. If it's an important client or your boss urging you to go out, you should probably suck it up and go, but know your limits. Having to work early the next day is a good excuse that will get you out of partying *and* make you look responsible (bonus!). Then again, if you're out with coworkers who know you don't roll in 'til noon, this maneuver may not work.

Business Travel

Getting invited on a first business trip can put a well-justified spring in a recent grad's step. The fact that your company values your contribution enough to put you on a plane and pay for a hotel room is a nice vote of confidence. However, a lot of people have no idea what to expect from a business trip, and expectations quickly turn to disappointment when they realize it's not all piña coladas, complimentary mints, and deals inked in front of the Taj Mahal. More often than not, it's just like a regular workday, only much more stressful because of the new environment and logistical challenges of doing business outside the office. But where a complainer sees an exhausting challenge, a savvy recent grad sees a chance to impress his or her boss. Performing well on a business trip speaks not only to your ability to represent your company on a client's turf, but also to your aptitude for navigating new situations smoothly. Whether you're a traveling salesperson heading to Cincinnati or a fancy consultant jet-setting to Germany, here are some tips for the road—play it right and you must just get those 15 minutes at the pool after all.

Travel arrangements. Prep work is crucial, as is knowing the company's reimbursement policies. What budget do you have for the flight and hotel? Can you rent a car or are you expected to use public transportation? Do you book your trip through a company travel agent or pay for it yourself (credit card reward points, what what!) and get reimbursed? If you're traveling with your boss, it's best to plan the trip together or with his or her assistant to make sure you meet any special needs (e.g., a hotel that's walking distance to meetings, yellow M&Ms upon arrival). If you're responsible for booking the accommodations, make sure there is a business center on the premises. You just never know when you're going to need to print a last-minute document, send a file, or even fax something (old school!). Prior to booking a flight, it might be worth checking Flightstats.com to make sure you aren't cutting a meeting close on a flight that's always 20 minutes late.

Prepare everything you'll need in advance. A few days before you leave, print out any important documents and copy all relevant files (and even tangentially relevant files) to a USB thumb drive. If you are giving a presentation, consider copying your Power Point slides and other materials to a CD, DVD, or other storage device. In the event that you're visiting multiple companies, split up the materials regarding each one so you don't fire up a CD at Company B and accidentally open up proprietary information about Company A, which just happens to be Company B's biggest rival (whoops!). In addition, don't get so caught up in the logistics and practical stuff that you forget to actually prepare to meet the client. If you've done your research and gone a step beyond what's asked of you, the chances of impressing your boss on the road will be much higher.

Find someone to hold down the fort. No matter how prepared you are, you'll probably leave something behind or realize you need a random file only after reaching your destination. To avoid a mad scramble, it's always helpful to have someone in the office covering your back. Show this person where all of your files are located (digital and printed) and make sure he or she is working on the days you're traveling. We're sure you'll be happy to return the favor, especially if your office bud helps you avert a disaster.

Do your research. Depending upon your company's style, you might want to research restaurant and entertainment options before leaving, especially if you're expected to go out with a client or you're attending a conference where you might meet people to network with in the evenings. More practically, be sure to locate a local copy shop or Kinkos in the event you need to print documents and your hotel's business center is closed. And since we're guessing you can't do your job without Internet, you might want to check out Jiwire. com and Wifinder.com ahead of time to find a few Internet hot spots (though maybe your company has those handy-dandy wireless Internet cards).

Packing. The art of packing is crucial for any trip, but particularly for a business trip. You want to travel like a ninja—stealth and maneuverability are important, but you also want to be prepared for the unexpected. Don't show up with a summer-camp style trunk, but give yourself a back-up plan in case you spill in-flight chicken piccata all over yourself. Check in with your boss or colleagues to see what the expected "away uniform" is. If you're given no guidance, you can always call up reception at your client's office and inquire about dress standards. "No-wrinkle" shirts are a traveler's best friend, and packing carefully can make the difference in how articles of clothing come out on the other end. In addition to clothing, be sure to pack a travel alarm clock, toiletries in a plastic bag (just make sure no liquids exceed three ounces and you have a zip-top, quart-size bag to fit them in to conform to TSA guidelines), a phone charger, and a laptop charger (plus AC adapter if you're going abroad). Last but not least, bring a stain stick—ones made by Tide work well—to ensure that you're prepared for any emergency, as well as some extra cash in the event you need to pay for a last-minute cab or something else.

Don't check your bags. If your boss isn't checking bags, you shouldn't either. It just takes more time upon disembarking from the plane, and there's always a chance they'll get lost. Going carry-on will force you to pack smarter, which always lends to easier business travel.

Stock up. While your company is apt to pay for most of the incidentals on your trip, the less money you spend, the better. Instead of cracking open the mini-bar upon arrival, consider making a convenience store the second stop after your hotel for any drinks or snacks you need to keep you going. Can we hear you say Red Bull and Gushers?!

Set more alarms than the Federal Reserve. Well, at least two. Nothing is more embarrassing than missing a morning meeting with a client. Whether you use your cell or BlackBerry and an alarm clock, or an alarm clock and hotel wakeup call, you should always "double up." We'd even recommend setting two wakeup calls 15 minutes apart just to be sure. And if you're going to use your phone or travel clock, make sure the time zone is correct. Ultimately, when it comes to alarms, being freakishly OCD is a good thing.

Save all receipts. You'll almost always need to hand in your receipts to get your money back at the end of the trip. When traveling, make sure to hold onto your receipts like they're worth the amount that's printed on them. If pretending you are literally holding a $75 bill makes it more fun, go for it.

Corporate Golf: A Crash Course

Transitioning into the workplace isn't all about getting the job done or even hobnobbing at the office party. There is also a phantom punch in the office politics repertoire that goes by the innocuous name of the "company golf outing." It sounds fun, but it can also be a bloody nightmare, especially if you have limited experience and your superiors are ex-jocks who mistakenly subscribe to the philosophy that sports are a training ground for life.

Actually learning how to play golf properly will take some time and require taking lessons or enlisting the aid of a friend, but learning how to avoid complete embarrassment is pretty simple. Here's a quick primer to get you ready for the various sand traps and water hazards of corporate golfing. Ninety-five percent of the time the outing will actually end up being a lot of fun, and hopefully pretty laidback. But if you do a little prep work, you might avoid the wrath of those one or two managers who take it just a little too seriously.

Dress code. Hopefully the venue is not some stuffy country club that just started opening its doors to minorities in 1999. Even if you're on a public course, though, proper attire sets a better tone than a sloppy tee shirt and mesh shorts. You can't really go wrong with simple khakis and a polo shirt.

Golf lingo. You can drive the cart, but can you talk the talk? Golf lingo is almost a foreign language, so sprinkle some key terms into conversation, but don't expose yourself by tossing around ridiculous phrases willy-nilly. One of our favorites is "afraid of the dark" (i.e., if the ball just misses the hole on a putt, it must be "afraid of the dark." Shout, "are you afraid of the dark," when your boss rims one out and he'll either be putty in your hands or think you're a maniac). Here's a quick list to help you get familiar with the fundamental terminology of the game.

- **Par.** The number of golf strokes considered necessary to complete a hole or an entire golf course in expert play. Holes are generally either par 3, par 4, or par 5 depending on their length and difficulty.

- **Birdie.** One shot under par.

- **Eagle.** Two shots under par—you'll probably never see this.

- **Bogey.** One shot over par.

- **Double bogey.** Two shots over par.

- **Fairway.** The area of the course between the tee and the green that is well-maintained—you want to hit your ball onto the fairway.

- **Rough.** The taller and coarser grass surrounding the fairway.

- **Bunker.** Sand traps—stay away.

- **Pin.** Slang for the flagpole marking the hole.

- **Handicap.** An amateur golfer's "handicap" is how many strokes over par he or she shoots on average. Either a golf club or national golf associations administer handicaps. Essentially it's the par for *you* rather than the par for the course. A low handicap is like a badge of honor in the business community.

- **Scratch golfer.** Someone with a handicap of zero. This person is getting the promotion over you!

- **Up and down.** When you hit one shot onto the green and then putt the next shot into the hole, you went "up and down."

Course etiquette. Proper etiquette is more important than a perfect swing. Brush up on the general rules of the game as well as the United States Golf Association's etiquette tips at usga.org. For the most part, keep this in mind: No noise, no sudden movements, no heckling. Golf is a very psychological game—you've got a lot of time to think about each shot, so focus and preparation are imperative. As in all situations like this, people will latch onto any excuse for why they screwed up. Whether you whisper a story to another player, open a soda, answer your phone, or let one rip while someone else is hitting a shot, you will soon make yourself *persona non grata* if you keep it up.

Gambling and tournament formats. If you're a recent grad, your salary is probably lower than anyone else's on the course, so no one's going to expect you to initiate betting at a corporate golf outing (nor should you in case it's frowned upon). That said, it might be worth knowing some of the popular forms of golf betting and tournament play just in case. One popular format in the business world is a scramble: Each member of a team of two or four people will tee off, and then everyone will all hit their second shot from wherever the best drive lands. The third shot is from wherever the best second shot ended up. You get the idea. This format is often used to move things along, even if no gambling actually takes place.

An easy out. If you've never played golf before and the company tourney is next week, is it really worth dropping money on lessons or hacking your way around the course just to save face? Remember, you can always volunteer and still be involved without playing.

Ten Steps to Take If You Lose Your Job

A lot of this book focuses on how to find your first job, but the unfortunate truth is that some readers are going to have to deal with a layoff (or firing) at one point or another. In a deep recession, the "next round of cutbacks" looms over companies like the grim reaper. Even during the best of times, no job is ever guaranteed—downsizing, new management, buyouts, and all sorts of other factors can leave you out on the chopping block. If it happens, don't despair. First, thank your lucky stars that you're a recent grad starting out your career and not a 50-year-old with a house and a down payment on a BMW. Then, make sure you take the following steps to mitigate the short- and long-term effects of a job loss.

1) If you were fired... The first step is to understand the firing. If you know deep down that you deserved to be fired, think about how you got into that situation and how you can avoid it next time. If you think there's foul play at hand (e.g., office politics, discrimination), now is the time when having a mentor (p. 250) could be crucial. If you really think you have a valid complaint, check in with the U.S. Equal Employment Commission (eeoc.gov) or see if you can speak with a lawyer. For most people, the main question is how to move on. As you start job hunting again, it's important to get your story straight. Depending on how long you were with the employer, you may consider leaving the job off your resume entirely—after all, you're a recent grad and there are plenty of other things you could have been doing during that time (like maybe you also volunteered, and you can make the volunteer work seem like a bigger commitment). If you do put it in on your resume or bring it up in an interview, be honest and straightforward. Don't dwell on it and don't be negative about your past employer. More than likely the company interviewing you will look into the firing, so a web of lies is the last thing you want to leave in your wake.

2) Prepare for an exit interview, and be wary about signing anything. The reasons for your dismissal are crucial to your ability to receive unemployment benefits (see #3), as well as your story moving forward. Stay calm and use your final meeting with your (now ex) employer to clear up any grey areas about why exactly you're being let go. You may be handed a severance/termination agreement to sign, but don't feel you have to do so before taking a very close look and, if possible, running it by a lawyer. It is equally important for you to be cognizant of any terms that could potentially limit your prospects moving forward, such as "noncompete" clauses regarding your ability to work for other companies in the same field.

3) Find out if you're eligible for unemployment benefits. If you were terminated through no fault of your own (i.e., you weren't straight-up canned for negligence) and you meet other eligibility requirements, you may be able to collect unemployment benefits. You can find out by contacting your state unemployment office. You should do this immediately because benefits generally last for a maximum of 26 weeks, and it may take a couple of weeks (or months—there are horror stories) for a check to start arriving. When you go to file for unemployment, you need the following information: your social security number; a mailing address and phone number; and the names, addresses, and dates of employment of all your past employers for the last two years.

4) Don't let your health insurance slip away from you. Losing your benefits sucks, but it doesn't mean you should let yourself become an uninsured, devil-may-care lunatic. In most cases, you can sign up for COBRA, which will allow you to maintain your employer-sponsored health plan at your own expense. However, most healthy twentysomethings can find a better deal on an individual plan they find themselves. The key is to maintain insurance somehow, as a large gap in coverage (over 60 days) could make it harder for you to get your next policy. Go to Chapter 7 to learn more about the importance of maintaining coverage, as well as ways to get health insurance when you don't have a job.

5) Avoid the temptation to go out in a ball of flames. Getting laid off definitely qualifies as uncool, and your first reaction may be Hulk-like anger or an overwhelming desire to slink off quietly and never speak to anyone from work ever again. But in the long run, the much more constructive course of action is to make nice with all your bosses and coworkers, because they can be crucial networking contacts down the line. If they walk you out with your belongings in a paper box, resist the urge to cry and/or yell, "You haven't seen the last of me! I am going to take you all down. Down to Chinatown!!!!!"

6) Gather all your files and any other work you don't want to lose. HR will probably say something to you on the last day about handing over any company property and not taking "proprietary" files out of the office. And yeah, you shouldn't take in-house documents and spread them all over the Internet in some sort of insane act of vengeance. But if you just want a file for your own personal use in the future, go for it. After all, you did the work, and it could save you a lot of time in the future if you end up working on similar things.

Any contacts you made while at work may also be valuable for networking, so make sure you make a record of your work address book.

7) Tell everyone you know you're back on the job hunt. It can be embarrassing or painful to tell people you got laid off. But honestly, most folks are more likely to be sympathetic than they are to call you a loser. And more importantly, if your network doesn't know you're looking for a job, the hunt is going to be a lot harder. So first things first: Throw up a Facebook status message letting people know your situation. Feel free to make it lighthearted. Here are a few examples:

- *Got the axe this week. Timberrrrrrrr!!! Seen any job openings in publishing?*

- *Anyone catch the front page article about me in* USA Today? *"600,000 workers laid off in February." Misery loves company! Anyone got tips for applying to business school?*

- *Remember when I worked for that car company? Yeah, me neither! Looking to switch modes—interested in marketing and branding. Holler if you've got any advice.*

8) Start making some money. The thought of ramping up for another job hunt may be overwhelming. The bad news: Any savings from the last job aren't going to last you that long (plus, they're supposed to be *savings*, remember?). The good news: There are plenty of ways to stay afloat before diving back into the fray. Check out page 27 for ideas on making money when you don't have a full-time job.

9) Don't feel sorry for yourself. Seriously, as weird as it sounds, there's no better time to lose a job. You have the least to lose at this stage in your career, so roll with the punches and get excited about the next adventure rather than wallowing.

10) Have a little fun. One of the toughest parts about transitioning from college to working life is severely decreased time off. If you're in a financial position that allows you to put off working for a bit—whether that's a couple of weeks or a few months—check out Chapter 1 and Chapter 9 for ideas on how to spend your time.

Beyond Your First Job

Depending on when you've come across this book, life beyond your first job might seem way too far off in the future to even begin contemplating. But since the Bureau of Labor Statistics reports that the average American works ten jobs between the ages of 18 and 40, it's likely that sooner or later, you'll get to the point where you will think about moving on to new pastures.

Whether you are considering switching jobs within the same field or trying something completely new, it can feel daunting (and sometimes a bit awkward) to get out of an existing gig that pays the bills. However, it's important to remember that now is a perfect time in your life to take calculated risks. Unlike cutting your own bangs or sledding alone, some risks have potential benefits.

If you can't afford to quit your current job until you've found a new one, job hunting can be a bit of a struggle, especially if you don't want your current employer to know you are looking elsewhere. In order to play it extra smooth, schedule interviews during your lunch break or take strategic vacation days to accommodate any traveling or interviewing that you might have to do. You can also utilize phantom doctor's appointments (be ready to explain what the hell's wrong with you) or squeeze in early morning breakfast meetings before work.

As for the interviews themselves, prepare yourself thoroughly for one inevitable question: "Why do you want to leave your current job?" The real reason might be that you despise your boss and feel degraded when he makes you expense his trips to the strip club. But being positive will leave a much better impression—say that you feel you've outgrown your current position, or that you are looking for a new challenge. However, don't forget to talk up all the stuff you've learned at the job you want to leave. You are evolving from a smart but untested college grad into a smart and semiexperienced twenty-something. And believe us, employers know the difference.

Good Reasons to Leave Your Job:

- You are chronically tired or depressed.

- You are being harassed.

- You are 100% sure you are in the wrong industry.

- You want to move to a new city.

- You don't think you would like doing what your boss or boss's boss do.

Bad Reasons to Leave Your Job:

- You just don't like working in general.

- You are in an office relationship that has turned sour.

- There is not a Starbucks close enough for your liking.

- You have done something illegal.

- Other offices have better vending machines. ■

Chapter VI: Money

Money

For the vast majority of recent graduates, life is not "all about the Benjamins, baby"—it's all about the Washingtons, Lincolns, and Hamiltons. As it turns out, starting salaries don't go all that far in the world of student loan repayments, health insurance, food, and rent. If you're lucky, your parents will help you out a bit. But the longer you stay dependent, the worse off you'll be in the long run. It's time to take responsibility for your own financial infrastructure as you make the transition into the world of self-reliance.

A lot of young people are understandably put off by the whole concept of personal finance. Getting a credit card, monitoring bank accounts, and "budgeting" can just feel like more things to worry about on an endless to-do list. But the important thing to realize is that there are aspects of personal finance that require a bit of forward planning. Between credit scores and compound interest, the American financial institution is designed to reward long-term saving and responsibility. The sooner you straighten out your current financial situation, start building credit, and begin stashing away some money (even $50 a month), the better off you'll be when it comes time to buy a TV, take out a mortgage on a house, and, eventually, retire comfortably.

The good news is you really only need to think about most of these issues once. Setting up a low maintenance system for your finances is easier than ever these days, so once you get your money train in motion, keeping the momentum going is pretty simple. That doesn't mean you have to plan your entire financial future today. Instead, try tackling a few aspects of your finances each month. Getting started, especially with saving and investing, is almost always the hardest part.

If you've never really thought much further ahead than how you're going to pay for the next burrito, don't worry—time is on your side. In this chapter, we will give you the foundation you need to make informed decisions with your money. We'll help you size up where you stand today, build credit, save money for the future, pay off your debts, and implement other tips and tricks to set you on the fast-track towards self-reliance. You could also read "Self-Reliance" by Ralph Waldo Emerson, but bear in mind that he once harbored known tax-evader Henry David Thoreau on his property. And you've got to ask yourself some serious questions about a man who lets another man live in a cabin in his backyard!

Personal Finance Is All About Perspective

Personal finance can mean a lot of different things to a lot of different people. To the ambitious, it's the road to a place where the streets are lined with gold and bums are encrusted with diamonds. To others, it's just a way of maintaining their current level of income. And for NFL players, it's something someone else worries about while they make it rain in the club.

As we jump into this discussion of personal finance, we want to make one thing very clear: What we mean by personal finance is being able to understand where you stand financially and establishing the appropriate financial infrastructure (e.g., credit, budget, bank account, debt repayment, savings, etc.) to optimize your cash, whether it's existing or expected. Personal finance will not make you rich—that's what working will do. But as you start bringing in a salary, it will help you maximize your money (and yes, earn even more) so that all those hours of labor don't go to waste.

Know Where You Stand Today

Whether you want to take the shortcut to personal finance bliss (see our cheat sheet below) or your goal is to really understand your money and begin making educated decisions about your financial future, it's hard to talk about personal finance without a sense of where you stand today. Do you know your credit score? How much debt do you have to repay? How much do you spend each month? Though we like to avoid financial exercises as much as anyone (unless they involve bench pressing gold bullion), it's extremely helpful to sit down and create a financial snapshot so you'll know how your financial decisions will affect your bottom line.

If you aren't sure how to pull this snapshot together, don't worry: As we cover each facet of personal finance throughout this chapter, we'll not only share tips on how to optimize your fiscal well-being in the future, but also explain how to figure out where you stand today.

> ### Personal Finance Cheat Sheet
>
> We recognize that most twentysomethings don't want to spend every Sunday rifling through their receipts for the week and cutting coupons

for a stock-up at Costco. And for some people, any mention of "APRs" and "index funds" sets off an inexplicable desire to drink heavily and/or fall asleep on the couch. So while we think it's important to understand personal finance (realistically, it's going to be a big part of the rest of your life), we're also of the mind that it's not nearly as complicated as all the punditry out there would suggest.

So forget about all the jargon for now. The basics are really pretty simple—you just want to make sure you're not 1) oblivious to your current financial situation; 2) losing money where you shouldn't be (e.g., dumb bank fees); 3) missing out on money you could easily be earning (e.g., interest); and 4) screwing up your ability to make major purchases like cars and houses down the line (e.g., ruining your credit). We think this stuff is so easy, in fact, that we want to put our money where our mouth is (get it?) by presenting you with eight steps to personal finance excellence.

> **Step 1.** Build a personal financial snapshot: Check your credit, compile your personal balance statement (i.e., your cash, stocks, bonds, debt), and get an idea of your cash inflows and outflows.

> **Step 2.** If you have any debt, create a plan to repay it on time (or even early) so that you'll be in a better position to improve your credit and financial health. To learn about debt repayment, see page 290.

> **Step 3.** If you don't yet have a credit card, make sure to get one, use it (even if you just spend $10 a month), and always pay off the balance in full. To learn about credit cards, see page 304.

> **Step 4.** Sign up for a checking account at a bank that either waives ATM fees and provides you with interest, like ING Direct's Online Checking Account, or one that has a prolific ATM network with no monthly fees, such as Bank of America. To learn about bank accounts, see page 298.

> **Step 5.** Once you have your spending money in a checking account, be sure to keep any extra funds in an Online Savings Account (e.g., HSBC Direct), which offers far better interest

Money

Personal Finance Cheat Sheet continued...

rates than regular brick-and-mortar banks. To learn about savings accounts, see page 300.

Step 6. Create a "plan" that will help you finance your current lifestyle. See page 316 for tips on budgeting.

Step 7. Begin to set yourself up for short- and medium-term purchases, like TVs and cars. To learn about saving, see page 321.

Step 8. If you receive benefits from a job, make sure to arrange monthly contributions to your 401(k). If you're unemployed or benefit-less, consider opening up a no-fee investment account with a brokerage house such as Ameritrade and make regular contributions to a Roth IRA. Or do both! (see page 328) To learn about long-term investing, see page 329. ■

It All Comes Down to Credit

Do you know your credit score? If you answered "no," you're not alone: Almost no one does, which is shocking considering that **credit is the backbone of your financial adulthood.** The problem is that people either have no idea what credit is or they choose to ignore it because it seems too scary to confront. Checking your credit can feel like getting a financial STD test. Chances are you're in fine shape, and if not, there are plenty of ways to start improving your situation. But you need to confront it now. Here's what you need to know.

What Is Credit?

Credit is an indicator of your financial decision making and trustworthiness thus far in life. In other words, do you pay people back on time when you borrow money and make good on contractual obligations? Before most third parties will enter into any significant financial agreement with you, they're going to check your credit score. Want to open a credit card? Rent an apartment? Purchase a cell phone plan? Credit will almost always come into play.

Many third parties will reward you for good credit (e.g., decrease your interest rates) and punish you for bad credit (e.g., a bank might reject a mortgage application). Not to harp on STDs (maybe we have a fixation, alright?), but it really is like getting to the point where you're about to hook up with someone and either saying "I'm clean and trustworthy!" or "Just FYI, I have a little bit of gonorrhea."

If you've never heard of credit (or worse, you know for a fact you have bad credit), consider this: 1) If your credit isn't up to snuff in situations where it's needed, you can always ask a friend or family member who has good credit to become a co-signer or guarantor on the transaction, which will get you over any credit humps; and, 2) You're young and time is on your side. You have many years to repair and/or build your credit before it can have any catastrophic impact on you. Presumably, you're not trying to cop a house today. But if you start thinking about your credit now, you'll have no problem doing so in a few years.

Components of Credit

Credit consists of two components: a **credit report** and a **credit score.** A credit report is a qualitative description of your financial history with regard to credit. It reflects what types of accounts you have open as well as any debt outstanding and late payments. A credit score, on the other hand, is a quantitative measure calculated by the Fair Isaac Corporation by aggregating the applicable pieces of your financial health that have been collected by the three main credit agencies: Experian, Equifax, and TransUnion. This credit score (also called your FICO) ranges between 300 and 850. A score of 700 is considered very good and will grant you all of the benefits good credit has to offer.

So what exactly goes into the calculation of a credit score? There are five elements, each impacting the overall score according to the following percentages:

Money

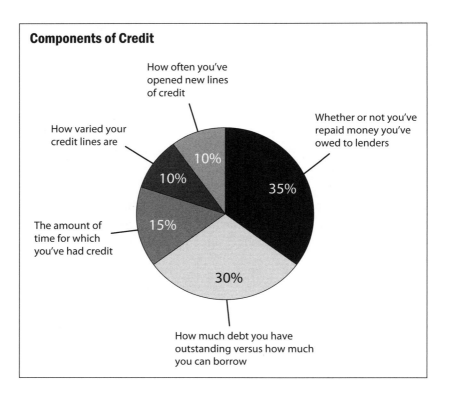

The important thing to notice here is that 65% of your credit is based upon factors that you can very easily control by paying your bills on time and by monitoring how much money you *have* borrowed compared to the total amount of money that you *can* borrow. It's also worth mentioning that credit pertains only to those applicable financial transactions that were in your name. So if you were one of the lucky few who in college toted a credit card your parents gave you, it won't have any effect on your credit if it was linked to their account.

Finding Your Credit

The good news is that the government requires the three main credit agencies to provide you with one free credit report each year via AnnualCreditReport. com. The bad news, as we now know, is that the report doesn't actually include your *score*. Thanks a lot, government! Retrieving your credit score is inexpensive and easy, though, so it's all good. Sites such as MyFICO.com will provide you with your score for $15—in our opinion, a $15 well spent. If you don't want to pay and are cool just getting a proxy of your score, you can use free services like CreditKarma.com or sign up for a free trial membership with Experian.

Word of warning: Experian is the company behind those sweet "Free Credit Report Dot Coooooom" jingles. Ever wonder how they can afford so many commercials? Hint: Their service isn't actually free. To retrieve your Experian proxy score, you have to give them your credit card number and sign up for a free trial membership. You can opt out before they start charging you, but they make it difficult for you to figure out how to actually cancel your trial. The easiest way to cancel is to just call customer service at 1-877-481-6826 and answer "no" to a bunch of questions until they agree to deactivate your account.

Just remember that the official Fair Isaac credit score your lenders will look at is a compilation of your Experian, Equifax, and TransUnion scores. Instead of aggregating all your proxy scores, we recommend just paying for the real thing.

> **Tips & Tricks: How cable can affect your credit score**
>
> Not every financial agreement you enter into will positively or negatively alter your credit score. In fact, many will have either no effect or a negative one. For example, the cable company might do a credit check prior to your signing up to make sure that you'll pay them, and they may even report late payments to credit agencies. But if you do what you're supposed to and pay on time, they won't pat you on the back or sing your praises to the credit bureaus. If you have no other ways of building credit (e.g., you don't have a credit card) there are ways to report good financial habits—like paying your cable bills on time—through an organization called PRBC. Check out page 290 if this applies to you.

Money

Building Credit

Remember that 65% of the pie that's easily in your control? Building your credit up is as easy as taking control of that piece o' the pie. For starters, always pay your bills on time—that's 35% of the equation maximized right off the bat. Don't get trigger-happy with credit cards and buy something you're not absolutely sure you can pay off. The other big 30% chunk that consists of how much of your available credit you're using (a.k.a. "credit utilization") is easily controlled as well—it's just slightly more complicated.

Credit utilization is simply a fraction: It's the amount of debt you have outstanding divided by the total amount of debt you can borrow. And the lower the fraction the better. If you have thousands at your disposal but you've only used $20 to buy dinner, you look like a responsible young lad or lady.

Fortunately, there are two ways to positively affect this ratio: 1) by decreasing the amount of debt you have outstanding, or 2) by increasing the amount you can borrow without actually borrowing any more.

Increasing the amount of money you can borrow—also known as your *credit limit*— is risky and should only be done by those who have their spending and debt under control. If you're a frugal type of cat, the best way to do this is to ask the credit card company to give you a higher credit card limit (see page 304 for information about credit cards). Don't ask as soon as you get the card—wait until you've had it for several months and paid all your bills on time. Then, call your credit card company and ask them if they can increase your credit limit. If they ask why, you can simply respond that you're considering making some large purchases, would like the limit increased, and are responsible enough to pay it off. Credit card companies are in the business of lending money and will most likely agree. Just don't ask for a $10,000 credit limit and then assume you can now afford a jet ski. Your limit has nothing to do with how much money you have, so spend according to what's in your checking account, not what your credit card can get you.

While we suggest focusing on the 65% of the pie you have direct influence over, we aren't suggesting that the remaining components of your score are not important too. They're just a bit harder to affect today. For example, you can't control how much credit you've had in the past. Instead, you can make sure that you start building credit today so that several years down the line when you attempt to purchase a house, you'll be in a position to take out a mortgage. The remaining two pieces—how varied your credit sources are and how much new credit you have—work hand in hand. A credit rule of thumb we endorse suggests having three sources of credit (e.g., three different credit cards). If you can manage this in your twenties, you're ahead of the game. But for most people it's much better to establish *good* lines of credit (even if that means just one) than have three bad ones. So don't go opening up tons of credit card accounts all at once, especially those ominously easy to get retail store credit cards. It will raise red flags and make you look as though you keep borrowing money because you can't pay off your original debts.

Fixing Bad Credit

No matter how responsible you are, it's easy to watch your credit score get dinged due to an oversight. Maybe you missed a credit card payment when you were on vacation, or you just had no idea your credit score was slowly dropping because you still had outstanding debt to pay off. The good news is bad credit is fixable. It just takes some time. (Note: No one can fix your credit overnight, so don't buy into late-night commercials that say it can be done for the "low price of $59.99!") Credit agencies have good memories, but they forgive and forget eventually. So while that unpaid bill looks like a scarlet letter now, a streak of responsible behavior will reduce it to a little blip on your credit report. Thus, **the only real solution for fixing credit problems is to pay your bills on time and make sure to keep your credit utilization ratio low.** Over time (from six months to a year or longer, depending upon how bad it really is), your credit will recover.

If your credit is being demolished by a loan you're having trouble paying off, try calling your lender to explain your situation and see if they can help you by either 1) lowering your interest rate, 2) decreasing your monthly payments, or 3) allowing you to seek deferment or forbearance. To learn about the pros and cons of these options, read more about debt repayment on the next page.

Money

Other Ways to Improve Your Credit

Okay, you've got your credit card, you're paying the bills, and you're dealing with your debt. Cool beans—these are the most important steps. If you want to be super proactive though, there's more you can do:

- **Check the accuracy of your credit report.** Talk about life being unfair—Bankrate.com reports that 70% of credit reports contain serious errors that may impact your credit. Once a year, you should check your report and make sure that nothing looks wrong (i.e., a service provider falsely claimed that you didn't pay a bill when you have proof that you did) and that the information is consistent across each agency. If you find an issue, send a letter to the credit agency requesting an amendment. Bankrate also provides a helpful letter template that you can find a link to via gradspot.com/book.

- **Don't authorize unnecessary credit checks.** Here's another thing that seems topsy-turvy: When a third party checks your credit score, the simple act of pulling your information can hurt your credit score. It's sort of like how even if you're innocent, having the cops show up at your house makes the rest of the neighborhood assume you sell drugs. There are **soft pulls** (e.g., you check your own score) and **hard pulls** (these happen when you apply for a credit card or activate a cell phone plan, for example). Only hard pulls can affect your score. Be vigilant about who checks your credit and never allow service providers to perform a credit check until you know you want to do business with them or you've narrowed your choice down to a select group and need to allow credit checks to move forward. No one can pull your score without your social security number, so as long as you keep it close to your chest you'll be safe from willy-nilly credit pulls.

- **Build credit in nontraditional ways.** Not all recent grads have the financial standing to get a credit card, but that doesn't mean they aren't being responsible with their money in other places. An organization called Pay Rent, Build Credit, Inc. (PRBC.com) recognized this oversight and worked out a system with Fair Isaac to improve it. Basically, you can report paid bills (e.g., cable, utilities) and other financial obligations that don't traditionally affect your credit to PRBC in order to benefit your score. Another option for getting past the credit card hump is to start with a secured card and then get a credit card once you've proven you can be responsible with it (see page 314).

- **Seek private (and free) counseling.** The Association of Independent Consumer Credit Counseling Agencies may be able to work with you on your specific situation, so if you're really in dire straits why not give them a call at 866-703-8787? They'll need to know some things about your financial health to be able to provide good advice, but don't fork over your social security number.

Repaying Your Debt

According to the College Board's 2009 *Trends in Student Aid* report, 65% of college graduates have student loans, and the average debt carried out of school is $20,000. In addition, Sallie Mae, reports that the average credit card balance is over $3,500. Bogey! If you're nodding your head thinking, "Yep, that sounds about right," hopefully you can find a little bit of solace in the fact that there are others out there in the same boat. But shared suffering eventually loses its appeal because, let's face it, we really only care about ourselves. Thus, you should find a lot *more* solace in the realization that you have plenty of options for dealing with your debt, and we're going to run through them in this section. Power to you (and those other people).

Money

Before you confront your debt situation, it's important to remember how debt works. Remember Economics 101? Of course you don't! But don't worry about that. All you need to know in this case is how loans work and how they affect your overall debt.

Loan Basics: Just Ask a Drug Dealer

There are three common types of debt that grads may have: credit card, interpersonal, and student. No matter whom you owe, repayment consists of two parts: **principal** (the outstanding amount of the loan) and **interest** (the "extra" on top of the principal you have to pay each payment period). Interest is derived by applying the interest rate to your current outstanding principal. Like our favorite textbooks of yore, let's consider an example:

Slim Charles took a loan of $10,000 from Proposition Joe to make a purchase in Bolivia. Being a savvy businessman, Prop Joe said he could afford to lend the money at a 7% interest rate. Slim went to Bolivia, made some purchases, and came home. When it was time to pay back the money, Slim didn't have the whole $10,000, so Prop Joe told Slim to pay him back $1,000 of the loan each year. So how much does he have to pay at the end of the first year? Unfortunately, it's not $1,000—he must also pay the 7% interest on the principal, which in the first year is still $10,000. So he must pay $700 of interest ($10,000 × .07) in addition to the $1,000 principal repayment. Thus, his total first year payment is $1,700, and his outstanding balance after this repayment is $9,000.

See how much interest can hurt? (This clearly was a very simplified example and assuming your debt is of the student or credit variety, there will be a minimum principal repayment each month that you won't get to choose. But we do think this example gets the point across.)

What happens if Slim misses his first year's payment? Well, it only gets worse:

Slim had a rough year on the corner and now he's broke. He still owes $10,000 and, as we know, was supposed to repay $1,700 this year (principal plus interest). But he can't pay anything. Like most lenders, Prop Joe decides to capitalize the interest payment. This means that the interest Slim should have paid (e.g., $700) will now be added to his principal, thus making the new principal $10,700. And guess what? Next year, Prop Joe will use this new principal to calculate the interest payment (e.g., 7% of $10,700), so Slim will be even deeper in the pit.

Money

Tips & Tricks: What's the deal with variable rates

While interest rates on your debt will generally be somewhere between 3% and 7%, they may be variable, meaning they can change every year depending on what's going on in the economy. For example, on July 1, 2008, the government decreased rates on Stafford and PLUS loans from as high as 8% down to as low as 3.6%. Needless to say, the best thing to do when interest rates drop is to lock in your rates by consolidating your debt (p. 294). Once you do that, your lender is obliged to honor that rate for the duration of your loan. The drawback? If rates drop any further, you can't take advantage of them. That being said, we think of the economy as a highly unpredictable beast and tend to discourage holding out for more favorable rates. However, if you have really good evidence that interest rates will be decreasing (e.g., the government publicly announces rate decreases before instituting them), then by all means hold off on consolidating until the drop, assuming you've already decided consolidation makes sense for you.

Among other reasons, **capitalized interest** is why you never want to skip a repayment installment. That's how debt balloons out of control (and, in Slim's case, how you might find yourself in an abandoned building on the wrong side of a nail gun). The finish line just keeps getting further and further away and begins to feel unattainable. To avoid going down this path to bankruptcy, be sure to, at the very least, make good on your interest payments each period.

Making a Repayment Plan: Every Little Bit Counts

The point of the examples above is to demonstrate a simple but scary fact: **The longer it takes you to repay your debt, the more interest you'll be paying to your lender over time.** Thus, repaying your debt an extra $50 to $100 per month in excess of the monthly repayments you've worked out with your lender can result in thousands saved in additional interest over time.

You're probably thinking, "Thanks geniuses, but if I had the cash to repay my debt I would have done it already!" Fair point. But look at your budget (p. 316) and we bet you can find a way to pay more each month, even if it's just $50. Remember: It's not just a matter of spending $50 today versus $50 tomorrow (if it were, we'd spend it now too). It's about spending $50 today versus hundreds over the additional months or years you hold your debt.

On the flip side, if you can't even afford your basic repayment (it's nothing to be ashamed of—a lot of people are also in this situation), there are ways to minimize your monthly repayments that we'll discuss in this section.

For specifics on repaying your credit card debt see page 315. For help with your student debt, read on.

Student Debt

As you've already read, there's a good reason pundits like to call us "Generation Debt." In fact, many grads fear they owe so much student debt that they'll be halfway through their working lives by the time they break even. But this isn't the time to herald the apocalypse—it's just time to recognize that it's possible to pay off your student debts and to get your act together.

The first step is to find out how much student debt you have. To do this, check in with the National Student Loan Data System (NSLDS) online at nslds.ed.gov to see where you stand. You will need to provide your social security number, but this is a trusted, government-run organization. While the NSLDS is accurate when it comes to whom you've borrowed money from, it isn't always so accurate with how much you owe them. Thus, after finding the who, the next step is to track down the what—reach out to each organization and find out exactly how much you owe, what your monthly payments should be, whether you have a grace period (see next page), and what your interest rates are.

Once you've done all of this, you should have all of your student debt details, and will recognize that you've fallen into one of two categories: 1) You can afford to pay off your debt as is, and possibly even prepay some; or 2) The payments are too taxing on your budget and you need some relief.

If you've fallen into the first category, then things are looking up—you can prepay your debt (and thus avoid losing money on interest), or you can just repay it on the original schedule provided by your lender.

If you've fallen into the second category, there are still options. For example, you can try to consolidate your debt, thereby decreasing your monthly payments and spreading your repayment schedule over many years. Or, if worse comes to worst, you can attempt to get your loans "forgiven." Regardless of where you stand, it's worth considering the pros and cons of all options.

Money

Prepaying Student Debt

Drumming up the money to prepay all of your debt today (or even a portion of it) may seem daunting, but it's the best way to minimize the net cost of repayment and move on with your life. Why? Because as we've discussed, you bypass all of the interest that accrues when you pay over time. Got money from grandma or a car you can sell? You might be able to wipe your debt clean and get on with your life in one swift move. This is particularly worth thinking about if your interest rate is on the high side (i.e., over 6%).

The "Perks" of Student Debt

In many ways repaying student debt is like going to a good massage parlor—quite expensive, but there are perks (like a sauna and free fruit—what were you thinking?). The first perk is the **grace period.** After you graduate, you can usually stall your debt repayment for up to six months (check with your lender before doing so). However, it's important to note that if any of your debt is unsubsidized, the unpaid interest during the grace period will be capitalized (i.e., added to your principal) unless you pay it yourself. By calling your lenders, you should be able to determine whether or not your debt is subsidized. The second "cherry on top" is the fact that a portion of your student debt interest is tax deductible (see page 339).

What Exactly Is Student Debt Consolidation?

In its simplest form, student debt consolidation on federal (e.g., Stafford, PLUS) and private loans enables you to do any or all of the following: 1) combine all of your loans into one loan, with one interest rate and one monthly payment; 2) decrease the amount of your monthly payment by repaying your loan over an extended period of time (up to 30 years); and 3) lock in your interest rates (many forms of student debt have variable interest rates attached and most people prefer to lock them in).

Consolidation may help you meet your monthly budget, but there's also a downside—the reason that consolidators are willing to allow you to pay less each month is because they can make more money off of your loan in the long run. In fact, over a 30-year period, you may pay up to three times as much as if you had repaid your debt on the original schedule, which is usually ten years.

When it comes to actual consolidation, there are basically three options: 1) a **standard repayment loan** that does not extend your repayment schedule past ten years but does fix your interest rate and combines your loans into one; 2) an **extended or graduated loan** that draws out the life of the loan—you can either make a consistent payment each month or pay less now at the expense of having to pay more in the future (when you're hopefully making more money); or 3) an **income contingent loan** where repayment is tied to—you guessed it—your income.

How to Pick a Student Debt Consolidator

Choosing a consolidator requires a fair amount of due diligence, but it's worth taking the time to do it right—after all, your relationship with the lender may last decades! As of the date of this volume, many of the lenders who consolidated government loans have left the market (e.g., Sallie Mae, NelNet) due to the credit crisis. Thus, if you have federal loans, you will most likely have to consolidate through the government. The website LoanConsolidation. ed.gov is a good place to start, but you'll eventually want to call one of the helpful attendants at the government's hotline (800-557-7392) to explore your options. Even though they'll ask for your social security number to explore your options, you don't need to provide it as long as you can tell them the types and amount of debt you have.

In terms of finding consolidators for your private loans, the first step should always be to call your lender. You'd be surprised, but many of them may offer to consolidate your debt rather then have someone else do it, or at the very least pass you along to a partner. However, whenever using a private (i.e., non-government) debt consolidator, look out for red flags like companies that resell your debt, non-fixed interest rates, and penalties for prepaying your loans.

No matter whom you consolidate with, you should expect some type of discount (0.25%) if you pay your monthly bill with automatic bill pay (p. 303), and possibly another discount of up to 1% if you make good on all your payments for the first 36 months.

Can I Really Get My Debt Forgiven?

If you *really* can't pay, then yes, forgiveness is possible. But understand that it's forgiveness in the way that your boyfriend or girlfriend "forgives" you for knocking boots with someone else—in other words, there are plenty of strings attached. Here are your three options.

Money

Tips & Tricks: Tax consequences of forgiveness

While debt forgiveness can be just what the doctor ordered for your financial health (and sanity), just remember that when it comes to the tax man, you can never get something for nothing. In fact, the amount of debt that will be repaid is viewed in the eyes of the IRS as income which you'll need to pay taxes on. Clearly debt forgiveness is a lot better than debt inflation, but whichever path you decide to travel down, just be sure to talk with an accountant before making any major moves.

Volunteer for Forgiveness

Your debt will be paid (usually up to $60,000) by a third-party if you provide services to their organization for several years. This includes full-time volunteering with organizations like Americorp and the Peace Corps (p. 150), enlisting for military service, teaching, or offering to help groups such as Equal Justice Works and the National Health Service Corps. Recently, the U.S. government institutionalized this practice of volunteer work in exchange for debt forgiveness by creating the Public Service Loan Forgiveness (PSLF) program, which you can learn more about via LoanConsolidation.ed.gov and 1-800-557-7392. In addition, some colleges may even offer debt repayment assistance, such as Low Income Protection Plans (LIPP), so check with your school if you're in need of forgiveness.

Income-Based Repayment

Another government-sponsored debt-forgiveness program that started in 2009 is the Income-Based Repayment (IBR) program. As unbelievable as it sounds, the government will actually repay a portion of your loan repayments based upon your income and family status. (Note: IBR should not be confused with an income-contingent loan, which is totally different and doesn't forgive any of your debt.) According to IBRinfo.org, you may be eligible for the program if the following criteria apply to you:

- You have federal student loans in either the Direct or Guaranteed Loan (FFEL) program.

- Your loans include Stafford, Grad Plus, and federal consolidation loans that do not include Parent PLUS loans. Perkins loans are eligible if you consolidate them into a Guaranteed or Direct loan.

- You borrowed either before or after IBR was created, for either graduate or undergraduate study.

- Your debt-to-income ratio qualifies you for reduced payments (a good rule of thumb is that if you make less than you owe each month, you'll qualify, but check out the calculator on the site to be sure).

Student Debt Forbearance and Deferment

While your grace period (p. 294) provides you with six months of payment-free bliss after graduation, you might be in a situation where you need to defer your payments even longer. Say hello to our little friends, student loan forbearance and deferment—both enable you to defer your payment of the loans (usually for up to three years). With deferment you don't have to repay the interest that accrues during that time, but needless to say, this added perk makes it harder to get than forbearance.

The qualification criteria for deferment and forbearance differ slightly and are also contingent on the type of loan you have. Qualifications for forbearance include the following:

- The inability to pay off the loan during its term
- Loan repayments equaling at least 20% of your monthly income
- Significant and unexpected personal problems
- Disability (including deteriorating health)

For deferment, you have to meet some of these less common criteria:

- Enrollment in a school at least part-time
- Unemployment (for up to three years)
- Experiencing economic hardship
- Military deployment
- Pursuit of an above-board internship
- Participation in national service

The best way to apply for deferment and forbearance is to check in with your lenders who will provide you with instructions. But once you have applied, don't jump the gun on skipping payments. Your deferment only kicks in once your lender alerts you that it does. And it's up to you to check in on your deferment status.

The Bottom Line on Student Debt

Student debt is no joke, and if you don't confront it now it can easily spiral out of control. In severe circumstances (e.g., you're completely broke and refuse to volunteer in Papua New Guinea), you can always come clean with your lender and see if you can work out an alternative arrangement. If you ever do get desperate, please talk to an accountant or lawyer before doing anything drastic.

Bank Accounts

Being suspicious of "banking" is a time-honored tradition that dates back to the days of ancient Greece, when gold was hoarded in temples by lecherous,

inbred priests…at least according to the movie *300*. Sometime later, Adam Smith used his "invisible hand" to invent capitalism, or, as it's now known, "eBay," and banks resembling the ones we know today were born.

Things are pretty well-regulated these days, but it's still good to bring a healthy amount of wariness to the process of choosing the right bank. Know that approximately 40% of banks' revenue comes from the fees they charge on consumer accounts, whether that's general monthly fees that are charged to just keep them open or "penalty" fees. Like going to the movies, the "feature presentation" (i.e., an account) lures you in and then they turn the screws with overpriced concessions like Swedish Fish and Milk Duds (i.e., service fees). Unnecessary fees that seem negligible can add up over time. With a little bit of research, however, you should be able to avoid most extra charges and find the right bank and bank account for you.

Choosing a Bank

The fact is, most banks offer pretty similar account options. But if you have a selection in your area, there are a few considerations that you should keep in mind.

- **Convenience.** This is probably the most important factor when it comes to selecting a bank. It's up to you, but we're guessing you'd prefer a bank that has a prolific ATM network (so that you don't have

Money

to rack up fees) and a brick-and-mortar branch nearby if you value being able to speak with someone in person.

- **Online Banking.** You should opt for a bank that provides online banking. Essentially, it enables you to check your balances, transfer funds, send checks, and more, all while sitting at home in your undies…and for free. Another major benefit is the ability to enroll in automatic bill pay, which we discuss further on page 303.

- **FDIC Insurance.** In the wake of the credit crisis, you want to make sure that your money is protected, and the best way to do this is to make sure that your bank has FDIC insurance (see below).

Types of Accounts

There are two main types of accounts you should consider: checking and savings. Here are some key things to look out for when comparison shopping for these accounts.

Checking Accounts

The most basic account offered by most banks is a checking account. This is preferable to keeping money under your mattress because you can write checks (usually necessary for rent), use ATMs to access your money anywhere, get a debit card (p. 301), and not get your cash stolen as easily. You receive no interest on your money, but you also pay minimal to no fees. If your needs are relatively straightforward (i.e., security and convenience), then your best bet is to just go with the most convenient bank, assuming it doesn't charge any general monthly fees. After all, there's no reason to pay for something that earns you no money.

Tips & Tricks: FDIC insurance

If the credit crunch taught us anything, it's that nothing is certain in the financial world and even the behemoths of banking can crumble to the ground. So while the chances of your bank going belly up all of a sudden are highly unlikely, you want to make sure you'll get your money back if it does. That's where FDIC Insurance comes into play. The government insures one account per person at each FDIC-insured bank for up to $250,000 (prior to the financial crisis that amount was only $100,000). There's no reason to go with a bank that is not FDIC-insured—even the Redneck Bank is (look it up, it's real).

Penalty fees to look out for when it comes to checking are ATM fees (i.e., paying to use another bank's ATMs) and bounced check fees (be wary of "bounced-check-protection" and instead opt for "standard overdraft protection"). An easy way to comparison shop is to head to Bankrate.com, which will give you the lowdown on every account from all of the major banks in your zip code.

Savings Accounts

As the name would suggest, savings accounts are built for money you save rather than spend. They offer the ability to earn interest on your money so it actually grows while it's sitting in the bank. Interest rates on savings accounts are not all that high, but why wouldn't you want your money to earn for you? Just be careful that you don't negate any earned interest by incurring penalty fees, because savings accounts have lots. Most notably, almost all savings accounts charge a penalty if you dip below a stated minimum balance, so you always need to ensure that you can meet the minimum, usually around $1,000, before opening one. As long as you pay close attention to your account's guidelines, you shouldn't have a problem avoiding fees.

Online Bank Accounts

The new kids on the block in the banking world are Online Checking Accounts and Online Savings Accounts, and they're making the traditional brick-and-mortar banks (Wells Fargo, Citi, Chase, Bank of America, etc.) look like chumps by offering some interest on checking accounts and an average of about 1% more interest on savings accounts. With no real estate, in-person bank tellers, janitors, or any other major overhead costs to deal with, these online banks save a lot of money that they then pass on to you in the form of better rates. New FDIC-insured online banks or branches of brokerage firms offering online banking accounts are popping up each month. The major players include ING Direct, Emigrant Direct, HSBC Direct, Ally, Charles Schwab, and Fidelity. When you start looking, use Bankrate.com to get a sense of what's competitive—you should be looking for the highest interest rate and a minimum balance you can sustain, as well as any other perks like waived ATM fees (since they most likely don't have their own ATMs).

The only catch with online accounts is that there are no physical locations so if you're the type of person that prefers visiting your bank and working with a banker, online savings accounts probably aren't for you. You also can't pop around the corner and withdraw or deposit funds; it usually takes a few days to send checks via mail or electronically to a checking account. Still, we think

Money

the positives—particularly for savings accounts—far outweigh the "negatives." See page 322 to learn about the power of compounding, and you'll understand why. Even just 1% makes a big difference over the long-run.

Opening a Bank Account

Getting a bank account is super easy. It requires filling out some basic information including your legal name, where you live, your phone number, email address, and so on. You'll also be required to provide your social security number, as well as either the number on your driver's license or another state issued identification card. Finally, you'll be asked to make an initial deposit, which can be as small as $1. When it comes to traditional banks, you can just pop into the closest branch, call the bank's phone number, or fill out an application online. With online banks, you can just do it on the website. And that's really all there is to it.

Using Your Debit Card

When you open up a bank account, you'll get a debit card that you can use for ATM withdrawals and on-the-go purchases. Debit cards don't solidify your "baller status" quite like a credit card (see page 304), but they're a great convenience. Unfortunately, they can also get you in trouble, so there are some caveats worth pointing out.

First, some merchants don't report debit card transactions immediately (especially if your PIN is not used in the purchase), so stay on top of your balance to avoid an accidental overdraft, which will result in a penalty fee and possibly even interest charges on the cash you didn't have. Furthermore, certain types of purchases (e.g., hotels, car rentals) can result in a "hold" or a "security deposit" that will tie up your funds until the transaction clears—your ears should perk up if you hear these words and you should realize that the deposit amount should not be considered usable money until it's been released back into your bank account. Finally, debit cards don't help you build your credit, and without credit you won't be able to do things like get auto loans and mortgages. So even though they're just as convenient as credit cards, they're not an alternative.

As always, comparison shop for debit cards to make sure you're getting the best option, though you probably won't choose your bank based on its debit cards. While most debit cards are the same, Citi's debit cards, for example, offer

Money

"Thank You" points which are redeemable for merchandise, travel, and other perks, so you might as well see what extras you can snag.

How to Write a Personal Check

One of the authors of this book (cough, Chris) didn't know how to write a check until he was 23-years-old. If you're in the same boat, just check out this tutorial showing you what to put in each section:

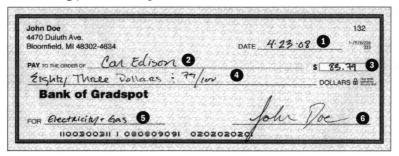

1) The current date

2) The full name of the individual or organization you are paying. Don't use nicknames or names you just made up

3) The dollar amount—be very clear with your decimal points and commas

4) The dollar amount written out in words—cents are written as a fraction in the form of "X/100." If there are zero cents, then write it out as "0/100"

5) Write what the check is for—this part is optional, but it can be helpful for your own record keeping

6) Your signature

Tip: When filling out amounts, avoid blank spaces (someone might sneak in some extra zeros). If you don't fill up a line, you can draw a line through the remaining space.

How to Endorse (or "Cash") a Check

So you have a check. Until you bring it to a bank it won't do you any good, and just bringing it to a teller without endorsing it won't either.

There are three different ways to endorse a check, and each is used for a different reason. The first way is to just sign the back of the check. If you want to either deposit it for cash or have it deposited into your account, this is all you have to do. It's best to sign it only once you arrive at the bank (or just before sending it to your online bank), because if you lose an endorsed check, anyone who finds it can sign their name below yours and cash it—no questions asked.

The next two options are applicable if you want to direct the check to someone else or mail it to your bank for deposit into your own account. To protect the check from ending up anywhere other than your bank account, write "for deposit only" and, below that, the account number that it can be deposited into. If you want to sign the check over to someone else (this traditionally occurs when you receive a health insurance reimbursement and need to transfer it to your doctor), sign the check on the back at the top and on the next line write, "Pay to:", followed by the person's or organization's name.

How to Void a Check

Sometimes you will have to provide a voided check to do things like set up direct deposit for your paycheck at work. To void a check, simply write "VOID" in large print across the face of the check.

Automatic Bill Pay

Automatic bill pay is a simple way to outsource responsibility and maintain good credit. There are two forms of ABP (not to be confused with the semi-delicious coffee chain Au Bon Pain). The more widely used one involves an arrangement between you and a company (e.g., your cell phone service provider) in which you provide them with your credit card or bank account number and they automatically charge you when a bill becomes due. The other, less widely known version of ABP is where you ask your bank to automatically send a check on your behalf to a vendor on a recurring schedule (e.g., your rent check every month). Setting up automatic bill pay just requires going to your online banking account or calling the bank directly. And it's a great addition to any automated financial system (see page 338). Think of automatic bill pay as a safety net: You should always review all bills before paying them (whether they're paid with automatic bill pay or not), and in the rare event that you forget to pay, automatic bill pay will be there to handle your business and save your credit rating.

Many people are hesitant to use automatic bill pay because they're worried about paying for something without seeing the bill. Conspiracy theorists have their value in certain areas, but we think there are some charges that just aren't worth the hassle and risk of a missed payment. For example, you know you're going to pay rent, so why not arrange for your bank to send a check the last week of every month? In addition, you know your cable bill should be consistent each month. Other places to consider using automatic bill pay are electricity bills (though you should stay on top of the charges to budget your usage) and any other monthly subscriptions. However, one area that we're on the fence about is your credit card(s) because who knows when someone will steal your identity and order half of the Sky Mall catalog. Create an online account through your credit card provider to receive e-updates when payments are due. If you then sign up for automatic bill pay for the card, you'll receive an alert telling you when the auto pay date is coming up so you can check the charges in advance.

Remember: You can always stop the automatic payments from going through if you need to do so. For example, if you had your rent in the queue and your landlord kicks you out of your apartment, you can stop the check from being sent (although stopping the check is now probably the least of your worries). In addition, companies usually provide a buffer between the dates when you receive your bill and when it is due, thus giving you time to stop it if need be.

Credit Cards

Can't get a job and your parents are kicking you out of the house? There's a simple solution: Apply for a bunch of credit cards, max them out on gear and non-perishables, and then fake your own death. Problem solved!

We're joking, of course—credit card fraud is not a foolproof plan. But it's a joke with a point: Credit cards breed extreme behavior, so beware. Spending that which does not immediately exist is inherently risky, and if impulsivity is the name of your game, it might be good to check yourself before you wreck yourself. **Credit cards should never be used as a way to get loans—at the end of the day, the interest rates that credit cards charge are not competitive.** It's basically like borrowing money from the mob. And while mobsters are very good in films, you wouldn't want to meet them in real life. If you don't think you will be able to make good on the payments, play it safe and opt for a secured card (p. 314) or a debit card (p. 301) instead.

So, what's so good about credit cards? Where to begin, kemo sabe. There are a multitude of important benefits to having credit cards, assuming you always pay them off on time. For a recent grad, the most important reason to have a credit card is that it will help you build your credit (see page 287). It's also nice to be able to cruise around without carrying huge wads of cash and to accrue perks such as air miles, free hotel stays, and cash back bonuses when you spend money. Another benefit is the insurance most credit cards provide on purchases. For example, if you buy something with your card and lose the item, or if your item breaks and customer support is giving you a tough time, the credit card company may actually reimburse you.

The Most Important Reason to Get a Credit Card

Let's just say it again for effect: Using a credit card (even if you're spending just $1 a month and repaying that $1) is the easiest way to build your credit. Building your credit allows you to do things like rent an apartment and purchase a cell phone plan in the short term, and take out mortgages and finance cars in the long term. It's better to start building credit today so that you have it when you need it instead of scrambling when you're trying to buy your first McMansion.

Choosing a Card

The three main things to consider when choosing a credit card are annual fees, interest rate, and rewards. You usually can't have all three, so it's up to you to decide which is most important. Assuming you always pay your bills on time and thus never pay interest, you should focus your attention on avoiding annual fees and snagging useful rewards. There are many credit cards that don't

Money

have annual fees attached—despite what rap music taught you, you don't need an AmEx Black Card. The only reason you should ever pay an annual fee for a card is if you know the rewards will far outweigh your annual fee, like in the case of a great airline rewards card for someone who travels a lot. Just keep in mind that it usually takes around 30,000 airline miles, or $30,000 spent on a card, to earn a free domestic flight. So, it probably only makes sense if you get to expense travel for work and accrue points for a personal trip. A more practical rewards option for most grads is cash back (for every dollar you spend on specific items, you'll receive 1–5% off, but just make sure that the items you receive this cash back on are the types of items you regularly purchase).

As mentioned, the interest rate shouldn't affect you because you're never going to charge more than you can pay...right?! But realistically, you might miss a payment, so the lower the fee the better—low-to-mid teens is about the best you'll get. Watch out for cards that boast an introductory 0% APR (i.e., interest rate) and no annual fee, because they'll usually increase both starting in year two. (For more tips on navigating credit card ads and terms, see our sample credit card ad on the next page.)

The best way to find a card is to browse your options on sites like CardRatings.com and CreditCards.com. These sites will allow you to compare hundreds of cards that are conveniently organized into categories like "Low Ongoing Rate," "Cards for No/Poor Credit," "Cash Back Rewards," and "Gas Rebate Cards." Also, check out "A Few Good Credit Cards for Recent Grads" on page 309.

Deciphering Credit Card Ads

Lawyers can barely decipher the fine print on credit card ads and even a math major would be hard-pressed to figure out how his or her bill is calculated. And at the end of the day, interest rates should be somewhat irrelevant since you'd ideally pay your balance in full every time. That said, here are a few key things to look out for when assessing a credit card offer.

BALLER BANK

"Charge It To The Game" Credit Card

BALLER BANK
CHARGE IT TO THE GAME

1234 123456 12345

YOUR NAME HERE

CARD OVERVIEW

- Earn up to 5% cash back **1**
- 0.00% APR*
- No minimum payment for 6 months**
- 0.00% balance transfers*** **2**
- No annual fee**** **3**
- $0 fraud liability for any unauthorized use if your card is lost or stolen
- 20 day grace period **4**
- Credit limit up to $20,000

Apply Now!

* 0.00% APR valid for up to 12 months; Prime Rate + 9.99% APR thereafter. **5** **6** **7** **8**

** No minimum payment for 6 months; 3.5% of outstanding balance thereafter. **9**

*** 0.00% interest rate until the last day of the billing period ending during June 2009; then the standard APR for purchases

**** Annual fee after first year is $95.

See additional terms and conditions on credit card application.

1)   **Rewards.** Air miles? Cash back? Hotel rooms? Are there any stipulations for redeeming the points? Do they offer something you would actually spend your money on otherwise?

2)   **Balance Transfer Fees.** Transferring debt between cards may seem like a useful move at times, but look out for the interest charged on these transactions.

3)   **Annual Fee.** This fee is paid each year simply for the convenience

of having the card. Unless you are receiving exceptional benefits, annual fees should be avoided. Beware of cards that tease with no annual fee for the first year only.

4) **Grace Period.** Kind lenders should offer a grace period, which is the period of time before the lender starts charging you interest on new purchases. You will want a reasonable grace period (e.g., 20–25 days) if you don't always pay your bill in full each month.

5) **APR.** This is the beginning interest rate that you pay on your outstanding balance. Usually, it is a "teaser rate" (e.g., "0% APR!") that will shoot up after the first year, or even sooner depending on your credit score.

6) **Prime rate.** A benchmark used by banks to determine the interest rate. Generally somewhere between 6-10%.

7) **Fixed rate.** This is ostensibly good, because the lender is claiming they won't change the interest rate (i.e., "fixed for life!"). The problem is, they can still just go ahead and change it whenever they want.

8) **Variable rate.** An interest rate that is tied to a standard index. This may sound good if interest rates are going down, but it's not like you can predict the movement of rates for the whole time you're going to hold the card.

9) **Minimum payment.** This is the minimum amount that you are required to pay that month in order for the credit card company to not report you to a credit agency. Remember, however, that the remainder is just racking up interest that you'll have to pay down the line.

Applying for Credit Cards Is Not Like Applying for School

These days, applying to over 20 colleges is considered standard, and Yale doesn't care that you also applied to Michigan and Pomona. However, applying for lots of credit cards in a short span of time makes you look desperate and can adversely affect your credit score. So where should you focus your efforts? For recent grads with no credit history and low income, your school may be your first port of call. Your alumni association might have an affiliate relationship with Visa or a bank and may be able to hook you up. Banks are also a good place to go. If you've been a loyal customer of your bank or any other financial institution over the years, they're likely to reward you with some plastic. And if no one's giving you a break, consider getting a secured card (p. 314) and then working your way up to a credit card.

Applying for a credit card is just like applying for a bank account. Whether you're going through your alumni organization, bank, or directly from a credit card company, you'll be asked for some personal information, identification, and your social security number. The only difference between applying for credit cards and bank accounts is that your credit rating may impact whether or not you are granted a card.

One last note: A fiscal mirage that derails many a thrifty spender is the store credit card. These are easy to get—maybe too easy. Myvesta, a nonprofit consumer-education organization, reports that each time you open a store credit card, 20 points are taken off of your credit score. If you legitimately buy half the J. Crew collection every season, then by all means get a J. Crew credit card. But in general, remember the old saying, "If it seems too good to be true, it probably is." Far too many people open store credit card accounts at the counter to get a discount, completely forget about them, and end up with late payments and a damaged credit score.

A Few Good Credit Cards for Recent Grads

When push comes to shove, there's no perfect credit card for a recent grad. Everyone has his or her own preferences. Maybe you have a fetish for hotel points, or maybe you're a bad grad and you need a low APR for that balance you carry on your card. To give you a sense of what's out there and provide some solid no-fee choices, here are some options to explore.

American Express Blue Cash. There's no annual fee, and you can earn up to 5% on many of your everyday purchases. It also provides American Express purchase protection, which is basically like built-in insurance on a lot of things you buy. The only negative is that after the intro period, the APR is between 17.24% and 21.24%.

A Few Good Credit Cards for Recent Grads continued...

Orbitz Visa. Rather than providing you with frequent flier miles for one specific airline, the Orbitz Visa gives you points that can be redeemed for anything on Orbitz.com (airfare, hotels, car rentals, vacation packages, etc.). In addition, for each travel booking made through Orbitz you get bonus points, and on eligible bookings, you get three points for every dollar spent. The card is supplied by Capital One and is part of its "No Hassle Rewards" program, so your points can also be redeemed for gift cards or cash. There's no annual fee and a pretty average APR of 13.9%. Though as a recent grad you might not earn a free ticket to Fiji, your points may be enough to get you home to visit your folks.

Fidelity Investment Rewards American Express. If you decide to begin depositing money into an investment account (p. 335), then this may be the card for you. Instead of providing you with cash back, it provides you with contributions to your investment account. For example, if you spend $2,500, Fidelity will contribute $50. It's an interesting way to force you to invest. While there is no annual fee, you are required to have a Fidelity investment account (which is one of the brokerage houses that we recommend later in the chapter), and there's also a low-ish APR of 13.99%. One other advantage is that if you really don't want to use your points for investment purposes, you can use them as World Points instead (which are redeemable for a variety of different items).

Citi Forward. This card is all about incentives for doing the right thing. For example, if for a few months you pay your bills on time and stay under your credit limit, Citi will reward you with a reduced APR. In addition, each month that you pay on time you earn 100 points, for signing up for paperless statements you earn 5,000 points, and if you spend $250 on the card within the first three months you earn 6,000 points. Points can be redeemed through the "Thank You Network" for merchandise, travel, gift cards, and so on. (Keep in mind, however, that a book costs around 2,000 points and a run-of-the-mill Gateway Desktop costs 70,000 points.)

Hopefully this gives you a good starting point for selecting credit cards. If you decide to look further (and we highly recommend that you do), be sure to carefully examine credit card terms and ads as you compare offers.

■

Proper Credit Card Maintenance

First and foremost, make your payments on time, every time. The main reason for having a credit card at an early age is to build credit, so your top priority should be to use it responsibly and always pay in full. If you have any old cards, don't cancel them as long as they don't carry an annual fee—building a long-term history with a card improves your credit rating, even if you are just spending $1 each month. Also, never max out a card or charge something that's over 50% of the limit—this type of behavior makes you look irresponsible to creditors.

While you can use your credit card for every little purchase, we think credit cards are best used for big-ticket items that you can easily keep track of, as well as online purchases because of the extra level of security that they provide. The negligible rewards you will earn on small purchases like lattes and gum may not be worth the risk of losing track of your spending and then not being able to pay the bill in full at the end of the month. On the flip side, if you direct all of your spending on your credit card, then you'll be able to easily see what you're spending money on each month, including the small stuff—you just have to be confident that you always have enough in your checking account to pay for it all.

Whichever credit card spending strategy you use, set up an online account for each credit card to receive alerts, avoid late payments, and ensure that you are rewarded for responsible behavior by requesting a credit limit increase every six months (see page 287). Check all your statements carefully for red flags like incorrect penalties, charges that are clearly erroneous (potential credit card fraud), and vendors charging you the wrong amount. If you are assessed any penalty fees or other charges from your credit card company, it's always worth asking them if they can remove them. Normally, if you ask, they'll do it. However, you need to call immediately after receiving the bill and you may need to respectfully talk your way up to a manager. While removing extra fees may work once or twice, it won't work forever, so don't think you can always be late and still get off the hook.

Deciphering a Credit Card Bill

It's one thing to have good intentions about properly maintaining your credit card, but follow-through is another thing altogether. If this is the first time you've owned a card (or have been responsible for paying it), it helps to understand what all the terms on your credit card bill mean.

Money

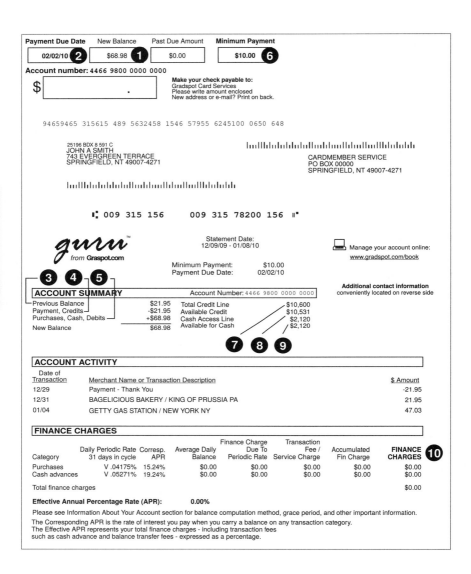

1) **Outstanding Balance.** This is the most important number on your bill. It's the amount that you owe your credit card company, and it's derived by taking the previous balance, deducting your previous payments and any credits, and then adding new purchases (all explained below). If you leave this amount outstanding, it will accrue crazy amounts of interest that you'll eventually have to pay as well.

2) **Payment Due.** The date when you have to pay up. As long as you pay the minimum (see #6) by this date you won't be charged a late fee. But we recommend always paying the full balance.

3) **Previous Balance.** This number was your ending balance from last month.

4) **Payment Credits.** This is the amount of the previous balance that you repaid (it can be the whole thing), as well as any credits the credit card company applied to your account (e.g., when you called and convinced them to refund a ridiculous charge).

5) **Purchases, Cash, Debits.** This is the aggregate of your purchases during the bill's period, as well as any cash advances you made or any penalties you received.

6) **Minimum Payment Due.** Hopefully you can ignore this number, but in the event you can't afford to pay your entire bill, this is the amount that you must pay the credit card company in order to preempt them from reporting your inability to pay your bill to a credit agency. Just remember: Interest will accrue (and ultimately compound, meaning you'll end up paying interest on your interest!) on the remaining unpaid balance.

7) **Total Credit Line.** This is the maximum amount of money you can borrow from a lender at any one time. After you've reached the limit, you have to repay that amount before you can borrow any more. So in the case of a credit card, it's the maximum amount you can charge in one billing cycle. Obviously you should never actually reach your limit. But it's an important number to recognize because it impacts your credit via your credit utilization rate (i.e., how much debt you have outstanding versus the total amount of money you can borrow). See page 287 to learn more about credit utilization.

8) **Available Credit.** Your total credit line minus your outstanding balance.

9) **Cash Access Line & Available Cash.** Please, please, please, don't ever worry about or use these figures, but if you must know....

Money

Essentially, in addition to enabling you to make purchases with a credit card, your credit card company may be willing to lend you actual cold hard cash. Warning: The loan will come with an outrageous interest rate. In fact, the terms will be so outrageous that this is just about one of the worst forms of debt. These transactions will be reflected in your "access line," which is the total amount the company is willing to lend to you, and your "available cash," which is that amount less what you've already (but shouldn't have) borrowed.

10)   **Finance Charges.** This section sends shivers down the spine of credit card debt survivors. This is where your credit card company details all of the interest you're racking up. You know you're a personal finance superstar when this section is blank.

What If I Can't Get a Credit Card?

Don't take it personally—credit card companies just don't really love recent grads. In college, companies probably threw credit card offers at you willy-nilly, even tossing in lame T-shirts and mildly inappropriate bottle openers for good measure. But really, they were judging you by your parents, as is the old American tradition. They assumed that daddy or mommy would be there to bail you out if need be. After graduation, however, you are judged on your own merits. Since the two main factors credit card companies consider are income and credit history, you now most likely look more like a pauper than a princess. For forward-thinkers, the power move is clear: Snag a good credit card right before you graduate. It won't expire for at least two years, and if you make good on all your payments, you shouldn't have a problem renewing it as a grad.

Should the options previously discussed (your bank, alumni association, etc.) lead to dead ends, you still have one option for snagging some slightly less awesome but still useful plastic: secured cards.

Secured Cards

Think of a secured card as a credit card with training wheels. When you sign up, the bank will ask you to put cash in an account linked to your card. That money, or some percentage of it, becomes your credit limit. If you think it sounds just like a debit card (p. 301), you're right. But unlike a debit card, a secured card can help you get a credit card—after a few months of using it without running over the limit, just call the bank and request an upgrade.

The danger of secured cards is that they allow you to carry a balance that accrues interest. But since your credit limit will be equal to the amount of money you deposited into the account, and most likely that amount won't be too high, you won't really risk that much damage from interest if you ever charge something to your secured card and then wait a month to repay it (i.e., the interest on a $50 balance is in a completely difference league than the interest on a $500 balance). That said, since the goal of having a secured card is to convince your bank to give you a credit card, you should never carry a balance. Use it frugally, pay it off, then upgrade.

When shopping for a secured card, you want to look for the same criteria that you do for credit cards: no fees and low interest rates (rewards aren't applicable here). Talk to your bank to learn about your options.

WARNING: The Dangers of Credit Card Debt

"A stitch in time saves nine" is not really an expression that's relevant to our lives anymore (who knows how to sew?). But the concept certainly applies to credit card debt, which can become a serious problem if you don't nip it in the bud. Remember our discussion of loans and interest payments on page 291? Here's a little recap to show you how debt can knock you upside the head: Let's assume that by the end of the first month that you have your credit card, you rack up some purchases and you don't have enough money in your bank account to pay them off yet. You clearly didn't take our advice, but we're not mad at you—it happens. Here's what really blows, though: When your second bill arrives, even if you didn't purchase a single thing with your credit card since the last billing cycle, your new balance will increase. Why? Because you pay silly amounts of interest on the money you didn't repay. Now, your new debt is the original debt plus the interest. And if you can't pay it again the next month, your debt will be even higher because you'll be charged interest on the original debt as well as on the interest you accrued in the second month! See the cycle? Credit card debt is the worst possible detriment to your financial health. No pair of shoes or new TV is ever worth the pain it can bring you.

Dealing with Credit Card Debt

Like all forms of debt, there's no quick fix here, so ignore those companies that claim they can help you repay your debt overnight. Instead, take an aggressive approach to paying it off, and do everything you can to make your situation more manageable. The first trick is to call your bank and request that they lower your APR. Worst case scenario they say no—at least you tried. If you keep pleading your case and stressing that a lower rate will help you pay off your debt (be clear you're not just looking for charity), things will probably go your way eventually. Another, more aggressive approach is to threaten to transfer the balance to another credit card with a lower APR. It's always easier to pull this move off if you actually know of a lower-interest alternative in the event they try to call your bluff. If you haven't done any research yet, you can tell the representative that you'll move it to "one of the many cards offered by your competitors that carry a lower rate." While it's a good bargaining chip, be very careful about going through with a balance transfer, because it usually carries fees and/or extra interest charges, as well as higher rates after an initial grace period.

Easy Budgeting: Audit Yourself

Setting up a solid personal finance infrastructure is all well and good, but it's really not much use if you don't have money moving through it. Once those paychecks start coming in, you've got to budget your income to make sure that the bills get dealt with, the savings account gets filled, the 401(k) gets some action, the bar tab gets paid, and so on and so forth. The problem is, the "B word" scares most recent grads off before they've even begun. So here's the deal: You don't have to write a journal entry every time you buy a smoothie, nor do you have to give up your Netflix subscription or haggle over the bill whenever you eat out with friends. Being that frugal can definitely save you money, but it's also annoying for you and everyone around you. Instead, your primary goal should be to get a realistic sense of what money is coming in every month and where it's going.

The best way to do that is to perform a self-audit. Aside from knocking you off the mental inner tube you're using to float down "denial," this process is relatively painless and, unlike with a real audit, there's no chance of jail time unless you perform a citizen's arrest on yourself. Here's what you do: For one month and one month only, keep close tabs on income you've got coming in, how much money you're using, and where that money is going. More than likely, your spending habits will have changed dramatically from what they were in college—regular expenses like pizza and $5 pitchers suddenly turn into rent, groceries, utility bills, transportation costs, and more. So check out your credit card bill, bank statement, and receipts to figure out the new lay of the land.

Now that you've braved this self-assessment, you can take two key steps. First, you can pinpoint places where curtailing your spending won't have any material affect on your life. You might think going out on the weekend is totally worth it for your sanity, but maybe that $50 "Cheese of the Month" subscription doesn't seem justified when you see it on your bank statement. Second, you can figure out how much money you have left over after expenses to filter into the savings component of your budget. These savings should

> ### Tips & Tricks: Set up an under-$5 fund
>
> Here's a simple way to save money without having to give up your daily latte. Instead of tossing your spare change around the house like you are living in a fountain, grab a bowl, a plastic cup, or any sort of reasonably sized receptacle and place it by the front door. This is your under-$5 fund, which you will use for any habitual purchases under $5. For most people, that means morning coffee, but it could also mean bagels, or the newspaper you bizarrely like to buy only three days a week, or anything else. The rule is that you can buy these things whenever you want as long as you draw the money from the under-$5 fund. If you forget to grab the $3.26 for your latte or there's no change left, then you're out of luck. Coffee from work will have to suffice.

Money

be broken down into two types: 1) savings for upcoming purchases such as televisions and medium-term purchases such as a house, and 2) savings for retirement (for both, see page 321). If you're maxed out every month, you're not ensuring that you'll be able to live the lifestyle you want down the road—we recommend that you save at least 15% of the money that's coming in. (For more advice on how your budget should break down, see "Budgeting Guidelines" below.)

And there you have it. That's really all you need to do to assess your budget. And now, if you want to get a little more nitty-gritty and really start to maximize your personal finance potential, let's dive into a few useful budgeting tips.

Budgeting Guidelines

It's one thing to look at what your past spending has been, but the real power of budgeting is in planning what you'll spend in the future. While there are no set rules for how money should be spent, you should expect to spend approximately 35% of your money on housing (depending upon your location of course, but it shouldn't exceed 50%), another 20% on other fixed costs such as food and debt, 15% on saving and investing, and the remaining 30% on whatever you want.

Get Ready for Grad Spending

Consumer product companies aggressively court recent graduates. Why? Because we spend a boatload of money becoming independent adults. A survey by Y2M Marketing found that 50% of newly minted grads purchase a new cell phone plan and 30% buy a car, and these expenses are just the tip of the iceberg. When you interview for jobs, you'll probably have to spend around $200 for interview clothes and shoes, $25 for a haircut, and another $25 for a nice portfolio and pad. We're mentioning this not to scare you, but rather to point out that these expenses might sneak attack you and throw you off your budget if you don't plan for them. To get a better grasp on the costs associated with setting up your apartment see page 109, and for setting up your kitchen see page 441.

Money

Budgeting Tools

Like exposing celebrities and "sharing" music, budgeting has been made much easier by the Internet. One great online budgeting tool is Mint.com, a website that automatically aggregates all of your financial information (e.g., bank accounts, credit cards, etc.) and enables you to set up a budget so you receive alerts when you overspend. If you're an Excel jockey and like building things yourself, Google Docs allows you to create spreadsheets that you can access from anywhere and use to keep

> ### Tips & Tricks: Reassess your cell phone plan
>
> College is all about off-hours—you study when most people are sleeping and mess around when most people are working. As a result, you often eat up cell phone minutes during the day by making calls between classes, parlaying with mama bear, arranging the night's festivities, and ordering calzones. But then employment comes along and changes the game. Non-work calls become fewer and fewer during the day, and you probably won't get out of work until after 7pm. Sounds depressing, but there's some good news: your peak cell phone usage just plummeted, so now you can decrease your monthly minutes and save some cash. After you get into a post-graduation rhythm, be sure to check your monthly cell phone usage, gauge how many minutes you really need, and adjust accordingly.

track of your money. And for those of you who aren't Internet-inclined, there's always a napkin. The last tool that most people ignore is your credit card. If you're responsible with your credit card spending and repayment, it sometimes make sense to use it for as many purchases as possible so all of your spending is tracked on one bill.

Coupon Cutting Isn't Only for Grandma

Coupons are free money. Why wouldn't you use them? These days, you don't even have to break out the scissors because so many companies offer coupons on the 'net. Before you purchase anything online, always be sure to Google "[fill in store name] coupon." Before heading to a brick-and-mortar store, it's also worth checking their website to see if you can either print out or send away for a coupon. Finally, if you sign up for company mailing lists, you'll most likely get coupons as well (along with a ton of spam).

Another way to get a break on prices in stores and sometimes even online is by furnishing a student I.D. at the time of purchase. If you held onto yours after college, see page 414 for tips on how to save money after graduation by using it.

see page 414

Money

Top Ten Things Grads Waste Money On

1) **Overzealous drinking/partying.** If you want to keep living "the dream" (perhaps something to reconsider regardless), you'd better wean yourself off Grey Goose and become a walking Wikipedia of happy hours.

2) **Coffee.** Some very bright people have done the math on coffee shop culture, and it's not as pretty as those hearts that some baristas draw in the milk foam. Assuming you average $3 on coffee per day, you could save nearly $700/year and direct that money into a savings account with a 2% yield. After doing this for ten years you'll have almost $8,000!

3) **"Shared" furniture.** A lot of people decide to split all apartment costs with their roommate(s), including furnishings. But what happens when one person owns a fifth of a television and half of

Top Ten Things Grads Waste Money On continued...

a dining room table? How do you calculate depreciation when buying out everyone else's share? Deciding beforehand who is responsible for different essential furnishings and then buying them independently allows each person to have ownership over something that they can later sell or take to a new apartment.

4) **Buying every cable channel.** Cable bills can easily reach upwards of $100 when you go all out. But do you really need the package with the foreign news and Showtime? If you only want the latter so that you can watch *Dexter*, perhaps you can wait until it comes out on DVD and then rent the whole season instead of purchasing a bunch of extra channels you don't watch. Or you can go cold turkey by canceling your cable television account and watching shows on the Internet. The ultimate grad entertainment package includes free access to Hulu.com, ABC.com, NBC.com, and other network sites, plus a $14.95 monthly subscription to Netflix for premium content.

5) **Enormous TVs.** Yes, a huge plasma flatty will make *Willow* look AMAZING, but is it really necessary in an apartment that costs about half as much per month? It's your money, but if you save it you will almost certainly be able to afford something top of the line by the time your surroundings warrant that sort of television experience.

6) **Cell phone perks.** If you have a job, daytime chatting is much reduced. Also, if you have a BlackBerry, are you really texting as much as you used to? Track your usage for a couple of months and consider scaling back your plan.

7) **Late payments on credit cards and bills.** Unless you have a very shady landlord, there are no massive Samoan men who will come around to break your kneecaps when you are late on rent. You may, however, incur penalties and damage your credit. Consider signing up for automatic bill pay to avoid late payments on all of your bills (see page 303).

8) **Extraneous subscriptions and memberships.** Gyms, university clubs, newspaper subscriptions…it all adds up. Think about how often you use these services and how much they're worth to you. Does your employer offer reduced-price gym memberships? Can you scale back your newspaper subscription to only get it on the weekends, and read it online the other days?

9) **Eating out.** Give a grad a fish, and he eats for a day. Teach a grad to cook a fish, and he saves sick amounts of money. Even making your own lunch or bringing leftovers to work a few days a week can make a huge difference.

10) **Energy expenditures.** Leaving the lights on all day, pumping the heat to sauna levels, and leaving plugs in the wall for no reason are not only bad for your energy bill, but also the environment. Do everyone a favor and budget your electricity and gas usage. To learn more about going green in your first place, see page 112. ■

Money

Saving & Investing

Let's face it: There's a lot of concern that the U.S. Social Security system won't be able to support us when we're old geezers playing futuristic bingo and trying to pawn off our Pog collections. And if the government doesn't come through, it's on us to make sure that we're bathing in the finest artisanal prune juices through our nineties. Even the smallest investment today (just $50 per month) can put you on course for a post-retirement summer house in Aruba—much better than porridge and terrestrial TV in a lonely bed-sit. Thinking shorter term, saving is what will enable you to buy that massive flat-screen TV for the living room or purchase your first home down the roads. And guess what? Saving doesn't mean just stashing some money away for a later date. It can mean putting money in a savings account so it earns some interest. Hence, saving is also really investing—whatever you want to call it, you should start doing it as soon as possible.

Admittedly, saving and investing aren't as simple as the other concepts we've discussed thus far in the chapter. From the constantly shifting financial landscape to the difficulty of adjusting your financial behavior to meet your savings goals, there's a lot to get hung up on. But you shouldn't. We're going to share with you approachable ways to get going with saving and investing so that you can start laying a foundation for the lifestyle you want in the future. The most important rule of saving and investing is, "Just do it." Making your money work for you is an acquired skill, and comfort with it takes experience. Getting started, however, can be easy and virtually risk-free. Let's get going.

Believe It or Not, You Already Earn Enough to Invest

Irony of all ironies, suckas: Just at the time in life when saving and investing benefits you the most, it's also the most difficult. You're finally making some money to store up for future winters, but new responsibilities like rent, car payments, and groceries hit your bank account hard. And unlike student loans, credit cards, and utility bill payments, saving and investing is optional, and thus usually ignored. But it's time to wake up and smell the money stacks. If you're able to contribute as little as $50 a month to an investment account, you'll have a sizable portfolio in no time. Coming up with $50 a month is as easy as buying cheaper beers, bringing a brown-bag lunch to work, or smoking less (see additional tips starting on page 319). Investing only $50 per month for the next 30 years while earning an average annual interest rate of 8% on that investment will yield $75,000 (even though you only put away $18,000). This is all thanks to the magical power of compounding.

Explaining the Power of Compounding

"The most powerful force in the universe is compound interest."

Who said that?

The answer, as you probably didn't guess, is Albert Einstein. Since everyone agrees he was a genius, we're going to go ahead assume that he was bang on the money.

Check it: As soon as you start investing, your own personal money tree will start sprouting new branches due to the fertilizing power of compounding. Peruse the chart below and see what happens when you invest $1,000 today and allow it to compound for 30 years, as well as what happens if you wait just a few years before making that same investment.

Case 1: Investment is made now (at time zero), with an 8% interest rate:							
	Year 1	Year 2	Year 3	Year 4	Year 5	>>	Year 30
Investment	$1,000	$–	$–	$–	$–	>>	$–
Value @ Year End	$1,080	$1,166	$1,260	$1,360	$1,469	>>	$10,063
Case 1: Investment is made now (at time zero), with an 8% interest rate:							
	Year 1	Year 2	Year 3	Year 4	Year 5	>>	Year 30
Investment	$–	$–	$–	$1,000	$–	>>	$–
Value @ Year End	$–	$–	$–	$1,080	$1,166	>>	$7,988
Difference:	**26%**						

The first thing to recognize about the above chart is that your money grows year after year without your doing anything but making the initial investment. Not only do you earn interest—in this case 8%—on your initial investment, but as your investment grows each year (from the interest you receive), you also earn money on that additional interest. Shake, shake, shake your money-maker!

As you can see, the earlier you start to invest, the better off you'll be. If instead of investing $1,000 today (start of year one) you wait just three years and invest that same $1,000 at the start of year four, by year 30 you'll end up with $2,000 (26%) less, assuming you're making both investments over the same 30-year period. To earn the same return by investing in year four that you would have earned had you started in year one, you would need to invest an extra $260, or 26% more money. Three years can make a pretty sizeable difference in the investing world.

This is all due to the power of compounding. Now imagine if you'd been investing money every year. That's a lot of money and interest working for you. It's up to you to decide whether you think you should start investing today, but by no means should you just have money sitting around. Take advantage of compounding, and make your money work for you.

Once you've gotten over the hump of getting started, the next challenge is to ballpark when you'll need cash and then place your money in specific financial vehicles that will ensure you'll have the amount you need when the time rolls around. Here's a quick guide to the different investing approaches.

Do I Pay Off Debt or Invest?

Let's say you have managed to save $10,000. We're not going to ask how you pulled that off—congratulations are in order! The question is what to do with it. Investing at least some of it would be the immediate answer, but what if you also have $30,000 in school loans? Now you've got to make a decision: Should you pay down your debt or invest your ten grand?

From a purely economical perspective, it depends on which is greater: the interest rate you're paying on your educational loans (after-tax, since some school loan interest may be tax-deductible) or the interest rate you'd get on your investments (also after-tax, as your investment gains will be taxed). Diehard investors would say invest, making the claim that you ought to be able to earn more on your money than the 5–6% you're likely paying on your loans. Plus, you'll become more comfortable and experienced investing your money, which is important to your fiscal future.

But let's entertain the realists as well. Assuming your debt has an interest rate of 5%, are you sure you can find investment vehicles that will pay more? Even if you can, do you think they'll pay that much for the entire life of the loan? Moreover, how do you feel about debt? Would you be a lot more comfortable if you got it off your plate sooner rather than later?

Clearly, there are solid arguments to be made on both sides of this debate. That's why we tend toward the middle ground—why not do both? Use some of the money you've saved to aggressively prepay your loan, and use some to invest. This way, you can start chipping away at your debt while still gaining important investment experience and making some money to boot.

That's just our two cents. If you're already confident investing or you know that it's important to you to knock out your debt and start fresh, you'll find the tools in this book to help you pursue either path. ■

Investing for Short-Term Purchases (i.e., Liquidity with Some Interest)

For investment n00bs, the easiest and least risky way to get in the game is a **savings account**. Money may not grow on trees, but it certainly does in banks. Determine a minimal amount of cash you can afford to stash away in a savings account each month (this can be $1, $50, or even $100—whatever you can stomach). Now, sit back and watch it turn into a new flat-screen TV. Savings accounts are best suited for situations in which you know that you'll be making a purchase in the near-ish future but need to keep the cash accessible in case you want it for something else soon.

> **Tips & Tricks: Risk vs. reward**
>
> Investing is the art of earning the highest return (or interest) on your money and making sure that your cash is available when you need it. But keep in mind that every investment option also has downsides. For example, higher returns are provided to you at higher risk. And longer-term investments, while usually less risky and with higher interest rates, mean the money isn't available to you on demand (i.e., it's "less liquid"). So when you consider any investment option, you need to be sure that there's a fair trade-off between risk and return, and liquidity is always an issue.

Because they are so low-risk and easy, it's not surprising that savings accounts ultimately have their limitations as investment vehicles. It's great to earn interest instead of letting your money sit around getting moldy, but the interest rates on savings accounts aren't always competitive with other forms of investing. Still, the reason they're popular is you get a rare combo—interest and the ability to get at your money when you want it. See page 300 for more on savings accounts.

Investing for the Medium-Term (i.e., Mostly Liquid with Medium Interest)

You may have heard parents or talking heads throwing around the phrase "fixed-income investments," but if you're anything like we were when we left college, you probably aren't quite sure what it means. Unlike a stock that varies in price and has liquidity because you can sell it at any time (see page 331 for more on stocks), a fixed-income investment is one that pays you a set amount of money over a set amount of time. Essentially, you're entering into a contract: You provide an entity with cash today, and that entity is obligated to return that money to you at a certain point in the future (i.e., the maturity date), plus make periodic interest payments to you during the life of the investment. While most fixed-income assets are designed to be held until their maturity date, you can sell them in the fixed-income markets the way you would sell a stock. However, since there are fewer buyers of fixed-income assets, they usually aren't as liquid as other investment options.

Certificate of Deposits (CDs) provide a happy medium between putting your money in a savings account and storing it for retirement. You can purchase a CD (no, not the Miley Cyrus kind) from your bank or investment brokerage firm, and it will provide a higher interest rate than a savings account. The hitch here is that you must keep your cash tied up in the CD until it reaches its maturity date (although often you can redeem your money prior to maturity in exchange for paying a penalty). CDs come with maturities ranging from six months to ten years, so you should be able to find one that meets your time horizon. Just know that shorter-horizon CDs tend to have similar rates to savings accounts; you need to dig into long-range maturities for it to make sense. So when considering a CD, you need to make sure that it not only pays off an interest rate that is attractive to you, but will also provide you with your cash back at the time you need it. Conveniently, CDs are also FDIC-insured (see page 299).

Tips & Tricks: The tax consequences of investing

Don't forget that any money you make on an investment is taxable, whether it's interest earned from a savings account or dividends from a stock. So while you might be earning 1.5% interest in an online savings account, just remember that after taxes, it'll be more like 1%, at most. There are, however, tax-free options such as municipal bonds (see next page) and tax-advantaged retirement accounts (p. 328). Ultimately, you shouldn't avoid taxable earnings just for the sake of giving the middle finger to the IRS—just make sure you factor them into any investment decision you make.

Government bonds, notes, and bills (all also known as "treasuries") are similar to CDs in that you need to hold onto them until their maturity date in order to guarantee the stated interest rate. This period can range from less than two years (bills), to between two and ten years (notes), to 30 years (bonds). The difference between treasuries and CDs is that treasuries are considered to be the safest investment in the world because for you to lose your money, the U.S. Government would have to default (if this occurs, you'll have a lot more to worry about than losing the money on your bond—head for the border!). Extra security, as usual, means lower rates of return.

However, the good news is that treasuries also have a market value, so there are instances where you can sell them for profit before they reach maturity.

Like the nation at large, cities also sell fixed-income investments in the form of municipal bonds (a.k.a., munis). They provide a higher return than treasuries (and are tax-free, which is huge), but it's more likely for a city to default on its bonds than the country. It's rare, but it has happened—in the '70s, Cleveland defaulted on its municipal bonds.

Treasuries and munis are a great compromise for people who want higher interest rates than savings accounts and CDs but don't want to risk their money in the stock market. You can get higher returns elsewhere, but you also stand to lose a lot more if the market doesn't go your way or a company goes bust.

On that note, it should be mentioned that large companies also issue corporate bonds that pay higher interest rates than government issues, but these are riskier and harder to evaluate than more vanilla government bonds (e.g., who knew in early 2008 that Lehman Brothers would cease to exist?). The benefit of buying a bond rather than a stock is that you're guaranteed a return since you are technically lending the company money. In addition, bondholders are considered to be senior to stockholders, which essentially means that in the event a company goes bankrupt, the company is forced by law to repay all of its bondholders in full before a single stockholder gets a penny.

Where can I buy this stuff? The quick answer is from a bank, TreasuryDirect.gov, or your brokerage firm, although you can only purchase corporate bonds from a brokerage firm (see page 335). To value a bond you use bond math, which is called "bond math" and not "simple math" for a reason. Instead of trying to provide a comprehensive overview here, we suggest you seek assistance from a service representative or adviser at whichever place you plan to purchase them from. Just keep in mind that since fixed-income investments aren't liquid, the maturity date for your investment should be before the date at which you'd need the cash. If you want to sell a bond before the maturity date, the easiest place to turn to is a brokerage firm. But again, it isn't always as easy to sell a bond as it is to sell a stock, and we suggest that you talk to a service representative or advisor.

Last, be sure that the actual interest you'll earn on the bond will outweigh your other investment options, and that you think the entity from which you're purchasing it will be around when payout time rolls around (clearly, the government should be...but will Citigroup?). If you do want to take a deep dive into fixed-income investing, then we suggest that you read the tutorials at TheStreet.com and Yahoo! Finance, or hold your breath for *Gradspot.com's Guide to Personal Finance*. (Whenever the $500k advance is ready, so are we!)

Investing for Retirement: 401(k)s and IRAs

Saving for retirement is the most important type of saving you can do. One day, you'll stop working but the bills won't stop coming, nor will your grandson's demands for PlayStation 25. Thankfully, Uncle Sam has lent us a hand and set up special types of accounts for retirement planning: 401(k)s and IRAs. These are the ultimate long-

term investment vehicles, and while it's tough to think that far ahead when you can't even decide what to have for lunch, we recommend giving them some serious thought. Why? Social Security aside, statistics show that you'll need about 70% of your pre-retirement income to maintain a similar standard of living (and we do assume you don't want to retire in order to lower your standard of living). In other words, if you're making $150,000 a year, retire at age 60, and live to be 90, then you'll need to have saved $100,000 for each year of retirement, or $3,000,000 total. That seems like a lot, but you have the most important element of retirement savings on your side—youth. The sooner you start, the better.

Employer-Sponsored Retirement Accounts: 401(k)s

A 401(k) is a conservative and diversified investment account set up by your employer. It doesn't require any action on your part aside from selecting some basic options when you first begin. Each year you'll be given an opportunity to invest part of your paycheck in the 401(k), and that money goes directly from your salary to your 401(k) before being taxed. Hence, any contribution you make to your 401(k) is tax-free. For example, if you pull in $45,000 a year and choose to contribute $2,000 of it, the whole $2,000 goes into your 401(k), and you will only be taxed on $43,000 of your salary at year-end. Taxes on the $2,000, as well as any investment earnings you make over time, are paid later when you withdraw the money at retirement age. At that point, your tax rate will most likely be less than it is today. By deferring taxes, you also get to put away more money *now*, and as we've seen from the power of compounding interest, that extra dough will grow significantly.

In addition to the tax benefits of 401(k)s, they are a great investment option because employers often "match" a portion of your contribution, sometimes even all of it—*cha*-ching! **If your employer matches your 401(k) contribution, we think you should max it out every time to squeeze as much free money out of the situation as possible.** You can invest up to $15,000 a year in a 401(k), and if that becomes $60,000, then you'll be big pimpin' at the retirement home. The only hitch with 401(k)s is that you can't withdraw the funds until you are 59.5 years old, unless you want to pay a 10% penalty. Although 401(k)s are set up by employers, there are no restrictions on moving them from one employer to the next, or even maintaining control of them in between jobs.

Self-Funded Retirement Accounts: IRAs

If your employer doesn't offer a 401(k) or you're self-employed, IRAs are for you—the "I" stands for individual. While contributions aren't tax-free, withdrawals are, which isn't so bad since you pay taxes on a small amount of cash today that will grow to be ten times its size down the line. The icing on the cake is that if you need to withdraw funds before the age of 59.5, there's no 10% penalty like with 401(k)s. There are many different types of IRAs, but ROTH IRAs, which usually require you to make less than $65,000 per year, are the current cool kids on the block. You can set up ROTH IRAs through banks and brokerage firms (see page 335).

Let's assume that you've decided to heed not only our word but the advice of just about every financial professional and stash cash away in a 401(k) or IRA. What next? In the case of a 401(k) you might not have a choice as to where the cash is invested—your employer may automatically put it into diversified funds, or you'll have a set of pretty limited options. When it comes to IRAs, however, you have to pick where the money is distributed. So keep reading if you want our two cents about where you could invest it. (Just don't pull the rookie mistake of making a contribution to your IRA and then not investing; you actually have to manage it!)

Long-Term Investing: Stocks & Funds

So you'd like your money to earn more than the almost risk-free returns provided by savings accounts, treasuries, or CDs? Then there's a world of

Money

options for you to consider: traditional stocks, mutual funds, index funds, electronically traded funds (ETFs), target-date funds, and so much more. (Of course, if you feel really lucky, punk, there's also the lottery. But rumor has it that your odds of being killed in a car accident on the way to purchasing a lottery ticket are higher than the odds of actually winning.) These investing options (minus the lotto) should come into play when you're dealing with retirement investing. Whichever route you choose, there are usually incentives for some degree of patience and stability with each of these options. For example, if you sell within a year of buying a stock, you will be taxed 50% on your profits, whereas the tax rate drops to 15% after a year. So don't spend all day watching *Mad Money* and driving yourself crazy, because patience is the name of the game for casual investors. If you diversify and maintain a long-term outlook, you should avoid the sick-to-your-stomach feeling caused by riding the Dow Jones minute by minute.

The Stock Market

Despite the pandemonium set off by the credit crunch and epic stock market crash that followed, we still think (as do the majority of finance professionals) that the stock market is a phenomenal long-term investment. The average annual return on the stock market, when reviewed over the long-term, has been 8%. The caveat here, however, is that over any short period (i.e., one or a few years), gains and losses have been anywhere between +20% and −20% (or more!). The key with the stock market is to invest in it for the long haul. If you're skeptical, then see the chart below of the S&P500, a main index and proxy for the market at large.

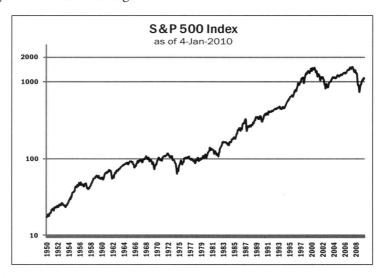

What you should take away from this chart is that over *any* 30-year period (roughly the number of years until you'll retire), the index increased dramatically. Hopefully this illustrates why as a long-term, conservative investor, you'll greatly increase the value of your assets if you invest in the market. In fact, since time has been shown to mitigate the extreme short-term fluctuations associated with the stock market by all but guaranteeing long-term 8% annual returns, most savvy recent graduates will invest all of their retirement money in the market. (When you get older—think forties, fifties, and sixties—and will no longer be in a position to stomach the short-term +20%/−20% swings, you can then take a more risk-averse approach and begin to transition your money into bonds and CDs…but, in our opinion, that doesn't make sense today.) The only way that the approach of investing in the stock market today would fail would be if, down the line, there were major problems with the U.S.—like nuclear winter–type problems. But if you're the patriotic type and believe that the U.S. will be just fine by the time you retire, then consider making long-term investments in the market.

Unfortunately, a lot of people got hit hard by the credit crisis because they did not take this long-term view of the market. They owned stock that plummeted in value over a short period of time, but instead of waiting for the market to rebound, they got nervous and pulled their money out. Now that the market has rebounded a bit (at least as of the writing of this book), those people are kicking themselves because they lost the opportunity for their investments to increase again. They locked in their loss and now they have to start all over again—maybe with less cash than they started with!

Obviously, it is possible to make a lot of money in the short term by playing the stock market. But unless you are a trader or you're best buds with Steve Jobs and he tells you when new products are dropping before announcing it to the public, it's very risky and time-consuming. So let's be clear that we're talking about long-term investing—if you want to get into gambling then turn on the talk shows and roll the short-term stock market dice.

Stocks

What is a stock?

Simply put, a stock is a small ownership stake in a company (another word you might hear for it is *equity*). Thus, if you buy one share of Google stock, you immediately become a partial owner of Google, right next to Sergey and Larry. (Needless to say, they have about a gajillion more shares than you do,

Money

but whatever—it's kind of a cool thought.) Each share has a value, known as its trading value or stock price, which is the amount that people are willing to buy and sell the stock for on the market. Since each share represents fractional ownership in a company, each share's value fluctuates each day based on news regarding how the company is doing. When a little start-up becomes a huge company like Starbucks, anyone who owns shares stands to earn a pretty penny. Welcome to the American Dream!

Some companies also offer **dividends** (i.e., optional quarterly payments) to their shareholders. These tend to be the more mature companies—like, say, General Electric—whose stocks have less room to grow. Some dividends can be pretty sizable. For example, Verizon pays yearly dividends equal to approximately 4–5% of the value of each share, which means you can earn 4–5% annually on each share you own, assuming the stock price itself doesn't decrease. If you're conservative, a dividend can be a very good reason to buy and hold a more mature stock because it serves as a middle ground between a riskier, non–dividend-paying stock and a fixed-income investment.

Now that you know how stocks work, the final question is where to buy them. In order to purchase stocks, you need to sign up with a brokerage firm (p. 335). To look up a stock's price, visit your brokerage firm's website, or check stock trackers like Finance.Yahoo.com and Finance.Google.com. All of these places will have a field to enter the stock's ticker (a one- to four-letter abbreviation of the company name) or the company's name. From there, you'll be provided with the stock's current price, charts showing past prices, news about the company, and all sorts of other information. For more in-depth analysis, you can also check the research section of your brokerage firm's website, as well as countless websites for investors. If you dig into this stuff, just keep in mind that research can be biased or flat-out wrong, and as you'll learn in the next section, we highly discourage investing in any single stock anyway.

The Importance of Diversification

As the old saying goes, you should never put all of your eggs in one basket. The same maxim applies to stocks. Imagine this scenario: You love Pepsi so you invest all of your money in Pepsi stock. But all of a sudden, Coke comes out with an unbelievable new drink that completely blows Pepsi out of the water. The stock plummets, and you lose your investment. But what if you had also invested in some other companies in different industries—you might have seen gains in those that would have cancelled out your big loss on Pepsi. Just as you can mitigate your market risk over an extended time horizon, you can also spread out your investments so one bad pick doesn't sink the ship. This investment principle is called "diversification."

You can diversify in many ways—among different stocks, different business sectors, and even different countries (if you're one of those people who thinks "China's on the rise"). You can also diversify amongst different asset classes, including stocks, bonds, CDs, real estate, baseball cards, and even cash. It all comes back to the same fundamental idea: If you spread your money around to many places, each one might not offer as much growth potential, but at least you can't lose it all at once. Just make sure you don't diversify to the point of "Default Credit Swaps," because while we don't understand them, apparently neither did the majority of Wall Street—or the world.

Of course, if you want to invest in a single stock because it's a company you love, then by all means go for it. In fact, it's a great way to dip your toes into the water of investing. But just keep in mind that you're venturing into shark-infested water, so don't want to swim out too far.

The Easy Way to Diversify: Index, ETF, Mutual, and Target-Date Funds

So how can you diversify? Well, you could spend days doing research and picking a ton of different stocks, each in a different industry and country… and then also buy some bonds and invest in some real estate while you're at it! But thankfully, the financial industry provides a much simpler solution: Index, Mutual, and Lifecycle (target-date) funds. These investment vehicles are valuable because they automatically diversify for you. Nothing personal, but as a recent grad, you probably don't have the skill set to figure out the accuracy of a stock price, let alone determine which companies/industries/countries will provide the best balance for your portfolio. Thus, if you're investing any significant amount of money (and that means significant by your standards, not anyone else's), we suggest you let the funds and the professionals do their thing.

Index Funds/ETFs

Dow Jones Industrial Average, NASDAQ Composite, and all of those other names you hear on the news are **stock market indices.** Basically, these indices group together a whole bunch of stocks that represent some portion of an economy; for example, the S&P 500 Index reflects the stock prices of 500 of the leading large-cap companies in the U.S. They are used as shorthand for the health of the economy at large, or the part of the economy they reflect. While

Money

you can't invest in the indices themselves, you can invest in their proxies, called Index Funds. For example, an index fund could track the S&P 500 (that index fund's ticker is "SPY"). As the S&P 500 rises, so does the value of SPY, and vice versa—this goes back to the idea discussed before of "betting on America." So instead of investing in a stock included in an index, you can—in a sense— invest in all of the companies in the index at once and thus easily diversify your investment.

ETFs don't necessarily track a public index, but they create indices of their own based on specific and publicly disclosed criteria and guidelines. Computers are then set up to automatically alter the portfolio every day, week, month, or year, to ensure it meets the preset criteria and guidelines. ETFs have been created to track the average performance of oil companies or even oil itself. So if you think a certain sector is a good bet, you could find an ETF that tracks it.

Both index funds and ETFs can be purchased through your brokerage firm, but you'll have to pay a pretty nominal cost of around 0.1%. Just keep in mind that even if you purchase an index fund or ETF, you still might not be diversified enough for your liking.

Mutual Funds

Mutual funds are like index funds and ETFs, except they are actively managed by humans rather than computers. So which do you trust more?! One consideration is that computers are willing to work for crap wages, whereas humans need to make a living. Thus, mutual funds come with fees up to 1.5% higher. Take a step back and think about what this means: If a mutual fund is outperforming the market (i.e., beating an index fund that tracks the market and has almost no fees), it actually needs to be outperforming the market by *at least* 1.5% to provide a better payout. Studies have shown that over 50% of actively-managed mutual funds underperform the market indices, so the computers have some reasonably solid ground to stand on. Moreover, in bad times, people with mutual funds will actually be losing more than the market due to the fees. This isn't to say that people haven't gotten rich by investing in mutual funds; they certainly have. And despite the potential drawbacks, most people invest in mutual funds because they feel more comfortable with the human component (at least you have someone to yell at when things don't go well!). In fact, savvy investors will actually invest in fund managers (i.e., pick a fund because it's run by a manager who has a successful track record) rather than studying the components of the fund. Ultimately, the choice between mutual funds and ETFs/index funds comes down to your willingness to pay extra fees to have a human who can speak with you about your money.

Target-Date (a.k.a. Lifecycle) Funds

Remember when we said that it makes more sense to be in the stock market today, but eventually, especially as you near retirement, you'll want to diversify into other, less-risky asset classes? Well, if you go the index fund and ETF route, then it's up to you to do so. However, once again, the financial industry has made the next step easier by offering target-date funds, the lazy-man's long-term financial retirement plan. These funds maintain a portfolio of stocks, cash, bonds, and other assets. However, unlike other types of investment vehicles, these funds target an end date meant to coincide with your retirement, at which point they'll cash out for you. In the near term, the investments mix will be weighted more heavily towards riskier assets (i.e., stocks) when you can afford to be more risk-tolerant, and when they approach their target date, they'll transition to more conservative vehicles (i.e., bonds and CDs). While target-date funds have very few expense fees (closer to 0.1% than the 1.5% of Mutual funds), they do have minimum investments. If you're interested in learning more about target-date funds, then look to Fidelity, Charles Schwab, T. Rowe Price, and Vanguard for just a few of the available options.

It should be noted that after the recent credit crunch and stock market crash, a lot of target-date funds got flack for losing their investors a lot of money. (Most other investment vehicles did as well though, so these funds aren't alone.) Some target-date funds were down 20% or more. This is because their stock holdings took a beating, like everyone else's. Those funds with target dates in the short term that weren't balancing properly and did take a dive do deserve that flack. But the funds with target dates in the distant future don't, especially if they were balancing properly for the long term. Nonetheless, just be aware that the only way to guarantee a perfect balance is if you do it yourself. Then again, will you really be any better?

Opening a Brokerage/Investment Account

Okay, now that you know what you're getting yourself into, it's time to figure out how to actually buy these stocks and funds. In the old days, you'd meet with a nice mustached man in a bowler hat and pinstriped suit who would help you distribute your cash to the appropriate places and charge you a fee for doing so. Fast-forward 20 years and, as you can imagine, the nice old man has been replaced by the Internet. Online brokerages enable you to buy stocks, bonds, and most of the funds we discussed above. They can also house your IRA. Some even have associated perks, like the interest-bearing checking accounts we mentioned on page 300. Grad-friendly online brokerage firms to check out include Charles Schwab, TD Ameritrade, E*Trade, Fidelity, and Scottrade.

You know the drill by now: Look for the accounts with the lowest fees (many brokerages even offer no-fee trading), then provide the same basic information (address, social security number, etc.) you would for a bank account. The only problem with online brokerage firms is that while most will provide you with research and a staff that can answer basic questions (e.g., how do I buy a government bond?), they won't offer any individualized advice. It will be on you to get familiar with the markets and your options before diving in headfirst. A full-service brokerage firm like Smith Barney can provide one-on-one guidance, but needless to say, you'll have to pay for the privilege of having someone tell you what to do with your money. Since you're probably not making any super out-of-the-box moves as a recent grad, we don't think it's necessary to go full-service (and you might not even meet the minimum required to invest with one of these firms).

A Final Word on Investing

Personal finance is a mammoth subject, and it's easy to see why there are countless books available on the subject (from classics like *The Intelligent Investor* to contemporary works like *Rich Dad, Poor Dad*), not to mention all the websites out there like TheStreet.com, MotleyFool.com, and SmartMoney.com. What we've tried to do here is to provide a basic outline of the investment ecosystem. You should now have all the tools you need to get started, but ultimately sound investing is about experience. Start small to get over the hump—eventually you'll gain the confidence and knowhow to be a little more adventurous. Look for additional guidance from family members and friends who you know are into the markets, and continue to educate yourself by reading and visiting websites. We also have some more resources for you at gradspot.com/money. Whatever you do, just remember that any small losses now are balanced out by the experience you gain for the future, when you'll have a more significant chunk of change to play with.

Your Investment Cheat Sheet

As promised at the beginning of the chapter, we want to provide an easy breakdown of the actions you should take with your hard-earned cash. To whit, here's a quick investment cheat sheet, organized by the amount of money you have available to save and invest.

$0 to $999. If you're in this range, you're probably either living at home or living paycheck to paycheck. Ain't nothing wrong with that. Find a checking account with no fees and you should be all set for the time being.

$1,000 to $4,999. With a few grand floating around, you should set up an online savings account so you'll earn at least 1–2% in interest. (That's $50–100 of free money each year!)

$5000, to $9,999. Get it in! With this type of money at your fingertips, you should consider getting some CDs from your bank in order to squeeze another percent or two in interest out of your savings. You should also make sure you're beginning to make some small investments into a retirement account. At the very least, open one up so you're ready to roll when the next big cash influx comes your way.

$10,000+. Congratulations! You're working with some serious cheese— it's time to open a brokerage account (e.g., TD Ameritrade). An index fund (e.g., SPY) is a good way to get started. Don't be timid; most brokerages grant you ten free trades or so, so you can buy something and change your mind next week. The important thing is that you gain experience researching an investment option and clicking "buy." It's fascinating to watch your investment gain or lose $5 in value each day, like a little money hamster. Eventually, though, it gets kind of boring— or nerve-racking. That's when you know you're an investor! Oh, and by the way: If you're in this range, don't forget to continue adding to your retirement account. ■

Money

Building a Financial Management System

If you've read everything in this chapter thus far, then you should have a grasp on what you need to know to effectively manage your finances. But it's one thing to "plan" to do it and quite another to actually do it. So how are you going to follow through? Ramit Sethi, the finance blogger and author of *I Will Teach You to Be Rich*, suggests setting up an automated finance system. And we cosign this approach for anyone who likes the concept behind the Show Time Oven—"set it and forget it!"—and who isn't afraid of running all of their finances through the Internet.

Essentially, his system takes the budget you've settled upon (i.e., how much money you want to divert towards debt repayment, nights out, saving, etc.) and automatically allocates the appropriate amounts to your different accounts each month. For example, your paycheck goes to your checking account through direct deposit, your automatic bill pay settings on your checking account distribute checks to the relevant places, a certain amount automatically gets redirected to your savings account, and so on and so forth…you get the idea. Your 401(k) is left out because that money gets deducted before you get your paycheck, but everything else gets dealt with automatically, and you're left with the money you've set aside to actually spend at your discretion. And as long as you take a second to check your bills and statements before the auto-payment gets fired off, you should be all good.

Clearly, there's a lot more to the system, and we'd highly recommend checking out Sethi's book and website for more tips. The fact that you barely have to think once you've set it up is awesome, but what we like most is the philosophy behind the system. It's driven by the idea that instead of spending every dime that comes your way, you should divvy it up amongst investments, savings, bill payments, debt repayment, *and* disposable income. Whether you use the tools of the 'net or create your own system doesn't really matter. The important thing is that you have a plan for your money. It doesn't have to be written in stone, but at least it's something to build on as you start making even more money and creating a financial foundation for yourself.

Taxes

Before we even know what a receipt looks like, it's ingrained in our young minds that "Tax Day" is the worst day of the year—even worse than January 1st, which is inevitably depressing. But there's really nothing to lose sleep over. Not only are you smart enough to do your taxes, but you also have it easier than most given that you presumably have nothing more than a modest salary and a little bit of income from savings and investment accounts. That said, don't treat your tax forms like a school assignment and start at midnight the night before they're due. This is more important than letter grades—it's about dollars and cents.

There are really only two ways to tackle taxes: Hire a professional or do them yourself. The D.I.Y. approach is not that taxing (pun intended!), but the problem is you may miss out on some of the tax savings that a hired professional could find for you. Given that a professional at H&R Block can walk you through your tax return for as little as $75 (treat the fee like insurance against messing it up on your own, not to mention that you might make that money back in deductions), we suggest the following strategy: Hire a tax preparer for the first go around (p. 342), but pay attention to the process, and take notes so you can pick up the reins in subsequent years. Whichever route you choose, here are a few things to keep in mind.

What You're Actually Taxed On

It's very simple: You are taxed on your income less any deductions and tax credits. This figure is called your Adjusted Gross Income, or AGI.

Tax Deductions

Deductions enable you to decrease the amount of taxes you owe by decreasing your AGI. To whet your appetite, try this on for size: Assuming your adjusted gross income is less than $65,000, you can deduct up to $2,500 in student-loan interest. Here's another: If you move a significant distance for a new job after graduation, the relocation expenses may be deductible. So in other words, if your AGI was $50,000 and you had $5,000 of deductions, you'd only pay taxes on $45,000. Another way to look at this is that the amount of taxes you'll have to pay is decreased by your total deductions times your tax rate. (That's as hard as the math gets.) Deductions come in all shapes and sizes, so it's worth browsing the chart on page 341 and poking around IRS.gov to see if you might be eligible for any before shelling out for a tax pro. However, good

Money

Tips & Tricks: Figuring out whom you owe

For recent grads cutting ties with their parents' tax return and moving to new states, the question of whom you owe (and who is going to pay) can be a tricky one. First and foremost, have a discussion with your parents to make sure they are not still claiming you as a dependent. You don't want to double-file, and they won't receive the W-2 form from your employer if you have started working. Next, think about where you have lived and worked in the past year. You will always have to pay federal taxes, so that's a given. However, you also have to pay the state where you are a resident, as well as the state where you work (if they are the same, then clearly you only have to file once). Note that some states take no personal income tax from residents (e.g., Alaska, Florida, Washington). If you've moved around a lot, you may want to check in with an accountant or tax pro to make sure you're not leaving anyone out or double-paying anything that's unnecessary.

tax preparers should be well-versed in all of these tricks, and might see things you might not. You just need to maintain a paper trail (e.g., check, receipt, email) for everything you purchase that may be deductible. If you say you gave $1,000 in cash to a charity, for example, you have to verify that donation to get a deduction. You can't just tell the IRS to "trust you."

Keep Good Records

A modicum of vigilance during the calendar year can go a long way toward making tax day manageable. Despite what you've seen in films, it is not wise to show up in an accountant's office with a duffle bag full of random receipts. So, what do you need to keep? First and foremost, your employer, as well as many of the organizations with which you do business (e.g., bank, brokerage firm), will send you forms at the end of the year that will be essential come tax time. But depending on your situation, you may need more than that as well. The following chart includes the most relevant tax forms and where to get them. Having these items in line will help you avoid a late filing and penalties of 5% each month past the due date. (Note: If the reason you're not paying on time is because you're low on fundage, arrange for a monthly payment plan with the IRS to avoid the late fees.)

Common Tax Forms & Deductions for Recent Grads

What	Who	Where to Get It
W2 Form from Employer (Annual Salary)	Anyone who is employed full time	Your company must provide this to you
1099 Misc (Freelance Earnings)	Anyone who has freelanced and earned an aggregate in excess of $600 from one source	Each entity who paid you more than $600 for the year must provide you with one
1099 Int (Investment Earnings)	Anyone who has a bank account, stock portfolio, or other investments	Your bank, investment company, and other institutions will each mail you one
1099 Div (Dividend Earnings)	Anyone who owns an investment that pays dividends	The dividend payer will send this to you
W2-G (Gambling Earnings)	Anyone who struck it rich at the casino or in the lottery	All depends upon where you won, but you should receive this from the casino or lotto authority
1098-E (Student Debt Interest Payment)	Anyone who has student debt	Your lender should provide you with this
1098 (Mortgage Interest Payments)	Anyone who has taken out a mortgage	Your lender or mortgage agent will send this to you
Moving Expenses (can write off)	Anyone who has moved in the past year	You must keep your receipts
Medical Expenses (can write off)	Anyone who is paying for CO-BRA, glasses, prescription drugs, or other medical expenses	You must maintain your own receipts
Job-Hunting Expenses (can write off)	Anyone who has looked for a job	You must maintain your own receipts
Charitable Donations (can write off)	Anyone who has donated to a government-recognized charity organization	You will receive an official receipt from each recognized charity

Money

Note: All tax documents that you are meant to receive should be mailed to you by **January 31st.** If you have not received any documents that you were expecting by the end of the first week in February, be sure to check with the companies that owe them to you. In addition, it is important to note that the information contained within the above table refers to the most common tax forms required and deductions taken for recent grads. But every case is different, so consult with a tax professional to ensure you aren't missing out on any other forms or deductions.

Hiring a Professional

Sometimes you've got to spend money to save money. Such is the case when you buy one of those travel fanny packs that goes under your pants, and also when you pay a tax preparer to work his or her magic and reveal tax loopholes you never knew existed. When it comes to finding a pro, H&R Block is the go-to for most people who don't have exceptionally complicated tax returns—their people are affordable and reliable; they offer the flexibility to work online, on the phone, or in-person; and they should teach you all the tricks you need to go D.I.Y. with confidence next time. However, you can also check the Yellow Pages for tax preparers, ask coworkers for recommendations, or just hand everything off to your parents' accountant if you're really lucky. An added benefit of hiring a professional is that you're less likely to miss the dreaded April 15 deadline or make a mistake.

Do It Yourself

If you've just got a W-2 form from work and a few 1099 forms from your savings and investment accounts, you might think you can handle your taxes on your own. More than likely you're right, but you probably still need a little more than a calculator and a pen. See if you can get a checklist of tax deductions from an accountant or check out the latest edition of the *Master Tax Guide* so that you're aware of things to look out for. Also remember that you have to file both a federal and a state return. Federal is usually easier, so you might choose to handle that yourself and then take your state return to a tax preparer

> **Tips & Tricks: Phone your friend VITA**
>
> If you have low-to-moderate income (generally, $42,000 and below), the good folks at the Volunteer Income Tax Assistance Program (VITA) will lend a hand with your tax return, for free. For more information, visit Vita-Volunteers. org or call 1-800-829-1040.

(H&R Block should only cost around $35 for state returns).

The most common option for filing on your own is to pick up some tax preparation software. It shouldn't run more than $30 and will make the process much smoother and less shady. Turbo Tax by Quicken makes filing your taxes as easy as completing an online survey—fill in the blanks and let the computer go to work. TaxCut can be accessed via H&R Block's website and is the cheapest option (starting at $15), but it can be confusing for more involved returns.

If your adjusted gross income is under $56,000, you can access some free tax filing resources through the government's "Free File" program. One is actually H&R Block's "TaxCut Free Federal Edition + E-File" service, and another is the humorously named TaxSlayer.com. Check out IRS.gov/efile for a full list of options and directions for using them. Again, just remember that these resources will only help you with your federal return, so you'll still have to deal with state taxes when you're done. (Note: In a few states, these services will offer free state returns as well, but it's not the norm.) They also might not point out deductions like the pay version of TaxCut, so either do your research beforehand or pay the extra money to make sure you don't miss anything.

With the help of one of these programs or websites, you should only have to commit two to three hours to this endeavor once you've pulled all of your forms together. Before you wrap things up, sign up for electronic funds transfer with the IRS so that they get your money quicker (and refund you quicker as well) and to ensure nothing gets lost in the mail. Finally, remember that taxes are something that everyone has to battle with, so you're not alone: Libraries, community centers, and college business departments often hold free Q&As and group help sessions during tax season. There's even a program called VITA to walk you through your returns (see "Tips & Tricks" on previous page). Just don't wander into AA accidentally…

Chapter VII: Health

Health

Nothing puts a damper on a recent grad's day quite like a broken arm or a root canal that he or she can't afford. Yet, the Independent Insurance Agents and Brokers of America reports that young people age 18 to 24 are less likely to be insured than any other demographic—nearly one in three lacks coverage, and that statistic only improves to one in four for people ages 25 to 34. Clearly, this lack of coverage is a huge political issue, but we're not really concerned with loading up the Uzi nine millimeter and heading to town hall meetings. What we want to focus on is helping you understand insurance and realize that even if you're unemployed, there are plenty of affordable ways to get a health care plan.

The most common misconception about health insurance is that it's not really a big deal if you're a healthy twentysomething. In fact, so many people maintain this crazy notion that the insurance industry even has a fun name for them: the "young invincibles." But guess what? Being healthy doesn't prevent you from falling off your single-speed Schwinn into a ravine or dropping the iron on your foot. Roaming around without basic insurance (sometimes called "catastrophic coverage") is like entering a Russian roulette league. Even if nothing happens in the first month or two, sooner or later your luck could run out and you'll find yourself with your leg in a sling and $15,000 in debt to the local hospice. That's where bare bones insurance becomes crucial—it's all about being prepared for a bullet (a figurative one, we hope), not being able to go to doctor for that little scratch in the back of your throat.

If you land a job with health and dental benefits, you've hit the jackpot. Your choices will be relatively straightforward, and you should have HR—as well as all your colleagues—to help you with any questions. Being uninsured because you're unemployed (or employed without benefits) is understandably intimidating, especially if getting kicked off your parent- or school-sponsored plan wasn't something you really anticipated when you were bonging Moët et Chandon on commencement day. But instead of ignoring the whole issue because it seems too confusing (a reasonable strategy in some situations, but not this one), we hope you'll take the time to read through this chapter and come up with a game plan. Not only is getting your own health coverage affordable when you're young and healthy, but it also has some important ramifications for your future insurability. If you're flummoxed by health care after college, don't worry though—you're not alone.

In the following pages, we'll clear out the debris and give you the tools you need to make smart choices about your health. We'll walk you through your insurance options, which are plentiful whether you are employed or not, and also tell you how to pick a doctor and a dentist.

As you read this chapter, please bear in mind that health care policy tends to change when presidents do. Keep your eye on the news for changes to the system that might affect your ability to find affordable coverage. We'll also do our best to keep you updated on Gradspot.com.

Why Insurance Is So Important

Needless to say, we wish everyone reading this book could be fully insured with a plan covering everything from check-ups to surgery to acupuncture. But we understand that the realities of the job market, and recent-grad finances don't make it easy for everyone to jump straight to health insurance heaven. Still, it's much better to wait it out in purgatory than hell—in other words, you need to figure out a way to provide yourself with basic coverage if a more comprehensive plan is not yet in the cards. If you're not convinced by the "accidents happen, and so does swine flu" argument, here are some further reasons for getting serious about insurance.

- **Unpaid medical bills are one of the leading causes of bankruptcy.** There are so many horror stories of twentysomethings being crippled by debt after an accident or sudden illness. Do you want to be on the local news when your unexpected appendectomy puts you $20,000 in debt and you have to leave your new job and move back in with your parents? Not only does getting smacked with massive hospital bills suck now, but it can also set your post-college plans back significantly as you struggle to recover from the hit. And even if it doesn't get that drastic, Experian reports that "unpaid hospital bills can affect your credit report if they are sent to a collection agency to recover the amount you owe." If you read Chapter 6, you know how strongly we feel about protecting your credit!

- **Without insurance, you could hurt your chances of getting insured in the future.** When you're young and don't have major health issues, insurance companies welcome you into the fold with open arms because they predict you won't cost them too much. But if you develop a chronic problem, they'll treat you like a leper and make it impossible or prohibitively expensive for you to get the care you need. The trick is to get in while the getting's good, because once you have consistent coverage, you are protected by the law against pre-existing exemptions (i.e., when a health insurance company won't pay your medical fees for a pre-existing condition). So don't wait until you're 30 and your body starts to go downhill! See "Tips & Tricks" on page 362 to learn more about HIPAA and how it affects you when you try to get a new policy.

- **Without insurance, you have to be more careful.** Do you want to live your young adult life in fear of sickness and injury? Of course not. You want to try that puffer fish sashimi that's offered to you, accept that invitation to a friend's ski house, and run that marathon. Life is full of risks, and obviously you would never want to do something where there's a high chance of getting sick or hurt. But there are a lot of fun things that get moved from the "responsible risk" category to the "dumb" category if you don't have insurance behind you.

- **Without insurance, you miss out on preventive care and screenings.** If you're uninsured you're probably not going to cough up the funds to have that physical or check-up that could uncover something at an early stage. And in the very unfortunate event that something does develop and you don't catch it until you get coverage later down the line, you may end up spending a whole lot more on treatment and premiums than you would have if you'd caught it early (and money's not even the biggest issue here).

Understanding Health Insurance

Newsflash: Despite what they'll tell you, no one—not even Nancy Pelosi—actually understands health care. For starters, who can really explain why it costs $20,000 to stay in the ER for a night? (It's not exactly the Four Seasons.) The real challenges for recent grads are twofold: 1) Getting a grasp on the lingo so you know what the hell's going on, and 2) Figuring out what you actually need in a health care plan. Then, once you know the nature of the beast you're dealing with, you can make more informed choices when you're choosing a plan through work (p. 362) or on your own (p. 357).

Health

Deciphering Insurance Lingo

The basics of health insurance are pretty simple: In exchange for a monthly premium, you can visit general doctors and specialists, and the insurance companies will pay for what they think it should cost. Sometimes, insurance companies will cover the whole bill, but they basically reserve the right to pay (or not pay, as the case may be) for whatever part of the bill they want.

Roger? Okay, let's take it to the next step. Most insurance plans also require a deductible, a copay, or both. A **deductible** is the predetermined amount that you have to spend on medical services in a given year before the insurance company starts to pony up. Then, even once you reach the deductible, the insurance company might still ask you to pay a small fee (usually between $5–$50) for each visit, called a **copay**. And as mentioned, the amount paid to the insurance company for your plan is called a **premium** (usually quoted at a monthly or yearly rate). Generally, the higher the deductible, the lower the premium. In the extreme, a High Deductible Health Plan (HDHP) with a very low premium is called "catastrophic coverage," since the insurance only kicks in when you need very expensive treatment. (In other words, you'd get bailed out of a $50,000 hospital bill, but might end up spending $5,000 of your own money on doctors' bills before you reach the deductible.)

So now we've covered premiums, deductibles, and copays—that's where the similarities end and the acronyms begin. Nowadays, almost every company or individual insurer offers a choice between a number of different plans called Managed Care, each of which has its own acronym that doesn't really correspond in any way to what it offers. Fortunately, we've provided a handy guide to acronymic decryption. CoverTheUninsured.com also has a helpful glossary of insurance-related lingo.

HMO. Health Maintenance Organizations place restrictions on the services a patient may receive. Under an HMO, the policyholder chooses a primary care physician

---

Tips & Tricks: Work freebies for your health

Check with your employer to see if they provide free medical services. These don't usually include the type of medical services you'd get from your general practitioner, but rather services like massages or shrinks. Some companies also offer free gym membership (or at least a sizeable discount), and most should have sign-ups for free flu shots in the fall.

Health

(PCP) from the HMO's list. After you choose your PCP, you must visit him or her for any medical issue. The PCP then decides whether your ailment is bad enough to warrant a visit to a specialist. But you are covered only if you see a specialist that is part of your plan. This system keeps costs (and the premium) low, but it can be annoying if you want to skip the step of visiting your PCP, or if you don't agree with a diagnosis.

PPO. Preferred Provider Organizations give you a choice of where to receive services, with the possibility of paying more out of pocket than an HMO, depending on where you choose to go. If you have a problem, you can go straight to a specialist without first getting approval from your PCP. If the specialist is a member of the PPO, insurance covers a high percentage of the services rendered (up to 100%). However, if you don't like the specialists on the list and just want to see the best orthopedic surgeon in the area (who happens not to be a member of the PPO), you will usually only be covered for a small percentage of the visit.

POS. Point of Service plans are the beautiful lovechild of HMOs and PPOs. As with an HMO, you choose a PCP and visit him or her for referrals. Once a referral is made, you can choose to stay within the network, or venture outside and pay more out of pocket. Sometimes, you can even skip the visit to your PCP if you know the out-of-network specialist you would like to visit.

EPO. An easy way to understand an Exclusive Provider Organization is to think of it as a scrawnier, whinier PPO. The list of providers you can visit is much smaller than with a PPO, and if you go out of network, your services may not be covered at all (except in emergency cases).

HSA. As the name suggests, a Health Savings Account is not actually an insurance policy, but rather a savings account into which you can deposit money on a tax-preferred basis (i.e., it's not taxed on the way in or out) and use to pay medical expenses. In order to open one, you have to have a High Deductible Health Plan—in 2008, that meant a minimum deductible of $1,100 for an individual. (Remember, HDHPs are cheaper than normal coverage since the insurance company only has to ante up after you've reached the high deductible.) So in practice, it's really an HDHP combined with a bank account. The idea is that if you can cover smaller expenses like check-ups with money from the account while still maintaining the "catastrophic coverage" provided by the HDHP, you'll end up spending less than you would on a more comprehensive health care plan. You can inquire about HSAs with banks, credit unions, insurance companies, and some employers—find

Health

options and comparison shop at HSAInsider.com. One caveat: Once the money is in the account you can't extract it for anything not stipulated by the terms of the account (doing so will bring a penalty if the IRS finds out). Also, if you move off your HDHP to a more comprehensive plan, you can no longer contribute to the HSA, but you still get to keep using the remaining money for the stipulated uses.

Figuring Out What You Need (and Want) from a Health Care Plan

Unlike the citizens who purchase them, not all health plans are created equally. At work, you might only have a couple of choices, making life a little easier. But in the D.C. zip code 20002 alone, there are currently 91 individual plans, so you should know what you're looking for before you get bombarded with irrelevant or overpriced plans.

The Necessities

Before you even think about your individual needs, there are several basic terms that you should have in any plan you purchase. Make sure you are covered for the following services:

- **Office visits.** When you stop by your doctor's office to check on your sore throat, fever, or anything else that doesn't seem right.

- **Surgical services.** Planned hospital procedures and examinations.

- **Inpatient hospital services.** Everything the hospital charges you for when you stay overnight—fee for the room you slept in, medication, gross apple sauce, etc.

- **Emergency room services.** Procedures and services when you enter the hospital through the ER without an appointment.

- **X-ray and lab services.** Anything from X-rays of broken bones to STD tests and biopsies on moles.

- **Prescriptions.** You want to only have to handle the copay (approximately $5 to $20), not the whole cost of a prescription.

The Costs

When comparison-shopping, you'll want to not only look at premiums, but also other fees and coverage limits that will determine the overall cost of your plan. Ronald Rosenfeld, president of North Shore Life and Health Agency, suggests looking closely at the following items:

- **Deductible.** How much do you have to pay out of pocket before the insurance company will start shelling out?

- **Copay.** What will you have to pay out of pocket for different services you might use in the next year?

- **Lifetime maximum coverage.** It should be at least $1 million.

- **Maximum hospital stay.** You want at least 180 days.

- **Out-of-pocket maximum.** Is there a maximum amount you'd have to pay in a given year? Pay attention to the fine print, as sometimes certain expenses like copays for out-of-network doctors will not count toward this spending.

Specific Needs

After you've made sure the basics are covered, you need to actually sit down and think about your medical needs. Many recent grads have never actually done this before—in most cases our parents picked a plan to cover everyone in the household, and that was that. But now that you're rolling solo, you need to take a look in the mirror and assess your own health care needs.

In addition to acquainting yourself with the acronyms on page 350, Bill Stapleton, president and CEO of Health Plan One and a 15-year veteran in the health insurance industry, recommends getting out a piece of paper to write down what you need, what you want, and how much you can afford to pay for monthly plan premiums, copays and deductibles. Once you've gone through this process, you'll know your needs, and you can question either HR or the insurance brokers you speak with about how best to fulfill them with your budget/options. (For example, if you know you need a preventative care screening or you need to make an office visit to discuss a problem with an allergist, you ideally want your plan to cover these things.) Calling up brokers is generally a good idea at some point in the process—you're not committed to do anything they say, but the conversation might bring up issues you didn't think of during your own research.

Got your pencil and paper ready? Here are some important questions to ask yourself:

- Does the plan cover annual check-ups?

  *While all plans should cover office visits, you may also want the ability to visit your doctor for a routine adult physical exam. If so, make sure that the plan covers **well patient care**.*

- Do you want a backup plan for when your doctor isn't available?

  *Some plans also cover **outpatient hospital services**, which enables you to visit an in-network hospital during its clinic hours and see the doctor on duty. Most people consider this their last resort after they are unable to schedule an office visit with their PCP because hospital waits can be upwards of six hours, even with an appointment.*

- What happened to me last year? How many times did I get sick? How many times did I visit a doctor? Am I a hypochondriac?

  *If so, maybe a **higher premium plan** is worth the peace of mind you'll get from being able to visit the doctor more often.*

- Do I want to be able to go directly to a **specialist** such as a gynecologist or dermatologist without first seeing my primary care provider?

  Some plans allow you to go to specialists directly, but they tend to be more expensive and have higher copays associated.

- Are my current **physicians** "in network?"

  If you have a primary care provider or specialist you really like, you might want to make sure you can continue to see that doctor without paying extra.

- Is my **local hospital** "in network?"

  While "in network" is a term often associated with doctors, certain hospitals will be in and out of your network. It's always good to know that a good local hospital is within your network.

- Do I or does my family have a history of **alcoholism**? What about **psychiatric issues**?

  Find out if the plan will cover treatments related to these issues.

- Are there things—e.g., maternity—that I'd like the option of adding onto my plan once I've already purchased it?

  *In insurance lingo, a provision in an insurance policy allowing for amendments to its terms and/or coverage is called a "**rider**." Make sure the provider can offer any features you might want to add to a policy down the line.*

And some more questions worth considering:

- Do I have **allergies or asthma**?

- Do I like to use complementary and alternative therapies, such as **massage therapy** and **acupuncture**?

- Am I comfortable accepting **generic medications,** or do I want to be able to purchase **brand name medications**?

- Do I care whether or not the plan provides **perks** (e.g., discounts on gyms) or provides general discounts on items such Lasik surgery?

- Am I **female**? (If you answered yes, see the next page for more specific tips.)

- Does the plan cover a **pre-existing condition** I have?

- Am I currently in the midst of an **extended course of treatment** (e.g., allergy shots, physical therapy)?

- Do I need a **case manager** to help me control a chronic condition?

- Will I be able to see doctors for **preventive care screenings**?

This process may sound a bit arduous, but it's a worthwhile time investment. "Too often, we file the paperwork away and take it out only after we have been denied services," says Stapleton. "Not only can this be costly, but we frequently do not utilize all the benefits we are paying for." Touché, dog.

Health

Women-Specific Health Care Concerns

The truth is, girls have to work a bit harder than guys when it comes to post-college health. In addition to getting insurance, finding a physician (see page 366 for tips on finding an OB/GYN), and tending to your pearly whites, you also have to figure out how to prevent yourself from inadvertently reproducing—not always a simple task. Luckily, many brave women have blazed the trail for you, and there is an abundance of health-related resources at your disposal.

Planned Parenthood

Regardless of whether you have insurance, Planned Parenthood (plannedparenthood.org) is an invaluable resource for all things woman-related. (Depending on what you got up to in college, this may be old news). In addition to offering annual pelvic exams and standard STD testing, Planned Parenthood's services include:

- Birth Control Services
- HIV Testing Services
- Hepatitis and HPV Vaccine Services
- Lesbian, Gay, Bisexual, and Transgender Services
- Men's Health Services (That's right, boys!)
- Pregnancy Testing & Planning
- Emergency Contraception Services
- Abortion Services & Referrals

The cost of services at Planned Parenthood clinics varies from community to community. Many centers charge according to income, so if you're yet to be employed (and/or insured), it's a great option. You may even qualify for a state-funded program or a lower fee scale. If you are insured, you can still elect to seek medical services from Planned Parenthood, as most clinics accept insurance.

Contraception / Emergency Contraception / Pregnancy

Sow your wild oats, but sow them carefully. And if you forget to sow them carefully, then have a back-up plan. You probably know all this by now, but just in case...

Contraception. Make sure to discuss contraception options with your doctor. And if you don't yet have a doctor, check in with a professional at Planned Parenthood (or your local reproductive clinic) to discuss options that might be right for you. Your insurance carrier may limit the amount or type of access you have to certain types of birth control (i.e., they will only provide generic birth control pills or they will only provide a one-month supply at a time), so make sure you are clear about what your policy stipulates.

Plan B. Plan B (a.k.a. "the morning after pill") may end up being an important weapon in your arsenal against having a kid. This medication is available over-the-counter for people over the age of 17 (be prepared to show photo I.D.) at most U.S. pharmacies or at Planned Parenthood. It generally costs between $10 and $50 (it tends to be less expensive at Planned Parenthood), and you need to take it within 72 hours of unprotected sex or contraceptive failure—but the sooner the better!

Pregnancy. If you meant to get pregnant, *felicitations*! If you didn't, trust us, you're not the first. There are plenty of resources at your disposal, and plenty of options from which you can choose. If you have a doctor that you trust, contact him or her to discuss options. If you don't, Planned Parenthood or a local reproductive clinic can help you research your options, make decisions, and take whatever action you deem appropriate.

Getting Health Care on Your Own

What if you're unemployed, or your employer does not provide health benefits? It's an intimidating situation to be in, for sure. But there are many affordable options at your disposal, and figuring out one that works for you is a lot smarter than eating Echinacea tablets, wearing a football helmet in the car, and praying for the best.

As Toni Frawley of Health Alliance Plan, a nonprofit health plan based in Detroit, explains, "Health care is out there and individuals can just go out and buy it." Sounds sort of obvious, but health care takes on such a mystique in this country that sometimes you forget that A) It doesn't have to be provided by someone else (e.g., parents or an employer), and B) You can shop for it just as you would any other major purchase. "Basically, you just need to do your homework," says Frawley. "So many grads are in the same situation as you and so many people have gone through this already—your friends included, probably. Talk to them and ask questions. Compare plans online and call up insurance brokers and carriers. You would research the TV you're going to buy the same way, so why not do it for your health coverage?" If you come across any unknowns during the hunt, CoverTheInsured.com and HealthInsuranceInfo. net are great resources for state-specific information.

Feel empowered? You should be—you're a consumer, the cornerstone of America! Now instead of rolling the dice by walking around with no coverage, let's consider some ways to stay insured when an employer isn't there to subsidize a plan.

Individual Coverage. Before you look to the options below, it's worth looking for individual plans in your state, as they can often be pretty affordable for a healthy twentysomething. You should definitely consider it as an option if you don't think you'll get benefits within the next year, but even if you think you might need coverage for only a few months, see what the payment schedule is for the plans you find—some charge monthly premiums and allow you to cancel at any time, which is a lot easier than tying together a bunch of short-term plans (see below) during your job hunt. For high deductible plans, individual insurance can be pretty manageable in some states. Using a healthy 23-year-old female as a test case, we found $2,500 deductible plans (with some basic coverage for office visits) ranging from $63 (WA) to $240 (NJ) per month, but most were in the $80–100 range. To compare quotes for yourself, type your zip code into eHealthInsurance.com or go straight to a provider (e.g., Anthem Blue Cross and Blue Shield). You can also just Google

"individual health care" and the name of your state to see who the providers are. Once you've found some candidates, run through the questions on page 354 and call up the individual providers or an insurance broker to see if they provide all the coverage you want.

Short-Term Insurance (a.k.a. "Bridge" or "Temporary" Insurance). Short-term insurance is an affordable holdover if you're looking for a job with benefits or you just need more time to weigh your options. In fact, even if you have a job, the benefits may take a month or two to kick in, so a temporary plan might still be necessary in the meantime. See page 361 for a full discussion of short-term health care.

Health

Pay to Stay on Your Parents' Plan (or Ask Them to Help You Out). If Mom and Dad can be convinced to help you out with one expense after college, it's probably health care—just use the argument that you "could die without it." Many states allow children to remain on their parents' plan until surprisingly old ages. In Texas it's 25; in New Jersey, believe it or not, residents can ride their parents' coattails until the age of 30! (Unfortunately, others cut it off at 19, so you need to see what's up.) If you can no longer be claimed as a dependent, maybe they'll help you pay for one of the other options in this section. And if Mom or Dad has covered your insurance through an employer-sponsored plan but you are now losing your dependent status, look into the possibility of continuing your coverage through COBRA.

COBRA. The Consolidated Omnibus Budget Reconciliation Act (better known as COBRA) has nothing to do with *G.I. Joe*, but it does enable people at companies with 20 or more employees to maintain health coverage (for up to 36 months) at their own expense after they have left an employer. In most states, it also covers young people who are kicked off of their parents' employer-sponsored plan when they can no longer be claimed as dependents. If you find yourself in this situation, ask your mom or dad to inquire with their employer(s) about this option, but understand that it will be very pricey since you'll have to pay the whole premium with no discounts. At your age, you can almost certainly go out and find a cheaper individual plan on your own. Should you decide you want COBRA to buy some time to figure out a sustainable alternative, be sure to act fast—you only have 60 days to announce your loss of dependent status, and then another 60 to elect COBRA.

Get a Job—Any Job. You're looking for a great full-time gig that will compensate you well and offer you all the benefits your heart desires. But in the meantime, why not make a little bit of spending money and gain access to benefits that could save you from bankruptcy if something goes wrong? Many temp agencies provide health benefits, as do Starbucks, Wal-Mart, and certain retail gigs. Check out Chapter 1 for more information on scoring one of these stopgap jobs, and see what big service sector companies can offer (in Hawaii, for example, even Häagen-Dazs offers health benefits).

Freelancer's Union. You might be making more than your friend who works for a Fortune 500 company, but you happen to be a freelancer or nanny and you don't have benefits. Enter the Freelancer's Union (FreelancersUnion. org). Through the Union you can get discounted health care for as low as $130/month (though the annual deductibles are as high as $10,000, so we're talking "catastrophic coverage" here). Coverage is not available everywhere in the country, but the easy-to-use website allows you to enter your zip code and get a list of available health, dental, disability, and life insurance plans. In order to qualify, you must meet their definition of an "independent worker" (e.g., freelancers, contract workers, temps) and work in one of the following industries or occupations: Arts, Design & Entertainment; Domestic Child Care Giver; Financial Services; Media & Advertising; Nonprofit; Skilled Computer User; Technology; and Traditional or Alternative Health Care Provider. You must also submit paperwork to show you've worked at least 20 hours in the last two months and earned at least $10,000 in the past six.

Alumni Association. The reason employers can get good insurance rates for their employees is because they offer providers easy access to a whole bunch of customers at once. The same goes for any organization that can pool together people to buy insurance at bulk rates—like your alma mater, for example. Contact your school's alumni association and see what it can offer in the way of temporary and individual plans.

Tips & Tricks: Flexible Spending Accounts (FSAs)

Another perk offered by some employers is a Flexible Spending Account, which allows you to deposit a portion of your pre-tax salary into a special account that can be used on certain expenditures. They include medical expenses, dependent care, and general health-related expenses (e.g., contact lenses, over-the-counter drugs). Medical expenses include any bills that aren't paid by insurance companies, and dependent care could cover things like day care for all those kids of yours. However, bear in mind that the money you don't use will disappear at the end of the year. Nine out of ten recent grads have never even heard of FSAs, but if you spend a lot of money at CVS filling the medicine cabinet, maybe they make sense for you.

City- or State-Sponsored Plans. In certain parts of the country, local governments have taken measures to help uninsured residents gain access to health care. For example, Healthy San Francisco is operated by the San Francisco Department of Health, and a program called Healthy NY provides coverage in parts of New York State (there are simple eligibility screeners on the websites you can check out to see if they're a possible option).

Note: When looking into individual plans, be wary of those that don't offer actual insurance coverage but rather discounts on health care services. CoverTheUninsured.com advises that "these plans are not a good buy, and many insurance regulators warn against buying them."

Short-Term Health Insurance

A lot of recent grads find themselves caught in health coverage limbo after graduation, waiting to land the job that's going to provide them with benefits. And even when they land that job, they often have to wait a month or more for their company-sponsored plan to kick into action. This risk is completely unnecessary and easy to avoid for most healthy twentysomethings with the purchase of a short-term health plan. For a healthy 23-year-old female, we found quotes between $23 (MD) and $127 (CA) per month, with most options falling in the $30–70 range. It's really not a high price to pay to protect yourself against a potentially catastrophic situation (plus you can often get a discount if you prepay up front).

In light of the preceding discussion of health care basics, short-term insurance can be explained thusly: A **low-cost, high-deductible plan** that covers you for a limited amount of time—the term is usually 30 to 120 days, and you should be able to renew a plan for up to a year before switching to a new provider. However, it's not ideal to jump around from one short-term plan to the next, so if there's no end to your uninsured days in sight, you should also take the time to research individual plans (p. 358)—some don't require a contract, so you can actually pay month to month and cancel whenever you want.

Short-term plans work best for generally healthy people whose main goal is to maintain insurability and avoid the crippling costs associated with a major medical emergency for a specific window of time and to maintain insurability. In practical terms, you get covered for injury and illness, and in the case of a major hospital visit, you'll be compensated up to a pretty high ceiling ($100,000 to over $1,000,000, the latter being preferable). So who is it bad for? People who visit the doctor often or need to buy prescription drugs don't get a great deal from short-term health insurance because of the high deductibles ($1,000 and up—lower ones will result in higher monthly costs) and the fact that it doesn't cover those prescription drugs (or OB/GYN visits, for that matter). You can check HealthInsuranceInfo.net to find state rules on temporary plans and the coverage they're required to provide.

When you're ready to find a provider, you can get short-term medical quotes specifically for grads from GradGuard.com, or compare quotes at eHealthInsurance.com to get a sense of your options. You can also just call up major providers and ask what they offer. Given the limitations of short-term health insurance for day-to-day stuff, your goal should be to find some reasonable balance between a low monthly premium and a high maximum

Health

Tips & Tricks: What's HIPAA?

The Department of Labor instituted the Health Insurance Portability and Accountability Act (HIPAA) in 1996 to protect people from being excluded for pre-existing conditions or other reasons when they try to move from one health care plan to another. A health insurance company can under no circumstance claim an exclusion if you've been covered under "creditable coverage" (e.g., COBRA, individual plans, and even some short-term plans) for the prior 12 months and you don't have a lapse in coverage from your old plan to the new one of more than 63 days. If you have a major gap (or you never had coverage in the first place) and you've received treatment for a medical condition at any time in the past 6 months, then that condition can be exempted as a "pre-existing condition," usually for a maximum of 12 to 18 months. Thus, while it's always important to maintain health coverage for the many reasons we've discussed, it's doubly so when you consider that a gap in coverage could leave you exposed to exclusions by future providers.

payout. Often, once you meet your deductible, the provider will pay 50–80% up to a certain level (e.g., $5000), and then 100% up to the ceiling (e.g., a million bucks).

Hold up! Where do you live? It's important to note that some states—including Connecticut, Hawaii, Massachusetts, and Vermont—don't allow short-term health insurance. There will be other options for the temporarily uninsured in these states, but if you are moving or have a temporary or permanent address in a different state that does allow it, you can carry an out-of-state short-term plan in some cases. Again, if you're in a bind, call up the major providers (e.g., Aetna, CIGNA, Oxford) and see what kind of solutions they can offer. However, these states might have their own subsidized plans for individuals (see page 360), so you still have options.

Getting Health Care through Work

If you're lucky, you won't have an option when it comes to picking a health care plan—you're just going to have to take the one your employer offers. It's a big perk that should not be overlooked during the job hunt. And even if you have numerous options through your job (probably HMOs or PPOs, for example), the other nice part about employer-provided benefits is that you have HR to guide you through the process. But before you go to HR, we suggest that you get familiar with the lingo explained (p. 350) and run through the questions listed on page 354. In addition, the first thing you should do when you get your offer is find out exactly when your company benefits kick in—some companies have a probation period before coverage goes into effect, so you may still need to talk to an insurance agent about an interim coverage policy or short-term insurance (p. 361).

Finally, let's be clear about one fact: Employer benefits do not mean that health care is *free*. It's just significantly discounted since companies can negotiate much better rates with insurance companies than individuals, and they also help you out with the costs. When you enroll, the money you pay toward your coverage is automatically deducted from your paycheck. To give you a sense of the discounts we're talking about, the Kaiser Family Foundation reports that, on an annual basis, a single worker contributes an average of $817 per year for an HMO plan, while the employer kicks in an average of $4,061. For a PPO plan, the worker-employer contribution split averages $860 and $4,116, respectively.

In some circumstances (e.g., you are a part-time worker), the employer will only offer partial benefits. Instead of blindly taking whatever's offered to you, make sure whatever they can provide—probably some sort of very spartan HDHP—works for your health needs. If you need more than just "catastrophic coverage," you may be better off seeking your own individual plan. And if you do end up going that route, see if the employer offers a Flexible Spending Account (p. 360), which will allow you to set aside money pre-tax for health care costs.

Choosing a Doctor

Just because you have insurance doesn't mean you're out of the woods. Now the fun really begins: You get to pick a doctor—most importantly, a primary care provider (PCP). If you are getting your insurance through work, someone from HR will likely sit you down after you enroll in a plan, hand you a book of 10,000 doctors, and ask you to pick one. Either that or you'll be forced to troll through your personal provider's website for a list of covered doctors. You might just lose hope and pick the one with the funniest name ("Methinks you're the one for me, Dr. *Lazarus Pinkerton*.") But it doesn't have to be that random, and you don't have to make the decision right away. There are a few simple ways to make an educated choice, so do the research and you won't end up with some wackjob who will try to kill you and harvest your organs.

Health

Before you do anything else, ask around. A good doctor embodies a perfect mix of professional know-how, geniality, and trustworthiness. So, while you can cast judgment on each candidate's med school degree if you want, the best way to find a good doctor is to talk to friends and colleagues to see if they can make a recommendation based on personal experience. Hopefully, any recommended doctors are included in your health plan (i.e., in that big blue book). If they aren't, it's not the end of the world—you can still go to them, you'll just have to pay extra. Only you can determine if you're willing to spend more money to go to an out-of-network doctor when you can probably find one that is just as good in network. In terms of what types of doctors you should consider for your PCP, the best bets are internists, gynecologists (p. 366), family practitioners, and GPs (general practitioners). The point is, you don't want a foot doctor dealing with your general health.

What if you can't get any recommendations? No need to fret. There are other resources at your disposal. Major metropolitan areas usually have magazines that release a "Best Doctors" report each year. If you aren't the magazine type, you can also browse WebMD and the American Medical Association's website. Whatever you do, avoid the Yellow Pages—it's not a good sign if a doctor has to advertise to get patients.

How to Evaluate a Doctor

Before committing to an MD, be sure to do a little digging first. Check the following background information by visiting the websites of your insurance provider, WebMD, Castle Connolly, and the American Medical Association (don't use any pay for services):

Status under your insurance plan. First things first: Is the doctor in network? If not, is there a particular reason you'd be willing to pay extra to see her or him? Check in with your provider for a list of practitioners covered under your plan.

Specialty and subspecialty. As noted before, find out what type of medicine the doctor specializes in, to make sure you're not wasting your time by seeing a podiatrist for a sinus infection.

Education. If the doc holds a degree from the University of Phoenix Online, don't line up to see him. There's no need to be snooty and only see Columbia grads, but try to set a reasonable standard to narrow down the most qualified candidates.

Credentials. Is this doctor "board-certified?" If so, it means she has full credentials. If she's only "board-*eligible*," it doesn't necessarily mean she's a quack, it just means she hasn't taken and/or passed her boards yet. Feel free to inquire why not, or if it makes you nervous, just steer clear.

Membership and appointments. Take a look at what organizations different doctors belong to and what board positions they hold. The more they're involved in the medical community associated with their area of expertise, the more likely they are to be up-to-date with treatments and procedures.

Hospital/Med school affiliations. Top doctors work at top hospitals; top hospitals offer top resources; and top resources mean that you get top care. If you can't figure out which hospitals are the best, any hospital affiliated with a university that has a good med school should rank well.

Disciplinary action. A lawsuit or two may simply mean the physician just ran into some bad luck or is willing to attempt more risky procedures. Ten or 20 and you're venturing into dangerous territory. Make sure that he or she has not been charged with serious transgressions, such as sexual misconduct or narcotic offenses (search Castle Connolly). Also, check if the doctor has been fined or had his license suspended or revoked for malpractice by contacting the respective state board of medicine.

Once you've found your doc and done your due diligence, there's one last step—call up the office and fire some questions at the secretary:

- Double-check that the practice does in fact accept your insurance.

- Ask if they are taking new patients, and find out what the wait time for an appointment is. The best doctors are often busier than the police at Mardi Gras, but waiting too long can be hazardous to your health. One to four weeks is a normal wait time; four months is not.

- Pay attention to office hours. If the physician only sees patients two days a week for two hours each day, you may want to find someone with better availability.

Health

- Ask how many patients are typically scheduled each hour. Three to five is a reasonable number. Leaving the office for an hour is acceptable, but leaving for four might get your boss asking questions.

- Inquire how after-hours calls are handled, and ask about the doc's availability in case of an emergency. Check if any back-up physicians will be accessible if your main squeeze heads to the islands.

- Even if the main office is conveniently located, ask where they do their blood work, X-rays, or other tests so that you don't have to go to the end of the earth for an endoscopy.

- Ask if they offer introductory meetings. It is perfectly acceptable to schedule an appointment to meet a new doctor before actually taking the plunge. By doing so, you can see the office and get a sense of whether it's a well-run operation. You may need to pay for this pleasure though, so figure out how much it will cost you beforehand.

Finally, understand that just because you saw a doctor once doesn't mean you have to stick with him or her forever. By law, doctors' offices have to transfer your transcripts to the next physician. We like to compare finding your doctor to finding a true love: It might take some work, and the first one isn't always the best, but once you find one, you'll have a really beautiful (and healthy) future together.

Choosing a "Lady" Doctor

For many girls, your gynecologist is going to be a hell of a lot more important than that other dude who hits your knee with a rubber hammer once a year. When it comes to health, the process of selecting an OB/GYN (or just GYN) should be one of your first moves. If you have comprehensive insurance, you can elect to choose one in the same way you chose a primary care doctor (see "How to Choose a Doctor" on page 363), but the thought of asking your boss and/or HR representative for gyno recommendations might not be so appealing. Don't worry—there are a number of additional ways you can zero in on a good doctor without having to announce to the office that you're having lady issues.

A few things to consider:

- **Gender.** Do you feel more comfortable with a female doctor?

- **Location.** How far are you willing to travel to get probed by a cold metal thing?

- **OB/GYN or just GYN.** Is it important for you to see a doctor who is an OB/GYN or would a standard gynecologist do? (The "OB" stands for obstetrics, i.e., prenatal care and baby delivery). Standard gynecologists will probably have shorter wait times because they won't be busy at the hospital delivering a baby when it's time to see you. Then again, when you all of a sudden get preggers, do you want to have to start looking for an OB/GYN? However, your gynecologist should probably be able to refer to you an OB/GYN.

Once you've got your needs lined up, start your search.

- **Search within network.** Much as you may have done when seeking a primary care doctor, consult your insurance provider's website for a list of in-network doctors. If you're choosing randomly, perform a thorough Google search and consult patient reviews before seeing a doctor.

- **Co-workers and friends.** Ask female co-workers for their recommendations, or if you have friends outside of work who are insured by the same provider, ask them for advice.

- **Other doctors and nurses.** If you currently have a doctor that you have a good relationship with, ask for

> **Tips & Tricks: The OB/GYN-PCP combo**
>
> It is possible to kill two birds with one stone by using your OB/GYN as your primary care physician rather than having two separate doctors. Many women choose this option for two main reasons: 1) They have a good relationship with their gynecologist and prefer not to see someone else, and 2) The have a lot more female-specific medical issues (e.g., annual exam, infections, discomfort, birth control) than other medical issues. And if you get lucky, your OB/GYN is an amazing generalist. On average, however, it would be a safe bet to assume that internists and GPs are probably better PCPs than gynos due to the more general nature of their work.

recommendations of colleagues who are covered by your insurance. Female nurses and physician's assistants can also be helpful in this regard.

- **Planned Parenthood.** Your local Planned Parenthood (or other family-planning clinics) is a great place to find a doctor, or you can ask the staff there to direct you towards other doctors within your community.

Dealing with Your Health Insurance Company

Tips & Tricks: When in doubt, get on the phone

Medical billing can be a nightmare. You may get a bill from your doctor or your insurance company or both, and sometimes it's not completely obvious whom you owe or how much. Instead of just sending off a check and hoping for the best, pick up the phone whenever you're confused. There's a number on the back of your insurance card, and while you may have to wait on hold for a bit, whoever's on the other side of the line is there to help you with any question you have regarding coverage or billing. Similarly, every doctor's office and hospital has a billing office that can assist you in determining what you owe and what the status of an insurance claim is. Call these people. Unpaid medical bills can eventually affect your credit if the doctor's office submits them to a collection agency, but there's no reason it should get to that point if you just communicate with the people who want your money.

If choosing a plan and finding a doctor wasn't enough of a pain, get ready for actually dealing with your insurance company. Figuring out what your provider will cover can often be a long, drawn-out affair, and the whole process of paying for medical services is about as labyrinthine as any transaction you'll ever make. That said, if you understand the basics of your insurance (and put your provider on speed dial for any questions that come up), you can avoid a lot of hassle. Experiences differ from company to company, but the way in which you interact with your insurer is essentially dictated by whether you have an HMO or a PPO plan.

HMOs

HMOs make insurance company interactions pretty simple. When you're interested in visiting a doctor, you always go straight to your PCP, even if you think you need to see a specialist. Since your PCP is already in network, you know his or her services will be covered by your insurance. If you've requested to be referred to a specialist, your PCP will have to approve your request. This process acts as a pre-approval mechanism, so your specialist care will also be covered by your insurance. Wham, bam, thank you ma'am.

PPOs

PPOs can get a bit more complicated since you can see a specialist without first being screened by a PCP. When you skip past the approval of your PCP, you have to answer some questions yourself about specialists: Are they in- or out-of-network, and how will that affect your copay? Is the purpose of the visit even covered under your insurance? There are two approaches you can take to making sure you are covered when you go straight to a specialist.

- **Option #1: Get pre-approval from your insurance provider.** If you're not in any huge rush to see the specialist, this route is probably the wisest. Follow the instructions provided by your insurance company when you signed up for your plan (ask your employer or check the company's website if you threw out all the paperwork). Most likely you'll have to call the number on the back of your insurance card and plead your case. If your visit is pre-approved, then the specialist should submit an insurance claim on your behalf, and the insurance provider will pay some if not most of your bill. Sometimes the check from the insurance company will go to the specialist, but in the event that it is sent to you, know that it's your responsibility to endorse it to your specialist and mail it in. (See page 303 to learn how to endorse checks.)

- **Option #2: Go first, then deal with the bill after.** If you just want to go to the doctor now and deal with the aftermath later, your specialist may submit the claim for you, or you'll be told you have to do it yourself. If the onus is on you, then most likely you'll be asked to pay for the visit in full and mail your receipt to your insurance company. When mailing the receipt, always keep a copy so you have records of your visit. You'll also have to include a reimbursement form (don't worry, it's really easy to fill out) that can usually be found in the "Forms" section on your health insurance provider's website. If you can't find the forms, then by all means call the number on the back of your card. Then you wait. And wait…And either get reimbursed or rejected. If you are in fact covered for the purpose of your visit and

Health

369

your claim is still rejected, then it just requires some wrangling with a manager at your insurance company over the phone and a lot of persistence until you finally get paid.

Dental Insurance

When most people think about setting up health care for themselves after college, managed care and general practitioners come to mind. But you can't forget the dentist, because otherwise your teeth will fall out, and then you will look sort of like that guy with "bitter beer face."

When it comes to the lingo (e.g., deductible, copay) and the fundamental need for coverage (one bar fight and a few root canals could leave you bankrupt), dental insurance is not so different from health insurance. (Note: The dental equivalent of an HMO is a DMO, or Dental Management Organization; PPOs in dentistry operate under the same principles as they do in health care). But if you thought a lot of Americans lacked health coverage, you might be surprised (or not) to know that there are 2.5 times more people who lack dental coverage—and over 40% of the country hasn't visited a dentist in the past year. Even amongst the employed population, far more people waive dental benefits than do health benefits. In our opinion, though, you should take dental benefits if they're offered to you at work.

If your employer does not offer coverage, you can get an individual plan for as low as $15 a month in some states (more commonly $20 to $35). Go to eHealthInsurance.com and type in your zip code to compare quotes. When it comes to deciding whether or not you need to pursue coverage of your own (or what type of plan you need), it's worth running through the following questions. Go through the list before calling up an insurance agent to find a good match.

- Does the plan fully cover office visits and preventative care (e.g., cleanings, check-ups), or only a portion?

- Is there a deductible?

- Is there an annual maximum benefit (i.e., a cap on how much the insurance will shell out for me in a given year)?

- Am I on a course of treatment (e.g., Invisalign) that I want to continue?

- Do I have any planned procedures (e.g., wisdom teeth removal, root canals, fillings) in the next year?

- Do I play sports where my teeth are particularly at risk?

- Do I want any cosmetic work now, or can it wait until later?

When looking for plans, you'll most likely come across the term **indemnity insurance.** Though it sounds sort of ominous, its alternative name—"traditional dental health insurance plan"—should calm your nerves. The general idea is that claim payments are made on a "fee-for-service" basis, which means that a set amount is reimbursed based on the type of dental treatment received. That set amount is based on what the insurance company thinks is, "usual, customary, and reasonable," for the particular treatment in your geographical area. When it comes to billing, you must pay the dentist directly and then file a claim with the dental insurance company to receive a reimbursement. As with a PPO plan, you can visit the dentist of your choice.

It is fair to say that if you have really good teeth, insurance might cost you more than the one check-up you get a year would cost out of pocket. But insurance is also about covering your butt if something unexpected happens, so in our opinion it's not worth getting hung up on that factoid.

How to Choose a Dentist

Finding a dentist isn't all that different from finding a general practitioner. The best bet is to ask coworkers, family, friends, and neighbors for referrals. You also want to make sure the practice accepts your dental plan, so you should check your provider's list of participating dentists. Another option is to do some searching on the 'net and call a local periodontist (gums specialists) or to ask for a

> **Tips & Tricks: Dental school clinics**
>
> The American Dental Associations advises regular professional cleanings and oral exams to fight tooth decay, which affects more than 90 percent of those 40 and older. If you don't have dental insurance, you're liable to say, "Whatever, I'll just chew some Trident White!" But what if you could get a cleaning and check-up for free, or at a very discounted rate? If there's a respected dental school in your area, you may be in luck. Student-run clinics will often offer basic screening and cleaning (as well as X-rays), all under the supervision of board-certified teaching staff. Check with your state's dental society to find a dental school, or search for a list at ADA.org. Damn it feels good to be a guinea pig.

recommendation. Finally, you can find out which lab a dentist uses for lab work, then call the lab directly to do a background check. Don your two-brimmed hat for this process to feel like a modern-day Sherlock Holmes.

Once you think you've found a winning ticket, it's time to run it through the wringer. Look out for malpractice suits, and call the state board of consumer affairs to find out if there are any records of actions against the dentist. Has the dentist's license ever been revoked or suspended? Do some Googling to find lawsuits and any other dirt. In this case, no results are a good result. You can also see if the dentist is rated on Dr. Oogle (which can be found at the amazing URL droogle.com).

Next, it's time to grill the dentist's office. Ask if the dentist owns the practice or if someone else owns it. If the dentist is an owner or co-owner, chances are he's more invested in his work and reputation. Also, find out how long he's been practicing. Don't sign up with a new dentist—it takes more than two years for a good dentist to really know what he's doing.

As with general practitioners, you don't have to stick with a dentist just because you go there once. Here are red flags to look out for on your first visit:

- You haven't had a filling in years, yet the dentist insists you need several fillings. (Bear in mind that if you've been sucking down six Cokes a day and you never brush your teeth, maybe he's right.)

- The dentist says you need to replace your silver fillings with plastic or "white composite" ones. Silver fillings last three times as long as plastic ones. And though silver fillings contain mercury, there's little scientific evidence that the mercury content in them is toxic to your body.

- The dentist says your gums aren't healthy and you need "root planing"—a deep-cleaning of tartar in hard-to-reach spots. Few healthy recent grads need such an intensive service.

- The dentist claims you need a crown or multiple crowns.

- Be wary of a zillion dental plans or tons of advertising: A good dentist doesn't need to advertise for patients.

Bonus: Life Insurance!

For some reason, people tend to associate life insurance with health insurance even though they have nothing to do with one another. (One is about staying alive without going broke, while the other is about helping out your loved ones if you kick the bucket.) But since it's another one of those wild cards that few grads anticipate, we think it's important to understand the basics. If it's being offered by your employer in the big box o' benefits, there may be compelling reasons to cash in—or even buy it on your own if it's not offered.

If you're like us, you probably thought that life insurance was only for wealthy fat cats and rednecks that want to fake their own death, collect on the policy, and escape to Mexico with their wife (who's also their aunt). That's certainly true, but it may also be for you. And guess what? Even if it's not, it's worth keeping on your radar as you start to do things like get married and (gasp) actually make some real money.

Here's the lowdown: Life insurance is a type of insurance in which an insurer (e.g., State Farm) agrees to pay out a sum of money to beneficiaries (e.g., mom, husband, mistress) of the insured (e.g., you) when the insured dies. So the logical criteria for needing life insurance are twofold: 1) You are actually making money (amongst other reasons, to pay for the insurance), and 2) Other people would be worse off, financially speaking, if you stopped making that money due to death. If you fit that profile, then you should consider opting for life insurance.

In brief, there are two types of life insurance: term and whole, which both pay out large sums of money to beneficiaries. There are two main differences. Term will cover you at a stable monthly premium (you can lock in a low rate now because you're young) over a specific amount of time (e.g., 30 years), at which point you'll be able to renew it at a higher premium. On the other hand, whole life insurance, once paid off, will cover you for the rest of your life and you can withdraw funds from it even before you croak. The kicker is that the cost of term life insurance is much lower than whole (e.g., $300/year vs. $3,000/year) and thus preferable for most grads. Ultimately, life insurance is a way to lock

Health

up funds for a very rainy day. Which means that if you don't like the concept of life insurance at all, you can take one more alternative approach: Just make sure to put money in a long-term investment account each month (or year) that you don't touch (this assumes you have the self-restraint).

Should you feel that this discussion is irrelevant to you at this point in life, just take one moment to consider two potential benefits of thinking about life insurance now versus ten years from now. Getting life insurance in your twenties is clearly a conservative move, but that's not to say it doesn't have its merits. Here are a couple key benefits to consider.

Locking in low premium rates and guaranteeing your "insurability." Assuming you're a relatively healthy twentysomething, the premiums you pay today will be much lower than when you reach your thirties, forties, and beyond. By purchasing a policy now, you can lock in those low premiums for life (or for a period if you select a term life policy). Not only that, but if you start now as a regular old officer worker, your provider will have to keep insuring you even when you decide to pursue your dreams and become an action movie stuntman.

Taking advantage of employer benefits. If your employer is offering you a policy with no strings attached (i.e., no extra monthly/yearly fees), then you should certainly jump on it. Even if they ask for you to slightly subsidize it (e.g., $10/month), it's still probably worth your while. Think of it this way: Isn't it worth one movie ticket a month to help out your loved ones if you kick the bucket?

If your employer doesn't provide you with life insurance and you're still interested in getting it, turn to the traditional insurance companies (e.g., MetLife, Prudential, State Farm), use comparison shopping engines such as Esurance.com, and call up insurance brokers to see if they can beat the rates you've found.

Chapter VIII: Cars & Commuting

Cars and Commuting

In order to be the consummate grad about town, it's sometimes necessary to have a car. How else are you going to get to work, pick up your furniture at Ikea, and still make an 8:30 rez at California Pizza Kitchen? Without a ride, it can be difficult to achieve this type of mobility. But convenience costs money, and being cool costs even more. Cars are usually the biggest monthly expense besides rent for fledgling graduates (and certainly the biggest purchase for a non-house-owning twentysomething), so make sure you assess your needs and know all your options before throwing your savings into that Mini Cooper.

Often, the post-college city that you choose will determine whether or not you need a car. Atlanta, Houston, and L.A. are typical "car towns," and they've got the traffic jams to prove it. Meanwhile, owning a car in New York City or San Francisco is a huge extravagance, and you may quickly discover that exorbitant parking fees and the fact that you never actually drive anywhere defeat the purpose of the investment. So, first things first: Do you really need a car? This question should act like a prompt in one of those "Choose Your Own Adventure" books: If you say, "No, I definitely don't need a car," then you can skip most of this chapter and turn to "Getting around without a Car" on page 400. If you choose, "Yes, I think I need a car," however, you've got quite the ride in front of you. But don't worry—we'll try to make sure there aren't too many unpleasant twists in the road. And if you already have a car, you should head to page 392 to make sure you own the appropriate car insurance.

For those entering the car market, the first step is to think about whether you are going to buy or lease. Insurance is another necessary issue to address, as is the question of where you're going to put the damn thing when you're not out rolling. And what about the thorny issue of financing? Presumably you are past the age where it is appropriate to have a bar mitzvah or apply to be on *My Super Sweet 16*. So unless someone gets extra generous with the graduation gift, you'll probably have to throw down some money of your own. And if you are already paying rent, a car might just be the straw that broke the bank account. Let's break down the math: A typical month of car ownership can run well in excess of $600 once you add up the car payment ($350), a few gas fill-ups ($100), insurance costs ($150), miscellaneous maintenance (a bunch), and fuzzy dice to hang from the rearview mirror ($5). That's a lot of dough that could be put into different pastures, like your savings or a vacation or delicious food.

Still, in spite of the financial drain associated with a good old-fashioned gas-guzzler, we can't deny the pleasure of rolling down the freeway at 66 mph in a 65 mph zone, bumping Vanessa Carlton and screaming into a Bluetooth receiver. We also can't deny that it's sometimes flat-out necessary to have a car.

In this chapter, we'll cover all the car basics you need to know in order to make an informed decision about riding dirty as a recent grad.[1] From looking for new and used cars to negotiating like a pro, comparison shopping for insurance policies, and staying safe on the road, we've got the car game covered. We understand that for some people, cars are more than just a way of getting from place to place—if there's a car you know you want to drive no matter what, then by all means do whatever you can (within the law) to make it happen. But for the most part, we encourage taking some time to find a solution that is as safe and affordable as possible. Scary as it sounds, it's very possible that you'll be riding this steel horse into your thirties, so make sure it's not a one-trick pony.

Buying vs. Leasing

While some of your more OCD friends will probably create models and Excel spreadsheets to determine whether they should lease or buy a car, the decision is not a complex one. You need to consider two factors: 1) How much money can you spend each month on a car (and how much do you expect to be able to spend over the next several years), and 2) Are you the type of person who would be content owning a car for a long time, or are you an A.D.D. type who would rather "try" a new car every two to four years without the hassle of ownership? As far as monthly expenses go, buying a new car is the most expensive option (roughly $600/month assuming a $20k car and a 6% loan), followed by leasing a car ($350 for the same car), and finally buying a used car ($280/month assuming a $10k purchase price and an 8% loan). But here's the kicker: At the end of a lease, you can't sell the car, thus you can't recoup any money—all the dough spent leasing it goes down the drain. After you're finished with a new or used car (5–10 years), however, you can resell it to earn a cash back bonus. Theoretically, if you purchased a car and then sold it at the end of your loan period, the total expense may be cheaper than the aggregate of the monthly lease payments on multiple vehicles over the same time period

[1] Don't actually ride dirty—we just like saying that. Riding dirty means driving in an illegal fashion, generally with no registration and/or with narcotics in the glove compartment. See: *Chamillionaire*.

(but we urge you to do the math on this one before assuming it to be true in all cases, as resale value will vary by vehicle).

As for what type of consumer you are, only you can really tell. Did you preorder the iPhone? Do you change your entire wardrobe twice a year? Does having a lower monthly payment *now* (when maybe you have a low-paying job and other expenses to worry about) matter more to you than the notion of long-term value? Do you like to test things out before you buy them? If you answered yes to any of these questions (especially the last one), you may be a leaser. Don't let the personal finance pundits tell you you're a "moron" for wanting to pay more in the long-run for lower monthly payments and a nicer car. The fact that 75% of luxury cars are leased should tell you that you're not alone; so as long as you're aware of the tradeoffs, you should do what you want.

While we genuinely think the "buy or lease" question is relatively straightforward, there are a few other things to consider when making this decision. For example, when you lease, all repairs will be under warranty for the term of your lease, whereas when you buy a car, all damage beyond the manufacturer's warranty is an out-of-pocket expense. In addition, there may be yearly mileage limits on a leased vehicle, but you'd only really hit those if you have a super-long commute or took road trips every weekend. If you buy a car, you'll have to lend special attention to maintaining it in order to preserve its resale value (e.g., wash and wax it, park it in the shade, change the oil regularly). And finally, regardless of whether you lease or buy, you still have to purchase insurance, pay DMV fees, and cover all of the other costs associated with driving. (For more information on the specifics of leasing, see page 389.)

Choosing a Car

After you've decided to lease or buy, it's time to hone in on the lot and see what kind of ride strikes your fancy. Go into the process knowing that it's going to be stressful. Besides rent, a car is most likely your biggest post-college expense, and it's also the one that will stay with you the longest. So yes, it's a big decision, and the process isn't as straightforward as buying a DVD player. But if you keep a cool head and think through it logically, you'll come out feeling confident in your choice. (If you freak out and buy a Mitsubishi Lancer with racing stripes, we can't really help you out.)

In terms of choosing a specific car, we're not going to sit here and tell you to "buy American" or drive a mini-van. However, it's pretty easy to narrow down

Cars & Commuting

the car field from hundreds to about five that are actually in your sweet spot. (For the top five new and used cars for recent grads picked by the editor-in-chief of *Car and Driver*, see page 382.) As you start checking manufacturer websites, reading online reviews, and scanning some dealership lots, keep the following concerns in mind. Be a huge dork and make a checklist if you want—trust us, thinking about these things will make you feel a lot better in the long run than walking into the Lexus showroom with a checkbook and a sheepish grin.

- **Cost.** As is often the case, the first way to narrow your choices is to knock out all the cars you can't afford! A reasonable budget dictates that monthly car payments should not exceed 12–15% of your after-tax income, so break out the calculator and figure out a price range (or use an online car payment calculator, like the one at Bankrate.com). It's important to note that this step is not just about looking at sticker prices. Instead, your concern should be the Total Cost of Ownership (TCO), which is an estimate of how much you'll spend over the life of a car. Take the models you're interested in and plug them into Edmunds.com's "True Cost to Own^{SM}" pricing system, which will provide a five-year cost breakdown for taxes, fuel, maintenance, insurance, and more. Clearly these are estimates, but the process is useful for revealing hidden costs, like the fact that a certain vehicle can reasonably be expected to cost you $1,000 in repairs three years down the line. Then go to page 389 to read more about financing, which will determine your upfront costs (i.e., down payment) and monthly payments (determined by the interest rate on your loan).

- **Insurance implications.** Related to the cost question is insurance (see page 392), which is required unless you want to go to jail. While you probably won't choose a specific policy until after you've sealed the deal on a car, it should factor into your choice rather significantly. Insurance fees are based not only on you as a driver, but also on the specific car you own. Vehicles with higher horsepower or cars that have a greater probability of being stolen will draw higher premiums from insurance companies. Used cars also tend to draw higher premiums. The difference may seem negligible, but even $40 a month can add up, so make sure you're factoring insurance into any "monthly cost of ownership" comparisons you make between cars.

- **Safety.** Do you need to drive in an armored tank? No, but that would be awesome. Do you need a car that handles well in the rain and isn't prone to flipping over on the freeway? Yes, that would probably be smart. Listen to mama bear on this one—a safe car is a cool car! Do some research to make sure you're not buying a death trap. Kelley Blue Book (kbb.com) allows you to compare safety features and ratings on any make and model, and it's worth checking out Safecar.gov for general vehicle safety information.

- **Specific needs.** Are you going to be stranded in the winter without four-wheel drive? Do you want enough space to handle weekend trips with friends or are you more of a solo road warrior? Are you planning to have a child in the next five years (seriously)? These types of need-based questions will go a lot further toward narrowing down a type of ride (e.g., sedan, SUV, drop-top) than thinking about your favorite color.

- **Reliability and efficiency.** Like a good BFF, a car that's reliable makes all the difference. And just as a lame but trustworthy friend always ends up being better than that cool, extra slick cat who wins you over and then stabs you in the back, a car you don't have to worry about will be a huge weight off your mind. Another concern that's particularly *en vogue* is fuel-efficiency. We've seen the country completely freak out about the future of gas prices, and it's not unlikely that it will happen again. Hybrids (e.g., the Toyota Prius) and other cars with high fuel-efficiency can make a big difference in reducing the overall cost of car ownership because you get more bang for your buck on each tank of gas.

- **Warranty.** A new car warranty is great for mitigating the cost of future problems with the vehicle. Just be careful about marketing ploys that sound sweet but really make no sense. For example, why would you need a "lifetime warranty" on a truck? No one owns a car for that long! (According to J.D. Power and Associates, most consumers get rid of a car five and a half years after they buy it.) It's pretty unlikely that you'll buy a car with major engine or transmission problems that don't show up in the first three to five years, so don't concern yourself with the length of the warranty so much as what aspects of the car it actually covers. As CNN Money advises, "No one should ever buy a car for the warranty alone, but if it is a consideration for you, look

Cars & Commuting

past the hype and think about real cars and real life. If you do that, it turns out there really isn't that much to think about."

- **Personal preference.** Don't discount your likes and dislikes. You're gonna have this puppy for a while, so make it count. If you only like Aston Martins, you may have to compromise. But driving a car you love will probably make you pretty happy, so be willing to stretch your budget where it makes sense.

Ten Great Cars for Recent Grads

We asked Eddie Alterman, editor-in-chief of *Car & Driver*, for his top five new and top five used car picks for 2010. Can you buy a jalopy for $800 on Craigslist? Of course. But if you're looking for great value and reliability at a reasonable price, check out these options.

New Cars (2010 Models)*

Honda Fit: Redesigned last year, the Fit offers a surprising amount of room inside and plenty of oomph from its 1.5-liter four-cylinder engine. Price: $16,000

Mazda 3: Available in sedan or hatchback body styles, the 3 is a solidly built and entertaining back-road companion. Price: $15,000

Volkswagen Golf: New this year, this hatchback version of the Jetta sedan is stout, roomy, versatile, and responsive. Price: $19,000

Honda Civic: This fun economy car handles beautifully, gives comfort to people and cargo, and offers faultless build quality. Price: $16,000

Nissan Versa: One of the roomiest entries in the subcompact class, the Versa is basic transportation, but it also offers the most power, with 122 horse power from its 1.8-liter four-cylinder engine. Price: $12,000

Used Cars**

Volkswagen GTI: The car that invented the term "hot hatch" is addictive to drive and able to accommodate an unbelievable amount of cargo. Price: $12,000

Mazdaspeed3: Fun galore. This car can hit 155 mph and still leave enough money in your bank account for a few months' rent. Price: $13,000

Mini Cooper: Find a two or three-year-old one, and no one will know the difference. The recent redesign hasn't strayed from the original British Invader. Price: $13,000

Subaru Impreza WRX: All-wheel drive, a rally-bred chassis, and extroverted looks. What's not to love? Price: $15,000

Honda Civic Si: With quick reflexes, unassailable build quality, and a great four-cylinder engine, the Civic Si will be fun for years. Price: $14,000

* Manufacturer's Suggest Retail Prices have been rounded.

** Rounded value via Kelley Blue Book Private Party Value with basic features, automatic transmission (when available), 36,000 miles, in fair condition, 2006 models (except for the Mazda which was a 2007 model), and Atlanta zip code 30322. ■

Cars & Commuting

Assessing Used Cars

The main reasons for buying a used car are either to save money or to achieve a little retro chic on the road. The two things to remember when jumping into the fray are 1) Used car salesmen have a bad reputation for a reason, and 2) An unreliable used car could end up draining more cash in maintenance and repair fees than a new one. However, not all used cars are jalopies, and when they work out, they are definitely the cheapest options. One obvious but important point is that there's a huge difference between a ten-year-old used car and a two- to four-year-old used car that has only 20–30K miles on it (the average car is driven for 12k miles per year). If you're shopping for value and reliability, you'll be looking at cars in the latter category. To find them, search around at car dealerships (watch enough local network broadcasts, and you'll see the commercials), peruse Craigslist and print classifieds, and check out websites like Carmax.com, ConsumerGuide.com, and AutoTrader.com. To get a sense for fair prices, go to Kelley Blue Book (kbb.com) and enter the year, make, mileage, model, features, the relative condition of the car you want, and your zip code. (The site will also provide local listings for the vehicle you want.)

Once you have the perspective to spot a deal from a rip-off, you can perform some due diligence on the ones that look fairly priced. In addition to accident history, you should research the number of previous owners, past mechanical problems, and maintenance history. Also, find out if the car has ever failed an inspection. Run a vehicle history report at AutoCheck.com using the Vehicle Identification Number (see below). A dealer should provide you a CARFAX vehicle history report, and if it doesn't, you should ask for one. This report includes vital info like accident and damage history, title problems (including salvaged or junked titles), frame damage checks, odometer readings (to make sure someone didn't doctor it), accident indicators like airbag deployment, and more. Look for cars that are Certified Pre-Owned (CPO), which means they have been inspected rigorously and are usually covered by a warranty from the manufacturer. CPO cars cost a bit more, but the added warranty and reliability may justify the cost.

Even with all these checks in place, you should always do your own inspection to make sure you don't get a lemon. Be as crazy about this as possible: Sit in every seat, turn on the car and play around with all its features, listen for ominous noises, get out and check all the lights, and so on. If you find anything that wasn't previously discussed and factored into the price, make sure the dealer will fix it at no extra cost to you; in fact, you should even demand they change the contract to say the problems need to be fixed before you have to pay. At the final stage of the sale, never agree to sign an "as is" statement, which means that as soon as you leave the lot the car is solely your responsibility. Instead, you should be given at least 30 days to make sure the car is in good condition.

Tips & Tricks: How to find the Vehicle Identification Number (VIN)

This useful number can be found in the following places: the previous driver's insurance card, the car registration, the VIN plate on the driver's side dashboard, and the certificate label on the driver's side doorjamb.

Cars & Commuting

Hitting the Dealership and Making a Deal

The Internet is only a means to an end—eventually you are going to have to get off your butt and get up close and personal with some cars. Word of warning: The only people who hate window shoppers more than 50 Cent are car dealers. As soon as you set foot on the lot, be prepared to get pitched to harder than David Ortiz with the bases loaded. But it's best to ignore all that jazz. Instead of letting a salesperson work you over, use the following plan of attack to ensure you get the car you want at the best price possible.

Step 1: Visit the dealership for a test drive. To avoid wasting time and getting pushed toward cars you can't afford, schedule an appointment and show up to the dealerships knowing what you want to see (utilize your Internet research here). When you test drive, take a ride that involves a variety of driving situations (e.g., stop and go traffic, tight turns, highway), then gather all the necessary pamphlets and pricing information and get out of there before a wheel falls off the "straight-talk express." The dealer may try to lowball you just to get you to come back, but realize that he or she has no intention of actually selling at that tantalizing price. Anyway, you shouldn't even be thinking about buying yet. The purpose of this visit is to make sure you really like the car, so just walk away if the salesperson tries to pressure you into making an on-the-spot decision.

Step 2: Do your research: After you've found "the one," head back to the lab and run the numbers on financing options (see page 389 to understand how financing works). Look up incentives and rebates on manufacturer websites and at Automotive.com, keeping an eye out for deals geared specifically toward recent grads and first-time buyers. Often, you will be offered either a cash rebate or low-interest financing options. Before grabbing the cash, use an online "rebate versus interest" tool to figure out

> **Tips & Tricks: Car deals for recent grads**
>
> In the hopes of building brand loyalty from the get-go, many car companies offer purchasing and leasing incentives to recent grads. All you need to do is to prove your graduate status from an accredited university (depending on how restrictive the program is), and the car companies will offer rebates, special financing rates, and a delayed first payment. Almost all companies offer incentives, so Google any car brand plus the words "graduate deal" or "college graduate" and shop around before making a purchase.

which is the better deal (Edmunds.com has a good one). You can then either call or email local dealers for price comparisons, or get multiple quotes at the same time using Edmunds' "Dealer Locator." Once you've gotten a grasp on the price range, you can go into the final stage…

Step 3: Negotiate. Since you're probably in the market for a pretty common car (as opposed to a 1-of-50 Lamborghini), you have a lot of room to flex your consumer muscles. Never settle for the sticker price. There are two approaches to the negotiating: the in-person method and the stay-at-home method.

- **In-person.** If you're a smooth operator or you can bring a friend/family member who is a bit of a jerk (in a good way), maybe you'll have fun going toe-to-toe with a dealership. It can be an arduous process, but there are certainly examples of success. When you go in, be prepared for the common dealership maneuver of asking what *you* want to pay for the car. They may even say, "Give me a number." Don't be afraid to throw out a lowball offer. For example, if the ticket price is $28K and you offer $22K, you might not get it—but you're a hell of a lot more likely to get it at $26K than if you said you were happy with the original price. For conversations like this one, make sure you're talking to a salesperson who actually has decision-making power, rather than someone who will keep walking into a back room to get a sign-off from some faceless (and potentially evil!) manager. When a

> ### Tips & Tricks: Networking your way to a deal
>
> In Chapter 4, we discussed the enormous value of networking during your job hunt. But out there in the "real world," building relationships can be useful in a lot of ways, not just in terms of your career. It's human nature to help out someone you're connected to (even if indirectly), and in spite of the stereotypes, car dealers are indeed humans. So, while it may be a long shot, it's totally worth seeing if you can network to a dealer in your area. Maybe you played high school sports with the kid of a local Honda dealer. Maybe your parents know someone. Maybe, after putting up a Facebook status message saying, "I'm looking to lease an Audi, anyone know where I can get a good deal?" you'll find out that your cousin used to date an Audi salesman. Because car purchases involve negotiation and fuzzy pricing, any way you can link your personal network with the dealer's will help you out. At the very least, it adds some accountability to the equation—a dealer will be much less likely to screw you over if he or she knows it will make its way back to a mutual acquaintance.

conversation does begin to hover around the price you want, don't be afraid to say, "If you give it to me for this price, I will sign right now." This premier league negotiating tactic tells the salesperson you are no longer comparison shopping, and he or she will be inclined to make you happy lest you walk away and never come back.

- **Stay-at-home.** Not the type to run a hard bargain? Find your savior at FightingChance.com. The bootleg feel of this website and all of the talk about a buying "technique" may seem incredibly ominous, but we've heard enough good reviews to be convinced. The blueprint is pretty simple: First, you pay $39.99 for a customized report of the make and model of the car you want. This report tells you exactly what dealerships are paying for the car, thus eliminating the information gap that allows them to overcharge. Armed with this trump card, you literally call or email a bunch of dealerships (maybe 5–15) saying you know how much profit they'll make off a sale and you're ready to sign with whichever one will give you the lowest price. Then, just crack a chocolate milk and chillax while the bidding war ensues. If the $40 you spent at the beginning snags you a $1,000+ discount on a car, you'll feel like a straight-up maven.

Signing the Contract

Once you've got your price nailed down with a dealership, it's time to seal the deal. Unfortunately, there's one more round of BS deflection to get past. Here are some ways to avoid getting screwed over:

- **Make sure you get the best deal on financing.** Make sure you know how you are paying for the car and exactly how much it will cost you per month. See page 389 for more on financing.

Tips & Tricks: When to car shop

Knowing the ins and outs of an enemy organization is a key to success in consumer battles. In terms of cars, this means realizing that most car dealerships impose yearly and monthly quotas on their salespeople, so if you shop in December (or at least at the end of the month), you might find yourself the happy beneficiary of some desperate deal making. The same goes for any day that will clearly be a slow one for sales on the car lot. Check the forecast for blizzards, hail storms, hurricanes, and tornadoes—the worse the weather, the better your chances of saving money on a car.

Cars & Commuting

- **Beware of extras.** Know exactly what features you want, because the salesman will try to throw in as many unnecessary extras as possible.

- **Protect your credit.** Don't allow the dealership to run a credit check using your license or Social Security number before settling on a price, as this information may be used to screw you on incentives and interest rates. However, as we'll discuss in the financing section, your credit will determine the loan terms you can get, so you'll want to know where you stand ahead of time.

- **Watch out for the factory fib.** Cars ordered from the factory should not cost more than those in the lot. Also, be careful about letting the salesman locate the car at another dealership; they often charge an unnecessary fee.

- **Trust your gut.** You're probably not buying a limited-edition Jaguar. The car you want will still be there tomorrow, and you can find it elsewhere. If anything feels fishy, trust your instincts and walk away. Don't let a salesperson pressure you or toss around jargon you don't understand.

- **Read the small print.** Once the papers have been drawn up, feel free to take them away so that you can review them with a fine-toothed comb. Like congressmen, car salesmen have been known to "earmark" a few extra clauses in the final copy.

Congratulations, you are now a car owner! You are probably feeling very protective, and maybe you have even named your car something like "Don Juan DeMarco" or "Desert Storm." But before you put the pedal to the metal, you've got a few more things to sort out, so keep reading.

Purchasing New and Used Cars with Financing

Walking into the car dealership can be pretty intimidating for most recent grads, since looking at the sticker prices alone probably makes it seem like even the fugliest car on the lot is out of your league. But that's where financing comes into play. Automobile financing is when you take out a personal loan to purchase an automobile, thus transforming that heart-stopping $20,000 into a manageable down payment and a monthly payment with interest. Unless you happen to have $20Gs ready to deploy right now, financing options are crucial to your purchase. The car payment plan you negotiate will determine both the total cost of the car over the long term and, more to the point, how you'll pay it off each month. Typically, the way it works is you make the down payment, pay sales taxes upfront or roll them into your loan, and then pay an interest rate determined by your loan company. The first payment is due a month after you sign your contract.

The most important thing you need to know about car loans is that you don't have to take the one offered to you through the car company, so you should comparison shop aggressively. Check with your local bank, Edmunds.com, and Bankrate.com to see what terms and rates you can get. (Note: a used car loan will always carry a higher interest rate than a new car loan.) It may end up that you can get the best deal through the car company, but don't assume. The second key to financing is that, as with all loans, your credit will affect the interest rates you can get. And it makes a real difference. Say you've got a $20,000 car, and you're going to pay it off over four years with an 8% interest rate. That means you pay $488.26 a month. But if a worse credit score boosts your interest rate just 2%, you pay an extra $20 per month. And over the course of the loan, you'll end up spending about $1,000 more on the car. While it's not a deal-breaker, remember how large you can grow $1,000 through a conservative investment vehicle? (See page 323 for a refresher.) If you don't know your credit score or can't fathom why the hell this has anything to do with buying a Civic, go to page 284.

Leasing Cars

On the surface, it's pretty simple: When you lease, you make monthly payments in return for the privilege of driving a car a maximum number of miles over an agreed-upon time period, generally two to four years. In some ways it's like a

Cars & Commuting

super long-term car rental, but what you're really paying for is the *depreciation* of the car over the period you drive it—in other words, the difference between a vehicle's original value and its value at lease-end, also known as its **residual value.** (Not surprisingly, the best lease deals are on cars with the lowest depreciation ratings. More often than not, Japanese and German cars trump American cars in this respect. As a rule of thumb, cars with 24-month residuals equal to at least 50% of their original Manufacturer's Suggested Retail Price value are solid deals.)

You don't need an advanced math degree to figure it out how the actual monthly payment on a lease is determined, and it's worth understanding the basics so you can spot a sheisty salesperson when you see one. There are two elements to a lease payment: the **depreciation charge** and the **finance charge**. To figure out the monthly depreciation charge, start with the **capitalized cost,** or "cap cost," of the car. This figure is not the Manufacturer's Suggested Retail Price, but rather the final price you negotiate with the dealer (hopefully less than the MSRP). Then, simply subtract the residual value and divide by the number of months in your lease contract. And *voilà*, you've just figured out how the leasing company is going to charge you for depreciation.

The finance charge is just like the interest you pay on a loan—in the eyes of the leasing company, leasing you a car is just like loaning you money, so it wants you to pay for tying up its funds. To calculate the finance charge, add the cap cost and residual value, then multiply by the money factor. "What the hell's the money factor?" you say. It's the interest rate divided by 2,400. "Why do I add the cap cost and residual value—isn't that like paying double?" No, this equation is just an easy shortcut for a more complicated calculation. Unless you're really into math, we suggest you just use it and not ask questions!

In addition to the depreciation and finance charges, there will also be an acquisition fee when you first get the car, typically in the range of $600 to $1,000.

The reason it's important to know all of this is so that you can check that everything you negotiate with the dealer actually makes it into the contract. Predatory salespeople take advantage by agreeing to your offer (and maybe even pretending they're giving you some awesome deal because you're so cool and smart), but then—whoops—the agreed-upon price is not actually reflected in the lease contract. Unless you're some sort of mental mathlete, you're not going to catch this trickery unless you do your own calculations and make sure everything adds up.

Unfortunately, fudged leasing charges are just one of the many ways dealerships can try to pull a fast one on you if you don't understand the elements that make up a lease payment. To further protect yourself, check out Automotive. com's "Car Leasing FAQs" (link via gradspot.com/book), which includes a simple rundown of the most common schemes.

Buying a Leased Car: Is It Worth It?

In theory, it sounds like an ace idea: Test out a car by leasing it, then buy it if you really like it. However, you need to do some research to make sure it's a deal worth taking. Here's how to think about it: When you get your lease, it has written into it a "residual value"—as mentioned before, whatever the leasing company predicts the car will be worth at the end of the leasing term, based primarily on the make/model and an assumption about how much mileage you'll put on the car (12,000 miles per year is standard). Many leases also come with a "buyout" price attached to them, and that price is usually determined by the residual value. You probably see the game by now: If the car comes back worth *more* than the residual value, you stand to snag a good deal by buying the car outright (assuming you like it). Of course, you could always go look for a used car of the same make and model and maybe get a better price. But if you already feel comfortable with your leased car, why not just stick with what you know? A used car could have all sorts of problems you didn't anticipate, whereas the one you've been driving for two or more years is more of a known quantity.

Once the end of your lease term draws nigh, the easiest way to figure out if an option to buy is worth exercising is to plug the

> ### Tips & Tricks: Car maintenance
>
> Now that you're responsible for a heavy-duty piece of machinery, you need to treat 'er right. Filling up the back seat with fast food containers is one thing—that can be rectified. But skipping oil changes and driving around like a destruction derby contestant is going to hurt you big time when you attempt to sell the car or return it after your lease is up. If you're an owner, check out the car's maintenance schedule in the manufacturer's instructions, then stick to it. Also, keep records of each service so that you can pass them along as proof of your good behavior when you go to sell. If you're leasing, avoid racking up extras that you'll have to pay off at the end: Stay within your mileage limit, make sure you know your repair and maintenance responsibilities as a leaseholder, and get the car cleaned and waxed before taking it back to the dealership.

car's details into Edmunds or Kelley Blue Book to get the market value and then compare that number to the residual value. Is it the same or higher? If so, you may want to consider purchasing. Just don't forget to negotiate aggressively, because the dealer probably doesn't want the car back on the lot and may be willing to cut a deal to make it go away.

Car Insurance

Auto insurance is required by law in almost every state, so dealing with it is less an option than an obligation. There are two main aspects of car insurance: protecting your car and protecting yourself. Whether your car gets jacked from the lot or you get into an accident that dents both your fender and your forehead, you are going to be glad you're covered. Indeed, driving without insurance is one of the least intelligent things you can do—if you get caught (or worse still, you get hurt), you may incur heavy fines and bills, lose your license, or even go to jail. So, put that college-educated brain to use and do some research to find a policy that works best for you.

When it comes to car insurance, comparison shopping is absolutely essential. Rubrics for calculating premiums vary considerably across different providers— in *The Quarterlifer's Companion*, Todd Morgano of Progressive Auto Insurance points out that "the cost of a six-month auto insurance policy for the same driver with comparable coverage varies from company to company by an average of $586." That's pretty insane, and it should provide plenty of incentive to consider all the options. For example, can you get onto your parents' policy? This setup is required if the car is registered in their name, but it may also be a good idea if they receive a multi-car or multi-policy discount. Furthermore, if you already have a policy, make sure that you are not wasting money by leaving it unchanged. First of all, it's more expensive to insure a 16-year-old Danica Patrick wannabe than a 23-year-old with a clean license. Moreover, premium prices tend to fluctuate yearly no matter who you are—if a large number of people in a given group (e.g., age, type of vehicle, number of accidents) file claims in a

> **Tips & Tricks: Double coverage = double payment**
>
> Before perusing prices, check any other insurance policies that you hold (e.g., health insurance, renters insurance); you may already be covered for certain aspects of a car insurance policy. For example, a person with comprehensive health insurance would probably only need to purchase the minimum personal injury protection (PIP) coverage.

given year, everyone's rates rise. Thus, you may be able to find lower overall premiums or discounts elsewhere due to changes in age, location, and other factors that determine your rates.

If you do decide to make a change or go it on your own, here are some things to consider.

The Bare Bones Basics

Before picking up the phone for a "15-minute call to Geico", take some time to familiarize yourself with the different types of coverage.

- **Liability.** Required by 47 states, liability covers accidental bodily injury and property damages caused by you in an accident (e.g., the woman in the other car's broken butt bone and the neighbor's flattened fence).

- **Collision.** Not mandatory (but purchased by most), collision pays for any repairs to your car after an accident, from a bruised bumper to a busted trunk. It does not pay for damage to the other person's car.

- **Comprehensive.** Also optional but popular (like parmesan cheese or pants), comprehensive pays for losses that are not the result of a collision, such as fire or theft.

- **Medical.** Pays all medical expenses of those your car regardless of fault. Does not reimburse those insured for lost wages or replacement services.

- **Emergency Roadside Service.** Covers situations like fixing a flat, getting keys out of a locked car, running out of gas, or using a tow truck.

- **Gap Insurance.** As soon as a car is driven off the lot, its market value depreciates 20–30%. In the case of an accident or theft, gap insurance pays the difference between what you owe (the actual market price) and what the insurance company says the car is worth. For example, if a $25,000 car is totaled and you have collision but no gap insurance, the insurance company will pay $20,000 rather than the full $25,000 that you paid for it. It is generally offered only on new cars, and leased cars usually have it built-in.

Cars & Commuting

- **Personal Injury Protection (PIP).** Being a PIMP is illegal in all states except Nevada, but having PIP is required by some. It covers medical expenses and lost wages for insured drivers regardless of fault.

- **Uninsured Motorists.** Pays for car damage when an accident is caused by someone without liability insurance.

- **Underinsured Motorists.** Pays for car damage when an accident is caused by someone with insufficient liability insurance.

- **Rental Reimbursement.** Dinero for a rental if the wheels on the car can't go 'round and 'round. (Sometimes credit cards provide this coverage, so check to make sure you're not doubling up on the same thing.)

Figuring Out What to Expect

The average policy containing liability, collision, and comprehensive coverage costs about $775 per year. However, that figure is dependent on a number of things:

- **Type of car.** Sports cars, large SUVs, and really small cars like the Mini Cooper may be the jam, but beware of the higher premiums that accompany these types of automobiles.

- **Car features.** Anti-theft devices, airbags, anti-lock brakes, and automatic seatbelts warrant an automatic price reduction.

- **Theft history.** Models with bad reps get bad rates. Check out theft history to get an idea of how a car will fare on the street. (According to the National Insurance Crime Bureau, the "most stolen cars" in 2006 were the '95 Honda Civic, the '91 Honda Accord, and the '89 Toyota Camry.)

- **Location.** Areas with high accident rates or incidents of larceny raise prices. (We know what you're thinking, but don't do it. Lying about where you live will allow the insurance company to shaft you down the line.)

- **You.** Not all drivers are treated the same. For example, young single males can expect to pay more just for being young, single, and male. At least the bathroom line is shorter!

- **How often you drive.** Long commute? Price increase is absolute.

- **Credit report.** If you missed your last two card payments due to a drunken visit to the L.L. Bean website, it could increase your premium by hundreds.

- **Driving record.** Clean licenses result in lower premiums.

- **Discounts.** Most companies offer sizable student discounts to those who maintain certain grades. You can also save if you have multiple cars insured (unlikely) or if you hold a renter's insurance policy with the same company.

- **Deductible.** A deductible is the amount paid out of pocket before the insurance company kicks in cash. A higher deductible will mean a lower premium price, but it also means that you must fork over more of your own money in the case of a calamity. Deductibles are usually offered in amounts of $100, $250, $500, or $1,000.

Finding a Policy

The first step in the search for auto insurance is learning your state's minimum requirements. Since safe is always better than sorry, most people go beyond the minimum to ensure coverage for a variety of problems. Initially, getting quotes online is a quick and easy way to make comparisons without the pressure of an agent. Have on hand your driver's license number; the year, make, and model of the vehicle; and the vehicle identification number (VIN). Geico, Allstate, Progressive, and all the other companies you've seen on TV are worth checking out, but be sure to do as much comparison shopping as possible. You should start at Esurance.com to get quotes and compare company ratings and also try Netquote.com. During this process, gauge the level of coverage provided by each policy against these recommendations from About.com:

- Bodily Injury Liability: $300,000 per occurrence
- Property Damage Liability: $100,000 per occurrence
- Medical Payments: $10,000 per person
- Uninsured Motorist Bodily Injury: $300,000 per accident
- Uninsured Motorist Property Damage: $10,000 per accident

Cars & Commuting

- Collision Deductible: $500
- Comprehensive Deductible: $0-100

Insurance lingo to a recent grad can be like AIM-speak to your grandmother, so you may want someone who can answer questions and walk you through the process. If this is the case, consider getting off the 'net and into an insurance agent's office (locate agents in your area by going to company websites or using Automotive.com's "Agent Locator"). When you finally make a decision, don't get off the phone or leave the agency without knowing exactly what you're getting (i.e., how much you are paying, what your deductible is, and how you are covered). Finally, familiarize yourself with the correct protocol should anything go wrong. How you handle the scene of an accident can make a huge difference in whether or not your claim is accepted.

Mileage Chart: How Much Do You Need for Gas?

Once you have a car, the cost of gas can really add up from month to month. Assess your commuting patterns and then use this chart to determine how much you should expect to spend filling up each week.

Miles driven per week ▶	100	125	150	175	200	225	250
Miles per gallon ▼	Cost per week (assuming $3/gallon)						
10 MPG	$30.0	$37.5	$45.0	$52.5	$60.0	$67.5	$75.0
15 MPG	$20.0	$25.0	$30.0	$35.0	$40.0	$45.0	$50.0
20 MPG	$15.0	$18.8	$22.5	$26.3	$30.0	$33.8	$37.5
25 MPG	$12.0	$15.0	$18.0	$21.0	$24.0	$27.0	$30.0
30 MPG	$10.0	$12.5	$15.0	$17.5	$20.0	$22.5	$25.0
35 MPG	$8.6	$10.7	$12.9	$15.0	$17.1	$19.3	$21.4
40 MPG	$7.5	$9.4	$11.3	$13.1	$15.0	$16.9	$18.8

Car Checklist

Just to make sure you are completely road-ready, we've compiled a quick checklist of car issues to deal with before driving. However, be aware that each state has its own unique regulations and standards (e.g., you may need to get a safety inspection in addition to an emissions test), so it's always a good idea to visit the Department of Motor Vehicles to make sure that everything is ready to go. Also, as a general rule, just make sure your tags, insurance, and registration are up-to-date and you should be fine.

- **Driver's License.** Presumably you didn't forget this little detail. Head to the DMV if your license has expired or if you need a new one. Remember, if you have moved, you can get a driver's license in your new state of residence (which, in turn, can help you register to vote there, but is not always a requirement).

- **Roadside Assistance.** Tow coverage is something most drivers don't actively think about too much…until they break down or their tire goes out in the middle of the freeway, at which point it becomes the most important thing in the world. The majority of new and certified pre-owned cars have roadside assistance tucked into the purchase price, so check with the manufacturer for the limits on how long the free service lasts. (One caveat: A tow provided through an automaker's plan will take your car to the nearest dealership, where parts and labor are probably more expensive, unless they're under warranty.) Beyond that, there are many roadside assistance plans you can sign up for, including AAA and OnStar. When comparison shopping, make sure the plan covers you (as opposed to the car), look at statistics like the average response time per service call, and find out any out-of-pocket expenses you'd be responsible for after a breakdown.

- **Camera.** Get your "citizen journalist" hat on and start carrying a disposable camera in your glove compartment. Photos could be clutch when it comes time to file a claim for an accident or dispute a parking ticket.

- **Cell Phones.** Find out if it's legal to operate a cell phone while driving in your state before you get caught looking like an a-hole. If it is illegal, hook up some Bluetooth and blab all you want!

- **Emissions.** There should be a little sticker on your windshield that says your vehicle fulfills the state's emissions standards. If not, or if the expiration date on the sticker has passed, you need to contact the DMV to find your local emissions testing station. Ask about exemptions (some states exempt new vehicles), and make sure you don't get caught driving with an out-of-date sticker.

Cars & Commuting

- **Insurance.** Don't get on the road without insurance—it's illegal and dangerous. See page 392 to learn about choosing a policy.

- **Roadside Emergency Kit.** Make sure you have emergency items (and a spare tire) in the trunk in case of a breakdown. You can find a list of useful items at Edmunds.com, but you should at the very least have flares, jumper cables, a map, a tire inflator, two quarts of oil, a first aid kit, and a flashlight with extra batteries. You can buy preassembled car emergency kits for around $25 to $75, depending on how comprehensive they are.

- **License Plates.** Having license plates is necessary. Get them from the DMV for $25–50, but be prepared to pay extra if you want them to say "OMFG" or "BALLER." If you re-register in a new state (see below) and receive new plates, make sure you send the old ones back and notify the tax collector in the town where the car was originally registered—some states charge property tax on cars, so you want to avoid paying if you don't actually live there anymore.

- **Oil Changes.** Again, there should be a sticker on the windshield telling you the mileage mark at which you should get your next oil change. Keep an eye on the odometer and don't go too far over this mark. Midas, Jiffy Lube, and local garages can all handle this task, so don't be afraid to shop around. Also, be wary when they tell you about the five other things that they can do to fix up your car while you're there.

- **Parking.** Make sure you have a reasonable and secure place to keep your car, both at home and at work. Some cities and neighborhoods require resident parking permits for street parking. If so, you will need to contact City Hall and apply for a permit, a process that generally requires a driver's license from the state you're in and proof of residency (e.g., gas/electric bill, bank statement, cable bill). Pay all parking tickets on time to avoid getting clamped by "the boot."

- **Registration.** Hit the DMV to register your vehicle, and keep the registration with you in the car at all times. If you move and have a permanent address in your new post-college city, you should almost always register your car in that state to avoid citations and unnecessary fines. However, it is worth noting that car ownership is more expensive in some states than others (e.g., California is pricey because they are

Cars & Commuting

so "green"), so if you still have a permanent address in the state where you came from (e.g., mom and dad's house), you can also continue to register there. Check the state's DMV website to make sure you meet various restrictions.

- **Miscellaneous.** Do you have enough windshield washer fluid? What about antifreeze? An ice scraper (if necessary)?

Top Ten Ways to Be a Green Driver

According to the U.S. Environmental Protection Agency, driving a car is the worst thing that most people do for the environment during their lifetime. (Yes, even worse than using aerosol deodorants!) Here are ten easy ways to reduce the harm of riding, many of which have the added bonus of saving you money:

1) Drive less. Use public transportation or carpool. Better yet, take a walk or hop on your bike.

2) Drive smart. Speeding not only gets the cops on your tail, but it also attracts the wrath of Captain Planet because high speeds produce greater emissions. Heavy braking and rapid acceleration also reduce fuel economy, so try to develop a smooth, safe driving style.

3) Don't "top off." When you fill up a tank of gas, don't give it that extra little pump at the end—gas spillage is not a good look. Also, always make sure the gas cap is secured tightly.

4) Perform regular maintenance. Another factoid, courtesy of the National Safety Council: Poorly-maintained vehicles can release ten times the emissions of well-maintained ones. Follow the manufacturer's instructions for routine maintenance and look out for red flags like reduced fuel efficiency, leaks, and black exhaust billowing out of the back of your whip.

5) Get an eco-friendly car. If you're in the market for a car, newer cars are better for the environment than older ones (hence 2009's federally funded "Cash for Clunkers" program). Check the fuel efficiency rating and look

Cars & Commuting

into trendy cars that people like Larry David drive. (As a bonus, these "green" cars are often cheaper than their competitors.)

6) Use clean fuels. Using "oxygenated gasoline" and alternative energy sources like electricity is way better than burning through tanks of premium unleaded in your Hummer.

7) Cool it on the AC. Pumping the air-conditioning while crawling through city traffic can increase fuel consumption by over 20%.

8) Avoid idling. Idling is wasteful, so avoid the Wendy's drive-thru and L.A. traffic jams. Also, don't sit around in parking lots blasting Joan Jett like a chach.

9) Get good tires. If you want to look like you got your car from the set of a music video, buy 22-inch rims. If you want to make the world a better place, use radial tires because they offer less rolling resistance and thus improve fuel efficiency. Also, make sure tires are properly inflated at all times.

10) Cut the dead weight. Have you driven around with golf clubs and an old bag of cement in your trunk for the past nine months? Extra weight means reduced efficiency, so treat your car like a professional athlete and shed those pounds. ■

Cars & Commuting

Getting Around Without a Car

Not having a car means less worry and more money saved. And even if you have a car, you don't necessarily need to drive it everywhere you go. People always think having a cool car will get them laid, but how many people have you ever met in a car that you didn't explicitly invite in? Now think about how many dudes and dudettes you can meet on a single train ride. Exactly. Let's consider some practical alternatives for getting around when you don't own your own set of wheels.

Commuting to Work

Workdays can be trying enough without traffic to contend with, so that's at least one silver lining to a carless commute. And trust us, there are many others. Here are some alternative transportation options to explore:

Public Transportation. In a place like New York or Chicago, the combination of great public transportation and sky-high parking fees makes it easy to choose the subway over a new Subaru. But even in more car-dependent locales like Los Angles and Denver, there are train lines and buses galore. As noted in Chapter 2, you may have to make some deliberate choices about where you live if you want to take advantage of public transportation. Just remember that in most major cities, a bus is never that far away. Even if they don't go all the way to your office, they should at least provide an easy way to get to mass transit stations.

By Bike, by Foot, or by Rollerblade. We know all the stereotypes about rollerbladers—neon spandex, old-school Walkmans…propensity to call *Starlight Express* "Andrew Lloyd Webber's best work." But we never let a little ribbing get in the way of an economical commute. There are many ways to get around under your own power, and they have the added benefit of providing a little exercise. A 25 minute stroll to work in the morning can really get the blood flowing and foster a much sunnier disposition than implanting your nose in the next person's armpit on the subway. If you live close enough to work to pull this off, the two other factors to consider are weather and hygiene. If you live in a place with extreme heat or cold during certain parts of the year, do you have a viable alternative for those days when even Lance Armstrong would rather drive? Also, if the walk/ride is arduous enough for you to break a sweat, are there facilities at your workplace for you to shower? B.O. will make you the office pariah quicker than hanging a poster of Mussolini in your cubicle.

Carpools. Zipping down the HOV lane, reading the paper, sipping a fresh Dunkin' Donuts coffee—talk about the life! Websites like RideAmigos.com, iCarpool.com, and CarpoolConnect.com

Tips & Tricks: How to sell your car

If you are moving to a new city or just can't afford the cost of ownership anymore, you may be looking to sell your car. For some people, this maneuver might even be a necessary step toward funding a move. But before you write FOR SALE in dirt on your windshield, do some research to figure out how to keep things kosher and how to make the biggest profit from the sale of your ride. Contact the DMV to find out about transfer of title, registration, and all that good stuff. Then research how much models from the same year with similar mileage are going for in order to price your car correctly (try Edmunds' "True Market Value" pricing tool, and enter your car's details into Kelley Blue Book to get a suggested retail value). Finally, advertise it on Craigslist, AutoTrader.com, and in front of your house. Then sell to the highest bidder. Once you get paid, head straight for the border (or wherever it was that you were going).

match up commuters with compatible routes and schedules. You can also ask around at work to see if anyone carpools or uses one of these services. Another option is the "casual carpool," an intriguing idea that is becoming more common in the United States. It's basically like Craigslist's "Casual Encounters," only instead of sexual deviance, complete strangers offer you a ride in their cars so they can use the carpool lane. Rather than picking you up at your place, casual carpool networks tend to have predetermined pickup points (e.g., "weekdays at 7:30 am at the Mobil station on Powell St. between Admiral and Commodore") that you can literally just go to and find a ride. Casual carpooling is prominent in the Washington, D.C., area (where it's called "slugging"), San Francisco, Pittsburgh, Seattle, and many other cities. Search around for options in your area, and be sure to read up on the unofficial code of conduct that has cropped up in this carpooling subculture (e.g., only speak when spoken to, don't bring messy/smelly food and drinks in the car, and accept NPR as the official soundtrack). If you're the only one there to get a ride, be smart and feel free to say, "Thanks but no thanks, chief," when a complete stranger rolls up in a two-seater car.

Joy Riding and Weekend Trips

Sometimes the weekday commute from your house only involves a hop, skip, and a jump, but you still want the flexibility to cruise to the strip mall, hit up an amusement park, or visit your significant other every weekend. If your leisure car use is exceptionally sporadic, here are a few alternatives to leasing and buying:

Car Rentals. Although the costs of renting a car can add up quickly (watch out for the crazy taxes tacked on to the quoted price), it is a viable option for the occasional three-day weekend getaway. If you need wheels, try Thrifty, Enterprise, or Dollar Rent-a-Car. Most major rental agencies have a hefty surcharge for drivers under 24 or 25, which can really hurt a budget-conscious grad. Call ahead before booking to find out what the real rate will be and to inquire about insurance options. Rent-a-Wreck waives the underage surcharge, but don't be surprised if you get a car that Xzibit would laugh at on *Pimp My Ride*. Finally, check to see if your employer gets special rates with any car rental companies.

Car Sharing. In a perfect world, you would be able to "own" a car for the few days a month when you need it and you would never have to worry about parking or maintenance. This is exactly the idea behind car sharing companies like Zipcar and Flexcar, which offer access to a huge fleet of autos positioned around most major cities. Yearly memberships start at around $50, and an hour of car use runs less than $10. Before committing, check the sites to see if you live in an area with a high density of cars. When you need one, you just find out where it's parked and then use the access card provided by the company to get into the car. Note that while the hourly rates are low, Zipcars are best used for short drives and errands of a few hours. If you are going away for the weekend, a traditional rental is more economical.

Trains, Planes, and Buses. They may not be glamorous, but Amtrak trains and Greyhound buses are two convenient, affordable options for getting where you need to go. Also, check for other regional bus services, like the (in)famous "Chinatown" services connecting DC, Baltimore, Philly, New York, and Boston. Many cities are also serviced by affordable shuttle flights that run on the hour, so don't rule out flying, either. Check out our online travel resources at gradspot.com/book for more tips on finding cheap flights.

Cars & Commuting

Chapter IX: The Grad 2.0 Plan

The Grad 2.0 Plan

*Grad 2.0 \ **grād too point o** \, noun:*

> *(1) A college graduate who exceeds the minimum requirements of life after college. Interests may include cooking, dating, and self-education.*

> *(2) A well-rounded, engaged twentysomething who evokes the traditional qualities of Homo universalis (i.e., the Renaissance person).*

During the 15th century, there were men in Italy who were good at everything: sculpture, painting, rowing boats, extemporaneous speaking…the list goes on to include most activities. They were called Renaissance men, and they were so remarkable that the entire century was named after them.

There are many lessons we can learn from these historical figures. But one stands out: The path to enlightenment is not found through narrow focus, but rather through well-roundedness. This perspective is what galvanized Renaissance men as the preeminent humans of all time.

Today, we all know that too much of a good thing is not in fact a good thing, especially when it comes to booze and snack foods. Yet we tend to become narrow-minded in other respects. Take careers, for example—they are generally cast in a positive light, but if you're not careful, you'll suddenly find yourself 30 years down the line with high blood pressure, a sexless marriage, and a laundry list of regrets. Even in the first year out of college, many recent grads obsess painfully (and unnecessarily) over jobs, apartments, and all the other issues discussed thus far. Those things are important, no doubt. But all that "setting up your life" should be a springboard for actually enjoying it, not becoming consumed by it.

The point is that taking advantage of life beyond work should be par for the post-college links rather than an anomaly. Staying in touch with friends— whether at a bar, through reunions, or on Facebook—is just fun, while other activities like reading, cooking, and checking out your city's cultural offerings can accrue fringe benefits in your professional, social, and romantic life. It's now up to you to find all those things that were served up on a platter in college (e.g., knowledge, food, and a well-stocked dating pool).

Clearly, there's no need to become a whole new person, nor should you feel pressure to be "highbrow," whatever that even means. And as much as we think

Tony Robbins is weirdly handsome, we certainly don't want this chapter to sound like self-help. Approach it more as a collection of things that it took us a while to appreciate after graduating—a head start, if you will. The main theme of Grad 2.0 is balance: All that yin needs a yang, and we hope this chapter will help give some ideas about where to find it.

Coping with the One-Year Rut

Before we get into the fun stuff, a little P.S.A. is in order to let you know you where we're coming from with these Grad 2.0 shenanigans. Part of the idea has to do with embracing your new freedom, but to be honest, it's also about staying sane in the emotional pressure-cooker of life after college. Here goes…

No matter what stage of the post-college transition you find yourself at, it's almost inevitable for a "grass is always greener" mentality to creep into play at some point. For one thing, missing college is totally normal. But there are also plenty of more complex reasons for hitting a rut. The people who have been working begin to feel burnt out and wonder if they should have taken time off. The ones who took time off fear that they have fallen behind. And the rest feel like they have toed the line between work and relaxation without fully accruing the benefits of either. The fact is that, to a certain extent, every recent grad is at the bottom of the totem pole, and that can suck. It can also be intimidating to adapt to environments populated primarily by older, more experienced people rather than by your peers. As a result, some grads even fall victim to "Imposter Syndrome": feelings of fraudulence and an irrational fear of being "exposed" as inept or incapable (see page 265).

If you are suffering an extended malaise, you are certainly not alone—whether they are willing to admit it or not, most grads experience some degree of discontentment by the 12-month mark. It's easy to become overwhelmed with the responsibilities and choices of post-college life, and these concerns can lead to exaggerated fears about the future. If you can barely juggle a boyfriend, an internship, and an apartment, how are you ever going to be able to handle marriage, kids, and mortgages? People do it, and so will you (if that's what you want). But you are probably not at that stage in your life yet, so why worry? Getting bogged down in the small stuff will only drive you crazy, as will thinking too far ahead. Instead, try focusing on means rather than ends and setting practical, achievable benchmarks for yourself (e.g., "How can I get my next story published?" rather than "Why am I not the editor of the *New Yorker*?").

Socially, the reality of post-grad life begins to sink in as it grows harder to stay in touch with friends, and demanding work schedules make dating and hanging out much more difficult than they were in college. Jealousy can also rear its ugly head, and it's definitely worth keeping that in check—just because your friend in a different industry got her first promotion already doesn't mean that you should have done the same. Rather than bemoaning this state of affairs, make a concerted effort to reconnect with old friends or go visit them in the cities where they've settled. Friendships and romantic relationships may require more work than they used to, but they can also be more rewarding as a result.

We won't lie: Post-college life isn't all fun and games. But remember that it's a time of *transition*. Embracing your Grad 2.0 potential in the ways suggested throughout this chapter will definitely help you to enjoy yourself and take some of the attention off work, roommate problems, and anything else that's getting you down. Rest assured that people bounce back from the struggles of this transitional phase, often with a new sense of purpose and recalibrated goals. How do we know this? Because we went through it ourselves, as did most of our friends. And you and your friends probably will as well. That's the point—it's nothing new and just like everyone before you, you'll bounce back. The important thing is that during "the rut" you maintain the perspective that you are not the victim of a massive anti–recent grad conspiracy—"the rut" is normal, and you're in control of your own life, so get out there and do your thing.

Staying Cultured

Recent grads who spend all of their time stressing about jobs, apartments, and credit card bills are sort of like those kids who spent all four years of college cloistered away in the math library. But while it's taboo to hate on huge nerds, transition-obsessed grads definitely get no love. After all, the newfound freedom of post-grad life should *expand* your capacity to pursue cultural endeavors, not limit it. No matter how brilliant and interesting the students were at your alma mater, college was probably a bit culturally insular since studying and partying trumped all other activities. Even though you probably have less free time now than you did in school, you may find that you have more flexibility in deciding how to use it. Now is the time to finally dig into new topics, not because they'll help your GPA or career prospects, but just because they interest you.

Oftentimes, the term *cultured* carries a lot of implicit value judgments about what counts as "culture." But as we like to say, "He who likes Zac Efron movies shall not throw stones." If you are into classical music, Impressionism, and ballet, then by all means foster those interests. However, if you're into German graffiti and late-eighties heavy metal, then don't feel you have to get into Handel. No one should be afraid to branch out and try something new from time to time, but at the end of the day, upgrading to Grad 2.0 is really just about doing things that *aren't* work. And while it's nice to go a step beyond *US Weekly* and *The Hills* from time to time, don't feel that traditional "high culture" is the only holy grail worth pursuing.

Things to Do

There are countless ways to be a cultured grad, and they don't all include looking at an upside-down urinal and pretending it's a magnificent *object d'art*. From museums to book clubs and cultural events, there are tons of places to see and things to do other than drinking a shot of beer every time someone drops an F-bomb in *Scarface* (fun about once every two years). And if you can leverage your student ID (p. 414) and cultural freebies, doing this stuff doesn't have to break the bank.

Museums & art galleries. Appreciating art does not have to involve flipping through flashcards and poring through semi-illegible notes. Why not get out there and enjoy it on your own terms? (As you know, it always looks better in real life than it does in the textbook.) A lot of museums are free (or free to

> **Tips & Tricks: How to find things to do**
>
> Finding interesting things to do around your city is not as difficult as it seems—you just need to know where to look. Start where our generation always starts, on the 'net. Browse local blogs (e.g., the Gothamist blog network), and sign up for email lists from your favorite institutions (e.g., bars, museums, concert venues). If you're brave enough to venture offline, check out the events section of the free local papers that are handed out at delis, coffee shops, and bars, or pick up local magazines with cultural listings.

the employees of many major corporations if you show your ID), and new exhibitions rotate through the halls several times a year. Many museums also offer free or very inexpensive lectures on topics ranging from the Renaissance masters to Pixar animation, or weekly classes taught by professors and historians. *But hey, I thought you said no more "learning"!?* In an attempt to get us twentysomethings through the doors, many museums offer free days and monthly parties where you can appreciate art, grab a drink, and maybe even find a date. If you are really into the scene, you can also get on the art gallery circuit. Better yet, stop by openings, where you'll often find an open bar and hors d'oeuvres, not to mention a lot of interesting and/or hilariously pretentious people. It's a great place to socialize or bring a date. To stay abreast of openings, just sign up for a gallery's newsletter, usually on its website.

Events at bars. Bars aren't just places to drink and pretend to watch sports while staring at people lecherously; many bars also hold monthly events such as poetry readings, art shows, trivia nights, and discussions on prearranged topics (e.g., time travel at a meeting of the Secret Science Club). The best way to find out about these types of events is by reading blogs, local magazines, and newspapers. You can even check to see if your favorite bars have websites with event calendars.

Organizations/Charities. Many charity events (particularly the ones called "galas" or "balls") have the reputation of being overly ostentatious, but it's important not to let the snootiness of some attendees overshadow the objective. Even though attending may cost more than a regular night out at a bar, at least you're supporting a good cause. In addition, everyone will be dressed to the nines, and it's a nice place to meet people if packed dive bars and dance floor conversations aren't your style. If you're more interested in the cause than the party, why not go ahead and volunteer? There are charities to fit anyone's interests, from working for a religious center to supporting the local public library or children with terminal illnesses. (See page 432 for more ways to contribute to charity.)

Concerts/Operas. You probably won't forget to see your favorite band, but don't rule out shows at smaller venues and local music festivals. Want a classy night out? Consider visiting the local philharmonic or opera. While ticket prices can hurt your bank account, rehearsals are usually free, and venues tend to sell tickets

Tips & Tricks: Finding new music in your post-grad city

If you're into music, one of the best parts about starting life in a new city is exploring the local scene. With record sales plummeting, acts are touring more than ever, which is good news for fans who like to see live shows. You can look for gigs listed in local magazines, but it's also wise to figure out some small to mid-sized venues that seem to cater to your tastes and sign up for their email newsletters to stay abreast of upcoming shows. If you're looking for new acts to follow, independent radio stations and music blogs are a great source of inspiration. Classics like Seattle's KEXP (streaming at kexp.org) and Los Angeles's KCRW (kcrw.org) constantly feature new artists, and many other cities have similar radio stations—often the local college stations—with live performances, concert news, and even exclusive deals on special events. And, of course, there are tons of places to listen to music for free online. If you don't have your own go-to websites yet, check out Hypem.com, Imeem.com, GrooveShark.com, Pandora.com, and MySpace artist pages.

at highly discounted prices the day of the performance (check each venue's website for details). Also, it never hurts to flash a student ID if you've still got one.

Film. There's more to film than Will Ferrell and CGI animals. Museums often show an interesting lineup of documentaries and other special-interest films that don't make it to the major cineplexes, and smaller independent theaters will give you a chance to brush up on your French (or your reading, as the case may be).

Sports/Parks. The fact that we now spend the majority of our days in stale, climate-controlled environments is all the more incentive to get out and enjoy the outdoor public spaces that your city has to offer. Watch street performers, bang a bongo in a drum circle, or just enjoy nature. Many parks also have sports leagues, courts, and fields that can be rented out by individuals or teams. There's always a range of leagues for everyone from novices to wannabe pro athletes, so make sure to check out local rags, league websites, and gyms. If you're not a team sports type of person, you can still search for running and biking clubs so you can meet new people and get motivated when you train.

Rediscover the Joy of Reading

A bizarre thing happens when you leave school—suddenly, you actually want to read all those novels and articles you were assigned in college rather than skimming them before class or stopping after the first five pages. In spite of ourselves, we all have that little rebellious streak in our minds telling us not to take orders. But without any assignments on your plate, it's easier to find time to read what you want, or at least snatch moments throughout the day (e.g., your daily commute) to dig into a book, magazine, or blog. At the very least, you can spend an absurd amount of time creating a list of books that will single-handedly make you incredibly wise and learned, as is the time-honored recent grad tradition. First up: *The Fountainhead*!

In addition to reading whatever the hell you want, it's worth tracking down relevant industry papers (e.g., the *Deal* for the

> **Tips & Tricks: The joy of podcasts.**
>
> If you have an MP3 player, subscribing to a free podcast is a great way to get news while multi-tasking. The *New York Times* has a whole slew of options, including one called "Front Page" that summarizes the major headlines every morning in about five minutes. BBC and CNN both offer a large lineup as well, though if you want to put your trust in some people who really know radio, NPR has the podcast game on lock. Getting a longer, weekly show like *Weekend Edition* and trying to listen to it in segments at the gym or during your commute will keep you well-informed as well. Depending on what your job entails, you could even listen at your work station while filling in Excel spreadsheets or mindlessly entering data.

investment banking industry or *WWD* for women's retail) once you've started your job. While the annual subscription rate might be steeper than that of *People*, having a subscription to an industry-specific publication will keep you in the know and possibly even give you a leg up on your coworkers or other job hunters. Another great way to stay on top of industry news is through Twitter (see page 215 for tips on finding the relevant people to follow).

Finally, don't forget the news. College can be a bit of a cultural bubble, and it was easy to get so wrapped up in writing term papers and partying with your friends that you literally had no idea what's going on in the world. You may already be a newshound, in which case you can tell us to piss off. But if not, there are plenty of painless ways to get your daily dose of news, including free daily headlines sent to your inbox from sources like Slate.com and the *Wall Street Journal*. If nothing else, a little current affairs savvy will help dispel the myth among older colleagues that our generation doesn't care about anything.

The Grad 2.0 Plan

Ways to Use Your Student ID

It may feel like the advantages of being in college (like sweatpants-all-the-time and sleep) have suddenly disappeared in a puff of smoke. But before cranking up "Glory Days" and shredding all college memorabilia in a violent fit of denial, know that there's one item not to scrap: your student ID card. You spent most of college trying to pretend you were 21; now you have to act like you're back in college to get deals on all sorts of Grad 2.0 goodies. Wearing shorts with writing across the buttocks will help, but ultimately the key is getting creative with your student ID, a magical piece of plastic that can help you save big in the real world (we're talking actual money, not dining hall points). Don't feel bad about this white lie—just claim you believe you're still a "student" in the European sense of the word (i.e., poor). Or get cracking on your own "D.I.Y. Education" (p. 418) and then you'll technically be a student in your own personal *L'école du Stuff I Want to Know*.

Note: If you're in grad school, you don't have to worry about faking the funk. And if you haven't yet left college, it's probably worth getting a new ID before you leave so you have one that doesn't look like it's been through four years of swiping already.

Tried and True

The following places are pretty lenient about offering student discounts. Remember the drill: Flash and proceed. Flash and proceed. Cool as a cucumber, you are.

Museums. Whether you're an art fiend checking out a Degas at the Getty in L.A. or an oddity fiend viewing the largest human colon at the Mutter in Philly, museums nationwide offer discounts and even free admission for students (or pretend ones).

Movies. If necking with the date you met at the museum isn't reason enough to go to the movies, a reduced fee should add some incentive.

Performing arts. Ballet, opera, symphony, theater, concerts—discounted tickets are often box-office-only, but the options are limitless.

Tourist attractions. View the world's largest Pez dispenser or smallest working sawmill—all at a reduced price!

Local businesses. If you live near a college campus, many restaurants, bars, and bookstores offer cheaper or tax-free goods. Support their business and save enough to support that coffee habit.

Worth a Shot

Getting these deals with an expired student card might be a stretch, but this is the real world, where smoke and mirrors can be the secret to your success.

Clothes. Just because you're no longer a student doesn't mean you can't dress like one. Retailers like J. Crew offer reduced rates to students (until graduation). As far as your wardrobe is concerned, if you hit upon the right salesperson, graduation may never come.

Vacation Deals. STA, Student Universe, and Travelosophy all offer student discounts on flights, hotels, packages, and tours. Consider getting an International Student Identity Card (ISIC), which offers savings everywhere from Seattle to Switzerland (and it's just $22 a year). The same company also has an International Youth Travel Card for non-students under 26. Go to Isic.org for more information.

Trains. Amtrak offers 15% off, but not only do you need a college ID, you must have either a Student Advantage Discount card or an International Student Identity Card. But just as two negatives multiply to produce a positive, two expired IDs can occasionally add up to one cheap train ride.

Buses. This form of travel is generally inexpensive to start with because it is about as fun as a Brazilian wax, but Greyhound offers 15% off tickets and 50% off shipping for students. The snag? You need a Student Advantage Discount card in order to get the deal.

Apple Store. You need Mac Books, iPods, and iPhones like nobody's business, but fundage is limited. Luckily, Apple offers student discounts, and the word in the blogosphere is that, if you hit upon the right salespeople, they barely check to make sure your student status is legit. If at first you don't succeed, try another Apple store.

Bank Accounts. Most banks offer no-fee accounts for students. Most banks also check to see if you're really a student. The good news: If you set one up when you really were a student, you can probably coast for years to come.

The Grad 2.0 Plan

Moving and Storage. If you're moving or storing stuff, inquire about potential student discounts. If you're like many grads, moving is going to become a major theme in your life over the coming years. The fact that you're moving from college or your parents' house might be a dead giveaway, but whatevs—no harm in trying.

Cell Phones. Beware: A lot of cell phone companies claim to have student discounts when what they're really offering is just a plan geared towards college-aged kids (more text messages, free ringtones, an anti-drunk dial device, etc.).

Public Transportation. Major cities sometimes offer major reductions on subway and bus cards. Don every item of university paraphernalia available and hand the attendant the card while singing the school's fight song. If "Hail to the Victors" does not make you victorious, nothing else will. (Note: You could get fined pretty badly for this one.)

Other Cards. The Student Advantage Discount Card only costs $20 a year and offers 20,000 discounts online and nationwide at places like Urban Outfitters, Dell, Barnes & Noble, Target, and Amtrak. Also, check in with your alma mater to see if they provide any discount cards for their graduates. UCLA offers special rates on plastic surgery, so you never know!

The Reunion Grad
by GRITZ

After college, one of the major changes to your social calendar will be the preponderance of reunion-oriented events that begin to crop up. Beyond the unforgettable Fifth Year High School Reunion, there's the football rivalry weekend, the freshman dorm get-together, the model congress rendezvous, and quality time with that family you started during your year abroad in Brazil. All of these reunions present a potential viper's nest of awkward situations and uncomfortable conversations. To keep your head above the fray, be sure to heed:

Gradspot's Reunion Commandments

Thou shalt not be the first to ask, "What are you up to now?" It's inevitable. You know it's coming. But you still don't want to be the one to admit you have nothing else to say. If someone asks you, then you are sort of obliged to reciprocate, but at least you can join in with the knowledge that you held out for a higher ground. A good tactic is to find an odd feature of the surroundings and comment on it—"James, look up there. Did you ever notice that remarkable gargoyle in all our years here!?" If you walk away soon after, you will leave the impression that you are now hilarious and maybe slightly insane.

Thou shalt not talk about thy job for over 60 seconds. It's amazing to me that when it comes down to it, people barely know what their best friends do at work. No matter how much they try, no one truly cares enough to figure it out. So the chance of being even remotely interested in what a casual acquaintance does is highly unlikely. As a corollary, it is reasonable to make up stories and spread various falsehoods about your life to spice up the proceedings.

Thou shalt not treat thy reunion as therapy. Apologizing for something that happened years ago is mad awkward, as is describing to people in intimate detail about how depressed you are. Keep it light—reunions are long, and you can't really afford to drag the mood down.

Thou shalt not get blackout drunk. This is controversial, but hear me out. There are some people you expect to wild out, and when you see them you'll laugh and say, "That dude is so good at partying!" But you don't want to be that dude. To most people, getting insanely wasted suggests that you are depressed and have adjusted horribly to life after college. Not a good look.

Thou shalt not blow up other people's spots. A lot of drunk people with very little to talk about are the WD-40 that keeps the gossip mill running. "Is your old roommate still addicted to heroin?" "Did you hear that James is a convicted sex offender?" People will pry at you for information about others, and you may even let things slip unwittingly amidst the mayhem, but it's a losing game. Better to just say that everyone's "doing great" and leave it at that.

Thou shalt not assume that everyone is the same as they used to be. Some people who used to be complete jerks may very well still be jerks, but at least give them a shot at redemption. This works best for high school, especially once the open bar kicks in—the biggest meatheads probably drank a lot in high school, but now they've had at least five

D.I.Y. Post-College Education

Unless you decide to go to grad school (p. 161), you may experience pangs of guilt about whether or not you fully took advantage of your college experience. "Uh oh," you might think to yourself while watching *Are You Smarter Than a 5th Grader?* "Has my window for enrichment passed me by in a haze of whippets and '80s parties?" Of course not. As Mark Twain once said, "I have never let my schooling interfere with my education." Now you have the opportunity to set a precedent for a lifetime of learning, and this time, there's no homework or tuition!

A little digging around online can reveal an endless fount of free content covering almost any topic imaginable, from the intellectual (e.g., university lectures) to the practical (e.g., how to fold a shirt like a Japanese store clerk). Even beyond your computer screen, there are plenty of ways to flex your brain muscles without paying tens of thousands of dollars for the privilege. Here are some great places to get your D.I.Y. education off the ground. **Some of the following URLs are too long to include here; to find these links and even more great resources, head to gradspot.com/book.**

College Redux

Justice (justiceharvard.org). The most popular class at Harvard is now available to everyone thanks to a partnership with Boston public television and a great website. The class broadly covers the question, "What is the right thing to do?" Through the lecture videos, you'll learn about the philosophies of such pivotal thinkers as Immanuel Kant, Aristotle, John Locke (no, not the dude from *Lost*), and John Stuart Mill, then watch as Professor Michael Sandel and a bunch of Harvard kids debate issues like affirmative action, abortion, and whether or not it's okay for Abercrombie & Fitch to hire only hot people.

Academic Earth (academicearth.org). Free video courses from leading universities, broken down by subject, university, and lecturer. Watch a Yale class on the Old Testament or find out what Guy Kawasaki has to say about entrepreneurship at Stanford.

100 Podcasts from the Best Colleges in the World. It's funny how much easier it is to listen to a lecture when you're not busy swinging crude text messages to your friend across the auditorium. Why not download an educational podcast once in a while and listen to it on the way to work or in the gym? Choose from subjects such as "The Future of the Internet," "Italian Culture," "Nintendo: A History of Innovation," and "String Theory." Or just keep listening to "Poker Face" instead. Whatever floats your boat.

Ten Places to Get Free Online Business Courses. If you listen to that guy from *Wired*, giving stuff away for free is the greatest business model of all time. So when places are giving away free lessons on everything from starting your own business to marketing, networking, and nonprofit management, we're inclined to think they probably know what they're talking about.

Ten Universities Offering Free Writing Courses Online. Some people think writing can't be taught, while others challenge that it might just be the key to unlocking the talent that's waiting to explode. Instead of investing $100K in grad school to find out, try checking out a UCLA screenwriting course or MIT's "Introduction to Fiction."

Free Berkeley Courses. The left-leaning university offers free video and MP3 lectures from a wide range of courses, including Chemistry and the Roman Empire.

The Gilder Lehrman Institute of American History (gilderlehrman.org). Fancy yourself a bit of a history buff? The Gilder Lehrman Institute was created in 1994 for the express purpose of "promoting the study and love of American history." It's not a college, but it does offer over 50 free podcasts and video lectures on the founding fathers, the Civil Rights Movement, and everything in between.

General Education

LibraryChick.com. This utterly overwhelming page is like an all-you-can-eat buffet of self-education. Check out free textbooks, audio books, and resources from this beneficent librarian. There's even an "Online Learning" section

The Grad 2.0 Plan

featuring links to courses, tutorials, and more.

The 60-Second Lectures. Every fall and spring, professors at the University of Pennsylvania are asked to give one-minute lectures on any topic of their choosing. Sometimes they run a little bit over, but for bite-sized snippets of high-minded intellectualism (topics range from the human brain to JFK's sex life), this archive is a great place to waste some time.

BigThink.com. Cut through the hot air of talking heads and commentators by finding out what "ideas" politicians, thinkers, and other doers have about the topics you care about. Check out short videos on everything from John McCain's thoughts on terrorism to Moby's advice for young musicians.

TED.com. Authors, politicians, designers, and other people with "ideas worth spreading" meet at conferences in Long Beach, CA, and Oxford, England, each year to give talks lasting about ten to 20 minutes on whatever they want. They all go up on TED's fantastic website, where you can watch Al Gore talk about climate change or see "mathemagician" Benjamin Arthur race a team of calculators to solve problems.

Fora.tv. More big names talking about big ideas. As the site explains, "We gather the Web's largest collection of unmediated video drawn from live events, lectures, and debates going on all the time at the world's top universities, think tanks and conferences." Deepak Chopra on the afterlife of Michael Jackson? Yes, please.

Lifehacker.com. Leading the charge in the "efficiency movement" is Lifehacker, a site where you can procrastinate for hours learning a thousand and one ways to…stop procrastinating. Irony aside, it features tons of great tips, as well as frequent links to how-to and free education sites.

Skill-Building

Learn a language. We all know the best way to learn Spanish is to go live in Spain (or El Paso). But whether you're trying to brush up your skills or start from scratch, there are plenty of online tools to help you get the ball rolling. Check out MyLanguageExchange.com to find native speakers who will be your email/text/video-chat pen pal. Also worth checking out is LiveMocha. com, which offers free online classes and the chance to interact with other speakers. If you're just looking for a little vocab building, Learn10.com will email you ten new words a day in whatever language you want.

Learn computer skills. Web skills are pretty bankable these days (see page 152 for more on freelance programming), and who knows—one day knowing computer languages could be just as important as knowing foreign languages. W3Schools.com has free web-programming tutorials that look pretty basic but definitely do the trick for beginners. For a monthly fee of $25/month (or $250/year), Lynda.com offers a wide variety of tutorials covering programming, design, Photoshop, Flash, digital photography, and much more. WebMonkey.com is the original free resource for web developers, offering a comprehensive list of tutorials and an easy-to-search "code library." Of course, you can always just try Googling what you want to learn along with the words "how to" or "tutorial."

Learn random skills. Want to know how to avoid wrinkles, start a fire with a battery, and fold a shirt correctly? Check out Howcast.com, Instructables.com, 5min.com, and VideoJug.com for short videos and posts on all sorts of stuff—both practical and useless.

Offline

One aspect of college you might be surprised to miss is the classroom environment—not so much the tests and grades, but rather the opportunity for discussion and shared learning. The good news is you can find similar settings in post-grad life. Head to your local library or look at ReadersCircle.org and Meetup.com to find book clubs and other intellectually driven groups, or just start your own with friends and colleagues. Libraries, as well as local museums and other cultural centers, are also a great place to find free lectures and events, and you can always look through local publications for interesting events in the area.

If you're willing to shell out a little money for the cause of self-improvement, try searching online and contacting local schools to find continuing education courses, language classes, or writer's workshops. Cooking classes are also increasingly popular, either through culinary institutes, up-market grocery stores, or other learning centers. In addition to learning something useful, you'll meet new people in a setting that's both encouraging and more diverse (especially age-wise) than your average college classroom. And if there's an offbeat skill or topic you want to pursue, it shouldn't be hard to find a reasonably priced tutor to help you out via Craigslist. Yurt-construction, anyone?

The Grad 2.0 Plan

Dating

The transition to life after college is hard enough without the added complication of figuring out how to woo potential mates. In some ways, dating will never be as easy as it was in college (although would you actually call what you did in college "dating?"). If we remember correctly, a combination of raging hormones, close quarters, and socially acceptable binge drinking meant that people were hooking up left and right. This is all well and good, but the transition to real life provides a great opportunity to meet people beyond the confines of the keg room. For some, it can be a rude awakening; for others, it's a breath of fresh air.

Beyond actually finding dates, one of the biggest challenges of post-college dating is simply making the time. Once you start working, your free time becomes more precious than ever, and it can be frustrating to waste it on one dud after another. In fact, some people become so career-oriented in their twenties that they only look for casual relationships, keeping any emotional investment that would take up too much time and energy at arm's length. Others feel like they need a stable relationship to counteract all the other uncertainties of life after college.

Honestly, we can't really get into all that—this isn't Dr. Phil! Relationship advice is a dish best served by friends. But before you throw on your "going-out shirt," we wanted to bring up some key aspects of post-college dating that tend to catch recent grads off guard.

Expanding the Dating Pool

In college, almost every class, party, and trip to the dining hall was a chance to lay the groundwork for a potential hook-up. Indeed, some people didn't even need to venture outside the dorm to find a little sugar and spice. In the post-college world, the demanding schedules of working life and the lack of communal living spaces can make it much harder to meet potential mates. The upside, however, is that you are likely to meet a broader range of people.

Ever wanted to date a musician? A cougar? A banker? An illegal alien? A dental hygienist? Now's the time to experiment. Just avoid going too young or too old—one is illegal and the other is just creepy.

Keeping an Open Mind

Many recent graduates say the hardest part about post-college dating is figuring out how, when, and where to meet people. You may find yourself wondering why dating seems to require so much effort and strategy. After all, you're young, you're cool, you're pretty good looking…what's the problem?

Often, it's a matter of expectations. It's possible that you and so-and-so will lock eyes and fall in love while reaching for the same box of Trader Joe's Os, but it's unlikely. While relationships may develop naturally for some people, others have to be a bit more creative. Picking up strangers in bars is not for everyone (nor is it as easy as it looks), and even more structured social scenarios can leave a lovelorn grad wondering how to make the first move. Without a built-in social scene at your disposal, you might have to think outside of the box when on the prowl.

The key is to stay open-minded about how and when you might meet people. In college, you may not have thought to put out the vibe until you were three drinks in on a Saturday night. In the real world, you are more likely to meet someone interesting when you least expect it: when helping a friend move into her apartment, or when your boss sends you to pick up a document from someone with a cute assistant, for example. You don't have to start dreaming about what your children will look like or whether a hottie is "open to adoption" every time you meet someone new, but keep in mind that sometimes love can bloom in the least likely (and most awkward) of situations.

Prime Prowling Grounds

If you know you're in the mood to dip into the dating pool, try attending cultural events, joining co-ed sports leagues, getting involved in your school's local alumni association, volunteering at a local nonprofit, or attending readings, screenings, performances, and lectures. Zeroing in on an activity or subject you love is a great way to connect with people who share your passion. Think about it: If you're hoping to find a girl who loves kickball as much as you do, your chances of meeting her are better if you actually join a kickball team (it can be one of those drunken-Sunday-afternoon ones, if that makes things easier). If you want a guy who appreciates art, start attending art openings and try to join a committee at a local museum or gallery. Bonus: When you're passionately pursuing your own interests, you appear that much more attractive to other people, and if no flames are lit you won't feel you wasted time doing something you didn't actually want to do. MeetUp.com is a great site for finding groups whose interests align with yours—from cyclists to classic film buffs, artisanal beer lovers to design junkies.

Online Dating

Young grads often make love connections through Facebook. If you fancy yourself a "Computer Love" aficionado, there is also the next level—online dating sites. These are a great source of contention among recent grads. To some, they are sketchy and sad—an admission that you've hit rock bottom and are ready to throw caution to the wind. To others, they make total sense. We live so much of our lives on the Web, and we're as adept as ever at making basic judgments about people from their online profiles, so why not move the awkward flirty stage of dating to the 'net to cut out a lot of hassle? The stigma is definitely fading—in 2006, a Pew Poll reported that 31% of adults in America knew someone who had used an online dating service, and the popularity of online dating continues to rise.

If this approach appeals to you, start by visiting the most popular sites like PlentyofFish.com, Match.com, eHarmony.com, and Yahoo! Personals. There are also options catering to individual preferences, such as a JDate.com (for Jewish singles), Adam4Adam.com (for gay guys), and Lesbotronic.com (for gay girls). In all cases, just remember why you're using these sites: The point is to expand your potential dating pool and eventually turn some of the connections you make into *offline* dates. It's easy to get bogged down in "winks" and other silly features without ever meeting anyone in the flesh.

Another option for efficiency freaks is speed dating, which offers the ability to meet a ton of people in a very short period of time. You may not fall in love, but you'll inevitably gain some stories that you can later use to regale your chums (and their single friends). Check out 8minutedating.com and HurryDate.com for events in your area.

Confessions of a Match.com User
by Arnold T. Pants

In an effort to meet women and expand my daily activities beyond reading, writing, rap concerts, and basketball games, I have joined Match.com. I have high hopes…well, not really. DC was recently voted as having an only slightly less unattractive population than Philadelphia, where most people look like Rocky Balboa used their face as a punching bag. Now, I am certainly no Fabio, but I am reasonably handsome. A few women have "winked" at me. I have "winked" back at some. I have even sent some introductory emails, which, for the most part, have yielded no response.

Could it be my tag line, "Moderately Interesting Man Seeks More Interesting Woman"? Could it be that I list my occupation as "Very Minor Internet Celebrity"? I mean come on—my blog on SocialConsumer.com is massive (at least in a very small niche). Perhaps it is just that I have uploaded only one picture.

Speaking of pictures, I find it troubling that, on a dating site, women post pictures of themselves hanging on OTHER MEN. Is this supposed to attract me? I am not interested in threesomes! (Not that kind, at least.) I will also judge a lady based on whom I perceive her to have been with in the past. Greasy-haired dude with striped shirt and black shoes? I will flat out assume she has questionable taste.

Another odd feature of these pictures is the preponderance of vacation shots. They are always of a beach. Do these women ever go anywhere interesting? They always list "travel" as a favorite hobby, yet they all seem to have been to Italy, the beach, and the beach. Personally, I would never list "travel" as a hobby. It seems ridiculous. And, I am convinced that if I list the places I have visited in the last year (Memphis, Vegas, Little Rock, Charleston, Boston, London, Oxford, Atlanta, New York, etc.) it would just make me look like I sell some weird stuff.

Most of the women list their drinking habits as "Social, one or two," and then have loads of pictures of themselves drinking giant margaritas that are in fact four or five drinks. As someone who has spent the last 18 months transitioning from an antisocial alcoholic guy to an antisocial sober guy, I find this troubling.

The Grad 2.0 Plan

Confessions of a Match.com User continued…

Selecting "turn-ons" from a finite list has also distressed me. Can I only be excited by flirting, public displays of affection, money, power, body-piercing, and skinny-dipping? Coincidentally, the first time I made out with a girl, she suggested skinny-dipping and I said, "Why don't we just get naked here?" Then we awkwardly fooled around on a lakeside dock. I guess that is another story altogether and I suppose skinny-dipping means that you are interested in risk-taking. On the whole, this is a pretty good trait.

Turn-offs are basically chosen from the same list. I simply selected body piercing, and then realized that on Match, all piercing (including ear) is considered body piercing. "Talking with one's mouth full" was not an option and neither was "wearing Ugg boots." The limits of Match are indeed frustrating. For body art you can select "none," "strategically placed tattoo," or "visible tattoo." Well, in my mind, all good tattoos are strategically placed. The logic behind this wording notwithstanding, the tattoo options are a prime example of Match using useless categories in an effort to define compatibility.

A lot of women list tattoos as a "turn on." I send them this email: "Hi, I see you like tattoos. I have a big one. Pause. Email me back." No responses yet. Sometimes I am more earnest and explain a little about myself. "Hi, I am the editor of a hip-hop studies journal and in my free time I write about antique furniture and tattoos." And, well, that just makes me look insane.

All in all, my experiment thus far with Match has been fruitless, save for one woman named "Tiny Tanya" expressing sincere interest. Since it took me three years to work up the nerve to tell the last girl I liked that I wanted to date her, I am a little apprehensive about Internet "flirting." But at the very least, I believe I can appear more confident from the comforts of my room than I can at a bar/bookstore/coffee shop. ■

The Bottom Line

Whether you're meeting a date online or in-person, it can be intimidating to put yourself out there. Keep in mind that there's a reason why half of every standup routine is devoted to relationships—dating ups and downs are something almost everyone has to encounter, and having a sense of humor and adventure will help you deal with any bumps on the road. Nothing ventured, nothing gained, right? (Of course, if you're setting up a date with someone online, use common sense and plan your first meeting in a public place with lots of other people around.)

The Importance of Matchmaking

Just as finding a job is more likely to happen if you are actively networking, finding dates is easier if you make it clear that you're in the game. Tell your friends you're open to being set up with people they think would be a good fit for you, go out with your coworkers and meet their college friends, or tag along with a friend to that random event even if you have no real "reason" to go. There may be another friend-of-a-friend there who also has no "reason" to be there…and *voilà*, there's your conversation starter. Better yet, host your own party/picnic/afternoon frisbee festival, and (discretely) let your friends know they're not allowed to show up without a sexy single friend in tow.

If you are the kind soul doing the matchmaking, don't be too heavy-handed about it. Instead of sending two people off on a blind date, try inviting them both to a party at your apartment or a group dinner to see if they hit it off.

> **Tips & Tricks: When it just isn't meant to be**
>
> One of the things that's both difficult and liberating about post-college dating is that you may date someone who has no ties to your social network. This can feel like an adventure, but it can also lead to anxiety and confusion. Out in the wider world, it becomes easier to make out one minute and then disappear off the face of the earth when you no longer want to see the former object of your (momentary) affection. That's not meant to be a depressing revelation, but rather a caveat for those who are used to the more insular dating pool college provides. Whereas mutual friends used to ensure that you knew what your college makeout buddy was thinking and where he or she lived, those you date in the real world may be less accessible. Sometimes romantic mysteries go permanently unsolved. Luckily, there are plenty of fish in the post-college sea. Eat a tub o' Chunky Monkey and keep it moving!

Tips & Tricks: Office romance

Now that you're out of college, office romance is no longer something that only happens on TV and in the movies. You might walk in on some risky biz in the copy room, or you might be the one who gets walked in on. Before you dip your hand into that honey jar, however, make sure you are familiar with all the consequences by turning to page 251.

Believe it or not, this is how many fruitful relationships are spawned. If love does blossom, the couple will probably make you a bridesmaid or groomsman at their wedding. If things go sour, they may never take your romantic advice again. Either way, it never hurts to try.

The Anatomy of a Date

When you do score a "real world" date, there are a few basics to keep in mind. Try to choose a spot or activity that is convenient and/or appealing to both of you. If you don't know the person that well yet, veer away from stuff that's egregiously guy-centric or girlie. Also, while group dates can work if there's some mutual acquaintance or it's billed as such beforehand, don't immediately throw your new date into a pressure situation where they have to hang out with all your best friends—wait until you know if you actually like the person to save everyone the effort of being nice to a new person!

Once you're out on your date, make like a Buddhist and be in the moment. While you might think that your BlackBerry's constant vibrating is a sign of your importance (and therefore a turn-on), it's actually more likely to distract than it is to attract. Turn off your technology, and turn on the charm. When it comes time to pay the bill, proceed with caution. It often makes sense for the inviter to pay for the invitee (at least at first). It's a modern world, and we don't want to imply that the guy must pay (particularly if there are two guys on the date), but a lady does like to be treated right. On a first date, it's a nice gesture if the guy offers to pick up the tab. Ladies, beyond the first date, it's considerate if you start pulling your financial weight. On a related note, don't choose a restaurant that's way out of your league just to impress someone on a first date. Keeping up the façade will quickly drain your funds, and besides—don't you want to find someone who loves you for you?

Long-Distance Relationships

If you graduated in love or somewhere close to it, you may find yourself in the extremely difficult situation of dating long-distance. Maybe your beau has yet to graduate, or maybe you and your mate have decided to pursue opportunities in different cities. There's no magic formula for a successful "LDR," but start off by having a candid conversation about your expectations and set a realistic timeframe for how long you will remain apart. Temporary distance really can make the heart grow fonder—or it can make the heart completely forget about the other person, which also simplifies things. Another issue to discuss is whether you are going to have an open or closed relationship. If it's the former, will you be expected to disclose your extracurricular activities or keep them to yourself? Going with the "let's see what happens" approach might work for some couples, but it also breeds suspicion.

Presumably one or both of you is moving to a new place and meeting lots of new people, so long periods of "radio silence" might not go over well, especially if someone's latest Facebook album features him or her doing body shots. Realistically speaking, however, these are all just things to think about. There is no set rulebook for LDRs, so the real key is just to be honest with yourself about your motivations and feelings. If you feel dissatisfied, is it because you wish you could be with your boyfriend or girlfriend, or because you wish you could see other people? Follow your gut rather than intellectualizing the situation to death, because there are few ways to rationalize a $200 phone bill (hint: get Skype) and months of loneliness.

Breaking Up in the Age of Gchat
by MARY KATHRYN BURKE

Two years post-college, I had my first real-adult dating experience. I was 24. It was about time. It was classically too-good-to-be-true, and I wanted to tell anyone who would listen: Doorman…drycleaner…butcher, baker, candlestick maker…you name it. He pulled out chairs and wore a suit to work and put his tasseled Cole Hahn loafers on shoe trees before flossing, perusing the *WSJ* one last time and going to bed at a reasonable hour. You know, a *real-adult* man. And with that came a subsequent, inevitable, real-adult breakup.

Breaking Up in the Age of Gchat continued...

Well, it's been a while now and from my toils, I offer a few humble tips for a more graceful breakup in 2010 and beyond. From someone who (hopes she) learned the hard way. As my dear friend and fellow Gradspotter Christine would say, "It used to be just tearing a photo in half. Now it's much more complicated to rid ourselves of the relationship residue." These days, comrades, it's everywhere. And it's your choice to pick a place to draw the line.

1) Texting/Calls. Eventually the goal is to stop. But let's be honest— it's going to happen. Especially if you're not teetotalling. While weaning yourself off your cell dependency, the next best step is warning your future 4 am self not to call or text him. Change the name in your phone from "John Perfect" to something that will make you think. Something like "Doyoureallywanttodothis?" This way, at least if you slip up you will first get a little reminder that you should feel guilty about it from your formerly sober self. It's like Nicorette gum except with words and without the chewing and the drug rush.

2) IM. Nobody goes on IM anymore. Just delete your account. Are you going to tell me you have AOL too?

3) Outlook. Dear innocent college kid on PINE, webmail, or Macmail: Someday you will sit in an office...in a cube. Like the one I am sitting in right now. And when you work in this cube you will undoubtedly email the coworkers 20 yards away from you all day in an email system known as Outlook. And Outlook, despite its many inefficiencies, is remarkably adept at remembering every damn person you ever emailed. One of those people is probably the boy you just broke up with. You may or may not have spent the better part of your days at work emailing him over Outlook at J.T. Marlin or wherever the hell he worked. Maybe you even sent him clever calendar reminders. Delete, delete, delete. Go into your address book at D-E-L-E-T-E. There is nothing worse than going to email your innocent intern Johnny and having John E. Breakup's email address come up. It's not worth it. Delete.

4) Blackberry Messenger. I don't do this, but I've heard stories and it sounds like trouble. See #1.

5) Gchat. Now we're talking. Something with nuance. Gchat has a lot of options, and the best thing to do is to try what is right for you. For a while you might want to go "invisible." You might be tempted to block him, but that's too transparent. Even more transparent than "invisible" if you can believe it. Do this: Hover over his Gchat name. Choose "more" and then "never show." He can see that you're online, but you won't have to stare at his name…and picture…and cutesy away-status. Tempting you. Mocking you. Added bonus: Make sure your picture is something fabulous you did in his wake.

6) iPod. Make an appointment at the Genius Bar at your local Apple store and have it reset. Seriously. This might hurt but it's for your own good. I promise that 500 of the songs have somehow become related to him. Or were literally put onto your iPod BY him. Or were on the radio the night you met, etc. Do it. Start fresh. Besides, the Genius Bar guy might be kinda cute in that hipster, Chuck Taylor, plaid shirt, black-rimmed glasses, *SNL* kinda way. Maybe. Here's what you can be sure of—he won't work at J.T. Marlin.

7) Twitter. Don't tweet unless you are a celebrity. If you are a celebrity, go on a date with some ladykiller your PR person calls, then have your assistant tweet Page Six and make sure your ex gets a link. If you must tweet, at least stop "following" him.

8) LinkedIn, MySpace, etc. Remove your connection to him on these sites. It might seem weird, but you know what's weirder? Looking at his page all the time and analyzing what he wore where, when, and with whom. Especially if the "whom" is a girl. Also, this will help prepare you for #10.

9) Online "Date." Or, rather, browse. You don't have to go on a date with someone from Match, JDate, or Eharmony—just look around. Get a feel. We have our entire thirties to date on these sites. But it's a better distraction than Facebook, phone, Blackberry, and iPod, tempting us to break rules 10, 1, 4, and 6, respectively. Have a coworker sign you up for one of these things and just look. Because eventually, you will be in your apartment, tempted to break rule 5. And you have to remember that there are other guys floating around whose hearts you have yet to break.

The Grad 2.0 Plan

Charity

Generation Y clearly has a social conscience. One must only log onto Facebook and look at all the groups about Darfur and bringing back *Arrested Development* to see that. The problem is that starting salaries don't stretch too far beyond the essentials, and many of us end up limiting our charitable endeavors to benefits/fundraisers that our friends are involved with. There's nothing wrong with that, and at least there's usually an open bar involved. But just because you're not Bill Gates doesn't mean you can't make an impact. Getting involved with charitable organizations is not only a nice thing to do, but it can also be a great way to meet new people, gain new skills, and build your job-hunting story (see page 122).

Charity on the Cheap: Giving Time and Other People's Money

Needless to say, complete selflessness in your twenties is not the best retirement plan. But that doesn't mean you have to give up on others. If you can't part with any of your hard-earned paycheck, consider volunteering or fundraising for a charity. If you've got the motivation, finding volunteer work is not that difficult. There are large-scale organizations like Habit for Humanity, YMCA, and Red Cross that are always looking for new recruits, and you can also search for local opportunities on sites like VolunteerMatch.org, Idealist.org, and 1-800-Volunteer.org. Just type in your zip code and keywords related to the type of charity you'd like to find (e.g., dogs, homeless, children). You can also check out the government's volunteer site (volunteer.gov). If you really get into the spirit, you can even look for full-time nonprofit work (see page 149 for job-hunting resources in the nonprofit sector). Perhaps the best way to make an impact is to take an in-demand skill you possess and bring it to an organization that can make the most of it. For example, if you do work that helps companies operate more effectively (e.g., legal, consulting, PR), you can do the same work—pro bono, of course—for a nonprofit. When digging into different organizations, look them up on CharityNavigator.com, a website that rates and evaluates charities based on their effectiveness.

In addition to volunteering your time, there's also a great tradition in this country of doing something completely unrelated to the work of a charity—like "blogging" or "running a marathon," for example—and convincing other people to reward your hard work by giving that charity some money. The bizarreness of the underlying psychology eschews close investigation because at the end of the day, everyone wins, so who cares? FirstGiving.com allows you to set up a fundraising page for almost any nonprofit, while Team in Training will help you raise money for the Leukemia & Lymphoma Society by participating in a wide range of endurance events, like half-marathons and triathlons. Indeed, races and walk-a-thons are very popular events for raising money. Whenever you sign up for a major marathon or race of any type, you will be given opportunities to raise money for a variety of charities. Often, they'll host training sessions and other get-togethers in the lead-up to the event, so in addition to getting into shape, achieving something you can be proud of, and helping a good cause, you may even meet some new people. For more options, check out the March of Dimes and the Avon Walk for Breast Cancer.

Of course, you can also create your own fundraisers. Are you an artist? Host a show or sell your pieces online for a good cause. Musician? Play a fundraising

> **Tips & Tricks: The benefit of charity**
>
> What's the best part about giving to charity? No, dum dum: Not feeling like you've made a difference. The tax break! Whenever you donate to a recognized charity, you can file for a tax deduction on your donation at the end of the year. The charity has to have received its 501(c) tax exempt status, and you will need to provide records of your donations. You can keep written documentation of cash donations, but if they exceed $250 you'll need official documentation from the charity. And remember: Donations to your alma mater are tax-deductible, as well! If you decide to volunteer your time instead of your money, you won't earn a deduction, but you can get cash back on travel, uniforms, and other expenses associated with charitable work. Check out Bankrate. com for more nitty-gritty tax tips.

The Grad 2.0 Plan

concert. You can even coordinate your office to have a charity event, which could range from something as simple as a bake sale to a more ambitious project (talk to HR about company fundraisers). Finally, if you're entrepreneurial and think there's an underserved cause out there, there's nothing stopping you from starting your own charity.

Giving Back to Your Alma Mater

When looking for nonprofit organizations to get involved with, don't forget your school, which will always be happy to receive your help even if it's not in monetary form. Take part in a fundraiser, help with a telethon, or reach out to a graduating student. Just pick up the phone and call the alumni association; it will surely find a use for you. If you've got a little money to spare, there are always annual funds (you'll get the emails, trust us), and you can also give directed donations that dictate how you want the money to be spent—just don't say "pizza in the vending machines." School giving isn't always that stellar for recent grads (the bigger checks come later on), so donating even $20 or $50 a year is greatly appreciated. Don't think you have to name a new science center to make a difference. We're talking "thanks for the good years" money, not "promise my kids will get in no questions asked" money!

The Post-Grad Facebooker

What NOT to Do on Your Facebook Profile

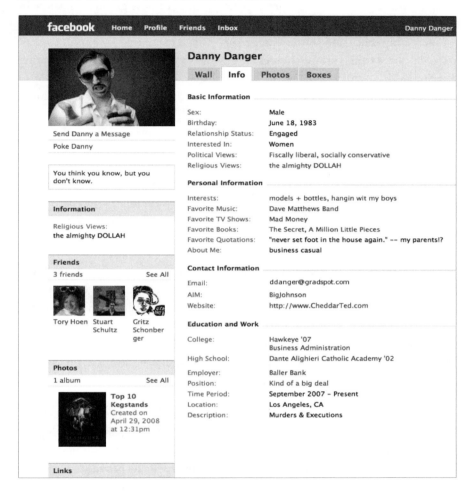

Danny Danger may be the man, but he's still lonely. Friend him on Facebook now!

As discussed in Chapter 4, making your Facebook profile work-appropriate is a pretty simple task: Change your privacy settings and try to avoid obvious red flags like bad-mouthing of employers, drug use, and racism. Gaining Facebook acceptance amongst your peers, on the other hand, is a complex and nuanced subject worthy of careful consideration. After graduation, many of the most "college" activities lose their cachet among more refined grads. By the same token, aggressive leaps into "adult" activities—e.g., getting married and having

The Grad 2.0 Plan

extravagant dinner parties—can be just as suspect to prying eyes. Here are a few pervasive social networking faux pas that everyone should try to avoid:

Late-blooming. We see this when a person displays a post-graduation surge in Facebook activity, furiously entering the public sphere under the guise of being an incredibly social and fun-loving person. This is evidenced by a multitude of tagged photos from various sources and excessive wall-posting. Late-blooming appears a bit alarming because in post-college life, it is almost impossible to party at such a high clip without the aid of drugs. Overall, this behavior is indicative of a person who has serious regrets and forgot to showcase his or her exceptional partying and socializing skills at the appropriate time.

Putting up an album for every weekend of the year. Much like *Real World* cast members, some people go to the same bar every weekend and apparently have an awesome time. Because the rest of us are very bored and voyeuristic, we will be forced to click through all 47 pictures of every album, even though they fill us with revulsion and acrimony.

Using the wall for private correspondence. Since its inception, the wall has been the cause of many of Facebook's most egregious faux pas. In post-grad life, walling what should be messaged remains an epidemic. Doing this is the online equivalent of shouting across the table. Even the notion of saying happy birthday publicly is self-congratulatory. It says, "Look at me everyone, I'm a good friend!" Use messages for private correspondence, and use the wall to publicly roast people. Because that's what it's for!

Posting uninteresting links. With the advent of the News Feed, Facebook users are able to push their agendas on you like never before. Posting an interesting link, or even a self-serving one, is not such a crime, but incessantly linking front-page news is offensive. If you are trying to prove that you are informed, that is obnoxious. If you think your friends need you to keep them informed, that is even more obnoxious.

Posting Facebook videos. Honestly, has anyone ever seen a good Facebook video? We reckon the answer is "no," because they are all terrible. This is a bizarre phenomenon, and it just goes to prove that no one on YouTube is actually an amateur. What a sham!

Including your entire CV under "Work Info." We've heard other people complain about this maneuver, and we can see how it might get one's goat. It is the most clear and distressing indicator of the transformation of Facebook from hilarious free-for-all to lame career networking tool. (See page 206 to learn about LinkedIn, where resumes are totally appropriate.)

Listing yourself as "engaged" or "married" to your best friend (or someone else to whom you are clearly not married or engaged). This was cute for about five minutes during sophomore year, but now that you've graduated, you're just going to end up confusing people and/or leading them to believe you've come out of the closet. If this is your intention, go for it. If not, reserve the irony for some other venue.

Updating your status every five minutes. Listing what you're thinking of having for lunch, how you feel about the weather, or how many days are left until Cabo is not interesting to anyone but you. And the truth is, we all know that the action of peoples' real lives is disproportionately correlated to their Facebook activity, (i.e., the more you update your status, the less you have going on outside of your cyber-social life). If you like status messages that much, just do the honorable thing and start a Twitter account. No one likes a monopoly!

Creating a Facebook group when you lose your cell phone. This is how it seems to work: Bill gets drunk. Bill drops his phone down a gutter. Bill passes out, wakes up, and immediately creates a Facebook group called "LOST MY PHONE—NEED YOUR NUMBERS." Who decided this was standard procedure? Please don't be this guy (or girl). If you lose your phone, email or message the people who matter to you, and then suck it up for a few months of mystery calls. If you never get that number back, then perhaps that's just the way things were meant to be.

Cooking

 One of the harshest realities of living independently is dealing with the necessity of feeding yourself. For many of us, dining hall meal plans only reinforced a lifetime of culinary ineptitude. Maybe you mixed a nice salad or figured out that making *matzo pizza* was not as disgusting as expected, but beyond these trial-by-fire experiments, most college students graduate with no basic grasp of how to buy, store, and prepare food. "Home economics" isn't at the top of the curriculum anymore and, let's face the facts: Some parents are horrible in the kitchen, as well.

One thing is for sure: You watched the Food Network. And it turns out that after watching over 1,000 hours of programming, you know how to properly remove the meat from a snow crab yet you still don't know how to boil an egg. There's no real shame in that—any self-respecting person would rather watch Gordon Ramsay tell someone to go screw himself than write down a Rachael Ray recipe. That said, a rotation of simple, quick recipes is essential to any budget- and body-conscious grad. This talent, in turn, has a trickle down effect into your broader life, allowing you to impress friends, dates, and colleagues with your culinary acumen.

Interview: Mark Bittman's Guide to Cooking at Home

Mark Bittman is best known as a food columnist for the New York Times, *a regular guest on NBC's* Today Show, *and the author of the classic cookbook* How to Cook Everything. *He's also traveled around Spain with Gwyneth Paltrow and Mario Batali for a television series on PBS and given a TED talk entitled "What's Wrong with What We Eat." We think he's pretty much the man, and his philosophy on his craft makes him the perfect guru for post-college: He rejects the notions that tools and ingredients must be expensive, that recipes must be followed to the letter, and that cooking isn't worth the effort. We caught up with him to get his advice for twentysomethings making their first forays into the kitchen.*

How did you start cooking for yourself?

My senior year of college and my first year after college I lived alone. I cooked every day—sometimes alone, sometimes with other people—and I really taught myself how to cook. In school I wasn't an over-achiever. I was always looking for shortcuts to get the grades I needed, and I approached cooking the same way: I never followed the directions exactly. I improvised as needed, and most of the time it came out okay.

What do you actually need in your kitchen to cook?

It's not $20 worth of stuff, it's more like $150–200 worth of stuff. Get stuff from your parents, grandparents, Salvation Army. Second-hand places are a good deal; if something was able to make it to the store, it's probably in pretty good condition. Even if it's rusted, you can literally throw it in a fire and the rust will burn off. You don't need fancy stuff when you're young; [the expensive things] only help when you're in your '60s and '70s and you're less likely to want to hold heavier things.

How do you figure out what to buy for the week?

The most important thing about shopping is the pantry. If you stock a good pantry, then you don't have to shop that often, and there's no excuse to run out to buy a slice of pizza at 10 pm. If you have grains, beans, eggs and onions, spices, and herbs—a very, very basic list–then you don't have to run out shopping. It can be a $25 investment a week until you build a full pantry. And then every now and then you have to run out and buy the fresh things, milk or lettuce, and that's how you take care of the fresh items. People always say, "Ahh, but I didn't have X, Y, or Z," and it's complete nonsense. There's no excuse not to cook. I have a small kitchen, I don't have a ton of stuff. I have maybe 50 things, $200 worth of things, and I can always cook whatever I want. Shopping is never a big deal.

What are entry-level things that grads should do if they want to start cooking?

People should always invest in a cookbook. These days you don't really need one because you can go online, but it's hard to judge if it's a good recipe or not. And if you don't have any cooking experience you really can't tell. You want to invest your time in learning to cook something you want to eat. Find a recipe, find how long it's supposed to take to make, and then double that time, because you have no idea what you're doing, and then go to work. It's not going to be Michelin-quality beautiful, but it's going to be fine. You just have to go for it. When people recognize how simple and straightforward cooking is, that's when they get into it.

Why do you think people eat healthier if they cook for themselves?

Well, there are many reasons—it's portion, it's ingredients, it's many things. I don't believe you can make yourself an 1,800 calorie salad. You look at what's going in there, and you think, "I don't even want to eat all that crap!" If you go to the store, you'll buy vegetables, and then you'll come home and cook them. You'll eat only what you buy. You can't possibly eat as badly as when you're not cooking. People who don't cook eat terribly. Two-thirds of Americans are overweight or obese—those are not cooks. I doubt even 10% of those people are real cooks.

Mark Bittman's Guide to Cooking at Home continued...

You have a daughter who's a recent college grad. What are your observations about people our age when it comes to cooking?

I'm optimistic about your generation because I feel like we've hit rock bottom. [Laughs.] I'm pessimistic about your generation because so many people of your generation grew up eating prepared food, take-outs, ordering in, and so much of this thinking is shaped when you're young. It's going to be up to you guys when you become parents to demonize over-eating. There was this ad with this kid saying to his mom, "Why are you smoking?", and the same is going to have to happen with over-eating: The kid has to be able to ask his mom, "Why are we going to McDonalds?" I think McDonald's is trying to change and I'm not saying those places are all bad. Those places are fine for a special occasion if you always eat at home, but to think of McDonald's as a staple place for eating? That's tragic. ■

Kitchen 101

More than likely, your kitchen looks more like a small closet than the *Iron Chef* Kitchen Stadium. But that doesn't mean you can't whip up a few well-practiced dishes. Before you get started, it's important to make sure your cooking area is clean. (*Ratatouille* is a bit unrealistic—having a rat infestation is not going to make you into a master chef.) Use a disinfectant to wipe down surfaces, especially after handling raw chicken. Clean all your cookware and utensils to avoid germs and food that always tastes like the *last* thing you cooked. ("I really want stir-fry on Thursday, so let's have it on Wednesday, shall we?") As annoying as it may sound, it

Tips & Tricks: Finding recipes

Along with Gradspot.com's "Recipe of the Week," check out these sites for recipes, tips, and cooking inspiration:

- Chowhound.com
- CookThink.com
- FoodNetwork.com
- Recipes.com
- Epicurious.com
- Mark Bittman's blog (bitten.blogs/nytimes.com)
- Rouxbe.com
- Cookstr.com

really is easier to give things a quick rinse and scrub immediately after using them than battling with a dried-up, filth-encrusted mound of dirty dishes at the end of each month.

All clean? Okay, let's proceed. Hopefully you have a stovetop, oven, sink, and refrigerator. If you're lucky you have a microwave and a coffeemaker, but those are luxuries. When push comes to shove, you can do most cooking with some pretty simple tools—don't be lured by the apple slicer and fresh yogurt maker when you reach the checkout at the kitchen supply store. Here are a few essentials that should serve you well. **Depending on where you shop, you should be able to outfit your whole kitchen for $150 to $200 total.** To reduce costs significantly, try to pick up as many items as you can from home (your parents or grandparents probably have stuff lying around), and try to find a local kitchen supply store for wholesale prices.

> **Tips & Tricks: The price of eating out**
>
> Take-out and delivery restaurants fuel the recent grad community, but they are also a severe drain on our collective wealth. Starting to cook, even just a couple of times a week, should help you keep a little more money in your pocket for other things. A more complicated aspect of eating out, however, is going to dinner with friends. These meals are about more than just the food, so instead of always saying no you just need to make a concerted effort to make it affordable without being a miser. If you are a barista and your friend is a hedge-fund analyst, make sure she knows that you don't want to go to $100-a-head dinners (unless she's paying). Don't get suckered into paying above your means out of pride, because the fact is that every American city has amazing food for cheap if you know where to look. *(continued on next page...)*

- **Large saucepan (3+ quarts; $14–25).** You want it to be big enough to cook a whole package of spaghetti or make a batch of sauce/soup.
- **Medium or small saucepan ($9–20).** For heating soups, sauces, etc.
- **10" frying pan ($13–15).** For cooking eggs, sautéing meats, making stir-fry, etc.
- **13"-by-"18 metal baking sheet ($5.75–15).** For baking and toasting bread.
- **Roasting pan ($6.50–10).** For roasting chicken, making lasagna, etc.
- **Mixing bowls (set of three; $5–11).** For preparing food, serving, and storing leftovers.
- **Measuring cup ($6.50–7.50).** For measuring out ingredients.

- **Peeler ($3–6).** For peeling vegetables like carrots, potatoes, etc.
- **14" colander ($7–10).** For draining pasta and other food cooked in water; washing fruits and veggies.
- **Wooden spoons (set of three; $3–10).** These are better than metal because they're easier on the surfaces of pots and pans.
- **Ladle ($2.50–3).** For serving soups, sauces, etc.
- **Bread knife ($3–8).** For breads, bagels, etc. Serrated edge also works well for cutting tomatoes.
- **Chef's knife (medium-sized; $10–13).** Good for chopping pretty much anything (including your fingers—be careful!).
- **Paring knife (might come with chef's knife; $3).** Useful for cutting small items and peeling.
- **Rubber spatula ($4.50–8).** For flipping pancakes, making scrambled eggs, sautéing, etc. Rubber is easier on surfaces than metal.
- **Whisk ($3–4).** For whipping up scrambled eggs and batters.
- **Can opener ($4–10).** That can of soup will taunt you if you can't open it.
- **Measuring spoons ($1–5).** For teaspoon and tablespoon measuring.
- **Cutting board ($6–9).** Plastic ones are a lot easier to clean (crucial when you're cutting raw chicken and other potentially dangerous foods).

Tips & Tricks: The price of eating out continued...

Choose your battles wisely, and find ways to cut costs, such as skipping appetizers and desserts or going to BYOB establishments. Then, when you do get yourself into a spot where the restaurant's more expensive than you'd hoped, suck it up and pay your share. No one likes people who haggle over the bill or itemize everything they ate to prove they owe $3 less than everyone else. And if you're planning a dinner or evening out, take other people's finances into account so as to avoid this sort of situation for others! Or make like the "The Situation" from *Jersey Shore* and just whip up some sausage and peppers at home. If your friends don't like it, you know what to say: "You are now excluded from surf 'n' turf night. You're excluded from ravioli night. You're excluded from chicken cutlet night."

Learning to Shop and Cook

Stocking "the pantry" (or the mini-fridge and cupboard, as the case may be) can be an inordinately onerous task for recent grads with no kitchen know-how. When you do a lap around the supermarket and end up with cereal straws, a steak, Kool-Aid mix, Double Stuf Oreos, Dave's Insanity hot sauce, and some Kraft Singles, you know you've got a little work to do. Putting some thought into your purchases beforehand (or even bringing—dare we say it—a *shopping list!?*) can help cut down on impulse buys and produce a more useful end result. So, what should you look for?

Beyond the obligatory salt-pepper-olive oil triumvirate, take stock of what you like to eat and build your pantry based on your preferences. Do you like hummus? You probably do. But did you realize that keeping garlic, oil, a few spices, and a can of chickpeas around will help you to make it whenever you want? The fun of learning to make your favorite foods from a few staple ingredients is threefold: 1) You save money; 2) You can experiment with a food that you already know; and 3) You can create a personalized version of a favorite dish that will wow your guests.

Rice, polenta, and oatmeal are other good stock items; they will never leave you hungry, and they are extremely versatile. Frozen chicken, pork, or sausage all serve a similar purpose in the kitchen—they provide a good base protein and can be deployed in a wide range of dishes. Pasta is also a major staple for the young adult, but unfortunately most pre-made sauces are gross. We recommend keeping a can of crushed tomatoes around at all times to make a quick sauce from scratch. Over time you will develop a "signature" sauce, and everyone will think you are either a) of Italian ancestry, b) the jam, or c) both. A basic tomato sauce is the perfect base for a variety of add-ons, and it requires only minimal cooking time. After you get a great multi-use sauce going, make a big batch and save it for pastas, pizzas, or whatever else you dream up.

Finding the Time to Cook

At the end of the day, it's important to remember that "when you're hungry" is not the only time of day to cook. Take an hour on the weekend to make a large casserole or chili that you can freeze and eat throughout the week. If you have roommates who are also interested in eating at home, set up a rotation where you cook for one another. Finally, don't be intimidated—with basic ingredients it is hard to make food that is inedible, and remember that, these days, you've always got the Internet as a resource to tell you the difference between frying and sautéing, or to provide simple recipes for almost anything. Once you nail one dish, you can build off that and mix and match with others—before you know it, you'll have a whole range of tricks up your sleeve.

The Grad 2.0 Plan

The Under-$50 Pantry

You don't want to be running to the store every time you try to make a recipe that involves "salt and pepper." There are some basic items that you want to keep on hand at all times—they'll last a long time and make your cooking forays a whole lot easier. (Prices vary according to geography and store, but these prices from a Safeway in the Bernal Heights neighborhood of San Francisco shouldn't be too far off what you can find.)

Olive oil (25 fl oz, generic) $9.99

Salt $0.89

Pepper. $3.79

Dijon mustard. $2.99

Butter (1 stick $1.49

Mixed Italian seasoning. $5.49

Balsamic vinegar $4.58

Soy sauce (10 oz $2.59

Red pepper flakes $4.61

Cumin $4.19

Chili powder. $4.69

Pam Cooking Spray. $3.99

Total. $49.29

Gradspot Recipes

One of the favorite features on Gradspot.com has always been the "Recipe of the Week." In spite of the cliché of recent grads subsisting on ramen packages, our peers are increasingly interested in food, and we have friends who not only cook at home frequently, but also make absolutely delicious fare. With our recipes on the site, we seek to celebrate the spirit of recent grad cuisine without resorting to the "Insert chicken breast into George Foreman Grill. Wait. Remove" formula (not that it isn't a useful formula to know—we just figure you can crack it yourself). Instead, our guiding principles are the use of budget-friendly ingredients, the ability to cook in bulk (i.e., cook once for several meals), and preparation that is quick and easy. We also encourage improvisation—once you make one of these dishes, you can easily add your own flair or adapt the basic elements to your own tastes.

In this section you'll find some favorites from the past two years of "Recipe of the Week." They cover the basics: chicken, fish, vegetarian dishes, and even simple dinners made from a few eggs or frozen meats and vegetables. We have created all these recipes with budget and time constraints in mind. You'll notice a strong trend toward recreating the favorites of childhood. What can we say—we're pretty nostalgic.

Note: Total costs based on prices at Safeway supermarket in San Francisco and assume you have a stocked pantry (see previous page); serving sizes based on average human beings.

Homemade Frozen Meal: Chili Macaroni

Serves 4; Costs $16

Back in the days of innocence and fast metabolism, we were all about Stouffer's frozen meals. Swedish Meatballs, Salisbury steak, chili macaroni—all are tasty and satisfying beyond your wildest dreams. But the problem with frozen meals in your twenties is that they are generally unhealthy and they carry a certain air of desperation. Thankfully, you can have your frozen meal and eat it, too. Make a big batch of this healthier recipe, and then pop it in the fridge or freezer for lunch at work or dinners throughout the week.

You need:

- 1 lb. ground beef/turkey

- 1 can black beans
- 1 large can crushed tomato
- 1 onion
- 4 cloves garlic
- 1 jalapeño
- ½ box macaroni
- Grated cheese (jack works well)
- Salt, pepper
- Cumin
- Chili powder

Dice the jalapeño, garlic, and onion. Toss all into a saucepan coated with olive oil. Cook down for ten minutes on medium heat. Add ground meat and cook until brown. Season with cumin and chili powder to taste. Pour in the crushed tomatoes. Cook down for 45 minutes. Re-season to taste.

In a separate pot, boil some water and toss in the macaroni. When it's cooked, combine with desired amount of chili and top with cheese. You have now prepared a frozen food classic at home. Pat yourself on the back and enjoy in front of *Gossip Girl*. Then freeze the leftovers.

Fish Night: Cod with Cherry Tomatoes

Serves 2; Costs $11

When Gradspot contributor Arnold T. Pants was a fellow at the New Bedford Whaling Museum, he ate a simple meal with Klaus Bartlemus, the world's leading expert on whaling. Klaus was also an expert on eating odd foods. He'd consumed the eye of a sturgeon and a whole small bird. He offered to cook us dinner, and to my surprise presented a very simple dish: roast cod with cherry tomatoes.

The meal is a truly lovely end to a cool spring day. Seasoned with olive oil, salt, and pepper and roasted for about 15 minutes, the fish comes out light and flaky. Serve it with steamed rice tossed with a bit of cilantro, as well as a side salad if you're feeling ambitious (see page 452).

You need:

- Cod (or any other white fish you want; two pieces)
- 1 package cherry tomatoes

- Rice
- Cilantro
- Olive oil
- Salt
- Pepper

Preheat oven to 375 degrees. While it's pre-heating, season the fish with olive oil, salt, and pepper. (If you froze the fish, let it thaw thoroughly before starting this process, and be sure to wash it by holding the filets under warm running water.) Place the fish in a deep baking dish and add the tomatoes—whole if you like, or halved. When the oven is ready, toss the dish in there and roast for about 15 minutes, or until the fish flakes easily.

For the rice, steam in a rice cooker if you have one. Otherwise, place two cups of water for each cup of rice in a large pot, bring to boil, and cook until the water has been absorbed. At that point, take it off the heat and allow to sit for 20 minutes or so—this will make it fluff up nicely. Toss in the cilantro and enjoy.

Pot Luck All-Star: Mexican Dip

Serves: A small army; Cost: Varies but buy the cheapest version of each item you can find

Whether you've got the crew coming over for football or you're heading to a friend's house for *Two and a Half Men* (you know you like it), it's great to have a hearty crowd-pleaser at the ready. When we were in high school our favorite game day (and après ski) meal was Mexican dip. Is it Mexican? No, it simply employs vaguely Mexican ingredients like refried beans and salsa. Is it filling and delish? Hell yeah it is.

You need:

- 2 cans refried beans
- 1 pound ground turkey (or beef... turkey seems to satisfy the dietary needs of more people, though)
- 1 package taco seasoning
- 1 small onion
- 2 packages of grated "Mexican blend cheese"
- 1 jar of sliced jalapeños
- 1 jar of taco sauce
- 1 jar of your favorite store salsa

The Grad 2.0 Plan

Preheat oven to 400 degrees. Dice onion and cook in a skillet, then add turkey and simply follow the instructions on the taco seasoning package. Once the meat is cooked, set aside.

In a Pyrex or other oven-friendly dish, spread out one can of beans. Top this with half the meat mix, half the salsa, half the taco sauce, and half the cheese. Toss in the jalapeños. Cover this with the second can of beans and repeat the layering. Bake until golden brown on top.

Why do two layers? Why not! But, really, one will suffice if you are not that generous or you only have a small party to feed.

Serve with tortilla chips or scoop the concoction into flour tortillas. Drink either Fresca, Pacifico, or tequila slammers.

Crowd-Pleaser #1: Hearty Pasta with Sausage and Eggplant

Serves: 4–6; Cost: $20

On a cold night when the sun starts to go down early, there's nothing like a hearty pasta dish to keep the engine purring. We experimented with variations of this classic Italian dish in the past, but eventually we chanced upon a combination that really seemed to knock our friends' socks off. Best of all, it's super easy and can easily be made in 20 minutes after work. The quantities below serve about three to four people, or alternatively provide you with ample leftovers.

You need:

- 2 eggplants
- 4 sausages (pick any variety you like from the supermarket fridge—my go-to is chicken and sun dried tomato)
- 1 large can crushed tomatoes
- Baby spinach leaves
- 1 box pasta
- Mascarpone cheese (or ricotta if you prefer)
- ½ medium onion
- 1 clove garlic
- Salt
- Pepper
- Crushed red pepper flakes

To get this show on the road, dice up half an onion and throw it in a wok (or pot) with some olive oil and some chopped up garlic. While it's softening up, cut your sausages into pieces. Throw those into the mix and cook until the sides of each piece are nicely browned. Add your eggplants (chopped into pieces as well) and cook until they've softened up. At this point, you can put some water on the boil in a separate pot for your pasta.

Now, add the can of crushed tomatoes to the wok and stir it up with the sausage and eggplant. This is the basis of your sauce so you can start seasoning to taste with some salt, pepper, and whatever else you've got on hand. I like to throw in some "BAM" with a whole bunch of crushed red chili flakes, but that's up to you. While it's simmering away on medium heat, put your pasta in the water and cook it. I think rigatoni or penne works best with this sauce, but it's up to you.

After you've drained the pasta, throw it right into the sauce in the wok or in a large bowl. Add two big spoonfuls of mascarpone (more or less depending on how creamy you want it—you can also skip this part entirely) and toss everything together until all of the pasta is covered and the soft cheese has spread around. Finally, throw in a couple handfuls of baby spinach leaves. As you toss the pasta one last time, the heat will wilt the leaves.

Serve with a bottle of wine (see page 454 to make a pick), and you'll be living large.

Crowd-Pleaser #2: Easy Chicken Picatta

Serves: 4; Cost: $11

Everyone loves some good breaded chicken, but who has time to do all the prep work? Not you, the busy budding executive (or whirlwind creative). Fortunately, there is an excellent alternative to egg washes, flour and breadcrumbs: prepackaged breaded tenders. (If you can find the variety from Bell & Evans, shell out the extra money—they're worth it.) With three simple ingredients and a few pantry staples, you'll literally be ready to eat in ten minutes.

You need:

- Olive Oil
- Breaded chicken tenders (12 oz package)

- 1 lemon
- Spaghetti

Start boiling some water for your spaghetti. While this is going, heat a large skillet coated with olive oil. Cook your tenders until they are golden and crisp and delicious. When you've cut one and determined that it's cooked through, squeeze in the juice of one of the lemons. Simmer on low heat as all the juices mix together. Cook spaghetti and then toss with olive oil and a little grated Parmesan if you've got any. Serve chicken on top of the spaghetti. Game. Set. Match.

Breakfast Any Time: Savory Scrambled Eggs with Goat Cheese

Serves: 2–3; Cost: $6

Having an ace egg dish up your sleeve is extremely useful for a budding chef. Whether you want to whip up a super easy "breakfast for dinner" or show your appreciation with a nice "morning after" brunch, you'll find plenty of opportunities to break it out. Assuming you or your patrons aren't lactose-intolerant, this easy scramble should do the trick for two to three people.

You need:

- 6 eggs
- ½ cup milk
- Butter
- Pepper
- Salt
- 2 ounces goat cheese

Whisk the eggs in a bowl with the milk, salt, and pepper. Add 2 tablespoons of butter to a large skillet. Add the eggs and cook them over medium-low heat, stirring constantly, until the desired doneness—if you don't like them wet, cook longer. When the eggs are done, remove the skillet from the heat, add the goat cheese, and fold it into the eggs. This will bolster the taste and texture and in one extra step turn your scrambled eggs into something quite special. Serve with some bread and a pot of coffee.

Easiest Date Night Dish Ever: "Loulé Shrimp"

Serves: 2–3; Cost: $13

Back when Arnold T. Pants was a little rascal nipping at his mother's heels, he was lucky enough to go on a family trip to Portugal. Because he was so young, memories of the trip are limited, but two stick with him to this day: 1) the time he roamed around wearing nothing but a headband and wielding a tennis racket (we know this because a photo of him naked now has a prominent placement on his mantle), and 2) an amazingly delicious dish called "Loulé shrimp" that has become a family staple ever since.

We're not sure if the people of the region actually called it "Loulé shrimp"—they probably just call it "shrimp." But that's neither here nor there. The important thing is that it's an incredibly simple dish (literally a 20-minute meal, if not less) that is both delicious and reasonably healthy.

You need:

- Large pre-cooked shrimp (1 lb; can buy raw or pre-cooked)
- Olive oil
- Crushed red pepper flakes
- Garlic
- 1 lemon
- 1 package rice pilaf

Start the rice pilaf following the instructions on the box. It generally takes about 20 minutes to cook down in water with a splash of oil or butter. As that's on the go, peel your shrimp. Chop up some garlic and sauté it in olive oil in a wok or frying pan. Then add the shrimp and cook until they're nice and pink. Sprinkle the whole shebang with crushed red pepper flakes (plus salt to taste) and squeeze a lemon onto the little devils to finish it off. If you're feeling really frisky, toss in some coriander leaves at the end for added taste.

And that's basically it. Serve with your rice pilaf and maybe some hunks of French bread for soaking up the sauce. A cheap white wine or a light lager works well to wash it down. Date night was never so easy.

The Grad 2.0 Plan

Healthy Choice: White Bean Salad

Serves: 2 as a main dish or 4 as a side; Cost: $7

In the heat of summer, a good salad makes an excellent meal. When it's this hot, your appetite can't handle Chipotle every day like it did in those "storing up for winter" days of late fall. Personally, we like a bean salad. Why? Because you still get protein but you don't have to futz around with cooking anything. All you need is three ingredients and five minutes to whip up a tasty light meal or a premier league side for another recipe.

You need:

- 1 can cannellini beans
- ½ red onion
- Arugula
- Garlic
- Olive oil
- Salt
- Pepper
- Balsamic vinegar

Drain the can of beans, wash with cool water, and place in large bowl. Then dice the red onion. Toss with beans and add the greens. Season to taste with salt, pepper, oil, and vinegar. It's also nice to squeeze a lime over the salad if you have one left over from your last Cinco de Mayo party. Crushed garlic is also an option, and one we usually exercise. If you've got a tomato on hand, feel free to throw that in there as well.

Go-To Dessert: Key Lime Pie

Serves: 4–6; Cost: $9

Pies are a good way to impress dates and your friends, but conventional wisdom suggests that they are bloody hard to make. Not so. Some are actually idiot-proof. So much so that even we can make them.

This Key Lime Pie recipe was devised and perfected by rapper Special Opp, of Community League fame. He cut his chops in the kitchen serving up quality fare to members of the Skull and Bones Society on their secret island hideaway. His desserts are brilliant, and his key lime pie has fans from Oxfordshire,

England, to Westerly, Rhode Island.

You need:

- 1 pre-made graham cracker crust
- 1 can sweetened condensed milk
- 2 limes
- 2 eggs
- Heavy cream

Preheat oven to 350. While it's heating, mix the juice of two limes, a little lime zest (little shavings from the peel), sweetened condensed milk, and eggs. Beat with a whisk (or a fork) until the mixture is smooth. Work the pre-made piecrust into an aluminum pie dish from the supermarket and then fill it up with the mixture. Bake until the whole thing ceases to jiggle—about 25 to 30 minutes. Let it cool old-school style on the windowsill, or throw it in the fridge if you are mad hungry for pie and can't wait. Once it's at room temperature, spray on some whipped cream and enjoy.

Drinking

The transition to Grad 2.0 may drive some recent grads to drink. But while shot-gunning Bud Lights and sake bombing were considered power moves in college, they begin to lose their cachet after graduation. Now's the time to add a touch of class to your alcoholic endeavors. Before you say, "Piss off!", and go out to buy a handle, let's be clear about one thing: This is not about being snooty—Natty Ice and Cuervo still have their place in our hearts (and at reunion tailgates). It's more about laying a foundation for a more long-term relationship with alcohol, developing the best hobby ever (i.e., "wine/beer/whisky/[insert favorite liquor here] enthusiast"), and being able to smoothly navigate new drinking situations like networking meetings, non–college-style dates, and coworker events. Wine is the official drink of the "adult world," but we'll also delve into beer, which is fast becoming a respected beverage at the dinner table.

Needless to say, not drinking is also a totally reasonable lifestyle choice (especially if you've discovered Abita Root Beer, perhaps the most delicious root beer ever made). You don't have to booze to be the consummate grad. The point is that if you are going to partake, it's worth expanding your horizons beyond Carlos Rossi and red Solo cups. So fill up your glass, light a fire, and let's talk drankin'.

Wine Appreciation 101

Whether you're looking to sound savvy at a business dinner or trying to impress that hottie from next door, a little wine knowledge goes a long way. There's no need to emulate that ostentatious guy from *Sideways* with his Merlot-phobia, but being able to navigate a wine menu can add an intriguing string to your post-grad bow. The world of wine is complex; the basics are not. Let us help.

Talking the Talk

There's no need to be overwhelmed when it comes to wine speak. When the waiter explains that a certain wine has notes of aged English leather and tiger lilies with a smooth, walnut-y finish, you may be tempted to opt for a mineral water instead. But don't let the pomp and circumstance deter you. Here's a list of the terminology you need to know. And even if you don't know it, you're still allowed to drink.

Old World. Generally refers to wines produced in regions with long histories of winemaking (e.g., Europe, parts of the Mediterranean basin).

New World. Generally refers to wines produced in "newer" regions such as the United States, Australia, South America, and South Africa.

Varietal. A fancy word for a type of grape and a way of classifying wines. Examples of different varietals include Chardonnay, Merlot, Pinot Noir, and Riesling.

Region. An indicator of where the wine was produced and another way of classifying wines. Examples of regions include Burgundy, Bordeaux, Chianti and Rioja. (Many European wines are classified according to region.)

Vintage. This refers to the year in which the wine was produced, and some years are better than others for specific wines depending upon the weather and other factors. That's not to say that 2005 was a great vintage for every wine, but it might have been for some. If you know the key years for specific wines, you'll be able to pick out some stellar bottles.

Blends & Table Wines. "Blends" and "table wines" are made by blending different types of grapes, which can yield delicious or disastrous results. Table wines are usually on the cheaper end of the spectrum and can be pretty tasty if you find the right one.

"Easy-Drinking Wine." This is one of those vague phrases that wine people like to throw around, but it basically means that the wine at hand is fairly innocuous, will please a variety of palates, and can be enjoyed alone or with food. It's smart to choose an "easy-drinking wine" if you're trying to please a group whose preferences vary from one person to the next. New World wines tend to be good crowd-pleasers.

Finish. A word used to describe the "impression" that a wine leaves as it's being swallowed. The finish is often described in terms of acidity or specific flavors (oak, fruit, spice, etc.)—or emotions if the person is a total BSer.

Full-Bodied vs. Light. A way to describe the "weight" of wines in your mouth. Does it feel inky? Watery? The more robust the flavor, the more "full-bodied" it is.

For more information on wine terminology, check out the helpful online encyclopedia at Wines.com.

Types of Wines

The three main categories for wines are red, white, and sparkling. (Note: Rosé is also quite popular as a warm-weather drink among Euros and wannabe-Euros.)

Within the three main categories, the options are endless, but here's a quick rundown of wines you are likely to find at restaurants and bars in the United States (where wines are generally categorized by varietal).

Red

- **Cabernet Sauvignon.** Generally full-flavored with a smooth and lingering finish.

- **Syrah (or Shiraz).** Tastes full-bodied with flavor notes of anything from raspberry to espresso to spice.

- **Merlot.** Has a medium body with hints of berry, plum, and currant, and a buttery finish.

The Grad 2.0 Plan

- **Pinot Noir.** A light crisp wine with an acidic finish.

Whites

- **Chardonnay.** One of the most versatile wines, it's often oaky, but it can also be soft with fruity flavors or smoky with flavors of vanilla, caramel, or butter.

- **Sauvignon Blanc.** Tastes crisp, dry, and refreshing with flavors ranging from grass to tropical fruit.

- **Pinot Grigio.** Can be good for beginners due to its sweet, light, crisp, and neutral flavors—but not all pinots are created equal.

Sparkling Wines

- **Champagne.** Designation reserved for sparkling wines produced in France's champagne region (the gold standard in sparkling wines). Think Dom Perignon, Moët et Chandon, and, of course, Cristal. Always go for "Brut" (i.e. dry) champagnes unless you like your bubbly very sweet.

- **Prosecco.** Italy's answer to champagne. Generally cheaper in price than actual champagne.

- **Cava.** Spain's version of champagne. Also cheaper in price.

- **Sparkling Wine.** The general designation for any carbonated wine.

Tracking Down Interesting & Affordable Wines

Drinking good wines doesn't require a lot of money. But don't be fooled by the hype of certain cheap wines. A little bit of hunting can open up the wine world without pushing you out of the under-$20 zone. Here are some tips for finding the good stuff.

Don't be shy. The staff at your local liquor or wine store is there to help. Chances are, they like to drink and have sampled many of the wines in stock. Tell them your budget and preference, and then put them to work.

Get off the beaten path. Sure, cheap Californian and Australian wines (think Yellowtail and Barefoot) are fine in a pinch, but did you ever notice they all kind of taste the same? It's because they are the same (i.e., they're mass-produced and don't vary much from year to year). Consider avoiding "brands" and, instead, try wines from more obscure regions. Look to wines from Portugal, Spain, and South America for great value.

"The wine next door." Rather than reaching for that pricey St. Emilion, try the bottle from Lussac-St. Emilion (a village five miles away). You'll find great wines while saving money and supporting smaller producers. Again, the staff at the store can help you fill in gaps in your knowledge of wine regions.

Poppin' bubbly. If you're like us, you probably aren't in a position to be popping Cris just yet. Opt for cheaper sparkling wines like prosecco (from Italy) or cava (from Spain).

Don't fear the box. Your days of playing "slap the bag" may have turned you off of boxed wine, but it's not as disgusting as you might think. Contrary to popular belief, you can find drinkable everyday wine in box form, and one box goes a long way (approx. three liters or four bottles). Look for French or Italian white wines for good value that will last a long time in the fridge.

Shop the Internet for deals. There are many different wine stores online that constantly offer up deals on great bottles, the most popular of which includes Wine.com and WineLibrary.com/WineLibraryTV.com. The latter also airs daily online wine videos hosted by a true, blue-collar NY Jets fan. It's just about the most approachable way to learn about and buy wine that there is.

How to Order Wine at a Restaurant

As an aspiring writer, Gradspot.com contributor Adam White has learned a thing or two about waiting tables. And with waiting tables comes the opportunity to try wines…lots of wines. We asked Adam rules of thumb for mastering the wine list (or just faking your way through it). You probably won't be going to too many sommelier-staffed restaurants with your friends, but you never know where your work and romantic life might take you.

1. Be confident in your knowledge level. You don't have to pretend to be a know-it-all. Even if you're telling your server, "I know very little about wine," engaging him or her on the subject will ensure that you end up with an interesting bottle.

How to Order Wine at a Restaurant continued...

2. Cheap is fine. Don't be intimidated by the high price tags in the Burgundy section—nobody ever orders the thousand-dollar Grand Crus (they're like the beautiful convertible in the window of a car dealership that's only there to lure prospective sedan-owners). Every wine list has hidden gems; it's your job to get the server to reveal them to you.

3. Ask for the somme. If you're at a fancier place with a sommelier, tell him or her what you're looking for (keep it simple: red or white, full-bodied or light, Old World or New World) and ask for a recommendation. Say, "I don't drink much wine, but I'm learning and I'd like to try something interesting—preferably for less than [insert budget here]." You're likely to come away with a beautiful bottle, an education, and maybe a new friend.

4. Just sniff. Until you master swirling and sipping (especially under pressure), smelling the wine will do. All you're smelling for is wet newspaper (which means the wine is corked) or an overwhelming molasses smell (it's oxidized). These are the reasons you would send it back. If you do taste, you are not tasting to see if you *like* the wine—you're tasting to make sure it's in good condition. A classic rookie move is to send it back because the taste is not what you expected.

5. Get drunk. Wine novices tend to sip slowly and tentatively. This makes no sense. Good wine is intended to be appreciated, yes, but it's also intended to make you feel good. Once you make it through the ordering, reward yourself by boozing it up.

Wine at Home: Serving, Storing, and Saving

Drinking wine at home is a great way to save money while still expanding your wine knowledge. In fact, a great weekend activity could be arranging a wine tasting with ten friends, where everyone pitches in to buy five bottles for $20 each. Before hitting the liquor store, here are a few ground rules to make your at-home wine-drinking experience runs smoothly.

Storing Wine. You probably don't have a wine cellar yet, but that doesn't mean you should abuse your wine. Store it horizontally (i.e., lying down) in a cool, dark place until you are ready to drink it. (White, rosé, and sparkling wines can be stored in the fridge).

Serving Wine. With some exceptions, reds should be served slightly below room temperature (54–58 degrees) and whites/rosés/sparkling wines should be served at cooler temperatures (the temperature of your fridge is close enough). Temperature extremes distort and/or minimize flavor, so avoid serving your wine *too* hot or *too* cold (unless they're crappy wines, in which case, chill that sauce).

The glasses used to drink wine also affect the experience. Larger, more spherical glasses are great for aromatic reds. Whites are generally consumed from smaller, less bulbous glasses. Sparkling wines are best enjoyed from "flutes," which help to make the bubbles last longer. If you only have Dixie cups, that'll have to do.

If you've never opened a wine bottle, you might want to try it a few times before inviting that special someone over for a romantic night in. There's nothing less suave than accidentally pushing the cork into the bottle and having to pick little cork chunks out of your teeth for the rest of the night. Remember to get the screw all the way in if you're using a traditional corkscrew, but we recommend "The Rabbit."

Saving Wine. While killing the bottle is probably not a problem for most recent grads, you can in fact save wine that you don't finish. To make your open wine last as long as possible:

- Refrigerate it (even if it's red).
- Seal it as tightly as possible. (You can force the cork back in or buy a reusable rubber cork.)
- Transfer it to a smaller container (less air in the bottle means less oxidation).
- Get creative. If your two-day old wine doesn't taste great on its own, you can still reincarnate it in the form of Sangria, or you can cook with it.

Get Your Taste On

Finally, the best way to learn about wines is to try, try, and try again. If you happen to live in a wine-producing region (northern California, the Pacific Northwest, or near the Niagara Peninsula), lucky you! Be sure to take advantage of local wine festivals and/or tasting events. If not, identify wine stores in your city that hold regular tastings and wine events where you can mix, mingle, and sample some new wines.

The Grad 2.0 Plan

Exploring the World of Beer

According to the Brewers Association, the total number of U.S. breweries on July 31, 2009, was the highest total in 100 years: 1,525. The craft beer industry has grown exponentially in the past ten years—beer bars are on the rise in every major city, more and more restaurants are offering beer pairings with their dishes, and innovative new beer styles are constantly being invented. If you're interested in drinking connoisseurship (a great pursuit to grow old with), you no longer have to feel like Joe or Jane Sixpack just because you'd rather grab a brew than a Bordeaux. Beer is *en vogue*!

Before you embark on your journey into the wide world of beer, let's get one thing straight: Drinking beer should be fun, enjoyable, and never stressful. Never drink beers that you don't like, unless there are no other beers available and you just want to get drunk. Some varieties are considered "trendy" and "refined" in the same way certain wines are, but if you are ordering a Tripel to look sophisticated, you may end up regretting the decision. Your best bet is to try a bunch of beers and see what you like (keep reading to learn about the best places to find them). Here's a very quick overview of some popular types of beers worth exploring, as well as some terminology that will help you ask for them at stores and bars.

Beer terms

Some lingo to help you navigate the beer menu.

- **Hops.** You'll hear talk of "hops" and "hoppy" taste when you're around beer drinkers. Hops come from hop plants (surprise!), and they are used as the primary flavoring agent in most beers. Hops add bitterness and act as a preservative.

- **ABV.** Alcohol by volume tells you how strong a beer is. Your average American lager (e.g., Miller) is about 4–5% ABV. "Ice" beers and malt beverages have higher alcohol content, and in general beers range from about 3 to 15% ABV, with higher alcohol content generally translating to a stronger taste. (Just to provide some context, the ABV of an average wine is 12%; hard liquor is 40% and up.)

- **Craft.** So-called craft beers are leading the charge in the quest to make people take beer seriously. These are brews made by independent (see below), traditional brewers on a small scale (e.g., less than two million barrels a year). The antithesis of Budweiser.

- **Microbrewery.** Sometimes called a "craft" brewery, these small breweries usually produce less than 15,000 barrels per year. They generally produce a wider, more interesting variety than their larger counterparts.

- **"Independent."** A craft brewery is "independent" if less than 25% of the craft brewery is owned or controlled by an alcoholic beverage industry. If you're more into indie bands than Top 40 radio, you're probably an indie beer person, too.

- **Head.** The foamy/creamy part at the top of the beer when your pour it. Most prevalent on stouts and bitters (think a pint of Guinness).

- **Imperial pint.** This means 20 fluid ounces, by the English measure. In the U.S., a pint is 16 oz. So if a bartender gives you the option of an imperial pint, you probably want to exercise it.

Types of beer

Ales and pale lagers are the most common families of beer, but there's a vast world out there to explore. Here's the tip of the iceberg.

- **Lagers.** Lagers are the most popular beers in the world, and probably what you've been drinking most of your college career (Bud, Miller, Coors, et. al. belong to the family of pale lagers). That said, the world of lagers is extremely varied, and each beer-drinking country has its own varieties. Light lagers are generally—but not always—lower in alcohol and more carbonated than dark lagers, which get their richer flavor and color from roasted barley and hops. Another popular variety is the pilsner, a light-colored lager hailing from Europe—it is generally hoppier and more bitter than its American cousin. (Note: When people talk about rich folks who drink "imported beer," they usually just mean European lagers like Stella Artois, Heineken, and Becks.) You might also run into German lagers of the "bock" family—you'll notice they're maltier and higher in alcohol content. Lagers are usually stored and served at cold temperatures, and in general you can expect an ABV of about 4–5.5%. **Where to start:** Too many to name—try to figure out if you like lighter, crisper lagers (e.g., Sam Adams, Stella) or a darker, richer incarnation (e.g., Saranac Nut Brown). Then mess

Tips & Tricks: Don't judge a beer by its color

A lot of people say, "I'm looking for a light beer," or, "Dark beers are too heavy for me," but the truth is the color of a beer has nothing to do with its alcohol content, taste, or heaviness. It's easy to see where this myth comes from—all mass-market "light" beers (meaning low in calories) are lagers that happen to have basically the same color, alcohol content, and flavor profile (i.e., "warm urine"). As a result, people associate the "look" of a light lager with something easy to drink and not too bold flavor-wise. But don't be a slave to color! Some light-colored beers are incredibly tough to drink, and some dark ones go down as smoothly as anything out there. Branch out, and you might find that you really love a black-as-night stout or an amber-colored ale.

with different countries and find a favorite.

- **Ales.** As with lagers, the diversity of ales is astounding. However, if you need some basic ways to differentiate, here goes: Ales are less carbonated, lower in alcohol, and have a stronger taste of malty hops. There are bottled varieties, but ales are really best when cask-conditioned and served from the tap. "English Bitters" are the kings of ales, especially when served at room temperature with a nice pie. Brown ales—most famously Newcastle Brown Ale—are also popular, and they're generally distinguished by their reddish-brown coloration and a sweeter taste of fruitiness or nuttiness. Darker "porters" are heavier and have a complex, chocolaty flavor. Finally, pale ales are generally known for their balance of malt and hops. **Where to start:** London Pride, Old Speckled Hen, Samuel Smith's Taddy Porter, Smuttynose IPA.

- **Stouts.** Technically, stouts are a sub-category of ales, but we think they're worth mentioning in their own right, mostly because a lovely drop of Guinness is always a great fallback. Stouts are dark, often with a creamy head and taste of roasted barley (think chocolate and coffee undertones). Oatmeal, chocolate, and oyster stouts are also interesting options. **Where to start:** Guinness, Beamish, Samuel Smith Oatmeal Stout, Goose Island Bourbon Stout.

- **Hefeweizen.** The hefeweizen, hailing from Germany, is the most popular variety of wheat beer. Wheat beers are highly carbonated and generally have a cloudy appearance when poured. The wheat provides a crisp, refreshing taste that makes these beers popular in summertime. (You'll often see them served in fruit varieties or with a lemon/orange segment.) American wheat beers can often be distinguished from their German predecessors by a hoppier flavor. **Where to start:** Paulander, Harpoon UFO, Erdinger, Rogue.

- **Belgian/French/Trappist.** Expect far higher alcohol content, stronger tastes, and funny glasses. Generally, these are considered "sipping" beers, so you won't find them in a standard Irish pub or late-night hot spot. True "trappist" ales are rare because they are literally brewed by or under the control of Trappist monks. Only seven of the 171 Trappist monasteries produce beer (six in Belgium, one in the Netherlands), the most famous of which are Chimay and Orval. The different strengths are generally labeled Enkel ("single"), Dubbel ("double"), and Tripel ("triple"). Belgian blonde ales, being lighter and more akin to a hefeweizen, are a good introduction to the often intimidating world of Belgian and French beers. **Where to Start:** Leffe, Chimay Rouge, Duvel Golden Ale.

- **Malt Beverages.** We're talking about malt liquor, people—not good or good for you, but fun to drink out of 40-ounce bottles in brown paper bags. If you're going to be "college," at least go all out: Buy malt liquor instead of a 30-pack of Busch Light. **Where to start:** Mickey's, Olde English, Steel Reserve.

Finding Beers

Exploring the world of beer is fun and, dare we say it, a bit more accessible than diving headfirst into wine culture. Best of all, it's pretty easy to do in most cities, and you don't have to drop an absurd amount of money to titillate the taste buds and get a healthy, responsible buzz on. Here are some ideas.

- **Go to local "beer bars" and attend beer festivals.** A beer bar sets itself apart by having a large, or at least distinguished, lineup of microbrews/craft/international beers on tap. Usually, the vibe is laidback—neither stuffy like a wine bar nor boisterous like a regular pub. They'll often have some mainstays coupled with a year-round schedule of featured beers, and they usually host special beer-related events and tastings. Festivals can be international in scope or focus solely on local producers, and they'll offer a great opportunity to taste a bunch of beers and speak with the people who make them. Check out free city papers and magazines (as well as BeerAdvocate.com—see below) to track down beer bars and events in your area, or search a large but incomplete list of bars on PubCrawler.com.

- **Cook with beer.** Beer can chicken (also known as "beer in the butt chicken") is a real crowd-pleaser, but there are many more ways to experiment with beer in the kitchen (it's great for marinades and stews, for one thing). Check out the cooking resources on page 440 and troll them for beer-related recipes.

- **Visit a brewery**. Visiting a vineyard can be time-consuming and costly—even if you don't go to France or Napa Valley, you usually have to get to some rural area where you clearly don't live. Breweries and microbreweries, on the other hand, are often right smack in the middle of cities. Midwestern cities are especially good for brewery visits, but it's worth looking into local options for a fun weekend activity. Find breweries on the Brewers Association website, then call up to see if they are open to the public—usually they'll offer free tours and tastings. Some even have restaurants.

- **Eat at a brewpub.** Again, brewpubs won't break the bank like a fancy meal with a $70 bottle of vino, but they are great fun. You can try some unique beers brewed on the premises and eat nachos— doesn't get much better than that. There are some chains (e.g., Rock Bottom, John Harvard's) and many local options. Find brewpubs at BrewPubZone.com.

- **Buy new beers to drink at home.** Maybe the 7-11 doesn't have a vast variety, but check out your local gourmet grocer or liquor store for a wider selection. Upscale supermarkets like Whole Foods and Harris Teeter also tend to offer a nice variety. Maybe you can even convince your grandma to get you a "Beer of the Month" membership for a graduation gift.

- **Try home-brewing.** No beer maven is worth his weight in hops until he's brewed his own. Take it back to the good ol' days by making up your own signature brew. Google John Palmer's "How to Brew" guide, and remember that it's illegal to sell your concoction.

- **Check out Beer Advocate.** The Alström Brothers have created a passionate community of beer enthusiasts at BeerAdvocate.com (there's also a magazine for $29.99 a year). It's a perfect place to start your journey with beer or foster a pre-existing propensity for the good stuff. Find an excellent "beer education" section—beer history, beer styles, food pairings, pouring techniques, and so on.—as well as encyclopedic reviews and a calendar of beer events across the country.

With the ranks of Duvel-quaffing beer geeks filling up fast (thanks hipsters!), the call has come to separate the wheat from the chaff in the beer community. No longer does "hating Coors Light" make you eligible for the club. So get out there and learn what great beer is all about!

Epilogue: The Golden Rule of Life After College

The Golden Rule of Life After College

Alas, fair graduates, we've come to the end of the road. We've talked about jobs and apartments, student debt and Facebook etiquette. Of course, there are many more issues that you'll encounter in your post-college life, but we can save those for another time and place (i.e., Gradspot.com and future guides). Hopefully, you've now got all the tools you need to lay a foundation for your new life of independence. Before we say farewell, however, we'd like to impart one last piece of advice that we hope you'll keep with you wherever you go: No matter what happens, always remember to keep it real. It may sound clichéd, but bear with us for a final moment.

"Keeping it real" lies at the very crux of the Grad 2.0 dilemma. The first few years out of college are a roller coaster of emotions and doubts, and it's incredibly easy to lose track of what's important. In an attempt to fit in, many working n00bs have the tendency to conform to the stereotypes promoted by their jobs. For example, finance types start using phrases like "models and bottles," and fashionistas become a little bit too obsessed with the September issue.

The new emphasis on money and salaries can make even the most down-to-earth grads begin to doubt themselves. And in some ways, the desire to assimilate is an inevitable byproduct of being at the bottom of the totem pole—everyone wants to move up and get recognized. But in the long run, compromising the person you really are will only draw you further and further away from the people and places that will make you happy.

So how do you keep it real? In his book *Reallionaire*, Dr. Farrah Gray details the amazing combination of positive thinking and entrepreneurial gusto that made him a millionaire by the age of fourteen. Starting out selling moisturizer on the street, Farrah caught the capitalist fever and began pitching ideas like he was Nolan Ryan in a pinstriped suit. Before he knew it, he had an endorsement from Oprah and more successful business ventures than he could count on his two well-moisturized hands. At the beginning of the book, he offers the following definition of a reallionaire:

Reallionaire: Someone who has discovered that there is more to money than having money. A person who understands that success is not just about being rich in your pocket; you have to be rich on the inside, too.

While Gray focuses primarily on balancing the power of money with the importance of staying grounded, his message is ultimately one of perspective. The emphasis on internal well-being that transcends traditional definitions of "success" is the key to Farrah's ethos. And, as a recent graduate in a world full of uncertainty, it should be yours as well.

Needless to say, keeping your head on straight won't be easy. If you can get through these years without encountering any earth-shattering doubts about your direction in life, you are either a professional athlete or unconscious. And at times (namely, when you see the biggest a-holes from your college trumpeting their successes all over Facebook), you'll genuinely wonder if nihilism is the only true path. But these years are way too valuable to concede to negativity. You're literally at the beginning of the ultimate life stage: You're youthful without being naïve or annoyingly earnest like a college student, yet independent without suffering from the pressures of a thirtysomething, who has to walk the sad tightrope between "settling down" and still pretending to be cool enough to dance at clubs.

In other words, this is the time when you can make real choices about your life and be treated like a serious person, but still feel liberated knowing that *nothing* about your career has to be set in stone. So focus on setting good precedents for yourself—precedents like enjoying what you do and solidifying valuable relationships—rather than obsessing over what other people are doing. It's true what they say: Life after college is a marathon, not a sprint. But that doesn't mean you have time to sit around drinking Haterade and feeling sorry for yourself. Get out there and do the damn thing, young graduate. You are ready to achieve greatness, and we look forward to hearing about what you accomplish. We wish you the nothing but the best. Thanks for reading, and remember: Whenever life after college throws you a curveball, you know where to find us.

Further Reading

These resources were extremely valuable in the process of putting this book together, and we recommend them to readers looking for further resources or different perspectives.

Bittman, Mark. *How to Cook Everything: 2,000 Simple Recipes for Great Food.* New York, NY: John Wiley & Sons, Inc., 2008.

Bolles, Richard Nelson. *What Color Is Your Parachute? 2010: A Practical Manual for Job-Hunters and Career-Changers.* New York, NY: Ten Speed Press, 2009.

Fischer, Kristen. *Ramen Noodles, Rent and Resumes: An After-College Guide to Life.* Belmont, CA: SuperCollege, LLC, 2008.

Florida, Richard. *Who's Your City?: How the Creative Economy Is Making Where to Live, the Most Important Decision of Your Life.* New York, NY: Basic Books, 2008.

Gregory, Michael. *The Career Chronicles: An Insider's Guide to What Jobs Are Really Like—The Good, the Bad, and the Ugly from Over 750 Professionals.* Novato, CA: New World Library, 2008.

Hassler, Christine. *20 Something Manifesto: Quarter-Lifers Speak Out About Who They Are, What They Want, and How to Get It.* Novato, CA: New World Library, 2008.

Levit, Alexandra. *How'd You Score That Gig? A Guide to the Coolest Jobs-and How to Get Them.* New York, NY: Ballantine Books, 2008.

Pollak, Lindsey. *Getting from College to Career: 90 Things to Do Before You Join the Real World.* New York, NY: HarperCollins Publishers, 2007.

Scheer, Marc. *No Sucker Left Behind: Avoiding the Great College Rip-off.* Monroe, ME: Common Courage Press, 2008.

Sethi, Ramit. *I Will Teach You To Be Rich.* New York, NY: Workman Publishing, 2009.

Thakor, Manisha, and Sharon Kedar. *On My Own Two Feet: A Modern Girl's Guide to Personal Finance.* Avon, MA: Adams Media, 2007.

Trunk, Penelope. *Brazen Careerist: The New Rules for Success.* New York, NY: Hachette Book Group, 2007.

Twenge, Jean M. *Generation Me: Why Today's Young Americans Are More Confident, Assertive, Entitled—and More Miserable Than Ever Before.* New York, NY: Free Press, 2006.

Wilner, Abby, and Catherine Stocker. *The Quarterlifer's Companion.* New York, NY: McGraw Hill, 2005.

About the Authors

Chris Schonberger (Harvard University, Class of 2006) is Editor-in-Chief of Gradspot.com. He has previously written for *Time Out New York, Entertainment Weekly, Let's Go,* and Forbes.com. When he's not helping recent grads transition to life after college, Chris devotes his efforts toward finding the best nachos in America.

Tory Hoen (Brown University, Class of 2006) is a freelance writer who splits her time between New York and Paris. She has written for *Time Out New York*, BusinessWeek.com, HipParis.com, and DossierJournal.com. When not writing, Tory spends her days haggling with Parisian street merchants over the price of cheese.

Stuart Schultz (Emory University, Class of 2004) is the founder of Gradspot.com and currently serves as the CEO. In his spare time, he enjoys playing soccer and is currently in training for semi-pro Wii Tennis tournaments.

Photographs by JOLIE RUBEN & GENEVIÈVE SANDIFER